Grand Strategy from Truman to Trump

Grand Strategy from Truman to Trump

BENJAMIN MILLER

WITH ZIV RUBINOVITZ

The University of Chicago Press
Chicago and London

The University of Chicago Press, Chicago 60637
The University of Chicago Press, Ltd., London
© 2020 by The University of Chicago
Published 2020
Printed in the United States of America

29 28 27 26 25 24 23 22 21 20   1 2 3 4 5

ISBN-13: 978-0-226-73496-5 (cloth)
ISBN-13: 978-0-226-73501-6 (paper)
ISBN-13: 978-0-226-73515-3 (e-book)
DOI: https://doi.org/10.7208/chicago/9780226735153.001.0001

Library of Congress Cataloging-in-Publication Data

Names: Miller, Benjamin, 1953– author. | Rubinovitz, Ziv, author.
Title: Grand strategy from Truman to Trump / Benjamin Miller ; with Ziv
Rubinovitz.
Description: Chicago ; London : The University of Chicago Press, 2020. |
Includes bibliographical references and index.
Identifiers: LCCN 2020013737 | ISBN 9780226734965 (cloth) | ISBN 9780226735016
(paperback) | ISBN 9780226735153 (ebook)
Subjects: LCSH: Security, International. | National security—United States. |
International relations. | United States—Foreign relations—1945–1989. |
United States—Foreign relations—1989–
Classification: LCC JZ1480 .M552 2020 | DDC 327.73—dc23
LC record available at https://lccn.loc.gov/2020013737

For Liora, Eti, Jacob, Adi, Tzuk, Ben, and Lia

Contents

Tables

Preface and Acknowledgments

I first encountered the consequences of grand strategy as a young draftee in the IDF (Israel Defense Forces). My armored unit was airlifted to the Golan Heights on the eve of the 1973 Yom Kippur War as a reinforcement to the units deployed there regularly. When, a day later, we confronted the invading Syrian military, our reinforcement was completely inadequate to face the much larger Syrian force. Thus, after my tank was damaged and ceased to function, I found myself—together with a few other soldiers—surrounded by a much larger Syrian force. These were extremely tough days—and nights—and I lost some very dear friends. This experience generated for me some initial interest in the big questions of war, strategy, and international diplomacy. It was only natural to also get interested in American foreign policy as, toward the end of the 1973 war, I became aware of the crucial importance of American statesmanship with both the US military airlift to the IDF and the shuttle diplomacy of the then secretary of state Henry Kissinger, who helped to end the war and then to initiate an era of diplomatic and military accords between Israel and the two neighbors that attacked it on October 6, 1973—Egypt and Syria.

My personal experience and interest in interstate diplomacy was further reinforced following my assignment to the UN as a member of the Israeli delegation to the UN General Assembly in New York. I was again impressed with the crucial role of the US, not only in Middle East diplomacy, but also in world affairs more generally. Thus, after this experience, it made a lot of sense for me to move to the University of California, Berkeley, to pursue a PhD in international relations. I was fortunate enough to have Professor Kenneth Waltz as a mentor, exposing me to the importance and the relevance of international relations (IR) theory for understanding all the subjects of war, diplomacy, and grand strategy that interested me.

My subsequent stints as a research fellow (at Harvard, MIT, McGill, Princeton, and Sciences Po) and as a visiting professor (at Duke; the University of Colorado, Boulder; Princeton; and Dartmouth) only reinforced my interest in both the big questions of international politics and in the American role in the international system.

The 2003 American invasion of Iraq was particularly puzzling: why did the US invade a faraway country that didn't pose a major direct threat to the much more powerful America? And why did it then try hard (even if not successfully) to do regime change in Baghdad and to promote democracy? What stands behind such a major policy decision, which became very costly in blood and treasure? Under what conditions would a regime-change strategy become the policy of the day? And then more generally—taking into account other major strategic changes—under what conditions does a grand strategy change? In other words, what is the most powerful explanation of such changes?

When I thought about this puzzle, the Waltzian education influenced me to try to do at least three things: first, to try looking at the big picture and to address the big questions; at the same time, to look for a relatively parsimonious answer, while developing a general model, which potentially applies to a great variety of cases; and finally, to bear in mind the potential influence of the international system (even if not precisely in the same way Waltz would have done it). In this way, I came to the idea that the combined effect of changes and variations in the balances of power and threat might provide a relatively parsimonious answer to the puzzle of changes in grand strategy. I apply it in this book to the case of American grand strategy since 1945 and until the second decade of the twenty-first century. But the objective is to introduce a parsimonious general model that also potentially explains changes in grand strategy in other cases of great powers or even regional powers.

Another key objective is to develop a general typology of grand strategies that will be applicable much beyond the American case by integrating variations in the objectives and means of the grand strategy. The presence of competing grand strategies helps to produce an ideational debate in different countries on which strategy to select. These various strategies are, in fact, competing ideas on how best to maximize the state's national security. While domestic politics and leaders' perceptions always play an important role in shaping the debate on the strategy selection, the variations in the international system play a key brokering role in at least some of the major debates. Importantly, some variations in the international system might lead the state to select a strategy that aims to shape the fundamental intentions and regimes of their opponents through an ideology-promotion strategy. Other systemic variations might encourage more material-oriented (realist) strategies. Similarly, some of these variations lead to offensive strategies, while others to defensive ones.

In the American case, realism and liberalism provide the major competing ideas on the desirable grand strategy. More specifically, the book highlights a novel fourfold distinction in the American case of offensive realism, defensive realism, defensive liberalism, and offensive liberalism. While the realist strategies are potentially applicable to other powers as well, instead of the offensive and defensive liberalism, other powers might select—according to their ideological preferences—offensive or defensive Marxist or offensive or defensive Islamic or offensive or defensive Confucian strategies. This book presents such a relatively parsimonious model to account for the key changes in American grand strategy since the end of WWII and until (and including) the rise of the America First/nationalist strategy under President Donald Trump.

During this long voyage of trying to understand the puzzle of grand strategy in general and in the American case in particular, I have accumulated numerous debts to colleagues and friends who were very helpful and supportive. Although I'll try to mention as many as possible of them, I apologize if I miss a few.

I'll start with some of the colleagues who provided insightful comments during the seminars where I presented the model, some of whom also provided comments on parts of the manuscript. In the Security Seminar at the University of Chicago, Charles Glaser, Robert Pape, and John Mearsheimer were especially generous in suggesting constructive comments. At the Duke University seminar, I would like to thank Joe Grieco, Chris Gelpi, Don Horowitz, Bruce Jentleson, Hal Brands, and particularly Peter Feaver, who has especially continued to be curious about this project. At Rutgers University, Professor Jack Levy was particularly helpful and supportive. At Columbia University, I appreciate the advice of Richard Betts, Bob Jervis, and Jack Snyder. Mark R. Bessinger made possible a one-year fellowship (with just a bit of teaching) at PIIRS (Princeton Institute for International and Regional Studies), which was very helpful for my research. At the Princeton Security Seminar, the suggestions of Tom Christensen were especially helpful. I also appreciate the support of Andreas Wimmer and the consultations with Keren Yarhi-Milo—both of them then at Princeton. Nuno P. Monteiro was kind enough to invite me to an IR talk at Yale and gave some good advice.

Steven Lobell invited me to a talk at Utah State University, where he and his colleagues raised some interesting ideas regarding this book's theory. My dear friend Jeff Taliaferro at Tufts—whose knowledge and wisdom on the subject of my book is second to none—was especially kind and supportive. In my one year of teaching at the University of Colorado, Boulder, Robert Schulzinger, a leading expert on American diplomatic history, was very helpful with regard to the book's project. Later on, Dartmouth College provided an especially supportive environment to work on this project and to receive some useful advice from Steve Brooks, Ben Valentino, Jenny Lind, Daryl Press, Jeff A. Friedman, Brian D. Greenhill, Steve Simon, and especially Bill Wohlforth. Mellissa Willard-Foster of the University of Vermont was particularly helpful in providing generous and very insightful comments. Ron Krebs showed a great interest in the project and gave a lot of encouragement even if he was critical of some of the arguments. Debby Larson gave some incisive comments on the model as the discussant in an American Political Science Association panel. Mike Desch showed interest in the project from its initial stages. In addition, I would like to note the encouragement and suggestions of my dear friends and colleagues T. V. Paul, Dale Copeland, Dov Levin, and Norrin Ripsman.

In addition to my highly supportive and encouraging colleagues at the International Relations Division and other colleagues in the School of Political Sciences at the University of Haifa, particularly helpful in Israel were my dear friends Korina Kagan and Galia Press Barnathan. Jonathan Rynhold, Israel Waismel-Manor, Doron Navot, Hillel Frisch, and Azar Gat provided useful comments. My friend Avi Kober was—as usual—very supportive and helpful. Ariel Kabiri and Carmela Lutmar were always cheerfully willing to help and to give advice.

My partner in this book project—Dr. Ziv Rubinovitz—was very helpful in collecting empirical material for the book based on the theoretical model, especially for chapters 4, 5, and 6. I very much appreciate his help.

The editors at the University of Chicago Press—initially David Pervin and later Chuck Myers and also Noor Shawaf and the copyeditor, Mark Reschke—were very helpful. I would like to thank them for their support and professionalism.

I am grateful for the generous financial support of the Israel Science Foundation (founded by the Israel Academy of Sciences and Humanities); the Israel Institute, its president, Professor Itamar Rabinovich, and its executive director, Dr. Ariel Ilan Roth; PIIRS at Princeton University and its director, Professor Mark R. Bessinger; and the Department of Government at Dartmouth College, its chair, Professor John Carey, and also Professor William C. Wohlforth who kindly sponsored my one-year visit there.

I have much revised earlier versions of some limited portions of this book, which have been published in "Explaining Changes in US Grand Strategy: 9/11, the Rise of Offensive Liberalism and the War in Iraq," *Security Studies* 19, no. 1 (March 2010): 26–65, https://www.tandfonline.com/; and "Democracy Promotion: Offensive Liberalism vs. the Rest (of IR Theory)," Special Issue on Liberalism, *Millennium* 38, no. 3 (May 2010): 561–91, https://journals.sagepub.com/. I would like to thank these journals for permitting me to use material that first appeared in their pages.

Finally, my immediate family—my spouse, Liora; my daughter, Adi, and her family; and my sister, Eti, and her late dear husband, Jacob Abiri—was always a major source of support and love, which made it possible for me to overcome the numerous crises during the various stages of the research and the writing.

Thus, I would like to dedicate this book to Liora, Eti, Jacob, and to the younger generation of my family: Adi; her husband, Tzuk; their amazing son, Ben; and their newly-born lovely daughter, Lia. Spending time with them is always a source of great inspiration and fun. Thus, I would like to thank them for all these precious and wonderful gatherings, and I look forward to continue them as much as possible.

Benjamin Miller

Introduction

The Puzzle and the Argument

The Puzzle

How can we account for variations and shifts in US grand strategy?[1] Namely, why does the United States adopt a certain grand strategy in a certain period, and why does it switch from one strategy to another? During the Cold War, the US changed its grand strategy several times, notably a few years after WWII and then after the invasion of South Korea by the North, after the Cuban missile crisis, after the Soviet invasion of Afghanistan, and then again, finally, following the change of Soviet policy under Gorbachev.

Following the end of the Cold War, we have witnessed two additional transitions in US grand strategy. The first transition took place from the Cold War period to the 1990s, and it was manifested in a greater US willingness to undertake limited humanitarian interventions. The second transition took place a decade later, following 9/11. The new strategy included, notably, a willingness to promote democracy by the use of force, as reflected in the 2002 Bush Doctrine and carried out in the 2003 invasion of Iraq. The United States intervened with a massive force in a sensitive region, in the absence of any immediate Iraqi threat to its security, with the explicit purpose of imposing democracy. This raises the question why democracy promotion by the use of force had become such a prominent objective of US grand strategy under the George W. Bush administration.[2]

Two basic puzzles are inherent in the various changes of grand strategy addressed here: why—and under what conditions—will a liberal power endorse a realist grand strategy such as the US did during the Cold War? And when—or under what conditions—will realist factors lead to the dominance of a liberal grand strategy such as during the post–Cold War era?

Rather than providing a comprehensive history of US grand strategy since 1945, this book focuses on explaining such key puzzles, while presenting a relatively parsimonious theoretical model. We argue that this model can provide a useful account of the key changes in American grand strategy even if it cannot explain all the details of the strategy.

In accounting for these puzzles, variations, and transitions in US grand strategy, we should consider some major debates in international relations (IR) theory in recent years. These debates revolve around the question of whether foreign and security policy (and especially the choice of grand strategy) is determined by material or ideational factors, and around the question of whether this policy is determined by external or domestic factors. While realism focuses on such systemic-material factors as the state's relative power and the presence (or absence) of significant external threats to its security in accounting for its choice of grand strategy,[3] constructivists attribute great importance to ideas, culture, and norms (both international and domestic).[4]

Different variants of liberalism attribute differential weight to material versus normative factors in affecting grand strategy. For example, the focus in a liberal grand strategy on the pacifying effects of economic interdependence has a powerful material dimension based on mutual benefits from international trade. At the same time, the focus on the peace-promotion effects of democracy in a liberal grand strategy has, at least partly, a strong cultural and normative aspect.[5]

Domestic approaches, for their part, focus on such factors as the domestic regime and internal politics of the state.[6] The individual level of analysis includes the belief systems of leaders and, in the US context in particular, the worldviews of particular presidents.[7]

Several major studies have recently dealt with the question of US grand strategy and the relative weight of external-material versus domestic-ideational factors affecting it. However, they are unable to account for the variations in US grand strategy mentioned above. Thus, Jonathan Monten develops a useful distinction between two variants of US liberalism in foreign affairs (parallel to what will be introduced here as "offensive" versus "defensive" liberalism), but is unable to account for the major change in the Bush administration's security policy before and after 9/11. By focusing on the continuous influence of liberal culture on US foreign policy (qualified by limited liability), Colin Dueck is unable to account for the differences in US grand strategy between the Cold War and the post–Cold War eras, let alone for the variations within each of these periods. Similarly, in concentrating on what he sees as the persistent US quest for hegemony stemming from the "open door" policy, Christopher Layne overlooks great variations in this quest during the Cold War and between the Cold War and the post–Cold War era, as discussed here.[8]

Barry Posen, John Mearsheimer, and Stephen Walt highlight "liberal he-gemony" as the post–Cold War grand strategy of the US, although they un-derestimate some of the key differences between the strategy in the 1990s and the post-9/11 strategy as analyzed in this work.[9] Moreover, these leading realist scholars, while heavily criticizing the "liberal hegemony" grand strategy, seem to understate the systemic-material explanation (which is usually associated with realist theory) of the change from a realist grand strategy during the Cold War,[10] to a liberal one following the end of the Cold War, as discussed in this work. This is one point that suggests that an explanation based on realist-related factors does not always coincide perfectly with a prescription of realist academics. As a systemic explanation, realism highlights that material fac-tors may compel or tempt the state to behave in certain ways even if realist thinkers may strongly believe that this is a mistaken policy because it doesn't serve well what they see as the national interest of the state.[11] We resolve this tension by presenting the systemic-material factors as explanatory—the key independent variables—while realism is introduced here as providing two of our four prescribed grand strategies, which constitute the phenomenon to be explained, or the dependent variables, of the study.

The Argument

In accounting for the puzzle of variations and changes in US grand strategy, this book proposes a theoretical model for explaining great-power choices of grand strategy.[12] The model is in principle applicable to any great power, but in this study it will be applied specifically to the United States—the key player in the international system since 1945. The model makes the follow-ing arguments. First, we distinguish among four possible ideal-type great-power grand strategies or approaches to security, according to the objectives and the means of security policy advanced by each approach. In the case of the United States, these approaches are offensive realism, defensive real-ism, defensive liberalism, and offensive liberalism (discussed in chapter 1).[13] These approaches are sets of ideas shared by policy makers about how to maximize their state's security, and thus they are an ideational factor.[14] Most of the contending approaches to security have been present in most US ad-ministrations, or at least in the influential foreign policy community. Their continuous presence under the same liberal political culture indicates that culture by itself does not determine the nature of US grand strategy.[15] There are often domestic debates within the US administration or in the policy community over the "correct" approach to security. However, one approach usually emerges as the dominant one in a given period (which does not mean that the others fade away). The changes in the relative dominance of the four ideational approaches to security (the grand strategies) are the dependent variables (the outcomes to be explained) of this study.

The second step of the argument addresses the question of what fac- tors—or independent variables—determine which one of these contending approaches to security will win in the domestic debate and emerge as the grand strategy that a great power, or specifically the United States, pursues at a given time. Rather than arguing that the outcome of the debate depends on such domestic-ideational factors as the vagaries of domestic politics or lead- ers' beliefs, we advance a material-systemic explanation of US grand strategy. Namely, we argue that international systemic factors broker between com- peting ideas. In other words, the international material environment works as the *selector* of ideas, and it determines which approach to security is likely to emerge as the winner and dominate US security policy in a certain period. The two systemic factors are the distribution of power in the international system and the degree of external threat faced by the United States. Various combinations of these systemic factors are conducive to the emergence and dominance of various grand strategies, and changes in these systemic factors lead to changes in US grand strategy over time. This does not imply that any security strategy is correct in any circumstance, but only that, given a certain combination of systemic factors, it is likely to prove more attractive to the policy makers.

The model combines systemic-material and domestic-ideational factors in an integrated theoretical framework.[16] Namely, while the ideational factors (the four contending approaches to security) are the dependent variables, the ultimate selection among them is made by the systemic conditions, and therefore it is these conditions that are the basic explanatory factors.

We should note that while realism is usually associated with independent variables, we use this term to indicate the dependent variable—that is, a par- ticular "realist" grand strategy or approach to security. Used in this sense, it represents an ideational rather than a material factor—namely, a certain set of ideas about how to achieve security. As an ideational approach to security (a grand strategy), realism is prescriptive—it suggests how the state should maximize its security. The systemic-material factors that are the independent variables of the model, on the other hand, are explanatory—they specify the material conditions under which each of the grand strategies is going to be the dominant one. Thus, the systemic conditions do not necessarily encour- age the emergence of realist grand strategies. Indeed, some combinations of systemic conditions are conducive to liberal grand strategies. Thus, whereas the dependent variables—the four grand strategies—are ideational, the independent variables are essentially material. This material international environment selects the dominant ideational approach to security or great-power grand strategy.

Two major intervening variables translate the systemic conditions into changes in grand strategy.[17] These intervening domestic variables are not the underlying causes of changes in US grand strategy, but they are part of the causal chain—that is, a description of how changes in the values of the independent variables change the values of the dependent variable.[18] The two intervening variables are decision makers' perceptions and beliefs at the individual level of analysis and the domestic balance of influence among the four grand strategies at the domestic level of analysis. The influence of these two intervening factors may be described in terms of two causal chains.

In the first causal chain, when an administration takes office, it will be initially guided by the belief systems of the key decision makers, notably, of course, the president and his close—formal and informal—advisors. Yet, major changes in the international system may compel the administration to change its initial foreign policy inclinations or worldviews in order to adapt to the new threats or opportunities coming from the changing environment. Under these changing conditions, it might be too costly to persist with the same grand strategy. Hence, changes in grand strategy under the same presidency suggest that leaders' preexisting beliefs by themselves do not determine the character of US grand strategy. Examples include the major changes in foreign policy under President Jimmy Carter in a more offensive direction following the growing Soviet expansion in the late 1970s and the opposite shift from an offensive to a more defensive grand strategy under President Ronald Reagan following the benign changes in Soviet behavior in the mid-1980s. We discuss both in this volume.[19]

In the second causal chain, systemic factors in the international environment help to determine the outcome of domestic battles among the advocates of the competing approaches to security.[20] One such mechanism is elections.[21] If foreign policy issues dominate the agenda, elections may be determined by international developments. One such example is the electoral victory of Reagan over Carter in the 1980 election discussed in the book. Another key example addressed in this book refers to external effects between elections—the effects of 9/11 on the rise of offensive liberalism in the US political system and policy-making community. While the offensive liberal approach to foreign policy was part of the US domestic debate in the 1990s, it was the changing international systemic conditions after 9/11 that made it much more appealing than it was previously and provided a great opportunity for this approach to dominate US grand strategy.[22] This does not mean

TABLE 0.1. Two causal chains

Causal chains	Independent variables	Intervening variables	Dependent variables
Chain I	Changes in the external environment	Changing decision makers' perceptions and beliefs	Changing grand strategy
Chain II	Changes in the external environment	Changing balance of influence in the domestic battles over grand strategy	Changing grand strategy

that this strategy was the correct one for maximizing US national security; it only means that the external systemic conditions increased the domestic attractiveness of this approach and thus allowed it to shape US grand strategy. The two intervening variables can work in tandem: we will show that in addition to increasing the domestic influence of offensive liberalism, the changing systemic conditions following 9/11 also brought about a change in the beliefs of the Bush administration with regard to security that resulted in its adoption of the offensive liberal program. Table 0.1 presents the two causal chains that can bring about changes in great-power grand strategy.

This book is organized in the following eleven chapters: the first describes the four competing grand strategies or approaches to security; the second presents the systemic model for the relative dominance of the four grand strategies; and the following eight chapters provide an empirical examination of the model, in explaining the key transitions in US grand strategy in the post–World War II era: four chapters deal with the Cold War era and four address the post–Cold War period. The Cold War chapters naturally focus on the strategy toward the key opponent—the Soviet Union; the post–Cold War chapters address especially US military interventions since the end of the Cold War.

More specifically, chapter 3 explains the key changes in US strategy in the early years of the Cold War (Truman): initially from defensive liberalism to defensive realism and then, following the onset of the Korean War, the shift to offensive realism. Chapter 4 accounts for the major changes following the Cuban missile crisis, essentially from offensive realism to defensive realism (Kennedy). The fifth chapter looks at the dramatic changes toward the end of the Carter administration back to offensive realism. The following chapter investigates the key changes in President Reagan's second term to defensive realism.

The last four chapters deal with the post–Cold War era. The seventh chapter discusses the decade of 1991–2001 and the emergence of defensive liberalism as a dominant US strategy (Bush Sr. and Clinton). The next chapter examines the post-9/11 rise of offensive liberalism and its application to US policy in the Middle East, especially regarding the war in Iraq (Bush Jr.). Even though the Iraq War is a single case, it is a crucial one for the Bush administration—it is the case that defined his presidency and his grand strategy in the area of security, with many far-reaching and continuous implications for the United States, Iraq, the Middle East, and the international system as a whole. This is the key case in which the post-9/11 Bush Doctrine played a major role, and it is important for the purposes of both theory and policy to understand the conditions under which this could take place.

Chapters 9 and 10 analyze more briefly some of the more recent developments. Chapter 9 overviews the key changes under Obama. Chapter 10 discusses the new approach brought about by Trumpism as a distinctive approach different from all the other four approaches, at least as it was reflected in the 2016 campaign and shortly afterward. The analysis of Trumpism is also useful for a comparative look at the competing approaches to American grand strategy and at the effects of the international system on their selection. The final chapter overviews briefly some of the key changes in the grand strategy under various administrations and also presents some of the key contemporary policy differences among the various schools in the age of Trump.

As we suggested, this book does not aim to provide a comprehensive and detailed history of post-WWII US foreign policy. While this history is obviously crucial for our analysis and we would like to highlight key elements of it, our focus is on explaining the key changes in American grand strategy since 1945. A key contribution is the introduction of a new classification of competing grand strategies and especially presenting a novel theoretical model that accounts for the changes in the grand strategy and examining the model by the empirical evidence. While we contribute to a greater understanding of the history of grand strategy, a major contribution is to the enduring debates in IR theory on the level-of-analysis question and on the explanatory power of competing material and ideational theories.

A key contribution of this study is also the applicability of its theory across system structures; thus, it is able to explain the variation between US strategy during bipolarity and the strategy in the unipolar era. We cited above some major studies that fail to do this despite their great contributions to the study of grand strategy. This also includes, among others, some leading realist accounts of US grand strategy, which are able to account for US behavior in the bipolar era but are puzzled by its behavior in the post–Cold War unipolarity, especially the post–Cold War military interventions. The model presented here is able to provide a parsimonious explanation of both the behavior during the Cold War and the changes in the post–Cold War era by using the same international systemic variables even if their values changed with the transition to unipolarity, thus causing the change in the American strategy—irrespective of whether we support or oppose the policy itself.

Between Offensive Liberalism and Defensive Realism—Four Approaches to Grand Strategy

Four Ideational Approaches to Security

As a first step toward explaining the dependent variables—the variations in US grand strategy—I distinguish among four possible ideal-type approaches to security or grand strategy, according to the objectives and the means of security policy advanced by each approach.[1] With regard to the objectives of security policy, the distinction is between strategies that focus on affecting the balance of capabilities vis-à-vis the opponent (realist grand strategies) and strategies that focus on ideology promotion (ideological grand strategies).[2] For example, in the case of a liberal great power, notably the US, ideological grand strategies focus on promoting democracy and free-market economies.[3] Yet, in the case of illiberal powers, ideological grand strategies focus on promoting illiberal ideologies such as fascism, communism, Islamism, or any other illiberal ideology—depending on the ideological nature of that specific illiberal power.

As for the means of security policy, the distinction is between offensive and defensive approaches to resorting to force. While the offensive security strategies advocate massive and unilateral use of military force, the defensive strategies support minimal and multilateral use of force. The distinction between unilateralism and multilateralism as employed here is based not on the number of coalition members, nor even necessarily on the blessing of the United Nations Security Council (UNSC), but rather on the extent of institutional freedom of action allowed to the most powerful member by its coalition. To qualify as truly multilateral, it is necessary for a coalition not to be only "a coalition of the willing" (that is, a coalition willing to follow the hegemon's lead), but to be able to impose institutional constraints on the hegemon's freedom of action. For the United States, it means, for example, working within the institutional constraints of the UNSC (with the veto power of the other permanent members), but also, notably, with NATO—where there is a need to reach a consensus with the allies.[4] In other words, while UNSC blessing is a sufficient condition for a military intervention to be qualified as multilateral, it is not a necessary one. If the coalition is unable to impose institutional constraints on the hegemon's freedom of military action, even if it has numerous members, the military intervention should be considered a unilateral action by the hegemon supported by a "coalition of the willing."

Whereas the distinction between offensive and defensive realism is a familiar one,[5] students of IR theory have tended to overlook the fact that a parallel distinction can be drawn within an ideology-promotion perspective. Most notably, it is possible to distinguish within the liberal perspective between offensive and defensive variants, or branches, of liberalism. Both liberal approaches focus on the benign influence of democracy on the external behavior of states and on international security and thus call to promote democracy, but they differ with respect to the means of doing so. While defensive liberalism favors the promotion of democracy by peaceful means, the offensive approach advocates democracy promotion by the use of force if necessary.

The various combinations of these two dimensions produce four ideal types of great-power approaches to security (see table 1.1): offensive realism, defensive realism, defensive ideology promotion, and offensive ideology promotion. Offensive realism refers to a combination of power maximization, including occasionally a maximal use of force, in a unilateral manner. This

TABLE 1.1. Four grand strategies

	Means of security policy: The approach to power and the use of force	
Objectives vis-à-vis the adversary	Maximalist/unilateral	Minimalist/multilateral
Focus on the balance of capabilities with the rival (realist grand strategy)	**Offensive realism** Quest for superiority/ hegemony, including by a unilateral resort to force	**Defensive realism** Focus on security maximization through balancing, deterrence, and multilateral arms control
Focus on ideology promotion (ideological grand strategy)	**Offensive ideology promotion** Emphasis on regime change through the use of force (ideological crusades)	**Defensive ideology promotion** Emphasis on soft power, international institutions, and the diplomacy of conflict resolution
	Offensive liberalism and imposed democratization in the case of the United States	Defensive liberalism and the spread of democracy and free trade by peaceful means in the case of the United States

strategy, which operates according to cost-benefit calculations, is aimed at affecting the capabilities of the adversary. Defensive realism refers to a minimal use of force in a multilateral manner for affecting the balance of capabilities; defensive ideology promotion emphasizes the spread of ideology multilaterally by peaceful means; while offensive ideology promotion focuses on effecting regime change unilaterally and by the use of force.

If ideology promotion is done by a liberal power, such as the United States, then defensive liberalism focuses on the use of "soft power" in a multilateral manner for promoting democracy, free-market economies, and international institutions, and thus affecting the rival's ideological character.[6] In contrast, offensive liberals are willing to use massive force in a unilateral manner in order to promote democracy and affect the rival's ideology.[7] This distinction is reflected in the longtime debate in US foreign policy between supporters of "exemplarism" (which is associated here with defensive liberalism) and "crusaders" or supporters of "vindicationism" (called here offensive liberalism).[8]

Since multilateralism tends to be associated with liberalism, readers might be puzzled by the link between defensive realism and multilateralism made here. However, defensive realists believe—similar to defensive liberals—that security should be achieved interdependently (that is, multilaterally) rather than unilaterally. In contrast to the defensive liberals, however, defensive realists emphasize hard power more than soft power. Defensive realists believe that no power can be secure if the military capabilities of other powers are vulnerable because, especially under crisis conditions, they might be compelled to strike first lest they "use it or lose it." Such a situation is unstable and dangerous to all parties involved. Hence, important components of security according to the logic of defensive realism are mutual security arrangements and confidence-building measures that enhance transparency and reduce the possibility of a surprise attack, thus mitigating mutual fears of being attacked. States should strive, through arms control agreements, to construct such a balance of military capabilities that no one has an incentive to attack first. Arms control, in this view, is intended to decrease the offensive capabilities of states while enhancing defensive ones in nonprovocative ways, and thus can reduce the security dilemma and the danger of inadvertent escalation and provide mutual reassurance.[9]

The four approaches constitute the ideational preferences or inclinations of various leaders and groups within a great power's policy community with regard to the choice of grand strategy, adopted on the basis of their values, belief systems, and worldviews. While only one of the approaches is likely to dominate the great power's grand strategy at a given time, the other approaches may be latent within its polity, as contenders in an ongoing domestic debate in the "marketplace of ideas" on the best grand strategy, namely, on the best way to maximize security.[10] As noted, both the realist and the ideological approaches are applicable to any great power. The liberal strategies are one set of ideological grand strategies that are suited to a liberal great power such as the United States, on which this book focuses. Yet the theory does not apply only to the US grand strategy. According to the model, a great power tends to adopt an ideological approach in accordance with its ideological preferences. Thus, illiberal great powers will adopt an ideological approach parallel to offensive or defensive liberalism, namely, one that focuses on the peaceful or forcible promotion of their ideology—be it Confucianism, conservative monarchism, Islamism, or communism.

The fourfold division is based not only on a distinction between realism and liberalism (in the case of a liberal power, notably the US), but also on an internal division inside each camp between offensive and defensive approaches. Indeed, beside the distinction between offensive and defensive realism, there also exists an overlooked parallel division between offensive and defensive liberalism. The distinction between offensive and defensive liberalism goes deeper and has lasted much longer than the recent debate on the neoconservative agenda during the Bush presidency.[11] While sharing the same liberal objectives, offensive and defensive liberals diverge sharply in the means they are willing to deploy to advance these aims, specifically on the desirability of the use of force in the democratization of nondemocratic countries.

I evaluate the advantages and the shortcomings of each approach and the grand strategy derived from its theoretical logic as an avenue toward protecting national security and toward fulfilling durable global or regional peace.[12] I focus on examining the prescriptions on maintaining peace and security that emanate from the theoretical logics of each of these approaches and the grand strategies that are thus inferred from each perspective. I subsequently briefly contrast the liberal and realist approaches with some constructivist ideas on peace. Finally, in order to clarify the differences among the four approaches, I apply their logic to a concrete issue at the center of major contemporary debates: democracy promotion and regime change by the US as the leading superpower. I open this final discussion by presenting the variations of ideal-type strategies toward regime change and conclude the chapter by linking these strategies and relevant examples to the approaches elaborated previously.

The post–Cold War spread of democratization, at least until recently, in particular has raised the appeal of liberal approaches toward promoting the vision of a global warm peace. Yet, the increased salience of democratization also poses some fundamental dilemmas within the global agenda. One key quandary concerns the means to advance democratization: should it be promoted by coercive measures—including the use of armed force—or through peaceful means alone? Should it only be imposed multilaterally, or is unilateral action also possible? These questions lie at the core of the debate between offensive and defensive liberalism. Another question—often posed by realist critics of the liberal argument—addresses the effects of democratization on stability: will democratization always bring about stability and warm peace, or might it produce a violent conflict or hot war—at least in some cases? Both realists and defensive liberals offer alternative ways to promote peace; offensive liberals, however, specifically insist that democracy is a necessary condition for peace and is the key to achieving it.

The Logic of the Fourfold Distinction and Approaches to Peace and Security

In the 1990s many realists introduced the distinction between offensive and defensive variants as one useful way to understand important differences within realism. Offensive realists argue that the best way to ensure state security is by maximizing a state's power until it becomes the superior power or hegemon. This approach asserts a hegemonic system or unipolarity as most conducive to national security and world peace, with small states able to enjoy stability so long as they bandwagon with the hegemon. Defensive realists suggest that states maximize their security and maintain their position in the international system by balancing their rivals' capabilities or by deterring them. Yet under anarchic conditions, arms buildups or alliance building—even if done only for defensive purposes—may still produce intense security dilemmas leading to instability and war. To avoid an inadvertent escalation, states should thus maximize security in ways that will be least threatening to the others' retaliatory capabilities and vital interests. In other words, a nonthreatening balance of power, built on defensive rather than offensive capabilities, is most conducive to national security and to world peace. Moreover, under such a balance, small states will be able to maintain their security and autonomy.

Students of IR theory have, however, overlooked the fact that a parallel distinction can be drawn along similar parameters from a liberal perspective. This theoretical paradigm specifically highlights the benign influence of liberal ideological tenets on the external behavior of states, and also has offensive and defensive variants, which share some fundamental common features alongside major differences. Liberals believe that a liberal world, with democratic market economies, will be most conducive to security and peace, but differ markedly on how to achieve this goal—more specifically in terms of the role of international institutions.

The following part of the chapter presents these four theoretical approaches and distinguishes grand strategies derived from their conceptual logic on the basis of two dimensions: the differing *goals* and *means* of preferred state policies for the advancement of peace and security. There are two types of security goals vis-à-vis other states: one affects the balance of capabilities; the other, the rivals' enduring intentions or preferences and domestic character.[13] There are also two ideal types of goal-oriented security strategies regarding the use of military force: either massive and unilateral or minimal and multilateral. Various combinations of these dimensions produce four types of approaches to international peace and security: offensive realism, defensive realism, defensive liberalism, and offensive liberalism.

A combination of power maximization and potential use of force, based on cost-benefit calculations in a unilateral way and aimed at changing the balance of capabilities with an adversary, constitutes an offensive realist strategy. Here the key to peace and security is hegemony and its preservation. Illustrations on the global level include Pax Britannica and Pax Americana,[14] the latter especially under the post–Cold War unipolarity.[15] Regional examples refer to the successful emergence of the regional hegemony of the US in the Western Hemisphere,[16] in Western Europe,[17] and in the Israeli-Egyptian context in the 1970s, later extended in the post–Cold War Middle East, at least in the 1990s,[18] and also Pax Sovietica under Soviet hegemony in Eastern Europe during the Cold War.[19]

Defensive realism refers to a minimal use of force in a multilateral way for affecting the balance of capabilities. Here the key to peace is cautious balancing and the formation of a world balance of power. Examples include balancing coalitions to preserve the balance of power in eighteenth- and nineteenth-century Europe and to prevent the emergence of a hegemon such as the anti-German coalitions in the two world wars and also mutual deterrence such as the MAD (mutual assured destruction) doctrine, based on the strategic situation that emerged between the superpowers during the Cold War.

Defensive liberalism focuses on the multilateral use of hard and soft power to affect a rival's fundamental intentions; offensive liberals are, by contrast, willing to maximize the unilateral use of force to affect those intentions. While the defensive version of liberalism stresses multilateralism as a way to advance peace, offensive liberalism relies on the assumed pacifying tendencies of democratization, displaying a regular willingness to consider the use of force toward that objective. Key examples of institutions driven by the logic of defensive liberalism in the area of peace and security include collective security arrangements, like the League of Nations and the United Nations. Prominent examples of events driven by offensive liberalism include the imposed democratization of Germany and Japan by the US after WWII.

Four Policy Approaches toward Peace and Security

One popular distinction between realists and liberals reduces their differences in policy objectives and means to the idea that realists focus on military security as the key state goal, while liberals have their eye on economics, social welfare, and human rights. With regard to means, realists allegedly emphasize the use of military force in a unilateral way, while liberals favor the resort to economic sanctions and incentives and the use of international institutions in a multilateral mode. Here, I advance different divisions, both within and between the two approaches (see tables 1.2 and 1.3).[20] First of all, both realists and liberals care about security and peace. Security is important both for its own sake and as a prerequisite for achieving other objectives. Indeed, the four approaches presented here all aim to enhance *state* security, as defined below, but they also argue that their prescriptions enhance

TABLE 1.2. Competing paths toward national security and world peace

	Means: Resort to force (hard power)	
Objectives vis-à-vis the adversary	Maximalist/unilateralist	Minimalist/multilateralist
Affecting the balance of capabilities	**Offensive realism** The way to world peace: **Global hegemony** (Pax Romana, Pax Britannica, Pax Americana)	**Defensive realism** The way to world peace: **A stable balance of power** (the balance of power during the Concert of Europe)
Affecting the rival's fundamental intentions/nature of domestic regime	**Offensive liberalism** The way to world peace: **Global democratization** (including by use of force) (imposed democratization of Germany and Japan and post-2003 Iraq)	**Defensive liberalism** The way to world peace: **Collective security** (the League of Nations and the UN; post–Cold War NATO; OAS; the Arab League)

TABLE 1.3. Is peace possible? Types of peace and disarmament

	Means: Resort to force (hard power)	
Objectives vis-à-vis the adversary	Offensive	Defensive
Realism	**Cold peace** through military and/or economic strength[1]	**Cold War/peace** by balancing/ deterrence and arms control
	(the Egyptian-Israeli peace under US leadership; Pax Sovietica in Eastern Europe)	(the US-Soviet nuclear MAD during the Cold War)
Liberalism	**Warm peace** (and disarmament) if all are democracies	**Warm peace** is reached by global/regional cooperation/ integration
	(post-WWII Western Europe)	Arms in the hands of a pacific coalition
		(the EU; ASEAN? Mercosur?)

1. *Cold peace* is a situation in which both war among, and threats to use force by, states are absent. The underlying causes of conflicts are moderated and reduced, but are far from being resolved. The danger of a return to the use of force thus still looms in the background. The category of *warm peace* refers to a low likelihood of war and to much more cooperative relations among the states than in cold peace. For an extended discussion, see Benjamin Miller, *States, Nations and the Great Powers: The Sources of Regional War and Peace* (Cambridge: Cambridge University Press, 2007), chap. 2.

world peace. Second, while military power is very important in the eyes of realists, many of them are reluctant to use it in an unrestrained way. Under certain conditions, some liberals might be much more eager than their realist counterparts to use force. Moreover, while many liberals are obviously true believers in multilateralism, there are some realists who also accept at least a certain type of multilateralism under some conditions, while some liberals are willing to resort to unilateralism in certain circumstances.

In asking how best to ensure national security and world peace, the four perspectives are distinguished by their responses to two major questions:

1. The *goals* of security policy: whether to focus on the balance of capabilities between the state and its rivals or on those rivals' fundamental intentions and domestic character.
2. The *means* of security policy: whether to focus on military power or non-military means and whether to do so unilaterally or multilaterally.

The various combinations of answers to the two questions spawn four approaches: Defensive and offensive realists and liberals (see tables 1.2 and 1.3). Let us start with a general distinction between realists' and liberals' conceptions of security and then address the different approaches of defensive and offensive within each orientation.

REALISTS AND LIBERALS: THE BALANCE OF CAPABILITIES VERSUS THE RIVAL'S INTENTIONS

A state may be secure under either of the following two conditions:

1. If threats of violence against the core values of the state are present, the state can be secure to the extent that it possesses the capabilities to defend its key values at affordable cost.
2. In the absence of a threatening intent to use violence against the state's major values. This condition fits in better with the vision of high-level "warm" peace, though addressing the first condition can also promote peace, albeit a "cold" one.

Competing realist and liberal approaches to security are ultimately distinguished by which of these two conditions they privilege.[21]

In contrast to liberals, realists are skeptical that it could ever be possible for states to avoid threats for an extended period so long as the international system is anarchic, that is, while states have to provide for their own security in the absence of world government or a global police force. Thus, for realists, since some level of external threat is given over time, the key to state security lies in possessing the capabilities essential to cope with such threats.

Realists argue that it is difficult to plan one's security according to an assessment of the intentions of other states, both because it is very difficult to know others' intentions due to their variability and because intentions can change very quickly.[22] In the eyes of realists, trying to affect or manipulate the basic objectives of powerful adversaries is an elusive goal, which might backfire and escalate conflict unnecessarily. Therefore, the assessment of intentions should be based on a cautious worst-case analysis (though, while the offensive realists focus uncompromisingly on the worst case,[23] defensive realists highlight the need for cautious behavior and restraint, in order to avoid unintended conflict). In contrast, there can be greater confidence in estimating capabilities, which are hard to change overnight. Indeed, for realists the key to security in a self-help system is the balance of capabilities—and it is this balance that shapes intentions.[24] As a result, for realists, an imbalance of power creates a temptation for aggression; thus, a powerful state facing weak opponents will abuse and coerce them. At the same time, equal or superior capabilities induce moderation in a rival because of the expected high costs of aggression. In other words, capabilities produce intentions.

In contrast to realists, who take the existence of some level of security threats for granted and therefore concentrate on the capabilities required to meet them, liberals focus on state intentions as the major factor affecting international peace and security. Liberals strongly believe in the independent effects of intentions: given benign intentions, states will not develop offensive capabilities, and thus, according to this view, intentions generate capabilities.[25] A key element in the liberal conception of peace and security is the "second image" in Kenneth Waltz's 1959 book *Man, the State, and War.* This "second image"—that is, the state's domestic character and dominant ideology—shapes actors' international behavior (an "inside-out" logic) in contrast to the realist "third image," according to which actor behavior is shaped by the anarchic international system, and especially by the distribution of capabilities in that system (an "outside-in" logic).

According to the most prevalent liberal theory of peace—democratic/liberal peace theory—liberal democracies do not fight each other.[26] As a result, liberals believe in the feasibility of enhancing peace and security through democratization. While for offensive liberals, democratization is the key to peace (and the resort to force to further its spread is not precluded), for defensive liberals international institutions, particularly those dealing with collective security, are the major peacemaking mechanism. In addition, liberals prescribe economic interdependence among states, since it not only provides material benefits but also a disincentive to unilateral military action. In the liberal view, trading states prefer "to trade rather than to invade." They are not interested in building invading armies and in occupying territory. A related argument is that free-market economies are more pacific and tend to focus on economic prosperity rather than on military buildups and wars, which are seen as wasteful enterprises.

Despite their general focus on state intentions, liberals agree that capabilities are crucial to security to the extent that their various prescriptions for violence-avoidance fail. This may happen among states that are nondemocracies, are not economically interdependent, or do not belong to international institutions. Democracies facing illiberal states, which are likely to produce offensive capabilities, will have to respond by building comparable capabilities.

In the following sections, I will discuss the policy implications for security and peacemaking strategies deduced from the competing logics of the four theories, starting with the contrast between defensive and offensive liberalism, then addressing the contrast between defensive and offensive realism, which is also closely related to the debate between the balance-of-power and the hegemonic approaches. Finally, I show how the theoretical logic of the four approaches informs competing strategies for regime change and democracy promotion.

COMPETING LIBERAL CONCEPTIONS OF PEACE
AND SECURITY: DEFENSIVE AND OFFENSIVE

Liberals suggest that liberalization is both desirable for the purpose of peace and security and attainable in different parts of the world.[27] Liberals argue that illiberal states are more likely to adopt aggressive strategies and try to accumulate as much power as possible. Liberal regimes, by contrast, are more pacific in general,[28] at least vis-à-vis other liberal states,[29] and tend to acquire only the capabilities necessary to defend themselves against aggression by nonliberal powers. Since the degree of threat in the external environment is a function of the proportion of liberal versus illiberal regimes, liberals agree that the more liberalism spreads, the greater the level of security of liberal states, irrespective of the balance of capabilities. Regime change— democratization—is most desirable. Economic interdependence (especially among free-market economies) and international institutions are other liberal strategies intended to moderate state behavior and create a more peaceful international environment.[30] Liberals believe that a more liberal world is not only desirable for security and other purposes, but also feasible. Liberalism, they maintain, has universal applicability, transcending national and cultural divides, and pacifying competitive relationships.

While sharing the assumption that liberalization makes the world safer and states more secure, liberals disagree among themselves over the means for reaching this desirable objective. Some analysts, especially realists, have recently underlined the offensive character of liberalism.[31] Others see liberalism as essentially defensive in character.[32] In contrast, I argue that rather than seeing liberalism as a whole as either offensive or defensive, there is a need to distinguish between a defensive as well as an offensive variant of liberalism. In the following sections, I outline some of the important differences between these two branches of liberalism.

Unilateralism versus Multilateralism

One key difference concerns multilateralism versus hegemonic leadership. Defensive liberals strongly believe in multilateralism in the sense that institutional constraints apply also to the freedom of action of the leading member of the coalition. Thus, strong limitations should apply to US unilateralism. In the opinion of defensive liberals, multilateralism enhances the legitimacy and effectiveness of the operation of international institutions in supplying a variety of collective goods in different domains such as security, economy, and environment. By this logic, defensive liberals maintain, US policies under multilateral restraints will also advance the true interests of the US while avoiding the expected opposition and balancing against it given US unilateralism.[33]

Offensive liberals, by contrast, doubt the effectiveness of international institutions in the absence of strong US hegemonic leadership. Powerful constraints on the hegemon make international institutions and collective action unproductive. Due to the problematic effectiveness of multilateralism, the hegemon must take also unilateral actions on occasion. In their eyes, US leadership, including by unilateral means, is the key to decisive and effective international actions for providing common goods such as peace, security, and other benefits.[34]

The Sources of Disagreements among Liberals

The sources of disagreement in liberal thought are not new, and go much deeper than the recent debate on President Bush's national security strategy.[35] Such differences are reflected in the divergences, for example, between Immanuel Kant and Thomas Paine with regard to military interventions aimed at spreading democratic rule.[36] Based on optimistic assumptions about human nature and progress, what Walker calls "Paine's revolutionary liberalism" (and we here call "offensive liberalism") advocates the use of force to impose democracy and global peace.[37] In contrast, Kant's cautious "evolutionary liberalism" (here called "defensive liberalism") opposes military intervention in favor of regime change and democratization: "no state shall forcibly interfere in the constitution and government of another state."[38] In complete contrast to revolutionary (or offensive) liberalism, evolutionary (or defensive) liberalism does not believe that external military intervention is a useful tool to advance democracy in nondemocratic states. This difference is derived from different conceptions of political change: while offensive liberals believe in easy transformation, defensive liberals subscribe to gradual institutional development.[39] In this sense, the neoconservatives are just the most recent wave (or incarnation) of offensive liberalism, but in no way created or invented it.[40]

Liberal Interventions

Although Woodrow Wilson exhibited a duality between "liberal internationalism" (his term for "defensive liberalism") and "liberal imperialism" or "liberal interventionism" (corresponding to "offensive liberalism"),[41] at least during the initial stages of his administration, he displayed strong offensive liberal tendencies, as manifested in numerous US interventions, especially in Mexico (1914, 1916) and Haiti (from 1915 to 1934) and also in Cuba, the Dominican Republic (1916 to 1924), Honduras, and Nicaragua (1912–22).[42]

Doyle points out that liberals face a dilemma between respecting states' right of nonintervention in domestic affairs (thus overlooking nonliberal states' violations of their citizens' rights) and advancing human rights in these countries (thus violating the norm of nonintervention).[43] Defensive liberals are relatively more respectful of the norm of nonintervention, especially when it comes to military interventions. In contrast, offensive liberals justify such involvement through similar arguments as those articulated by one of its early advocates—long before the US neoconservatives—who asserted that "barbarous nations" do not have the rights of civilized nations, "except a right to such treatment as may, at the earliest possible period, fit them for becoming one."[44]

A key distinction in this respect is between "cosmopolitan Liberals," who are generally interventionist, and "national Liberals," who tend to be noninterventionists, except in a few extraordinary situations;[45] in terms of the classifications employed here, the former could be described as offensive liberals, and the latter as defensive liberals. There are two types of cosmopolitans: right-wing libertarians, such as Hadley Arkes,[46] who focus on intervention to promote political rights and freedom, while left-wing egalitarians, like David Luban,[47] focus more on intervention to promote social rights such as rights to food, shelter, clothing, and security—for instance, to be free from arbitrary killing. Key examples of national liberals, on the other hand, include J. S. Mill and Michael Walzer.[48]

Defensive Liberal Mechanisms

Defensive liberals are committed to the idea that the spread of democracy and capitalist systems can and should be accomplished peacefully, including by the "power of example" and what Joseph Nye terms "soft power," that is, the ability to shape the preferences of other states through nontangible resources such as institutions, culture, and the attractiveness of ideas, regimes, and economic performance.[49] Other defensive liberal methods include trade agreements; economic incentives such as foreign aid to support transitions to democracy and the free market; the assistance of international institutions, for example, in the supervision of elections; engagement by a great variety of nongovernmental organizations that provide aid and know-how to groups that are interested in democratization, such as the media, trade unions, opposition parties, human rights and women's groups, and so on.[50]

Defensive liberals also believe that free trade, economic interdependence, and association with international institutions can change state preferences and make them more pacific and less able and inclined to resort to force. Defensive liberals particularly believe that economic interdependence, and to some extent international institutions, foster democratization. As a result, there is less need to exercise outside pressure on reluctant regimes to democratize, and they are, in turn, more receptive to free trade and membership in international institutions because of the associated economic benefits. Liberals aim to create economic interdependence among states, so as to make them prefer "trading rather over invading," for in the liberal view, trading states have no interest in building invading armies.[51]

Liberals also believe that enhancing the power of international institutions or regimes will increase the incentives of states to cooperate with each other and will thus produce more benign state intentions.[52] In the area of security, the most relevant institution is a collective security system under which all peace-loving states are committed to come automatically to the defense of any state attacked by an aggressor irrespective of previous particularistic ties, affiliations, and alliances with the victim. It is a system based on the universal norm of "one for all and all for one." Key examples include the League of Nations, initiated by Woodrow Wilson, and the UN, led by the Security Council, though both organizations, especially the former, do not have a very good record in making and keeping the peace.[53] Defensive liberals might argue, however, that in the post–Cold War era, the UN became more relevant for peacekeeping missions around the globe.[54]

Other liberals might point out that regional organizations are more effective for collective security than a global organization, pointing to the more successful records of the Organization of American States and, especially, post–Cold War NATO, with its successful interventions in the Balkans: Bosnia in 1995 and Kosovo in 1999.[55] More generally, defensive liberals can highlight the warm peace reached by regional cooperation and integration in Southeast Asia (ASEAN, the Association of Southeast Asian Nations), South America (Mercosur), and most notably the European Union. Consistent with their focus on democracy as the key variable affecting the likelihood of peace, offensive liberals would argue that it is not surprising that the most successful of all these regional organizations are the EU and NATO, being composed solely of liberal democracies. Defensive liberals, for their part, are more open to the possibilities of high-level regional peace based on regional institutions and economic interdependence—even if not all the regional states are currently liberal democracies.[56]

Defensive liberals also engage in multilateral diplomacy to resolve conflicts, attempting to reduce the likelihood of hot spots escalating toward violence. The 1991 Madrid Conference on Arab-Israeli peace and the 1995 Dayton Agreement on Bosnia are examples of this kind of multilateral diplomacy.[57]

Offensive Liberal Methods

Like defensive liberals, offensive liberals also believe that affecting the basic intentions and internal regime of the adversary in the direction of liberalization constitutes the most effective and fundamental solution to the security and peace problem. In this respect, their views are diametrically opposed to those of realists. Yet, they differ from the defensive liberals in the means that they think are sometimes necessary to reach this objective. In contrast to the strong emphasis of defensive liberals on soft power, they are much more receptive to the use of hard power. They are more skeptical about the utility of the peaceful means advocated by the defensive realists, especially vis-à-vis totalitarian and tyrannical regimes. While they may accept the logic of the balance of power in order to avoid war, if possible, with other great powers, they are more ready than defensive liberals to resort to force against a weaker tyranny with the aim of installing a democratic, or at least a freer, regime.[58] At the same time, offensive liberals are more inclined than realists to embark on wars of choice— "ideological crusades"—without looming "clear and present" security threats (as the defensive realists would insist) or opportunities for material profit (as the offensive realists would prefer). Offensive liberals are not interested only in a change in the political regime of potential opponents, but also in a transformation of their economic system. They believe that free-market economies are not only better for business, but will also behave more peacefully. In other words, they strive to impose a Western-style liberal regime.

Moreover, in their view, economic liberalization is likely to promote political openness—resulting in eventual democratization—as a growing middle class demands increasing political participation. Besides imposing democracy, then, offensive liberals are also willing to apply coercive pressure on countries to open their economies to free trade, the so-called Open Door policy.[59] They focus mainly, however, on the political regime in line with Woodrow Wilson's democratizing crusade—"to make the world safe for democracy."[60]

US Hegemony and Regime Change

Like offensive realists, offensive liberals also strongly favor US hegemony, which they believe leads to weaker powers bandwagoning with their strongest counterpart. The benign hegemony of a liberal US, they also suppose, will generate less opposition than the hegemony of a nondemocratic regime.[61] Indeed, we should expect substantial support for US hegemony from both fellow democracies and freedom-loving people in nondemocracies, hoping for US help, including coercive measures, to free their countries from tyranny. In the offensive, as opposed to the defensive liberal view, the US does not need to legitimize its use of force through multilateral institutions, such as the UN, especially if they are populated by nondemocracies. Lacking legitimacy at home, how can such nondemocracies confer it abroad?[62]

The differences between defensive and offensive liberalism manifested themselves most clearly in the debates preceding the Iraq War between the Europeans, led by defensive liberal France and Germany, and the Bush administration, intellectually informed by neoconservatives—who had risen to prominence after 9/11 and shared in the long-standing tradition of offensive liberalism in the US. Although the Europeans were all in favor of democracy in Iraq in the long run, in principle, they were reluctant to use force to institute regime change. In contrast, the US—mindful of 9/11—adopted the offensive liberal view that regime change is necessary in the case of tyrannical regimes that constitute a security threat to the US, either because they sponsor terrorism, or because they develop weapons of mass destruction, or both.[63]

Liberalism and constructivism   Both liberalism (including, notably, the offensive variant) and constructivism share a lot in common by attributing great importance to the role of ideas in foreign policy, in contrast to the realist focus on material factors.[64] Still, there are some key differences:

1. While constructivism focuses on ideational elements, both variants of liberalism do highlight *material* factors, such as economic interdependence and its pacifying effects (defensive liberalism) and the military power of democratic great powers, notably the US, which preserves its primacy in a unipolar system and also spreads democracy by the use of force (offensive liberalism).
2. Constructivism is not a definite IR theory in the way that liberalism and realism are. Rather, it advances a general, even philosophical framework for *understanding* by highlighting the critical role of ideas, norms, and identities; moreover, in principle, it is open to pointing out the influence of a great variety of different sets of ideas and norms, including antiliberal ones. In contrast, liberalism is committed to a certain set of ideas and norms of specific substantive content, which is expected to influence the behavior of liberal states. Obviously, those constructivists who underline

the effects of liberal norms and ideas share a lot with liberals, but other constructivists might highlight the effects of completely different ideas as diverse as Islamist, communist, or Confucianist, which supposedly influence the behavior of nonliberal actors. In this sense, it is impossible to deduce a specific type of grand strategy from the logic of constructivism as is the case with the four perspectives discussed here: defensive/offensive realism/liberalism.

3. Accordingly, liberals and constructivists diverge with regard to the key mechanism to achieve peace: while for liberalism these are specific liberal mechanisms—democracy (particularly for offensive liberalism) or collective security institutions (defensive liberalism), constructivists highlight the more general effects of identities and normative and ideational factors such as "mutual identifications, transnational values, intersubjective understandings, and shared identities" on the emergence of peace.[65] In particular, the focus of offensive liberalism on the state differs from much of the existing constructivist work, which highlights the importance of transnational social networks and international institutions.[66]

OFFENSIVE VERSUS DEFENSIVE REALISTS; HEGEMONY VERSUS THE BALANCE OF POWER

Although they identify the same basic security problem, the responses of offensive and defensive realists are completely different.[67] Offensive realists make a direct connection between power and security.[68] They believe that in order to ensure security, the state has to maximize its relative power and achieve superiority vis-à-vis its opponents. The more power it possesses, the greater the margin of security the state enjoys. Maximum security is achieved through full-blown hegemony in the international system, or at least in the region under consideration.[69] Under these conditions, the hegemon can deter potential rivals and compel others to make diplomatic, economic, and strategic concessions so as to maximize its power. Without such superiority, rivals will grow stronger at its expense and pose a threat to its security. If a challenger emerges, the hegemon may resort to preventive war to meet the danger.[70]

Defensive realists, by contrast, do not make a direct linkage between maximizing power and security; power maximization might even harm state security under certain conditions.[71] While offensive realists view the great powers as revisionist and expansionist, defensive realists see them as status quo oriented, with survival or security—and not power maximization—as their primary objective. States defend themselves against threats and minimize relative losses, and attempts at expansion are both unnecessary for state security and even likely to backfire. Accordingly, for security purposes, states should behave moderately and avoid threatening others. In the defensive realist view, an accumulation of power beyond what is needed to defend the status quo—especially through the acquisition of offensive capabilities— might make the state less secure through the familiar workings of the security dilemma. Such an arms buildup, even if only for defensive purposes, might frighten other states, when, perceiving a threat to their security, they arm themselves in response. What is known as the offense-defense balance is thus a critical factor in determining the intensity of the security dilemma, which is especially intense when the offense has the advantage and it is impossible to distinguish between the two. Under these conditions, a likely outcome might be a costly and dangerous arms race leading, in extreme cases, to inadvertent escalation and war—even when both sides seek only to protect the status quo.[72] Offensive realists, by contrast, highlight the likelihood of premediated wars due to the revisionist aims of the great powers.

Defensive realists believe that security should be achieved interdependently rather than unilaterally. No power can be secure if other powers perceive themselves to be vulnerable because, especially under crisis conditions, the latter might be compelled to strike first, having been put before the choice to "use it or lose it." Such a situation is unstable and dangerous to all parties involved; hence, states should strive, whether unilaterally or through mutual security arrangements and arms control, to construct a balance of capabilities that discourages everyone from attacking first, that provides an advantage to the defense and allows all to distinguish as much as possible between defensive and offensive capabilities. In this way, peace may be achieved— albeit a *cold* peace based on a certain balance of power. In contrast to the situation of high-level warm peace, moreover, armaments will remain an important component of such a peace, although arms control agreements, which reinforce defense at the expense of offense, are desirable for the prevention of war.[73]

Defensive realists believe that the defense usually has the advantage, and that bullying is not profitable in the international system as a countervailing coalition will be formed against the most threatening power to prevent it from achieving its hegemonic objectives.[74] Offensive strategies, therefore, are unlikely to succeed, and as a result of learning, such strategies are likely to lose their attraction over time. In contrast, offensive realists believe that the offense usually has the advantage and that states bandwagon with the stronger or most threatening party rather than balance against it.[75] Hence, an offensive strategy to achieve hegemony and maximize power can succeed by exploiting opportunities to expand at affordable cost. Such maximization and expansion, in turn, leads to bandwagoning with the superior power rather than balancing against it.[76] Security and peace are reached through strength and superiority rather than through balance and restraint as advocated by defensive realists.

Important components of security, according to the logic of defensive realism, are security arrangements and confidence-building measures, which enhance transparency and reduce the ability to conduct a surprise attack, mitigating mutual fears of being attacked. These fears are a major source of insecurity, especially if offensive capabilities have an advantage over defensive ones (and consequently there are advantages to preempting the opponent by attacking first), or if it is impossible to distinguish between offensive and defensive capabilities.[77] Arms control, in this view, is intended to decrease the offensive capabilities of states while enhancing defensive ones in nonprovocative ways. It can reduce the security dilemma and provide mutual reassurance by sharply distinguishing offensive from defensive capabilities.

In the eyes of defensive realists, confidence-building measures and arms control can signal defensive intentions of states and thus reduce the likelihood of escalation. This provides a major way for rational actors to avoid wars. Wars might rather occasionally occur due to various domestic pathologies.[78] In contrast, offensive realists highlight the great uncertainty about other states' intentions, while it is impossible to distinguish between the offense and defense as most weapon systems can serve both offensive and defensive purposes. Such uncertainty and the impossibility to distinguish between military systems increase the level of conflict under international anarchy. In contrast, the belief of the defensive realists in the possibility to distinguish between revisionists and security seekers increases the likelihood of international cooperation and of effective arms control accords.

Defensive realists view nuclear weapons as the ultimate guarantee of security by providing states with the ability to deter each other with the threat of unacceptable damage. Yet, mutual security is enhanced only in a situation of mutual assured destruction (MAD), in which all parties have a secure second-strike capability, meaning that they can absorb a massive surprise attack and still inflict unacceptable damage on the opponent, giving none of the parties the incentive to preempt and strike first.[79]

A related conceptual and policy question concerns the potential trade-offs between deterrence and defense: will the deployment of a defensive antimissile system like the Strategic Defense Initiative (SDI, or in its popular name—"Star Wars") or national missile defense reinforce US security and world peace or jeopardize it? Defensive realists, who tend to be deterrence purists, argue that a defensive buildup, which makes the state less vulnerable to attack and therefore more capable of preemption, increases the opponents' security dilemma, thus leading to an arms race and greater mutual insecurity. Since the potential deployment of missile defense systems in Eastern Europe and East Asia would have led to arms races with Russia and China—who would have feared the loss of their retaliatory capabilities—the US should avoid the buildup of such defensive systems. In opposition, advocates of missile defense assert that in the absence of defense, deterrence can fail with catastrophic consequences. The logic of offensive realism suggests that the combined effect of nuclear deterrence, antimissile defense, and overwhelming, sophisticated conventional capabilities will ensure US military superiority, which, in its eyes, is the best guarantee of both national security and world peace. Even if this peace were cold and heavily armed (especially in the case of the hegemon), it would at least result in the avoidance of wars between the great powers.

Realism and constructivism   These approaches seem to be further apart from each other than liberalism and constructivism, since realism is essentially a materialist approach, whereas constructivism is an ideational one, while, as noted, liberalism has some strong ideational components.[80] Yet, constructivists can potentially advance an underlying explanation of supposedly "realist" behavior and outcomes (such as balancing, hegemony seeking, armament, the security dilemma) by showing that they are the result of the dominance of "realist" (or "Hobbesian")[81] ideas held by leaders and societies due to cultural effects, at least in certain periods of time. The counterrealist response would have to demonstrate then that these outcomes are indeed the result of anarchy as a material-situational constraint (rather than as a shared idea) and of the distribution of the material capabilities in the international system.

At any rate, constructivists challenge realist prescriptions for peacemaking by suggesting that "security communities" exist in the international and regional arenas and these communities do not need balancing or hegemony to achieve and maintain peace.[82] Their mutual identifications and shared identities are likely to produce high-level warm peace also in the absence of balancing and hegemony. Yet, realists counter that even the "poster child" of the constructivist case—the Western European high level of warm peace—could not be achieved in the absence, at least initially, of balancing against the common Soviet threat during the Cold War and the pacifying role of US hegemony as the security provider to Western Europe against this threat. Realists themselves, however, are divided on the effects of hegemony and balancing.

TABLE 1.4. Differences between offensive and defensive realism

Issue	Offensive realism	Defensive realism
Anarchy > war	Premeditated wars	Inadvertent wars
Military capability	Advantages to offense	Advantages to defense
Other states' intentions	Uncertainty	Signaling defensive intentions (including by confidence-building measure)
Distinguish offense vs. defense?	No	Occasionally yes
States' orientation	Great powers are revisionist	Security seekers
Rational actors?	Yes	Occasionally domestic pathologies
Does aggression pay?	Yes—frequently	No—countervailing coalitions
Alliances	Bandwagoning/buck-passing	Balancing
Which balances matter?	1. Balance of power	1. Balances of threat
	2. Overall military (and economic) power	2. Offense-defense balance, affected also by geography and technology
Anarchy > behavior	Conflict dominates	Potential for cooperation
Nuclear weapons	First strike	Second strike
Use of force	Maximal	Minimal
With others?	Unilateral	Multilateral/arms control
When secure?	Being the hegemon; superior offensive power	Mutual deterrence; balance of power; defense is superior and possible to distinguish from offense enhanced by confidence-building measures

HEGEMONY VERSUS BALANCE OF POWER

While some offensive realists focus on the contribution of hegemony to the national security of the hegemon itself,[83] others emphasize the utility of hegemony for world order.[84] This is partly related to hegemonic-stability theory, the logic and implications of which for world peace are contradicted by balance-of-power theory associated with defensive realism. Despite their common roots in realism and structural analysis, the basic premises of the hegemonic-stability school directly contradict those of the balance-of-power school. The first assumption of the hegemonic-stability school is that order in world politics is usually created by a single dominant state.[85] This assumption rests on the logic of collective-goods theory;[86] hegemons are both more able and willing to provide public goods than other states, which prefer to free ride rather than share in the costs. Hegemons, for their part, will be more willing to pay these costs because they benefit greatly from a well-ordered system.

The second assumption is that continuing order depends on the persistence of hegemony, so that the emergence of powerful challengers undermines the established international order.[87] Contrary to traditional balance-of-power expectations, Organski's "power transition" model, for example, suggests that growing equality in the distribution of capabilities among the great powers will make the international system less rather than more stable and increase the risks of a major war. The classic historical illustration of the hegemonic-stability argument is the nineteenth-century "Pax Britannica," which was supposedly guaranteed by Britain's predominant economic and sea power.[88] Rising German capabilities at the end of the century, so the argument goes, posed a challenge to the British-led international order; this challenge culminated in World War I and its destructive aftereffects. After 1945, and especially in the post–Cold War era, the hegemonic-stability school maintains, it has been US preponderance that has ensured peace and prosperity through Pax Americana, and the emergence of equally capable powers, notably nowadays China, could undermine this order.

The balance-of-power school disagrees, arguing that hegemony is not feasible because of the effective functioning of the equilibrium mechanism;[89] nor is it conducive to either preserving the autonomy of states or advancing peace and stability. In this view, the inherent balancing tendencies in world politics have two major implications: first, states will tend to join the weaker coalition;[90] second, an imbalance among the major powers will trigger great efforts by the lesser among them to catch up with the "hegemon" through alliance building and expansion of their power base. Thus, the end result of disequilibrium could be more intensive competition and a more dangerous situation than in a state of equilibrium. In contrast, the achievement of rough equality would reduce the incentives for a rising power to challenge the status quo. Hegemony is also undesirable, as a marked imbalance of forces creates a temptation for aggression against weaker states.[91]

Thus, the balance-of-power/defensive realist school argues that every major attempt at reaching hegemony has led to the emergence of a countervailing coalition[92]—as in the cases of Philip II, Louis XIV, Napoleon, the German kaiser, Hitler, and the Soviet Union—at least in Europe (as manifested by NATO). At the same time, when the great powers took care to preserve the balance among them, peace was maintained. A major example is the nineteenth-century Concert of Europe that both maintained the balance among the five great European powers and succeeded in keeping the peace starting from the 1814–15 Congress of Vienna and at least until the eruption of the Crimean War in 1853.[93]

Applying this debate to the current international system, offensive realists would argue that US hegemony and the unipolar structure of the international system guarantee peace. A good example of this argument refers to the pacifying effects of US-led NATO interventions in the Balkans in the 1990s. At any rate, it is not feasible in the foreseeable future to balance the United States' hugely superior capabilities,[94] although some analysts challenge this argument by highlighting the major increase in Chinese economic—and to some extent also military—capabilities.[95] Others see a transition to a multi-polar world.[96] Defensive realists, in fact, have anticipated the emergence of a balance since the Soviet collapse in 1991 even though they could argue that until 9/11, and especially until the invasion of Iraq, the US behaved moderately and avoided giving others sufficient incentives to form a countervailing coalition. Defensive realists expected such a coalition to be more likely following the Iraq War given unilateral US behavior and resort to preventive war and regime change by force, increasing the perceived threat posed by US behavior to other states.[97] This threatening behavior could lead at least to "soft balancing" by other powers, that is, diplomatic opposition to US policies and lack of cooperation with them so as to constrain its freedom of action.[98] Moreover, in defensive realists' eyes, it is the marked imbalance in world power in favor of the US that permits such aggressive behavior and abuse of superior power. Defensive realists conclude that the emergence of a balance is not only to be expected, but is also desirable for world peace and security as a constraint on the unnecessary US resort to force (thus it is also good for the US national interest).

IR THEORIES AND THE POSSIBILITIES
AND THE CONDITIONS FOR PEACE

Liberals are more open to the possibility of the highest level of peace—warm peace including disarmament—if the conditions they highlight are present. Realists believe in the possibility of peace, too, but it will be at best a cold armed peace based on a certain balance of power. For defensive realists, arms control might be achieved under certain conditions.[99] Yet, for all realists, complete disarmament seems to be a dangerous illusion. Under anarchy the fears associated with the security dilemma are more likely to spawn arms races rather than enduring disarmament (defensive realists). Revisionist powers might take advantage of such supposed disarmament at the expense of status quo powers (offensive realists).

Liberals are not pacifists, and they do allow for the use of force for self-defense. Still, defensive liberals are skeptical about key realist instruments—the balance of power, deterrence, and preventive war (although some of them might be more receptive to a preemptive strike when there is an immediate, clear and present danger).[100] The combination of self-defense and caution is typical of defensive realists who draw on the deep insights of this school to advise statesmen to pursue moderation and restraint in foreign policy. This might also seem like liberal advice. Yet, the liberal vision is bolder than realist prudence alone—it is a world of high-level peace, which eschews an armed balance as even a defensive realist would have it. Moreover, the road to warm peace goes through "second image" characteristics—states' internal beliefs and attributes, notably successful democratization and a market economy, which are more supportive of peace and security than a realist emphasis on the balance of capabilities under anarchy. Indeed, to reach a high-level warm peace, there is a need for "regime change" based on human rights and the consent of the public. Crucially, however, liberals differ with regard to the key question of whether this change of intentions and beliefs should take place through the use of force (offensive liberals) or by peaceful persuasion, the power of example, and soft power (defensive liberals).

For realists, such domestic changes are not the key to the question of war and peace. Democratization is going to have either marginal effects or destabilizing consequences. At any rate, realists argue, liberal great powers should not be in the business of democratizing other states. This might be a futile or even dangerous enterprise. It is also unnecessary. If these states are important for security purposes, the focus should be on issues related to the balance of power and deterrence rather than on the domestic character of these states; and surely the uncontrolled dynamics of democratization should be avoided.

Illustrating the Logic of the Four Approaches: Strategies toward Regime Change

This section illustrates the logic of each approach—and the grand strategies derived from them—by briefly discussing the variations in regime-change strategies. From the point of view of a liberal democratic great power (like the United States), there are four potential ideal-type policies toward regime change, each informed by a different conceptual framework—as shown in table 1.5.

TABLE 1.5. Continuum of variations of policies toward regime change and the conceptual frameworks informing them

Grand strategy	Imposed democratization	Partial/gradual democratization	Nonintervention/ abstention	Democracy removal
Approach informing it	Offensive liberalism	Defensive liberalism	Defensive realism	Offensive realism

1. Imposed democratization   The great power (the US in our case) uses coercion to impose drastic/comprehensive regime change toward democratization of the country at stake manifested by holding free general elections in short order. Such an endeavor includes major investment in the political, military, and economic spheres. This grand strategy is derived from the logic of *offensive liberalism*. We argue that this strategy especially guided the behavior of the Bush Jr. administration following 9/11.

2. Gradual/partial/peaceful promotion of regime change toward democratization   The great power (i.e., the US), in close cooperation with other like-minded states and international institutions, helps both to build up state institutions and to create a political environment, which are necessary prerequisites for democracy (for example, state building, promotion of human rights and independent judiciary and media, and transition to market economy), but are not sufficient conditions for the emergence of a full-blown democracy. This grand strategy is deduced from the rationale of *defensive liberalism*. The strategy also focuses on reducing the barriers to international trade and foreign investment. With regard to the use of force, this strategy encourages humanitarian interventions as defensive moves to protect persecuted people everywhere on the globe from genocide and ethnic cleansing. Democracy is not imposed; instead the intervention is supposed to help to create some of the conditions for the emergence of democracy later on. We'll argue that this was a major strategy during the 1990s.

3. Nonintervention   The great power stands on the sidelines—an abstention from an intervention in domestic affairs of nondemocratic states even if an authentic democratic revolution is suppressed by force by these states. This grand strategy is based on the logic of *defensive realism*. This strategy was followed throughout much of the Cold War. Defensive realism, as a whole—together with other components of this approach—was especially prevalent during the détente era of the 1960s and 1970s, and also in the second half of the 1980s.

4. Democracy removal   This grand strategy involves deposing democracy and replacing it by a pro-US authoritarian regime. The weaker form of this strategy is to actively support the continuation in power of a friendly authoritarian regime. This grand strategy is based on the rationale of *offensive realism*. Several cases during the Cold War could fit this strategy.

The next sections discuss the links between the approaches and the variations in regime-change strategies and illustrate them very briefly.

1. Offensive liberalism   Since democracy is a necessary condition for an enduring and stable peace and for a complete removal of security threats, according to this approach, democracy promotion is a key component of its grand strategy. More specifically, when confronted by illiberal powers, which pose major security threats, offensive liberals recommend imposed democratization as such a regime change supposedly removes the security threats coming from these countries as soon as they become democratic. This can be done either directly by the occupation of the country at stake—which makes it possible for the occupier to try to impose democracy—or indirectly by providing support, including military aid, for groups that try to replace the authoritarian regime with a democratic one.

> *Empirical examples*: In addition to the somewhat controversial cases of democratization by Woodrow Wilson in Central America mentioned above, the US imposed democratization—while allocating huge resources—in defeated, but still potentially powerful post-WWII Germany and Japan at the beginning of the Cold War. The post-9/11 attempt to democratize Iraq was also informed by an offensive liberal strategy to eliminate in the most fundamental way terrorism and weapons of mass destruction in Arab countries with authoritarian governments, starting with Iraq as a hoped-for successful "model" of "peaceful democracy."[101] The logic was that the illiberal character of these Arab regimes supposedly produced large-scale terrorism—due to the absence of peaceful channels to express political grievances. Illiberalism was allegedly also the source of the quest for weapons of mass destruction—reflecting the aggressive character of these regimes. The Iraq intervention will be discussed in chapter 8.

2. Defensive liberal   This grand strategy advances some of the conditions for peaceful democratization, but does not pursue a full-blown imposition of democracy on the country at stake. Such an imposition, in this strategy's view, is likely to generate a nationalist backlash and strong international opposition to the imposing power, leading to a failure of the attempted democratization. Instead, there is a partial/gradual approach focused on creating the prerequisites for democracy (humanitarian intervention to protect human rights, promotion of a market economy and assistance with institution building, starting with the rule-of-law aspects of statehood). Defensive liberals also use soft power and the "power of example" for democracy promotion, which, it is argued, will over time advance peace through full democratization.

> *Empirical examples:* The limited democratization by the US, for example, in the Philippines.[102] In this case the US encouraged only limited political reforms while in Germany and Japan, following the offensive liberal logic, it also advanced fundamental socioeconomic reforms.[103]
>
> Examples of humanitarian interventions without imposed democratization — to be discussed in chapter 7 — include Somalia (1992–94), Haiti (1994), Bosnia (1995), and Kosovo (1999). Thus, for example, democracy was not imposed on Serbia after its defeat in the Kosovo War; later, however, the Serbian public — at least partly due to the external US-led NATO intervention — removed Milosevic from power and installed democracy. These interventions were multilateral — either through the UN or NATO.[104] Another defensive liberal option is using the dynamics of "the power of example" of American "soft power"[105] to encourage peaceful democratization and transition to market economy, which is, however, initiated and led regionally and locally such as in South America in the 1980s and Eastern Europe in the 1990s. According to the defensive liberals, both soft power and multilateralism enhance the legitimacy of US actions to promote democracy in peaceful ways.

3. Defensive realism   This approach suggests a cautious policy, avoiding pro-democratic interventions in order to steer clear of unnecessary dangers and the cost of confrontations and war, and this rises out of the belief that the character of the regime is at any rate not a crucial factor in shaping foreign policy. Moreover, the likelihood of success for externally driven regime imposition is quite low due to the nationalist resistance it will generate.

> *Empirical evidence:* A key example is addressed in chapter 3: the refusal to "roll back" Soviet influence in Eastern Europe by the US in the 1950s,[106] although Soviet control over domestic affairs in that region, and its insistence on a closed sphere of influence, prevented an explicit spheres-of-influence agreement.[107] The avoidance of "rollback" culminated with the nonintervention in Hungary (October 1956) even though the revolution there seemed to be promoting a genuine democracy with widespread popular support.

4. Offensive realism   The great power's key concern is to advance its material national security interests irrespective of ideological considerations. Thus, according to this approach, the great power could under certain conditions engage in removing a democratic regime, even if the great power affecting regime change were itself a democracy—if this democratic regime seems hostile to the great power and to its material security and economic interests. Instead, the great power could install a friendlier authoritarian regime contributing to its power and security. A somewhat weaker version of this logic leads to supporting an existing allied authoritarian regime, especially when it has strategic and economic importance, and avoiding exerting pressures on it to democratize and to protect human rights irrespective of its abusive behavior.

> *Empirical examples*: Iran in 1953, Guatemala in 1954, and Chile in 1973 are cases of a US strategy of democracy removal in accordance with its realpolitik interests in the framework of the Cold War competition.[108] US policy toward the Arab and Muslim world, especially Saudi Arabia and Egypt (also Pakistan during some periods), fits the weaker version of supporting friendly authoritarian governments already in power and avoiding exerting pressures on them to democratize despite their major human rights abuse—as long as they continue to serve the US strategic interests (such as supplying oil at an affordable price and making peace with Israel).

Variation in regime change and democracy promotion is one of the dimensions in the US grand strategies we're going to examine in this book. A key challenge for this book is to try to account for the variations in the application of the competing grand strategies in different periods. The task is to find the most powerful explanation for the selection by US administrations of a certain grand strategy in one period, while a competing strategy (informed by a competing approach) was selected in another period. Under what conditions is each of the grand strategies (and the related approach) more likely to be selected and applied? What is the best explanation of these variations: is it the decision-maker/individual level of the president and his worldview, or domestic political pressures and incentives, or the opportunities and constraints of the international system, or some combination of these causal factors? These are some of the major questions addressed in the remainder of the book, which will further develop some of the novel concepts, issues, and theoretical distinctions among IR approaches—and their derived grand strategies—addressed here. The next chapter presents the explanatory model—the conditions under which each of the competing grand strategies is selected. The following chapters examine the theory by analyzing some of the key changes in the post-1945 US grand strategy.

2

Explaining Changes in Grand Strategy

The Model: The Systemic Conditions for the Rise of the Four Strategies

While some existing studies distinguish between competing grand strategies, they fail to provide a parsimonious theoretical explanation for the key question: under what conditions is each of the competing strategies likely to emerge as the dominant strategy, at least for a certain period of time?[1] To the extent that there are explanations of the choice of a grand strategy, they are usually associated with the incumbent president and his worldview and maybe also that of his key advisors.[2] This makes a lot of sense in the American political system based on the president's wide authorities, especially in foreign and defense policy. Thus, observers attribute great importance to the initial views of the president when he comes to office and formulates the initial grand strategy.

What we show in this study, however, is that at least some of the key changes in US grand strategy occurred *during* the terms of some of the presidents—and frequently they generated markedly different strategies than those advanced at the beginning of the term. For these kinds of changes, we need a different type of explanation, which will not be based solely on the individual or even the domestic level of analysis.

Our explanation is based on the combined effects of two key systemic factors: the global distribution of capabilities and the balance of threat confronting the great power. Variations in these two factors can account for changes and variations in the American grand strategy. While elements of realism and liberalism are always present in US grand strategy, these systemic factors determine the relative dominance of each of the four approaches in the foreign policy of the United States at a given time and the likelihood of its acceptance by the US domestic political system. Thus, for example, while both realist and liberal components were present in US grand strategy during the Cold War,

TABLE 2.1. Systemic conditions for the dominance of the competing grand strategies: The case of the United States since 1947

	Global distribution of capabilities	
Balance of threat	Hegemony	Great-power parity
High external threat	Offensive ideology promotion → offensive liberalism	Offensive realism
	Post-September 11 (key case: the invasion of Iraq)	Height of the Cold War (1950–62, 1979–85)
Relatively benign environment	Defensive ideology promotion → defensive liberalism	Defensive realism (early Cold War: 1947–50)
	1991–2001	Détente (1963–78, 1985–90)

generally realpolitik considerations overrode liberal impulses when it came to the grand strategy vis-à-vis the key opponent—the other superpower.[3] At the same time, liberal elements dominated the US grand strategy during the post–Cold War period (see table 2.1). We start with an analysis of the first explanatory factor: the balance of capabilities.

THE GLOBAL DISTRIBUTION OF CAPABILITIES

This factor distinguishes between a situation of great-power parity (bipolarity or multipolarity) and the presence of a single predominant power (unipolarity)—that is, a global hegemon. In general, the distribution of capabilities selects between the realist and the ideological approaches to security. When there is a single hegemon, the costs of pursuing an ideological security strategy that accords with its domestic values and preferences are much lower than in a situation of great-power parity, because of the high freedom of action the hegemon enjoys in the absence of a powerful countervailing rival or coalition. As Waltz argues, "in the absence of counterweights, a country's internal impulses prevail, whether fueled by liberal or other urges."[4] In other words, it is mainly under the conditions of hegemony that the regime type of the great power significantly influences its choice of grand strategy. Hegemony is a permissive condition for pursuing an ideological foreign policy (which in the case of a liberal hegemon means liberal foreign policy, but if the hegemon follows a different ideology, then its foreign policy will tend to advance that ideology). Thus, when there is a global hegemon with a strong liberal orientation, liberalism may have a field day.

Why would a hegemon try to transform the domestic character of other states—defensively or offensively? One explanation might be that the hegemon supposedly can do it. But why invest resources in such an enterprise, especially when the hegemon doesn't face a major threat? This might be related to the consideration of a future decline of the hegemon and the rise of other powers. If this power transformation takes place when the rising powers have already adopted the ideas and values of the declining hegemon, then they are supposedly less likely to pose a major threat, as they would have done, had they still advocated a contradictory ideology.

More specifically, a liberal hegemon tries to make the world in its own image because of ideological, economic, and security considerations. Ideologically, liberals believe in the universality of their ideas, and this encourages them to spread their ideology. Economically, liberals believe that the spread of market economies and free trade will benefit the hegemon's economy—as well as the world economy more broadly. International peace will also be strengthened by the rising economic interdependence when free trade and capitalism spread all over the world. Finally, based on the democratic peace theory—that democracies do not fight each other—the liberal hegemon believes that if other powers liberalize, they will not pose a security threat to it even when they become stronger in the future. Based on liberal tenets, the expansion of democracy will also reinforce world peace.[5]

However, in a situation of great-power parity, realist approaches tend to dominate and override the ideological ones. The competition with other great powers compels the state to focus on the balance of capabilities with the rival powers that possess the capacity to harm its security, either in order to balance their capabilities (defensive realism) or to surpass them and reach superiority (offensive realism). Attempts to influence the rivals' ideology in such a situation may seem both futile and dangerous. The external constraints on the great power's freedom of action reduce the appeal of costly ideological crusades, which are seen as a luxury in such a situation. The second key causal factor refers to the balance of threat.

THE DEGREE OF EXTERNAL THREAT
FACING THE GREAT POWER

The second systemic factor distinguishes between a benign international environment and an environment laden with high external security threats to the great power. The degree of threat may be assessed as follows: a high-threat environment is present when the opponent is both able (that is, has an offensive power-projection capability) and willing (as demonstrated by aggressive behavior) to inflict heavy damage upon the great power. If only one of these necessary conditions is present (power-projection capability or aggressive behavior), or if none of them is present, then the system is benign or at least relatively benign.

Thus, the degree of threat variable we employ is based partly on a material component, namely, offensive power-projection capabilities (which are distinctive from the overall aggregate balance of capabilities).[6] Accordingly, the presence of rivals who possess such capabilities is a necessary, though not sufficient, condition for producing a threatening environment. However, the threat variable is not a purely material one, because in addition to material power, it is also based on the state's perception of the opponent's aggressive intentions. The opponent's intentions introduce a perceptual component into the discussion of threat, but we assume that the state's perception of the rival's intentions is primarily influenced by the rival's own behavior— whether it is aggressive or benign. The perceptions of the rival's intentions are often shaped by a formative event such as a major international crisis, which may persuasively demonstrate its aggressive or benign intentions.[7] Thus, benign or cautious behavior in a crisis and a willingness to make concessions to avoid war may signal benign intentions on the rival's part. Another costly signal to convey moderate intentions is by a willingness to implement a major cut in offensive weapons.[8]

In contrast, crossing international boundaries with military power in an offensive way by another great power or its allies is likely to signal a high level of threat even if it happens in remote regions. This is because boundaries are crucial elements of the international multistate system, separating between the key actors in the system—the sovereign states. An offensive crossing of the international boundaries violates a key post-WWII international norm designed to maintain stability and to prevent wars—the norm of respecting states' territorial integrity.[9]

A similar signal is a major military buildup by the rival that focuses on first-strike, counterforce nuclear weapons, which are able to deny the second-strike retaliatory capabilities of the other side, notably by constructing multiple-warhead, high-precision land-based missiles. On the conventional level, a major buildup of power-projection capacity such as a blue-water navy may signal a threat. Unilateralist behavior—without taking into account the views of numerous other states, notably allies, or of international institutions—might also signal a threatening behavior.

The main influence of the degree of threat variable is on the choice between offensive and defensive security strategies. A high level of external threats encourages offensive policies in order to cope with these threats. There is a greater willingness on the part of the elites and public opinion to endure sacrifices and bear heavy costs in the face of such high threats.

The international environment is seen as dangerous, and thus it seems appropriate and sensible to act in aggressive ways to cope with it. In contrast, when the international environment is benign, a greater weight is given to defensive strategies. These are seen as the most appropriate ways to cope with the relatively peaceful external system. The main danger in such a situation is seen as stemming from the unintended escalation of conflicts rather than from the aggressive intentions of powerful enemies. As a result, the focus is on preventing such escalation by defensive behavior rather than on prevailing over an aggressor by an offensive strategy.

There might be some variations in the level of threat among different regions under the same international system, depending, first and foremost, on the degree of proximity of the region to the most powerful opponent(s). The level of threat will be higher in regions that are proximate to the powerful opponent than in regions that are remote from it because power projection is less costly to proximate regions.[10] Thus, the various combinations of these two systemic variables affect the relative dominance of each of the four competing approaches to security, as follows:[11]

1. A System of Great-Power Parity Laden with External Threats Increases the Likelihood That the Great Power Will Pursue an Offensive Realist Grand Strategy

Facing other powerful states (under either bipolarity or multipolarity) that limit their freedom of action, the great power is compelled to resort to realist strategies. The threatening nature of the system provides incentives to pursue offensive strategies in order to cope with the high threats. An empirical example is the US grand strategy at the height of the Cold War, as analyzed in chapter 3. Thus, while toward the end of World War II, President Franklin Roosevelt aimed to pursue a defensive liberal strategy (as demonstrated in his idea of the multilateral "Four Policemen" concert of great powers),[12] the United States had to change its initial postwar inclination due to systemic pressures, irrespective of the worldview of the person in the White House. Thus, facing a powerful Soviet Union with major offensive capabilities in Europe and perceived aggressive intentions demonstrated in a range of international crises in 1946–50, namely, a highly threatening environment, the United States in the late 1940s and the 1950s adopted an offensive realist grand strategy. As Dueck suggests, this strategy "was not a strategy of balance, but of preponderance."[13] Layne similarly argues that "when World War II ended, the Soviet Union was the only obstacle to U.S. global hegemony, and in the first postwar decade Washington's principal grand strategic goal was to secure that hegemony by removing the Soviet Union as a peer competitor."[14] Thus, in the early 1950s, the United States embarked on a massive program of military buildup and adopted the doctrine of massive retaliation. As one historian defines it, "in what was technically peacetime," the United States "embarked on military preparations comparable to those undertaken during the Second World War."[15] In other words, we will show that the alternative defensive approaches—both realist and liberal—even if initially supported by key decision makers, were eventually rejected during this period because of the rising balance of threat. At the same time, the post-WWII changing international structure—from multipolarity to bipolarity—led to the marginalization of the liberal strategies in the superpower context. Specifically, due to the Soviet countervailing power, the United States was unable to pursue an offensive liberal strategy of "rollback" (that is, regime change in Eastern Europe), even if there was some domestic ideological support for such a policy, and had to be content with the offensive realist approach of surpassing Soviet capabilities.

A non-American example of a great power that pursued an offensive realist grand strategy under a multipolar and high-threat international system is Germany on the eve of WWI, especially between 1890 and 1914.[16] An example of a small state pursuing an offensive realist strategy in its own neighborhood during some periods of its post-1948 history is Israel.[17] The Jewish state has aimed at military superiority (at least a qualitative one) vis-à-vis a potential Arab- or more recently Iranian-led coalition in the high-threat environment of the multipolar Middle East.

2. A Combination of Great-Power Balance with a Benign Environment Encourages Defensive Realist Strategies

A situation of great-power parity encourages the powers to adopt realist strategies to cope with one another. The benign nature of the international environment encourages defensive measures and a search for ways and means to prevent the eruption of costly and dangerous arms races and inadvertent wars. An empirical example is US policy toward the Soviet Union in the 1960s and 1970s culminating in the détente period. Following the Cuban missile crisis, as discussed in chapter 4, in which the Soviet Union demonstrated cautious behavior and a willingness to avoid war, the United States was faced with a relatively more benign environment, in which both superpowers shared the common fear of inadvertent escalation. In other words, while one of the necessary conditions for a high-threat environment (Soviet capacity to inflict heavy damage on the United States) was present, the other necessary condition—aggressive behavior by the opponent—was missing, or at least declining, and thus the system could be defined as relatively benign. In response, the United States adopted a defensive realist grand strategy composed of deterrence (the mutual assured destruction [MAD] doctrine) and arms control with the Soviet Union, designed to avert inadvertent escalation and an expensive and destabilizing arms race.[18] Thus, both superpowers responded similarly to the shared threat of an inadvertent escalation by following the defensive realist strategy of mutual deterrence and arms control.

Still, taking advantage of its growing power-projection capabilities in the late 1970s, including a blue-water navy, the Soviet Union once again became more expansionist outside its traditional sphere of influence (culminating with its 1979 invasion of Afghanistan, which resulted in a major crisis with the United States). Thus, the international environment facing the United States once again became less benign, and in response the Carter administration, despite its initial defensive liberal inclinations, as discussed in chapter 5, reverted to a more offensive realist strategy that continued in the early 1980s under the first Reagan administration. As the Soviet Union adopted a more moderate posture under Mikhail Gorbachev in the mid-1980s, the global arena once again became more benign, and the second Reagan administration (again, despite its initial hard-line preferences), as addressed in chapter 6, shifted from an offensive realist strategy to a defensive realist policy of arms control with the Soviet Union.

An example outside of the US is Great Britain, which traditionally played the role of the "balancer" in a multipolar Europe of the eighteenth and nineteenth centuries.[19] This balancing role led Britain to join the weaker coalition in order to maintain the balance of power on the European continent, while helping to reduce the quests for superiority there and thus supposedly increasing European stability. Consequently, we might say that Britain usually followed a defensive realist grand strategy vis-à-vis the continental European great powers.

Following the surprise attack of the Egyptian and Syrian militaries against Israel on October 6, 1973, which started the Yom Kippur War, Israel seemed to adopt a defensive realist strategy of security arrangements with its two Arab neighbors. Israel seemed to realize that the costs of trying to maintain deterrence through superiority—the offensive realist strategy it followed until the Yom Kippur War—were too high and too dangerous and not necessarily successful as the surprise attack by the Arab armies clarified. Thus, the goal became to reduce mutual fears of surprise attacks and the related security dilemma and inadvertent escalation. This was accomplished by various steps such as establishing demilitarized zones and areas of reduced military forces. Another major move was the deployment of third-party monitoring or peacekeeping forces, separating the military forces of the rivals, and observing their compliance with the security accords signed after the 1973 war under US mediation.[20]

3. When a Global Hegemon Faces Low External Threats, It Will Tend to Select a Defensive Ideological Strategy

The material-systemic variables, specifically an overwhelming preponderance in all components of material capabilities, give the hegemon leeway to promote its agenda—a strategy that would be self-defeating (if not suicidal) for a great power to pursue in the less permissive, international environment of great-power parity. In the case of a liberal hegemon, it will promote a liberal agenda. When the external environment is benign, it will encourage the liberal hegemon to pursue defensive liberalism, which seems under these conditions to be a suitable strategy—that is, the peaceful and multilateral promotion of liberal democratic regimes, free trade, and international institutions, using soft power and the "power of example," as discussed in chapter 1. Thus, the Clinton administration, addressed in chapter 7, tried to promote democracy and free market in Russia and the integration of China into the global economy and its key institutions (notably the World Trade Organization). A key use of force under defensive liberalism is for "doing good," notably, leading humanitarian interventions all over the globe. Chapter 7 will discuss the defensive liberal dominance of the first decade following the end of the Cold War, starting shortly after the collapse of the Soviet Union, that is, with the transition to unipolarity and the absence of major external security threats. One piece of evidence that indeed systemic factors—and not the initial worldview of the president—led to the dominance of defensive liberalism refers to the start of the conduct of humanitarian intervention under the (defensive) realist (rather than liberal) administration of President Bush Sr., notably the 1992 Somalia intervention.

A different version of a grand strategy of defensive liberalism took place in post-WWII Western Europe in the benign environment created since the 1950s under the American security umbrella in the region. Thus, the two leading regional powers—and former enemies—France and West Germany initiated a process of gradual integration starting in the 1950s with the European Coal and Steel Community (1952) and later the Common Market (1957), while involving more and more European states, leading eventually to the formation of the EU with a common currency for most of its members and the free movement of people among many of the member states.[21] This process of integration was based on three key liberal principles: enhancing economic interdependence, constructing common institutions, and promoting democracy—all steps were taken in peaceful and cooperative ways, usually using soft power, thus fitting the logic of defensive liberalism. Moreover, this process showed the "power of example"—the EU in its various stages became attractive to more and more European countries, which wished to join voluntarily, enlarging the membership to twenty-eight states, including most of the postcommunist countries of Eastern Europe.[22]

While Israel has pursued realist strategies in large parts of its history, in the 1990s—at least in its first half—it pursued what we might call a defensive liberal strategy of the "New Middle East." This strategy focused on promoting peace with the Arabs—and thus transforming the whole region—by attempting to build the two defensive liberal mechanisms of economic interdependence and some regional institutions in the Middle East.[23] The architect of these ideas, then foreign minister Shimon Peres, was seemingly influenced by the power of the example of Franco-German reconciliation and the closely related process of European integration.[24] The two conditions of our model seem to be applicable in that period: a relative Israeli superiority and a relatively low-threat environment. This combination was the result of the end of the Cold War, which terminated Soviet support for Israel's Arab rivals (notably Syria) and the defeat of a key enemy—Iraq—by the US in the 1991 Gulf War. This defeat also weakened the Palestine Liberation Organization (PLO), which supported Iraq in the Gulf crisis.[25] At the same time, another potential enemy—Iran—was still quite weak following the 1979 Islamic Revolution, which ended US support for Iran, and the bloody eight-year war with Iraq (1980–88).

4. A Combination of a Global Hegemon with a High-Threat Environment Encourages an Offensive Ideological Strategy on the Hegemon's Part

When a global hegemon confronts a high-threat setting, it will tend to pursue an offensive ideology-promotion strategy, notably by imposing a regime change according to its ideological preferences. Thus, when a liberal hegemon faces a hostile and violent international environment, it will tend to adopt an offensive liberal strategy, namely, use its superior capabilities to find a fundamental solution to its security problems by transforming the ideological character of its opponents through regime change—if necessary by force. The threatening environment will help mobilize domestic support for such an offensive strategy, with its attendant costs and sacrifices.

Thus, in regions where the United States was hegemonic, and where there was also a major proximate security threat (notably in Western Europe in the early Cold War), the United States did promote liberal ideology, including by the use of force, culminating with imposing democracy on West Germany when it was under US occupation in the years following the end of World War II. The same policy was applied toward Japan in East Asia. However, in regions in which the United States was the hegemon, but where there was no major proximate security threat, like Latin America, no major attempt at democratization was made.

Chapter 8 will analyze the transformation of the grand strategy of the George W. Bush administration following the 9/11 attacks. These attacks provided fertile grounds for the invasions of Afghanistan and Iraq. The invasion of Iraq especially was under the offensive liberal belief that the most fundamental way to minimize security threats is to democratize the political system from which the threat emerged.

In a comprehensive study, John Owen analyzes quite a few historical and more recent cases of forcible regime change.[26] He underlines that such regime changes are usually done by great powers, usually in their empires or sphere of influence.[27] We would like to refer briefly to the Nazi German case in WWII and two post-WWII examples, while mentioning the conditions for such a grand strategy as specified in this study. Nazi Germany imposed fascist regimes under its hegemony in Eastern Europe during the high-threat environment of WWII.[28] The two post-WWII cases are the Soviet Union and Israel.

Parallel to offensive liberalism, which the US pursued in Western Europe in the aftermath WWII, notably imposing democracy in West Germany,[29] the hegemonic power in Eastern Europe, the Soviet Union, pursued an offensive ideology promotion in its own sphere of influence, thereby imposing its own ideology, communism, on Eastern European states occupied by the Red Army in WWII. After the bitter historical experience of invasions from the western side of its border (notably, the German invasion in June 1941 on top of the 1812 Napoleonic invasion of Czarist Russia), it is not surprising that the Soviets were concerned about potential security threats from west of their European border. Not only did Stalin, however, create a security belt in Eastern Europe to avoid hostile regimes allied in their foreign policies with its enemies—a "security-seeking" outcome that could be acceptable to the Western powers as suggested in the Yalta Summit.[30] Stalin went well beyond that by doing regime change and imposing Marxist-Leninist regimes in the area west of the USSR.[31] For his part, the Soviet leader after Stalin—Khrushchev—intervened in Hungary in 1956 to depose its reformist government and to restore a communist government in the Soviet ideological style.[32]

Israel also pursued a forcible regime change when it invaded Lebanon

in 1982 and tried to establish what it considered to be a friendly Maronite/
Christian dominance in the country. Israel expected that the new regime
would advance peace between Lebanon and Israel and especially the ideological preferences of the Israeli nationalist government at that time. The
expectation was that the newly installed regime would help to remove the
Palestinian refugees from Lebanon. These refugees would then be resettled
in Jordan, transforming it to a Palestinian state. This would supposedly make
possible for Israel to annex the West Bank and thus would enable the fulfillment of the nationalist ideology of the then right-wing Israeli government.
The favorable regional conditions for such a strategy included at that time
a superior Israeli military position in its immediate environment following
the removal of its most powerful rival—Egypt—from the Arab-Israeli conflict in the aftermath of the 1978 Camp David Accords and the 1979 peace
treaty.[33] At the same time, the animosity of the still powerful at that time
"Eastern front," notably, Syria, Iraq, and the PLO, made the environment a
high-threatening one.[34]

The American changes in grand strategy in the last decade will be addressed relatively briefly. While evaluating the grand strategy of the Obama
administration, chapter 9 will ask, was Obama a defensive liberal or a defensive realist, and to what extent did changes in the external environment
influence changes in his grand strategy?

In chapter 10 we'll assess how the current changes in the international
environment affected the 2016 elections and the rise of President Trump and
how they influence the grand strategy of the Trump administration. In the
concluding chapter, we'll summarize very briefly our key findings in relation
to the theoretical expectations of the model and present the current policy
debates according to the logic of the approaches discussed in the book.

Summary: What Are the Indicators for International Systemic Influences?

In this section we summarize the indicators for when we will know that the
international system exercises major influence on the formation of the grand
strategy. Following are the criteria for the influence of the international system. The more prevalent these conditions, the greater the effects of the systemic factors:

- The greater the variation from the decision makers' original ideas/views,
  the greater the systemic effects.[35]
- Timing: This policy change can be reasonably traced to systemic inputs,
  especially if the change in views follows the systemic stimulus.

- If views popular at home are turned down following systemic developments.
- International systemic effects on the domestic-ideational competition: The continuous domestic competition of ideas on grand strategy is likely to be influenced by the external changes, and this influence might also be reflected in election outcomes.

The Rise of Offensive Approaches:
- A systemic explanation of the rise of offensive approaches is more applicable—the greater the gulf between initial willingness to cooperate (joint great-power policemen or cautious balancing/spheres of influence) and eventual adoption of more hard-line approaches (either a quest for superiority or regime change).
- Offensive approaches (either realist or liberal) are more likely to dominate the grand strategy—the greater the gulf between the initial willingness to cooperate with the opponent and the emergence of threatening signals from the international system in favor of conflictual approaches manifested by rising security threats and aggressive behavior by the opponent (such as crossing international boundaries militarily).
- Offensive approaches are also more likely to dominate if initial expectations of a benign international environment are falsified by large-scale violence against the great power or its allies.

The Rise of Defensive Approaches:
- Systemic explanations of the rise of defensive approaches are more applicable when the opposite takes place—the greater the gulf between initially hard-line policies and eventual endorsement of soft-line approaches.
- Defensive approaches (either realist or liberal) are more likely to dominate the grand strategy—the greater the gulf between the initial willingness to compete and the signaling from the international system in favor of cooperative approaches.

The Rise of Realist Approaches:
- Systemic explanations of realist approaches: if initially liberal ideas (multilateral institutions or promotion of democracy/human rights) are sidelined and realist approaches are endorsed.
- Realist approaches (either offensive or defensive) to grand strategy are more likely to dominate the grand strategy if the signaling from the international system does not seem to favor initially liberal ideas (such as multilateralism, international cooperation, or promotion of democracy/ human rights), which are sidelined by major security threats.

The Rise of Liberal Approaches:
- Systemic explanations of liberal approaches: if initially realist ideas (superiority or balancing) are sidelined in favor of liberal approaches (such as

democracy promotion, humanitarian interventions, and working within multilateral institutions).

- Liberal approaches (either offensive or defensive) to grand strategy are more likely to dominate when realist expectations about the dominance of international politics by great-power competition seem to be out of touch with what is going on in the real world—either because such competition does not take place (notably because of the transition to a unipolar world with only one superpower) or because the key security threats come from non–great-power sources.

We turn now to the first empirical chapter, which analyzes the US strategy in the early years of the Cold War.

3

The Road to Offensive Realism:
The Evolution of US Grand Strategy
in the Early Cold War, 1945–50

The Puzzle: Why Did America's Soviet Policy Change
Twice in the Five Years Following World War II?

In this chapter, we will explore the evolution of US grand strategy toward the Soviet Union in the formative years of the Cold War (1945–50).[1] Within five years from the end of World War II, the US changed its grand strategy twice. While starting with a conciliatory, cooperative strategy toward the Soviet Union (what we call "defensive liberalism"), roughly two years later a more hard-line policy took over, though still relatively moderate with a focus on diplomatic and economic means of containment ("defensive realism"). Yet, three years later, in 1950, the US shifted gears again to a much more hawkish policy of seeking military superiority and embarked on worldwide commitments and forward deployment of its military forces ("offensive realism"). The strategy of offensive realism that emerged in 1950 continued to guide the US throughout the 1950s and early 1960s. These significant successive shifts in grand strategy between 1945 and 1950 and their timing provide a major historical and theoretical puzzle in need of explanation.

Before explaining this puzzle, we need to address alternative interpretations of US grand strategy that the scholarly literature has offered. Indeed, three major theoretical works in international relations have interpreted US grand strategy in the early years of the Cold War. What these works have in common is that they present a picture of a single US grand strategy in these years and do not note the changes it experienced over time. In addition, they present competing and mutually exclusive versions of the grand strategy that the US followed. Thus, while one study claims that the US followed a defensive realist "offshore balancing" strategy since 1945, the others present liberal conceptions of US grand strategy, both defensive and offensive. In this chapter, we will present a more nuanced picture of successive changes in US grand strategy that is in better accord with the historical record.

The changes in US grand strategy during 1945–50 have been detected long ago, but their origins were widely attributed to the change from Roosevelt to Truman. That is, while Roosevelt is perceived as having supported an accommodative, cooperative (defensive liberal) approach toward the Soviet Union, Truman had other ideas and preferences and changed the approach to a more hard-line (realist) one. According to this perspective, the explanation for the change in US grand strategy (and for the escalation of the Cold War) lies in the personal preferences of the president.[2] We will present a different explanation in accordance with our theoretical model. Namely, it is the international system that serves as the selector of competing ideas on national security. More specifically, it was the combination of the military might of the Soviet Union and the growing threat it presented to the US (deduced from aggressive Soviet behavior) that determined US grand strategy. Thus, Truman initially continued Roosevelt's conciliatory policy toward the Soviet Union and allowed it the benefit of the doubt. Only after it gradually became clear to him during 1946 because of the Soviet Union's own behavior that it was an expansionist power and a rising threat to the US did he switch his strategy to a more hard-line one—defensive, not offensive, realist. He switched it once again in 1950 following the North Korean attack on South Korea, which was a key event that was perceived as the final proof of the Soviets' expansionism and aggressive nature. The fact that Truman did not follow his initial preferences but rather changed grand strategies twice due to external events shows the dominant role of the international system in determining grand strategy.

This chapter is organized as follows. First, we briefly discuss three leading explanations that were published in the last twenty years of American grand strategy formation and show the limitations to these interpretations. We will then discuss the US "marketplace of ideas" and the domestic debate concerning the strategy toward the Soviet Union in the first decade of the Cold War. US officials and commentators offered four key ideas regarding the most effective and desirable grand strategy that should be followed to maximize US security and to construct a more peaceful world order. Each of these key ideas, which were advocated by leading spokesmen and competed for dominating US grand strategy at the end of World War II and the beginning of the Cold War, fits the logic of one of the four ideal types of grand strategy defined in this study—defensive liberalism, defensive realism, offensive realism, and offensive liberalism. More specifically, defensive liberalism was exemplified by Franklin Roosevelt's multilateral, cooperative, and conciliatory approach toward the Soviet Union and his idea of "the Four Policemen." The epitome of defensive realism was George Kennan's conception of containment, as expressed in his "Long Telegram" of 1946 and subsequent 1947 "X" article in

Foreign Affairs,[3] and developed during his tenure as director of policy planning in the US State Department in 1947–48. Offensive realism was represented in the approach of Paul Nitze, Kennan's successor as director of policy planning and the leading author of the seminal National Security Council (NSC) report 68 (NSC 68) in 1950. Finally, offensive liberalism is associated with the "rollback" doctrine of John Foster Dulles, the secretary of state in the Eisenhower administration.

We will then trace the evolution of US grand strategy under Truman and explain which idea was selected and why. We will demonstrate how the US shifted its grand strategy from defensive liberalism in 1945–46 to defensive realism in 1947–50 and to offensive realism from 1950 onward. The causes of these successive shifts had to do with the growing perception of improving Soviet military capabilities and the rising Soviet threat (which was based primarily on Soviet aggressive behavior). These two factors in combination ultimately resulted in the choice of the offensive realist strategy that continued to guide the US throughout the 1950s and early 1960s. As for offensive liberalism, despite the anticommunist ideological preferences of the Eisenhower administration, the core idea of the liberation of Eastern Europe ("rollback") never became a major part of US grand strategy due to power considerations, namely, the military might of the Soviet Union, and the consequent US unwillingness to risk the eruption of a major (nuclear) war on behalf of Eastern Europe. Thus, the international systemic factors of power and threat served as the brokers or selectors among several available approaches to the Soviet Union. More specifically, considerations of Soviet power affected the change from defensive liberalism to defensive realism, and eliminated the offensive liberal option. The rising Soviet threat brought down in turn both defensive liberalism and defensive realism. The combined effect of Soviet power and Soviet threat brought about the ultimate triumph of offensive realism as the US grand strategy toward the Soviet Union from 1950 onward.

Alternative Interpretations of US Grand Strategy during the Cold War: Mearsheimer, Layne, and Dueck

The scholarly literature concerning the early Cold War and US grand strategy is immense. Rather than attempting a comprehensive review, we will focus here on three major theoretical works by leading international relations scholars—John Mearsheimer, Christopher Layne, and Colin Dueck—all of whom present their own theoretically informed interpretations of US grand strategy in the formative years of 1945–50.[4] A brief review and critique of these works clarifies how our interpretation of US grand strategy differs from theirs. In terms of the present study, two of these works present a liberal conception of US grand strategy (either defensive or offensive), while the third presents a defensive realist interpretation.

John Mearsheimer presents a defensive realist conception of US grand strategy.[5] He describes American behavior vis-à-vis Europe as consistent and unchanging for the period of 1900–1990, and he defines it as a strategy of "offshore balancing." In other words, the US has consistently maintained the European balance of power by actively intervening to prevent a single great power from taking over Europe and emerging as the hegemon in Eurasia. It only deployed military forces in Europe when there was a danger of a rising hegemon whom the regional powers were unable to balance. Thus, the US intervened in both world wars when there was a serious danger to the European balance of power and a rising threat of German domination, and the regional powers were unable to maintain the balance. Similarly, in the Cold War, the establishment of NATO and the long-term US commitment to Europe that followed was because the Soviets controlled Eastern Europe and no Western European power could face them, leaving the US as the only power that could balance Soviet power. This is a defensive strategy. Although Mearsheimer is considered the leading offensive realist, in fact his theory with regard to US intervention in the Cold War is not different from defensive realism because it conceives of US behavior as balancing and not defeating the Soviets.[6]

Mearsheimer's defensive interpretation of US grand strategy is questioned by Christopher Layne, who argues that the purpose of the US strategy during the first decade after World War II was not to secure the balance of power.[7] Rather, the US followed a much more ambitious plan to secure American superiority and global hegemony "by removing the Soviet Union as a peer competitor."[8] While pursuing global preponderance seems in accord with offensive realism,[9] in fact Layne's conception is closer to offensive liberalism, in that, according to his interpretation, the US pursuit of global hegemony was driven by economic and ideological concerns. He claims that the main purpose of the US in its quest for preponderance was not military security, but rather economic and ideological expansion and securing an "open door" for US economic interests. In other words, the US used all the means necessary (including military ones) to assure the global triumph of economic liberalism, that is, free trade. In this way he interprets the US insistence in the early postwar years that Eastern Europe should be open (and not a Soviet sphere of influence).[10] In addition to maintaining an open international economic system and demanding that other states open their economies, the "open door" policy also included a political-ideological component based on the worldview of US leaders—spreading democracy and political liberalism abroad and demanding that other states adopt US ideas and institutions.[11] Containing the Soviet Union was a relatively secondary and minor objective in US grand strategy compared to assuring the US global economic access to foreign markets and raw materials. The US grand strategy, according to Layne, stemmed from domestic and ideological US interests and beliefs, and not from the external factor of Soviet behavior; indeed, he claims that in its quest for hegemony the US disregarded signs of Soviet weakness and moderation.[12]

The concept of "open door" and Layne's entire interpretation of US grand strategy is heavily based on the revisionist or radical school of Cold War US historiography.[13] This school presents a sinister picture of the US trying to advance and support its business interests worldwide, including by military means, and thus it fits the offensive liberal approach in the terms of this study. The debate between Mearsheimer and Layne is thus a new incarnation of the classic debate between the orthodox and the revisionist historiographical schools of Cold War origins—with the orthodox school presenting a defensive realist conception of US grand strategy striving to balance an aggressive Soviet Union, while the revisionist school offers an offensive liberal interpretation of the US aspiring for an "open door" due to its economic and corporate interests. The orthodox school argues that the US was in fact being defensive, only responding to Soviet aggression, while the revisionist school argues that the US was the aggressor and tried to change the Soviet Union and its bloc to fit into its preferred political and economic order.

Dueck agrees with Layne that the US was seeking preponderance rather than balance of power in the postwar era.[14] He presents a cultural-ideological interpretation of US grand strategy based on American liberal norms and ideas, namely, its belief in spreading democracy and open markets.[15] Dueck argues that US grand strategy was liberal in that it strove to remake the world in the liberal self-image of the US and build "an international order characterized by free trade, national self-determination and liberal democracy."[16] Thus, he claims that the US rejected the option of an explicit realist spheres-of-influence arrangement in Europe due to a liberal opposition to Soviet domination of Eastern Europe. However, he presents a more defensive conception of US strategy than Layne, arguing that the US enthusiasm for spreading liberalism abroad was curbed by its unwillingness to expand large resources and a desire to limit the costs of international commitments ("limited liability"), resulting in a tendency to strive for "liberalism on the cheap."[17]

Layne and Dueck provide a useful corrective to Mearsheimer's defensive realist interpretation of post–World War II US grand strategy. Indeed, as we will discuss below, it is difficult to characterize US strategy after 1950 as defensive and aspiring to maintain the balance of power; it was indeed an offensive strategy that was aimed to achieve superiority rather than balance.[18] However, unlike Layne and Dueck, we will show in this chapter that this strategy was realist rather than liberal. It was based on security considerations and chosen primarily because of the combination of the vast Soviet power and a high degree of perceived Soviet threat and not because of US liberal ideology and "open door" economic interests.[19]

Indeed, like the revisionist/radical school of US Cold War historiography on which his "open door" argument is based, Layne's interpretation overstates the importance of economic and ideological motivations in US grand strategy and downplays security considerations, the influence of external events, and the factor of the Soviet threat.[20] Thus, he fails to note that the US commitment to Europe (expressed in the establishment of NATO in 1949) was not a purely American initiative designed to achieve domination in Western Europe; it can be argued that the US was invited or even dragged back into Europe by its Western European allies.[21] Thus, Dueck notes that while the Europeans pressured the US for a military alliance and wanted it to play the leading role in NATO, the US Congress was initially reluctant to fund extensive US troop deployments overseas.[22] The European allies were motivated primarily by their fear of the Soviet Union. The fact that the perception of the Soviet threat was shared by US allies shows that this threat was not manufactured by US elites to justify policy based on other (economic and ideological) considerations.

Similarly, the Truman Doctrine of 1947 was not simply an American initiative and an expression of US ideological preferences, but rather was a result of several processes and events. One significant event was Great Britain's statement in 1946 that it could no longer maintain Greece, and its subsequent withdrawal from involvement there.[23] Thus, the US was compelled to assume an active global role by the combination of the rising Soviet threat, the weakness of the European states, and the decline of Great Britain. Likewise, Layne and Dueck's argument that the US rejected an explicit spheres-of-influence arrangement with the Soviet Union in Europe because of its liberal economic and ideological preferences assumes that the Soviet Union would have agreed to such an arrangement and ignores the difficulty of cooperating with Stalin and his lack of responsiveness.[24]

Another problem with Layne's conception of US grand strategy concerns the issue of timing. Layne contends that the US aspired to reach international hegemony since the early 1940s.[25] This interpretation, however, fails to account for one major fact (duly noted by Mearsheimer), namely, that following Germany's defeat, the US rapidly demobilized its forces and cut its defense budget, so that by 1950 only about eighty thousand US troops were left in Europe.[26] Only gradually and reluctantly did the US increase its military commitment to Europe by the formation of NATO in 1949 and by deploying considerably more military forces on the continent after 1950. In 1953 US troops in Europe numbered 427,000, and throughout the Cold War, their number did not fall below three hundred thousand. The US also deployed nuclear weapons in Europe during the 1950s and early 1960s. This pattern of events makes it difficult to claim that the US quest to achieve military preponderance was planned in advance,[27] and indeed that it pursued hegemony in Europe before 1950.[28]

A major issue with the liberal conceptions (either offensive or defensive) is that they overlook the fact that while the US was conducting regime change during the Cold War, the regime change was, at least in some notable cases, in an illiberal and antidemocratic direction rather than democracy promotion, such as in Iran and Guatemala in the early 1950s (and later Chile in 1973).

Contrary to Mearsheimer, Layne, and Dueck, we argue that US strategy changed twice in the first formative years of the Cold War. In 1945–46, the US followed a liberal strategy (albeit defensive rather than offensive), but in the 1947–50 period it switched to a more hard-line defensive realist one. Then, following the North Korean attack on South Korea in 1950, its grand strategy changed once more—this time to an offensive realist one. None of the three studies discussed above captures these variations because they all regard US grand strategy in this period as constant and unchanging.

In addition, in contrast to Layne's and Dueck's interpretation, we argue that the main causes for the adoption of these various strategies were not domestic or ideological, but rather external, more specifically, the realization of the military might of the Soviet Union (its control of Eastern Europe and its ability to occupy the rest of Europe) and its rising threat (as deduced by the US decision makers from aggressive and expansionist Soviet behavior). The combined effect of Soviet power and high threat led to the ultimate adoption of offensive realism as the grand strategy that guided the US throughout the 1950s and early 1960s.

The differences among the studies discussed in this section, and their problems are summarized in table 3.1.

Thus, to sum up, the present study differs from the three studies discussed here on the following points related to the grand strategy that the US followed:

TABLE 3.1. Competing interpretations of US grand strategy in the early Cold War

Scholar	Which grand strategy did the US follow in 1945–50?	What factors explain the choice of US grand strategy?	Critique
Mearsheimer	Defensive realism (preventing the rise of a potential hegemon in Eurasia)	Material-external—the balance of power	• Does not see variations in US grand strategy over time • Fails to see that the US strove for hegemony rather than balance after 1950
Layne	Offensive liberalism (spreading economic and political liberalism)	Domestic-ideological—the beliefs of US elites and US economic interests ("open door")	• Does not see variations in US grand strategy over time • Overestimates the influence of domestic-ideological factors on US grand strategy • Underestimates the role of material-external factors in the US choice of grand strategy • Fails to see that the US did not aspire to hegemony before 1950
Dueck	Defensive liberalism	Domestic-ideological—US liberal beliefs and norms (moderated by a domestic unwillingness to expand resources)	• Does not see variations in US grand strategy over time • Overestimates the influence of domestic-ideological factors on US grand strategy • Underestimates the role of external factors in the US choice of grand strategy
Present study	1945–46—defensive liberalism; 1947–50—defensive realism; 1950–1962—offensive realism	Material-external—Soviet power and threat	

- Contrary to all three studies, we claim that the US did not follow a single strategy toward the Soviet Union in the 1945–50 period.
- Unlike Layne and Dueck, we argue that the US did not pursue a liberal strategy toward the Soviet Union after 1946.
- Unlike Mearsheimer, we argue that the US only pursued defensive realism for a short period in 1947–50; after 1950, it pursued superiority and hegemony rather than balance (offensive realism).
- Unlike Layne, we claim that the US pursuit of hegemony was not planned since the early 1940s, but emerged only after 1950.

Concerning the explanation for the US choice of grand strategy:

- We agree with Mearsheimer that the main factors behind US grand strategy were external/material rather than domestic/ideological. To Mearsheimer's factor of the balance of power we add a second external component—the degree of threat.
- Unlike Layne's and Dueck's domestic/ideological explanation of US grand strategy, we advance an external explanation for the US pursuit of hegemony after 1950.
- The brokering role of the international system is demonstrated by causal links between changes in the international environment (the growing Soviet threat according to its actions); and changes in the balance of power—Great Britain's withdrawal and decline; loss of atomic monopoly; communist successes in Europe and Asia; and changes in US grand strategy shown, for example, by consecutive time links between the changes in the environment and changes in US grand strategy.

The phases of the evolution of US grand strategy are based on the combined effect of the two propositions introduced at the beginning of the chapter:

1. 1945–46: Defensive liberal grand strategy due to the perception of the Soviet Union—a WWII ally—as not threatening and relatively weak because of the war devastation.
2. 1947: Transition to defensive realism due to a bipolar system (British decline and Soviet Union powerful in Europe)—culminating in the Truman Doctrine.
3. 1950: Growing Soviet threat (the Korean War) led to a shift from defensive realist to offensive realist strategy[29]—founded on NSC 68.
4. The grand strategy overall 1950–62: Offensive realist—the quest for and the maintenance of US superiority due to the combined effect of Soviet power (under bipolarity) and high threat.

The next sections analyze the ideational competition on the best grand strategy in the early Cold War.

The Four Competing Ideas during the Beginning of the Cold War

We start with presenting what kind of empirical evidence could meet the expectations of each one of the four approaches. Thus, the presence of this evidence, if it dominated US policy, would show that the grand strategy that the US pursued was guided by this approach. We then discuss the various alternative ideas raised by US elites about the desirable US grand strategy in accordance with the different approaches.

TABLE 3.2. Competing explanations of US grand strategy in the Cold War

	Mearsheimer	Layne	Dueck[1]	Leffler[2]	Present study
Which grand strategy did the US follow in the post-1945 era?	Defensive realism	Offensive liberalism	Defensive liberalism	Offensive realism	Offensive realism
Did the US strive for hegemony in the post-1945 era?	No	Yes	No	Yes	Yes
Which factors explain US grand strategy?	External— security factors stemming from balance-of-power considerations	Domestic— ideological factors stemming from the "open door"	Domestic— ideological factors stemming from US liberalism	External— security factors stemming from a "conception of national security"	Systemic— the balance of capabilities and balance of threat
Role of the Soviet threat	Major	Minor	Relatively minor	Relatively minor	Major—a key factor
Was the US strategy a reaction to the Soviet threat?	Yes	No	No	No—it went much beyond that	Yes

1. Ikenberry has a partly similar argument to Dueck's; see G. John Ikenberry, *After Victory: Institutions, Strategic Restraint, and the Rebuilding of Order after Major Wars* (Princeton, NJ: Princeton University Press, 2001).

2. Melvyn P. Leffler, *A Preponderance of Power: National Security, the Truman Administration, and the Cold War* (Stanford, CA: Stanford University Press, 1992).

Next, we show that even if parts of these ideas became important components of US grand strategy, the idea that became dominant in relation to the key rivalry with the Soviet Union was the quest for superiority related to offensive realism. The most powerful explanation for the selection of this option is derived from the international system even if domestic politics and decision makers' perceptions also played significant roles as intervening variables.

How does each grand strategy look according to the competing approaches?

Offensive liberalism would promote democracy, including by use of force, and it would push for an "open door" policy, namely, opening markets in different countries to foreign goods and investments. Such a strategy is conducted unilaterally, which means that the US would be willing to go it alone or lead a coalition in which its investment is far more significant than that of its partners.

Defensive liberalism promotes the same set of values but through multilateralism, which means cooperating with other powers and not leading alone.

This could be done in the form of a great-power concert or collective security. This strategy promotes action through international institutions;
using economic cooperation/international trade; and a gradual promotion in peaceful ways of the prerequisites for democracy.
Defensive realism advocates cautious balancing. The power should be cautious in its use of force, interventions, and forward deployment. It should
aim to establish an explicit great powers' spheres-of-influence arrangement of the international system or—if among ideological rivals—more
likely a tacit spheres-of-influence arrangement. Under this strategy, there
are no interventions for democracy promotion; but arms control would
be preferred for strategic and crisis stability.
Offensive realism suggests a massive buildup, armament toward superiority
(including of the great power's allies), global deployment, and worldwide
alliances. This strategy is unilateral by nature, and regime change may be
done toward nondemocracy, according to the material interests of the
great power vis-à-vis its global rival.

THE AUTONOMY OF IDEAS AND IDEATIONAL APPROACHES TO SECURITY

The first few years following the end of WWII witnessed an intense debate
among alternative ideas on how to maximize US security and to shape
the postwar order by promoting peace and preventing the dominance of a
single power over the resources of Eurasia. Each idea is organized according
to the objectives of the grand strategy and its major means.

1. DEFENSIVE LIBERALISM: MULTILATERAL COOPERATION—THE FOUR POLICEMEN[30]

FDR's grand design for the postwar order was premised on the collective en-
forcement of peace by the great powers.[31] His "Four Policemen" concept is
based on great-power cooperation derived from shared interests in maintaining world peace. The great powers (the US, Great Britain, the Soviet
Union, and China) should also enjoy special managerial privileges in exchange for maintaining their collective responsibilities to enforce the peace.
FDR believed that the four great powers should jointly manage the peace
after WWII.[32] He preferred collective decision making to unilateral action.[33]
The Four Policemen would not limit their cooperation to managing immediate threats to peace, but would devise a peace settlement for the war's aftermath, and then continue to consult about the maintenance of peace in the
postwar era.

Collective security or balance of power   FDR believed that peace would be preserved by a system of collective security maintained by the wartime allies acting in concert and sustained by mutual goodwill and vigilance.[34] The victorious allies would supervise the disarming and portioning of Germany and subject various other countries to their control. One of his ideas was that the Big Four would remove from the hands of other nations, friendly and hostile alike, all weapons more dangerous than rifles.[35] More precisely, FDR's Four Policemen was seemingly a compromise between Churchill's balance of power and the unconstrained Wilsonianism of his advisors such as Secretary of State Cordell Hull, who opposed power politics, spheres of influence, alliances, balance of power, and territorial change by force.[36]

Yet, in fact it was more collective security than balance of power. FDR was informed by the concept of collective security, modified by the idea of the Four Policemen as the enforcers of collective security, instead of the traditional balance of power. To FDR, the purpose of the war was to remove Hitler as the obstacle to a cooperative international order based on harmony, not on balance of power.[37] He wanted to destroy the balance of power and didn't fear the implications of balance-of-power logic, notably Soviet expansion to the vacuum created in the middle of Europe or the collapse of the alliance in the aftermath of victory. FDR didn't favor preserving the balance of power (including against the Soviet Union) following the war, but he sought to pursue a state of universal peace; thus, the US should disengage its military forces following the war rather than stationing them in Europe,[38] because in his view the US public wouldn't accept this; he also rejected US responsibility for the economic reconstruction of Europe.

Domestic- and Individual-Level Sources for the Defensive Liberal Approach

Domestic politics and the ideational approach   The integration of the Four Policemen concept in a collective security framework is at least partly due to the domestic power of defensive liberalism in the US. Indeed, internationalist groups in US domestic politics advocated the defensive liberal approach. In response to their pressures, FDR agreed to a new international organization—if the four great powers continued to be in charge of enforcing the peace.[39] Thus, FDR later incorporated his Four Policemen concept into a collective security framework acceptable to Wilsonian idealists even though he continued to insist on the centrality of power.[40]

Belief system and the ideational approach   FDR firmly believed that the Soviet Union could be persuaded to assume the burdens and responsibilities of a great power for maintaining world order.[41] FDR's preference was for an explicit spheres-of-influence agreement, but he expected public opposition to an internal interference in European states, while competitive balance of power would be unstable and might lead to war.[42] Thus, both FDR and much of the public supported collective security.[43] A universalist vision of collective security was the official policy of the US since the middle of WWII.[44]

Overall, the bureaucracy (State Department and the Joint Chiefs of Staff) and the public shared FDR's optimism about the postwar order. In a November 1944 public opinion poll, 44 percent believed that the Soviet Union could be trusted to cooperate with the US; 35 percent didn't; 11 percent didn't know. The Joint Chiefs did not even consider locating permanent bases in Europe. In April 1945, when Truman replaced FDR, he believed he should continue FDR's policies.

2. OFFENSIVE LIBERALISM:

ROLLBACK ("LIBERATION")[45]

The objective of rollback was the liberation of Eastern Europe from the coercive Soviet rule. The logic of the strategy was based on the advocates' argument that containment is too defensive and didn't challenge the Soviet Union. Such a defensive posture would only generate further retreats by the US and its allies. So long as the communist regime stayed in place, the Soviet Union would continue to constitute a threat to the US and the West. Thus, rollback supporters prescribed regime change, including a strategy of military intervention to help anticommunist revolts in Eastern Europe and potentially to attack the Soviet Union itself.[46]

Key advocates and supporters of offensive liberalism included a variety of individuals, groups, and organizations, while the call for the liberation of Eastern Europe culminated during the 1952 presidential campaign. The most important advocate was John Foster Dulles, the chief foreign policy advisor to the Republican platform committee.[47] He helped shape the platform's pledge to "revive the contagious, liberating influences . . . [which] will inevitably set up strains and stresses within the captive world which will make the rulers impotent to continue in their monstrous ways and mark the beginning of the end."[48]

In a May 1952 article in *Life*, entitled "A Policy of Boldness" John Foster Dulles called on the US to make "it publicly known that it wants and expects liberation to occur."[49] Only rarely did he point out concrete steps to advance liberation such as an intensification of Voice of America broadcasts to stir up resistance, then air supplies to the freedom fighters, and eventually acceptance of the liberated states into the free world as the Soviets disengage. Both Kennan (the major representative of defensive realism) and Dulles saw opportunities for undermining Soviet rule in Eastern Europe. While Kennan wanted to do it by taking advantage of latent differences within the international communist movement, Dulles was more interested in overthrowing communism in Eastern Europe.[50]

Another key offensive liberal advocate was political theorist James Burnham, who called for the "liberation" of Eastern Europe from Soviet influence via direct backing of anticommunist revolts—the position approved by the 1952 GOP convention. Not only did he call for liberation from Soviet rule, but advocated the establishment of full-blown liberal democracies,[51] though in practice he suggested carrying out mostly propaganda and symbolic acts. The popular criticism of Truman/Acheson as too soft on communism and of containment as too defensive (fed by communist triumphs in 1948–50)[52] was manipulated by the Republicans for political reasons and culminated in the 1952 presidential campaign as appeals to liberate the satellites had deep resonance.[53]

A moderate offensive liberal advocate was Republican Senator Robert Taft. Despite his concerns about US overextension, he believed in the possibility of encouraging love for freedom in the Soviet Bloc while spending relatively small amounts of money. Though universal democracy was desirable, the US could not impose it and spend a lot of resources on it.[54]

In the bureaucracy, there were two prominent groups of rollback advocates: The first group was composed of State Department officials who were dissatisfied from deploying abroad only the nonnuclear components of atomic weapons, authorized by Truman on July 28, 1950, at an NSC meeting.[55] They insisted that military capabilities provided the shield to protect the West, while the US enacted a positive program to project its influence into the Soviet world, roll back Soviet power, and promote internal changes within the Soviet Union itself. The second group included the Central Intelligence Agency (CIA) Special Operations Group, who were conducting clandestine/covert operations in Eastern Europe (see also below).

As Mitrovich uncovers, the practical means suggested by supporters of rollback inside the Truman administration focused on psychological warfare, including propaganda and covert actions (see below in the discussion of actual policies).[56] The reasons, which the advocates of this policy suggested for adopting such rollback policies, were its successful application in WWII and that it would mitigate the danger of war with Soviet Union.[57]

Realists have not always been united over the issue of how much intervention in global affairs was enough.[58] Neither are they so united even now over the issue of restraint in the early period of the Cold War. As Patricia Roberts points out in a capsule history of the development of the realist school, realism began as a philosophy of intervention. Before World War I, nascent realists like Theodore Roosevelt, Alfred Thayer Mahan, and Walter Lippmann believed that American security depended on a balance of power in Europe and keeping a large portion of the continent in hands friendly to the United States. A balance of power was important because a united Europe in unfriendly hands was the one entity capable of invading or otherwise threatening the United States. Thus, Lippmann believed that the United States had to intervene in World War I on behalf of Great Britain. Subsequently, during and after World War II, he joined other academic realists like Hans Morgenthau, George Kennan, and Reinhold Niebuhr in urging the United States not to repeat the mistake it made after World War I by retreating into isolationism. All of these realists urged the United States to remain involved in Western Europe and to help it rebuild so that it would not fall into the hands of communists who might invite Soviet influence into the Western sphere. It was only later in the Cold War that these realists, whom we call here defensive realists, began to drift away from the consensus urging greater US intervention to limit the Soviet sphere—Lippmann in his famous dissent from Kennan's Mr. X article, Kennan from what he considered the misinterpretation of his containment doctrine, and Morgenthau even later, concerning Vietnam. Meanwhile, other realists—whom we see as offensive realists—like Dean Acheson and Paul Nitze believed that they were following Walter Lippmann's realist principle of balancing goals with the power available by expanding American and European military power to achieve the necessary goal of preventing communist expansion into the rest of the world. For many years, then, the realist school was divided between "hard" (or offensive) realists, who advocated increasing Western military power to achieve their desired goals, and "soft" or "restrained" (or defensive) realists who advised the United States to reduce its goals to match its available power.[59]

3. DEFENSIVE REALISM: PRESERVATION/ RESTORATION OF THE BALANCE OF POWER

The realists viewed the Cold War as a great-power struggle for hegemony.[60] The threat was posed by the Red Army at the heart of Europe, and it was derived from Russian imperialism, not communist ideology and world revolution.

The grand strategy's objectives   The US should focus on the restoration of the balance of power, which was distorted by the defeat of Germany and Japan and the expansion of the Soviet Union. The concept of the balance of power is the key idea in the defensive realist policy analysis and prescription. This concept is viewed as the most appropriate way of reconciling national aspirations with the national interest.[61] The realists, especially defensive realists, are against making the world in the image of the US, but rather prefer preserving its diversity against attempts to remake it in the image of others.[62]

Instead of a universalist vision of collective security, George Kennan, as a leading defensive realist practitioner, prescribed a strategy of preserving a global equilibrium, namely, balance of power, especially in Europe and Asia within the existing international order rather than trying to reach a "one world." The key goal was to prevent Soviet domination of areas of great potential power in Eurasia, which would enable its superiority and pose a major threat to the US.[63] If a balance of power is restored in Europe, there is a chance for conflict reduction, although not a comprehensive settlement so long as the current regime/ideology of Moscow persists.

The conception of interests, threats, and intervention is seen in the context of the balance of power: Interests must be finite because capabilities are also finite; a distinction must be made between what is vital and what is not; threats must be determined against this criterion of interests; to be serious, threats had to combine hostility with capability, namely, industrial warmaking potential; thus a communist regime in the nonindustrialized Asian mainland is not a serious threat that requires preventive action; considerations for intervention are a combination of interests and costs—the importance of interests and the ease (costs) with which they could be defended; there are five vital power centers that affect the world balance of power—US, Great Britain, Germany/Central Europe, Japan, and USSR; the key threat to the balance of power is the possibility for the USSR to control (at least) two of these world power centers, thus, the balance of power is not feasible so long as Germany and Japan remain power vacuums; and focus on the defense of the power centers—"strongpoint defense" rather than "perimeter defense."[64] The key point is that the balance of power can be maintained by denying the key centers of military-industrial power from Soviet hands.

The Defensive Realist Conception of Soviet Intentions

In Kennan's Long Telegram (February 1946), fear and insecurity are the key Soviet motivations: "The sources of Soviet conduct could be best understood in term of psychopathology . . . the Kremlin's neurotic view of world affairs is a traditional and instinctive Russian sense of insecurity."[65] In this view, diplomacy is the best instrument to deal with the Soviet paranoiacs. Containment was not aimed so much against a Soviet military attack or international communism. Communist ideology does not guide Soviet behavior; therefore, the objective of containment should be to limit Soviet expansionism, while communism posed a threat only to the extent that it was an instrument of that expansion. The key opportunity for Soviet expansion is provided by demoralization, deprivation, and instability in regions bordering the Soviet sphere of influence.

The Means of the Defensive Realist Grand Strategy

The restoration of the balance of power will be done by reassuring the states, which are under the Soviet threat, especially in the key areas of Western Europe and Japan. For defensive realists, however, the key means for doing it should be economic and technological instruments such as the Marshall Plan in Europe in 1947–49: economic rehabilitation as a key means/priority of containment even if that meant deferring military preparedness based on an estimation that the Soviets are unlikely to resort to war in the near future (due to the US atomic monopoly and the Soviet control of Eastern Europe without war).

Military force is important for the balance of power, thus some military deterrence is necessary, though Kennan was against excessive reliance on the military. The strategy should promote selective engagement in the industrial centers (Western Europe and Japan) and selected nonindustrial regions around them (Turkey and Greece, and the Middle East because of its oil), but not beyond that to wherever communism expands—like in mainland Asia such as China.

The defensive realist approach accepts spheres of influence in terms of the balance of interests and in contrast to offensive liberalism. It avoids direct military intervention to prevent communist takeovers and avoids calling for the overthrow of communist governments in Eastern Europe—because Moscow would be willing to go to war over maintaining its sphere of influence in Eastern Europe.[66]

Churchill (who was an indirect participant in the US ideational debate) called for a traditional balance-of-power system. Such a system should include rebuilding Great Britain, restoring France to great-power status, and even the inclusion of a defeated Germany. German inclusion would mean resisting its dismemberment so that along with the US, it would counterbalance the Soviet Union, while reducing the latter's excessive demands for reparations.[67] A balance-of-power system would also include a spheres-of-influence agreement such as the percentage attempt with Stalin.[68] There was also support in the US for such an arrangement of an explicit spheres-of-influence agreement, including notably Kennan, Bohlen, and Lippmann.[69]

Defensive realists opposed a universalist strategy: The assistance to Greece/Turkey was part of the United States' assumption of Great Britain's responsibility to contain Soviet encroachment into the Mediterranean and preserving the European balance of power. But in Kennan's view, due to domestic considerations, the administration misrepresented it as a moral, universalist struggle between good and evil—which as a realist he saw as a dangerous, unworkable policy.[70]

The approach favors a multipolar world: Rather than a division into US and Soviet spheres of influence, the US should be interested in the rise of independent centers of power—Japan and Western Europe and the emergence of balance of power among all of them.

Nationalism can be useful for the strategy if the US takes advantage of tensions between the Soviet Union and the communist movement due to Soviet intolerance, thus reducing its ability to expand. At that time, it would mean an encouragement of Titoism—cooperation with Eastern European communist governments independent of Moscow for containing the Soviets. Nationalism would help to contain communism.

Defensive realists also opposed a preventive war against the Soviet Union. At the same time, an extreme version of defensive realism called for disengagement:[71] Avoiding new strategic commitments on the Eurasian continent was a position that appealed to many Americans because of classical liberal concerns,[72] and was supported by both conservative Republicans like Herbert Hoover and Robert Taft and progressives such as Henry Wallace.

OFFENSIVE REALISM: SUPERIORITY

Offensive realism argues that state security can be maximized only by being the materially superior power. Maintaining the balance of power is insufficient. An offensive realist strategy includes ideas of a preventive war. Marc

Trachtenberg demonstrates the prevalence of preventive-war thinking within the upper echelons of the Truman and Eisenhower administrations.[73] Thus, Eisenhower asked Dulles whether "our duty to future generations did not require us to initiate war at the most propitious moment" and raised the idea several times at meetings of the NSC between 1952 and 1954.[74] There were quite a few proposals to destroy the Soviet atomic plants before bombs could be produced or even afterward. For example, the navy in 1948,[75] and even State Department moderates (Bohlen in 1949 and Kennan in 1950),[76] thought in terms of war with the Soviet Union before it had nuclear weapons. Churchill thought alike.[77] A major source of preventive-war thinking was the air force—there was widespread support among high-ranking officers for a preventive war via strategic airpower.[78] Both the secretaries of the navy and air force called for an air strike on emerging Soviet nuclear weapons capabilities.[79] Preventive war—a major idea of offensive realism—has to be distinguished from a key idea of offensive liberalism: rollback; the former focuses on the balance of capabilities, while the latter idea addresses change in the regime/intentions of the opponent.

The key document that prescribed an offensive realist approach at the beginning of the Cold War was NSC 68, whose leading author was Paul Nitze. It advanced a range of positions that differed considerably from the defensive realist strategy led by Kennan.[80] We'll discuss next some of the key differences.

I. THE CONCEPTION OF SOVIET OBJECTIVES: INTENTIONS VERSUS CAPABILITIES

According to Paul Nitze and Dean Acheson, Moscow aimed to weaken, if not destroy, the US and to reach world domination by all possible means, including by demonstrating that force and the will to use it were on their side.[81] In contrast, Kennan argued that the Soviet Union was already overextended. As an example, Kennan presented the Yugoslav leader Tito who demonstrated independence from Stalin; Titoism offered opportunities for the US to exploit tensions within the Eastern Bloc.

NSC 68 was more pessimistic and suggested that Soviet expansion produced strength. Kennan focused on the evaluation of Soviet *intentions*. He estimated that the Soviet Union was cautious and would not take advantage of its superior conventional power as there was little to gain from it. NSC 68, for its part, focused on Soviet *capabilities*: when the Soviet Union becomes superior and expects to win, it will go to war in the form of a surprise attack; in other words, capabilities shape intentions; until then, there is a danger of war by proxy.[82]

II. ARE INTERESTS DIVISIBLE?
EXPANSION VERSUS MINIMAL

Kennan: Yes. Since not all of its interests were equally vital, the US had a lot of freedom of action whether and how to respond to a proxy war authorized by the Soviet Union.

NSC 68:   No. Interests are indivisible. Thus, it is imperative to respond to any challenge even in the periphery—otherwise the US would eventually sacrifice vital interests. The Eisenhower administration held a similar position.

In Kennan's view, however, maintaining a balance of power (and thus to safeguard diversity) required only to deny centers of industrial-military capability from the Soviet Union, which means in practice that it was necessary only to defend selected strong points.[83] In contrast, NSC 68 called for the expansion of interests, while taking into account also considerations of prestige and credibility, and as a result leading to an increase of defense spending:

(1) Perimeter defense—all points along it are considered of equal importance, blurring the distinction between vital and nonvital interests.[84]

(2) Changes in the balance of power could occur not only as a result of military or economic actions, but from intimidation, humiliation, or even loss of credibility. In other words, the balance of power depends on perceptions, including of the public and issues like prestige and credibility.

(3) Increase in defense spending in contrast to the administration's position. According to NSC 68, the US could afford the higher defense spending by governmental "management" of the economy via application of Keynesian techniques, namely, higher growth rates by governmental stimulation of the economy.

(4) The threat defines the interests: Expansion of interests according to the Soviet threat. US interests couldn't be defined apart from the Soviet threat to them; "frustrating the Soviet design" became an end in itself, not a means to a larger end.

III. CAN MILITARY SUPERIORITY BE TRANSLATED INTO POLITICAL ADVANTAGES?[85]

Kennan: No—the US should respond asymmetrically: strengthen itself and its allies, but no need to duplicate Soviet capabilities.

NSC 68:   Yes—even without war the Soviet Union could use its excessive military to challenge the US and its allies' position. Accordingly, NSC 68 called for military superiority.[86]

Table 3.3 overviews the key differences between the two realist approaches of balance of power versus dominance. NSC 68 was explicitly against a preventive war.[87] It saw preventive war as a negative option—both not feasible and morally repugnant. It favored only a preemptive strike.[88] Still, it can also be defined as an offensive realist document (see below and Snyder, *Myths of Empire*) because some of the report's key points echoed the conventional preventive-war arguments, especially that the US is moving to a period of high danger.[89] While NSC 68 was against relying too heavily on nuclear weapons, it approved of the H-bomb. In contrast to Kennan, the document opposed "no first use," and supported what would later be called "flexible response."

What are the main defensive realist criticisms of NSC 68?[90] First, it expanded unnecessarily both defense spending and the conception of "national interests." Second, it did not take advantage of fragmentation inside the communist movement/world. Third, it did not introduce an effective combination of objectives and capabilities. Fourth, it advanced rhetoric of a universalist approach of democracy promotion.

NSC 68 was essentially offensive realist, though it had some rhetorical elements of offensive liberalism. Thus, Nitze suggested that while the goal was not to democratize everyone, in order to mobilize domestic support, there was a need to make the case that the objective was not only repelling an invasion, but also "creating a better world."[91] NSC 68 and its primary author Paul Nitze (though others were not sure) approved of rollback—to replace communist governments with anti-Soviet, democratic ones.[92] Still, the practical priority was to increase the military budget and to reach military superiority.

The Dependent Variable: The Selected Grand Strategy, 1945–50s

I. FROM WWII UNTIL THE END OF 1946—DEFENSIVE LIBERALISM: THE ACCOMMODATIVE APPROACH

The selected grand strategy evolved in three stages.[93] In the first stage, toward the end of WWII and in its immediate aftermath, having in mind the postwar world order, the US followed a cooperative approach toward its wartime partner. Both FDR and Truman in the first phase of his term,[94] at least initially, led a cautious and accommodative policy toward the Soviet Union based on the willingness to accept legitimate Soviet security interests.[95] FDR sought to maintain the Grand Alliance as a great-power concert in the aftermath of the end of WWII, which meant mainly preserving friendly peacetime relations of mutual respect with Stalin.[96]

This accommodative policy had several foundations. First, FDR planned

TABLE 3.3. Differences between Kennan (DR) and NSC 68 (OR)

Item	Kennan—DR Minimal deterrence and balancing	NSC 68—OR Peace through strength
Are interests divisible?	Yes—distinction between vital and nonvital	No—even peripheral can challenge/undermine reputation/credibility, thus eventually eroding vital interests
Importance of credibility/reputation	Low	High
Is the periphery important/fragility of the BOP[1]	No	Yes[2]
Likelihood of war initiated by Moscow	Low—Soviets are cautious; war only by miscalculation	High—Soviet Union has superior capabilities, which will lead it to initiate war
Political utility of superior military capabilities, affecting the balance of resolve?	No—US can respond asymmetrically Resolve derived from the importance of interests	Yes—translated into strategic advantages; An indicator of resolve/willingness—thus a need for military buildup also to show political will[3]
Relations among capabilities, interests, and resolve	Level of vital interests determines resolve	Military capabilities are a signal of resolve
Intentions vs. capabilities	Intentions are important[4]	Only capabilities matter; intentions are unknown—then worst-case analysis re Soviet intentions (including resort to nuclear weapons);[5] even if intentions could be estimated, they could change overnight; thus, it is essential to have the capacity to use force that could be measured and treated as constant[6]
Nature of interests	Objectively determined irreducible interests	Determined by the perception of the Soviet threat: Any interest threatened by the Soviets becomes vital—interests are a function of threats > great expansion of interests
Military means/defense spending	Limited	Unlimited
Type of means to contain the Soviet Union	A great variety: political, psychological, economic, nationalist, and military	Military superiority > big expansion of the defense budget[7]
Use of force—"flexible response"[8]	"Horizontal"—limited military, but greater use of economic, diplomatic, and psychological means	"Vertical" from deterrence to nuclear weapons
Is the response symmetrical?	No—acting only when interests are vital, conditions favorable, and means accessible	Yes—responding whenever the Soviets challenge interests
Commitments and resources	To limit commitments according to resources	To mobilize resources to meet commitments

(Continued)

TABLE 3.3. (*Continued*)

Item	Kennan—DR Minimal deterrence and balancing	NSC 68—OR Peace through strength
Should the US exploit fragmentation within the communist bloc by cooperating with independent communists to contain the Soviet Union?	Yes—it is the USSR, not international communism, that threatens US security, thus cooperating with communists independent of Moscow, to contain the Soviets	Assumes continuous Soviet control over communism; any communist victory appears as a US loss, at least in the short-run
Negotiated settlement with the Soviet Union	Conflict management, though not resolution, is possible	Impossible without a change in the nature of the Soviet system; negotiate only from a position of strength, but the US is in relative decline and Moscow has inherent advantages in negotiations without taking into account its disadvantages[9]
Roots of Soviet conduct[10] See below on the image of the opponent	Defensive—Soviet Union paranoid; The challenge: Long-term and political	Offensive— the danger: immediate and military (1954—"the year of maximum danger"—Moscow will have major power—projection to the US by their bombers)
Direction of the military BOP	Soviet Union is the weaker party[11]	West is disarming, while the Soviet Union fully armed (threat, or capability, inflation[12]—a tendency to exaggerate the opponent's capabilities and intentions)
Cognitive explanation: Image of the opponent	Status-quo power; Defensive motivations; Possibility of reaching a political agreement	Offensive, very aggressive, revisionist, willing to use force, including nuclear weapons; Settlement impossible

Source: John Lewis Gaddis, *Strategies of Containment: A Critical Appraisal of American National Security Policy during the Cold War* (Oxford: Oxford University Press, 2005), 95–103.

Note: DR, defensive realism; OR, offensive realism; BOP, balance of power.

1. Gaddis, *Strategies of Containment*, 200–1.

2. Eisenhower (and also Khrushchev) believed that events in the Third World could tilt the BOP. Gordon S. Barrass, *The Great Cold War: A Journey through the Hall of Mirrors* (Stanford, CA: Stanford University Press, 2009), 126.

3. Strobe Talbott, *The Master of the Game: Paul Nitze and the Nuclear Peace* (New York: Knopf, 1988), 57.

4. Talbott, 57.

5. Talbott, 58.

6. Talbott, 57; Barrass, *The Great Cold War*, 93: both superpowers thought in this way.

7. Gaddis, *Strategies of Containment*, 97–98.

8. Gaddis, 99.

9. Gaddis, 102–3.

10. Talbott, *The Master of the Game*, 55–56.

11. Talbot, 56.

12. Talbot, 56.

TABLE 3.4. Summary table: The competing visions of US grand strategy

Vision	Defensive realism (Kennan)	Offensive realism (Nitze)	Defensive liberalism (FDR / Wallace)	Offensive liberalism (Dulles)
Major strategy	Contain the Soviet Union by economic and political means	Contain the Soviet Union through military superiority	Manage the international system jointly with the Soviet Union and through international institutions	Rollback communism in Soviet-dominated states
Ultimate US goal	To hold on until the Soviet Union mellows or collapses from within	To win the Cold War	To achieve international peace and stability	To defeat and rollback communism to be replaced by liberalism (regime change)
Image of the Soviet Union	Enemy/competitor: hostile but cautious; opportunistic; revisionist but with limited ambitions	Enemy: implacably hostile; revisionist with unlimited ambitions (bent on world domination)	Partner in managing the international system; a normal status-quo power	Enemy: implacably hostile, bent on spreading its communist ideology throughout the world
Sources of Soviet conduct	Insecurity and fear of the West stemming from Russian history, exacerbated by communist ideology	The expansionist nature of the communist regime that cannot abide coexistence with the democratic West	Legitimate security concerns	Ideological— spreading communism by any means at its disposal
Nature of the Soviet threat	Primarily political— might take advantage of weakness or dissention in the West to expand	Military— potential attack on US allies (and conceivably on the US itself)	There is no threat	Military and ideological—a threat to Western security and way of life
Can the Soviet Union be accommodated?	Partly; deterrence should be coupled with reassurance; the Soviet Union should not be provoked unnecessarily in order not to exacerbate tensions	No—it should be contained (and if possible, pushed back) through military superiority	Yes—through accommodating its legitimate security concerns	No—it should be checked and rolled back

to demobilize the army rapidly and bring it home.[97] While the US did not favor spheres of influence due to domestic and liberal considerations, it was aiming initially at a far-reaching move of a military disengagement: In Yalta FDR promised the withdrawal of US forces from Europe within two years of Germany's surrender.[98] At the Tehran conference (December 1943), FDR admitted to Stalin that Congress might not approve the deployment of US troops in postwar Europe; FDR wanted only a limited US postwar occupation zone.[99]

Similarly, Truman didn't respond favorably to Churchill's request that US forces stay longer than that date. Truman continued a dual approach: trying to convince the USSR that a comprehensive European settlement is preferable to spheres of influence, while starting to prepare such a division in order to deflect Soviet inclinations in that direction.[100] The US was not inclined in the early postwar months to challenge the reality of Soviet hegemony in Eastern Europe directly; rather it was willing to recognize the interests of Moscow in Eastern Europe if they avoided interference in domestic affairs.

Second, Stalin was misperceived as a pragmatist and moderate ("Uncle Joe"),[101] while FDR didn't distrust Stalin almost until his death.[102] FDR's postwar plans were based on the assumption that the Soviet Union would be willing to collaborate with the West in preserving world peace.[103]

Third, a fundamental basis of the accommodative view was the US acceptance of Soviet security interests—the US was willing to be cooperative so long as the Soviet Union seemed to be a security seeker. A key distinction regarding the Soviet policy toward Eastern Europe was whether it was interested only in influencing Eastern European foreign policies (a security seeker) or in extending the totalitarian coercive Soviet system with secret police (an expansionist/greedy/non-security-seeker power).[104]

At this stage the dominant view in Washington was that the Soviet Union was a security seeker. Thus, FDR and Truman in his first few months subscribed to the explanation of Soviet behavior as a security seeker, defensively motivated by insecurity, which can be overcome by reassurance.[105] This policy included gestures of good will and restraint toward Moscow during and immediately after the war.[106] Thus, Harriman began his tenure as the ambassador to Moscow in 1943 as a firm advocate of FDR's policy of US-Soviet cooperation. US policy makers attached great importance to cultivating a lasting cooperative relationship with the Soviets.[107] FDR enacted a soft-line toward Stalin to overcome his lack of trust in the West and to show that collaboration was in their best interest.[108] At the Tehran Summit (November 28 to December 1, 1943), FDR did his best to accommodate Soviet security requirements.[109] During World War II, the Soviet projection of power into

Europe was seen as defensive.[110] This soft-line continued as the war neared its end and in its aftermath.

Accordingly, the US initially accepted the Soviets' security demands to have a sphere of influence in Eastern Europe for foreign policy purposes—a policy of reassurance as was expressed by Ambassador Harriman (April 1945) and Secretary of State James Byrnes (October 1945).[111] In other words, the US did not object to regional arrangements for legitimate security interests, only to intervention in internal affairs by the dominant state. Thus, the Soviets had a right to "friendly" neighboring states.

Until late 1946 Truman continued FDR's road of belief in great-power co-operation. Only then, slowly and in a rather disorganized way did the US object to Soviet policies that it deemed threatening to its interests. From late 1945 to the end of 1946, the Truman administration awkwardly moved away from FDR's policy of accommodation toward a more hard-line strategy vis-à-vis Moscow; the administration's view shifted from perceiving the Soviet Union as a tough ally to a potential opponent.[112] Responsiveness to domestic politics couldn't play the decisive role in this shift as the public also had an informal defensive liberal orientation. In the eyes of the public, the Cold War came as a surprise to most Americans. There were expectations that issues would be addressed within the UN.[113]

II. 1947–49: FROM DEFENSIVE LIBERALISM TO DEFENSIVE REALISM—KENNAN'S CONTAINMENT

According to Miscamble's study, what is striking is not that Truman abandoned FDR's policy, but that he sought to maintain it for so long in the face of Soviet behavior.[114] Although at several points Truman lost his patience with Stalin, he soon regained it and continued his quest for agreements and understandings, a policy he abandoned only in 1947. However, Truman's progression from conciliation to containment was not direct and unidirectional. Instead, Miscamble adds weight to the argument previously made by Deborah Larson that at least until early 1947, Truman vacillated, sometimes offering concessions and at other times refusing to yield. Over time, the policy drifted toward the latter, but the progression was not smooth. The defensive liberal approach was already in trouble during 1946,[115] even though its final collapse occurred only in early 1947: "Beginning in 1947, the Americans finally recognized with some clarity that the 'hoped-for new order' of FDR's and Cordell Hull's soothing, wartime assurance was 'an illusion.'"[116]

The key objective of the first stage of Kennan's strategy was the restoration of the balance of power, while focusing on nonmilitary means. One com-

ponent of the new grand strategy was containment embodied in the Truman Doctrine. In early 1947 the US replaced Great Britain as the dominant
sea power in the Mediterranean and as the one intervening in European political affairs.[117] Truman proposed assisting Greece and Turkey so that their
governments could fight the domestic challenge posed by communists. He
stated: "I believe that it must be the policy of the US to support free peoples
who are resisting attempted subjugation by armed minorities or by outside
pressures."[118]

A key element came later in 1947—the Marshal Plan, expressing US commitment to fund European economic recovery in order to stabilize Europe
and to prevent the rise of pro-Moscow communist parties.[119] Another motive
was to detach the Eastern Europeans from Soviet control by offering them
Marshall Plan aid,[120] but the Soviets and the Eastern Europeans—obviously
under Soviet instructions—refused to take part. Thus, the plan assisted only
the noncommunist part of the continent, a region that was a key center of
the global balance of power; thus, the plan was a major component in the US
strategy to preserve the balance of power as a part of the Cold War struggle.[121]

The US commitment to protect the key center of power of West Germany
was demonstrated in the Berlin crisis. When the Soviets closed the border
between the two parts of Germany and besieged West Berlin in the summer
of 1948, the US showed its resolve by carrying out a round-the-clock airlift to
West Berlin. The commitment to the defense of Western Europe culminated
with the establishment of NATO in 1949.[122] Maintaining the atomic monopoly was also an important element in the strategy; there was also a serious
consideration of preventive air strike against the Soviet Union, although not
selected eventually and rejected by the administration.[123]

The grand strategy's logic at this stage was largely based on Kennan's conception of containment. The Truman administration implemented the first
stage of Kennan's strategy—restoration of the balance of power based on a
distinction between vital and less-vital interests. Thus, only the industrial
regions of Western Europe and Japan had to be protected.

The conception of threats combined hostility with a considerable material capability. The Truman Doctrine could create the basis for a universal
intervention in favor of any "free people" or "democracy," slogans that can be
manipulated by any leader who aspired to get US assistance.[124] Still, following
the announcement of the doctrine, the administration clarified that it opposed universal interventions, that is, in places not crucial for the balance of
power. Rather the administration favored selective engagement: strongpoint
defense of building up positions of strength, while rejecting intervention in
the mainland of Asia, from Afghanistan to Korea.[125]

The Means for the Implementation of the Grand Strategy

Based on Kennan's defensive realist advice, the focus in 1947–49 was on economic means — especially the rehabilitation of Europe, while deterrence and covert actions were secondary.[126] It was not a military-centered strategy so long as the threat was not high: "If Truman was always ready to give the military a budgetary boost in time of crisis, he usually backtracked once tensions eased."[127] Thus Truman turned down various Pentagon proposals for a major increase in defense spending and for a considerable defense buildup.[128] Economic rehabilitation as the key means and priority of containment was accepted by the administration — even if that meant deferring military preparedness based on an estimation that the Soviets were unlikely to resort to war in the near future (due to the US atomic monopoly and Soviet control of Eastern Europe without war).[129] The administration employed economic and technological means selectively to reinforce power centers not under Soviet control. At the same time, the administration had made some use of non-economic instruments, notably, atomic deterrence, psychological warfare, and covert action.[130]

While US policy was to deny the key power centers from Soviet control, the strategy was not based on US control of the allies; that is, Washington pursued nonintervention in internal affairs. The administration was willing to tolerate diversity, even if not communist regimes, by accepting the potential for multipolarity, namely, the rise of independent centers of power (notably, Western Europe and Japan) as a development that would serve US interests better than dominating spheres of influence. The idea was to empower Europe and Japan so that they would be able to withstand communist pressures without an enduring US security commitment.[131] As Kennan suggested in November 1947, and Secretary of State George Marshall accepted, "It is urgently necessary for us to restore something of the balance of power in Europe and Asia by strengthening local forces of independence and getting them to assume part of the burden."[132]

According to the balance-of-power criteria, these forces included Western Europe and Japan, but not China. Thus, the anticommunist assistance was denied from those places not considered critical for the balance of power, especially if the anticommunists were at any rate incompetent while the communists were not expected to be Soviet puppets. A key example was the case of the Chinese nationalists.[133]

In a following stage, Kennan's strategy aimed to fragment the international communist movement: it can be seen as defensive realism (supporting Titoism) with some offensive realist tendencies.[134] Thus, Marshall Plan aid was offered to the Soviet Union and to Eastern Europe, to the latter in order to spoil its relations with the USSR.[135] The administration also conducted in 1948 a rapprochement with Tito despite the internal character of the regime—due to his breakup with Stalin.[136] The following year the US attempted to encourage further dissidence in Eastern Europe by establishing the Voice of America and by economic pressures and covert action. The strategy manifested, moreover, tendencies toward offensive realism. NSC 58/2 ("United States Policy toward the Soviet Satellite States in Eastern Europe," December 1949) called for the elimination of Soviet power from Eastern Europe even if that meant cooperation with communist regimes if they were not subservient to the USSR. This logic also applied to potential cooperation with, notably, Mao's China.[137] The strategy called for using Titoism to roll back Soviet influence in the communist world by encouraging nationalist movements within world communism, which tended to weaken the Kremlin control of this world. In other words, the US should align with the forces of nationalism to weaken Soviet imperialism (the same logic as supporting independent centers of power in Europe and Japan).[138]

Finally, Kennan's strategy aimed at a behavior modification of Soviet policy so that they will learn to live with a diverse world rather than remaking it in their own image, namely, to make them behave according to the UN charter and thus to reach a negotiated settlement with them. This required responding positively to Soviet conciliatory moves while resisting aggressive moves. This approach was endorsed by the administration and translated to NSC 20/4 (November 1948).[139]

At the same time, Kennan opposed both offensive liberalism and offensive realism; rather, he favored a cautious (defensive) strategy: avoiding direct military intervention to prevent communist takeovers and avoid calling for the overthrow of communist governments in Eastern Europe—because the Soviets would be willing to go to war for maintaining their sphere of influence in Eastern Europe.[140] The strategy was also not offensive liberal because of his willingness to work with communist regimes so long as they were not subordinated to the Soviet Union.

The administration's strategy, however, partly shifted toward a more assertive defensive realism, including moves that Kennan opposed such as the establishment of NATO, the formation of an independent West German state, persistent deployment of US forces in postoccupation Japan, and developing the H-bomb.[141] Kennan viewed these steps as enhancing the security dilemma by encircling the Soviet Union with military alliances. These moves were designed to build "situations of strength" (advocated by Acheson)—strength came to be viewed as an end in itself, not as a means for a larger end of changing Soviet objectives and behavior. This was based on a focus on the rival's capabilities rather than intentions, assuming that capabilities are more measurable, while it is harder to identify intentions, which can also more easily change overnight.[142]

III. THE SELECTED GRAND STRATEGY, 1950: NSC 68 AND KOREA—FROM DEFENSIVE TO OFFENSIVE REALISM[143]

The transition from defensive realism to offensive realism in the second half of 1950 is manifested by the quest for achieving US military superiority in accordance with the spirit and the prescription of NSC 68. Historians agree that preponderance became national policy following the onset of the Korean War.[144] It was a vision that called for ever-more armaments. US leaders believed that both the industrial core of Eurasia and the raw-material-producing periphery had to be included in the US sphere for the Soviet Union not to win the Cold War. This was a costly strategy.[145] Secretary of State Acheson believed that "through military superiority the US would wrest the initiative from the Kremlin and multiply its options for waging the cold war."[146]

A key expression of the quest to reach superiority is the enormous jump in the defense budget for 1951 in comparison to previous years. Truman asked for more money for defense for 1951—from $13.5 billion to $48.2—a 257 percent increase.[147] This was a dramatic change in light of Truman's earlier persistently strong opposition to any rise in defense spending and also his related lack of endorsement of NSC 68 until the Korean War.[148]

Although US officials talked about "restoring the BOP [balance of power] in Europe and Asia,"[149] Dueck suggests that under containment US officials did not seek balance of power with the Soviet Union,[150] but rather predominance: large defense spending and commitments.[151] Containment went far beyond balance of power—it was not a strategy of balance, but of preponderance.[152] This applied, however, to the post–Korean War period. In *Preponderance of Power*, Leffler highlights the US quest for superiority.[153] Particularly, two strategic considerations influenced the development of a comprehensive overseas base system: One was the need for defense in depth—the US must encircle the Western Hemisphere with a defensive ring of outlying bases. The other was the need to project US power quickly and effectively against any potential adversary.[154] Both Acheson and Nitze supported a major military buildup: America's own risk-taking had to be supported with an ever-larger array of military capabilities.[155]

The new offensive realist grand strategy—the search for superiority—

was guided by the logic of NSC 68, which was adopted by the administration in September 1950. NSC 68 was essentially an offensive realist document, even though it also included some offensive liberal elements, but they were less integrated into the actual grand strategy. NSC 68 called for "a build-up of military strength by the United States and its allies to a point at which the combined strength will be superior . . . , both initially and throughout a war, to the forces that can be brought to bear by the Soviet Union and its satellites."[156]

What was new about NSC 68 was that it called for more and more money to implement the program and to achieve the goals already set out.[157] It also concluded that no parts of the world were now peripheral and that no means of protecting them could now be ruled out.[158] NSC 68 prescribed to the US to behave as a revisionist power. It was not a defensive/status quo document— but rather an offensive one, making the retraction of Soviet power the US objective, to force the USSR to recede by creating situations of strength.[159] The offensive character of NSC 68 was manifested in its divergence from NSC 20/4 (November 1948). It called for the projection of military strength to combat the Soviet threat, and it recommended a massive military buildup.[160]

Before Korea, Truman rejected this prescription and tried to reduce military expenditures.[161] The balance on the eve of Korea was of US atomic superiority, but of conventional inferiority. The US had a total of only seven active divisions, the nearest of them to Korea was in Japan.[162]

But following the North Korean invasion, the Truman administration initiated a major buildup of US military, aiming for preponderance.[163] This huge military buildup was intended for reaching superiority over the Soviets in reaction to Soviet-sponsored communist aggression, notably the North Korean invasion of June 1950: by 1953 US military production was seven times that of 1950.[164] This chain of events contradicts Layne's argument that the US aspired for hegemony already before the Cold War and irrespective of the Soviet threat.[165] The eruption of the Korean War convinced Truman and his advisors that the authors of NSC 68 were right: any part of the world threatened by the Soviet Bloc would have to be protected, whether it was industrial or not.[166]

The Manifestations of Offensive Realism: Establish
and Maintain US Superiority, 1950–62

The offensive realist strategy adopted with the outbreak of the Korean War had two dimensions: to strengthen the US by a more militarized and globalized containment in order to reach a preponderance of power and to weaken the opponent—the Soviets. Policies to strengthen the US included primarily a major increase in the defense budget as both Nitze and Acheson—the two leading offensive realists in the Truman administration—called for.[167] Soon after the war, the budget tripled to nearly $50 billion per year. National security obligation would total about $69.5 billion in fiscal year 1951, level off to about $56 billion for fiscal years 1952–54, and decrease to about $45 billion in 1955. Most of the funding would be earmarked to the military establishment. While in 1946 US defense spending was less than 5 percent of the gross national product, in 1953 it was 17 percent of the GNP.[168]

A related development was a rapid expansion of the armed forces from 1.5 million to 3.6 million men (the Soviet Union expanded its own to five million). Each of the three services had greatly expanded: the creation of seventeen army divisions—compared to ten authorized in June 1950; 322 combatant ships—compared to 238 authorized in June 1950; seventy air wings—compared to forty-eight in June 1950.[169] NATO also went through a major strengthening,[170] notably by a major permanent deployment of US forces in Europe.[171] More specifically, there was a push for a full war-fighting force by 1954 (thus Stalin feared an attack by 1954).

Specifically, the number and power of nuclear weapons increased rapidly as well as the production of uranium and plutonium, leading to an increase in the output of atomic weapons. The strengthened arsenal included more powerful atomic bombs (seven times more powerful than Hiroshima), a total of eight hundred bombs that could destroy the Soviet Union in two hours, and culminated with the production of the H-bomb—a thousand times more powerful than the bomb dropped on Hiroshima (by late 1952, the Soviet Union had seventy bombs and a small number of slow-moving planes that could reach targets around the Soviet periphery).

Truman approved another massive manufacturing of nuclear weapons;[172] the US enhanced its ability to destroy, not only Soviet industrial targets, but also a wide range of military targets, especially nuclear weapons. Overwhelming nuclear superiority had become the objective of US strategy.[173] Strategic superiority was Eisenhower's goal as well; during the first five years of Eisenhower's presidency, the number of US nuclear warheads increased from about 1,000 to about 5,500, along with 1,200 B-47 bombers that could bomb the Soviet Union from bases in the US.[174] Thus, in 1956 there was no "bomber gap" in the Soviet favor,[175] and in the late 1950s, neither was there a "missile gap."[176] The arms buildup of Eisenhower and Kennedy demonstrated that "the concept of deterrence was yielding to one of absolute security."[177]

Additional elements of offensive realism included the establishment of worldwide anti-Soviet alliances, which surrounded and encircled the Soviet

Union with US bases and also the expansion of war aims in Korea. In addition to its own bases, the US encouraged West German rearmament in May 1955,[178] and stepped up military help to France in Vietnam and to Taiwan.[179]

Under Eisenhower containment became more assertive, with America's security being based on an imbalance of nuclear terror—at the expense of a large conventional army.[180] The offensive realist strategy, rather than promoting democracy, advanced the removal of elected governments from power: Iran (August 1953) and Guatemala (1954).[181] In other words, within the framework of the keen Cold War competition, the offensive realist logic led the US to promote illiberal regimes instead of liberal ones, and rather than promoting democracy, to install autocracy by force. Regime change by the US during that era was intended to replace democratically elected regimes that were unsettling to the American security interests with more compatible ones for the American interests. A common element to all offensive realist administrations: "Kennedy and his advisers, like John Foster Dulles and the drafters of NSC-68, differed from Kennan in their conviction that the balance of power was fragile"; small fluctuations in its distribution—or even the perception of such shifts—could have major repercussions across the world.[182]

Key Dimensions of Offensive Realism: Policies
Designed to Weaken the Soviet Union

Offensive realism was augmented by some components of regime change ("liberation"), including elements of offensive liberalism in the strategy.[183] Critics of containment argued that it was too defensive and didn't challenge the Soviet Union. Such a defensive posture would allegedly only generate further retreats by the US and its allies. In *Undermining the Kremlin*, Gregory Mitrovich argues that following the Allied victory in World War II, the United States turned its efforts to preventing the spread of communism beyond Eastern Europe. The policy of containment was, however, only the first step in a clandestine campaign to destroy Soviet power. Drawing on declassified US documents, Mitrovich reveals a range of previously unknown covert actions launched during the Truman and Eisenhower administrations. Through the aggressive use of psychological warfare, officials sought to provoke political crisis among key Soviet leaders, to incite nationalist tensions within the USSR, and to foment unrest across Eastern Europe. Mitrovich demonstrates that inspiration for these efforts did not originate within the intelligence community, but with individuals at the highest levels of policy making in the US government starting as early as 1947.

Mitrovich and Grose highlight the US propaganda and political warfare of Radio Free Europe/Radio Liberty and a variety of cultural and intellectual front organizations and also subversion by agents parachuted behind enemy lines. Mitrovich focuses on attempts to exploit vulnerabilities in the Soviet Union: programs to disrupt Kremlin decision making (Operation Overload), to encourage Soviet officials to defect (Operation Engross), and to take advantage of Soviet disorientation after Stalin's death (Operation Cancellation).

NSC 20/4, approved by Truman in June 1948, called for planting disinformation and supporting armed resistance groups. The main strategy was to take advantage of the "paranoid nature" of the Soviet power structure to encourage conflict within the leadership and between the party and the military and the security services and the army.[184]

Specific policies to weaken the opponent focused mainly on propaganda and psychological warfare, though they also advanced some subversive and covert operations. C. D. Jackson, the president's special assistant for Cold War operations, was eager to use psychological warfare and covert actions to roll back Soviet power.[185] Yet, the Eisenhower administration used rollback rhetoric essentially as part of "psychological warfare" against the Eastern Bloc;[186] indeed, the administration's abortive proposal for a congressional "captive nations" resolution in early 1953 was justified off the record by Dulles as a psychological weapon.[187]

Still, there was also some component of subversion/covert operations in the Eastern Bloc.[188] NSC 10/2 empowered the CIA to conduct covert operations through the Office of Special Projects (later renamed the Office of Policy Coordination), which dealt with "subversion against hostile states, and support for indigenous anti-communist elements."[189] NSC 20/4, which was approved in revised form by the president in November 1948, placed a high priority on generating resistance behind the Iron Curtain and exploiting the disparity between Soviet and national communist interests.[190] NSC 68 itself called for a continuation of offensive-minded strategy.[191] The general policy objective was to further stimulate Titoism, but during 1948–52, the CIA initiated some support for resistance movements in Poland, Ukraine, the Baltic states and Albania.[192] The most far-reaching operation was to dislodge the communist regime headed by Enver Hoxha in Albania. The CIA sponsored Albanians who parachuted into their homeland, but they were captured. It shows how difficult it was to overthrow regimes in police states; it proved impossible to transform the passive resistance of the population into an open rebellion.[193]

The CIA established front organizations for underground political groups and potential subversion and guerrilla activity in Eastern Europe.[194] On June 18, 1948, NSC 10/2 called for covert operations to attack the Soviet Union around the world. The Pentagon wanted "guerrilla movements . . . underground armies . . . sabotage and assassination." The CIA's mission was to roll back the Soviet Union to Russia's old boundaries and free Europe from communist control.[195] There was a plan to recruit legions of exiles for armed resistance groups to penetrate the Iron Curtain, though only a few were found.[196] "In World War II, the United States made common cause with communists to fight fascists. In the Cold War, the CIA used fascists to combat communists,"[197] such as the Ukrainian Mikola Lebed against the Soviet Union. "By 1949, the US was ready to work with almost any son of a bitch against Stalin. Lebed fit that bill."[198] The CIA used former Nazis because they convinced them that they "could run missions aimed at the heart of Soviet power."[199]

Several works showed that contrary to what had been believed, the Anglo-American attempts to weaken or overthrow the communist regimes in Eastern Europe and even in the Soviet Union were serious, were conducted on a large scale, and were central to the strategy for waging the Cold War.[200] "They also revealed the father of many of these efforts to have been George Kennan, something that did not fit well with the picture of him as the mastermind of containment or with his later critiques of belligerent American policies."[201] "It is too simple to see this period as characterized by containment, even if we view this approach as being quite capacious. From the start, holding the line against further Soviet expansion vied with the strategy of forcing a retraction of communist power, and after the split with Yugoslavia, of encouraging other Titos which meant accepting (at least temporarily) communist governments as long as they were not subservient to the USSR."[202]

The new evidence on offensive liberalism shows rollback-related policies as early as 1947. This data on US covert actions highlights the offensive component in US grand strategy, but it does not prove the dominance of offensive liberalism in the strategy. While it aimed also at regime change, for practical purposes, it was political and psychological warfare to undermine and weaken the opponent—thus fitting nicely with offensive realism.

As Robert Legvold argues, Mitrovich's characterization that "rollback" was "the be-all of US policy" was "overdrawn."[203] Similarly, Garthoff suggests that apart from identifying the existence of these operations, Mitrovich has not been able to learn whether they eventually led to any active efforts, much less any identifiable results.[204]

The Explanation

The evolution of US grand strategy is based on the combined effect of the two propositions introduced at the beginning of the chapter: First, during

1945–46 the dominant strategy was defensive liberalism based on the perception that the Soviet Union was not threatening (a WWII ally) and was relatively weak (as a result of the war devastation). Second, in 1947 there was a transition to defensive realism, articulated in the Truman Doctrine due to the emergence of a bipolar system (British decline and the Soviets emerged as powerful in Europe), augmented by some components of offensive liberalism as the Soviet threat grew in 1948.[205] Third, the growing Soviet threat (manifested in Korea 1950) led to a change from a defensive realist strategy to an offensive realist one as expressed in NSC 68, augmented by some components of offensive liberalism (psychological warfare), which were abandoned in 1955 with the growing Soviet capabilities.[206] The grand strategy of offensive realism was based on the quest for and the maintenance of US superiority.

THE INTERNATIONAL SYSTEM AS THE BROKER OF THE MARKETPLACE OF IDEAS

The effects of the international system on grand strategy are demonstrated by causal links between changes in the international environment (the growing Soviet threat based on its actions and changes in the balance of power manifested by Great Britain's withdrawal and decline, the loss of atomic monopoly, and the communist successes in Europe and Asia) and changes in US grand strategy. These effects are shown, for example, by consecutive time links between the changes in the environment and changes in US grand strategy.

Facing other powerful states that limit their freedom of action, the great powers are compelled to resort to realist strategies. The threatening nature of the system provides incentives to pursue offensive strategies in order to check the high-level threats. The US grand strategy at the height of the Cold War illustrates this point. Toward the end of World War II, President Franklin Roosevelt aimed to pursue a defensive liberal strategy (the multilateral Four Policemen concert of great powers),[207] and President Truman at first planned to follow suit. But systemic pressures after World War II had forced the US to change course, irrespective of the president's worldview.[208] The Soviet Union had major offensive capabilities in Europe and demonstrated aggressive intentions in a range of international crises in 1946–50—thus creating a highly threatening environment. Facing such an international environment and for the sake of its security, the United States was compelled to adopt an offensive realist grand strategy. Due to Soviet power, offensive liberal strategies like "rollback" were impossible to implement, thus the goal was to surpass Soviet power.

Explanation of the Selection of the Grand Strategies

EXPLAINING THE DEFENSIVE LIBERAL APPROACH IN 1945–46: LOW SOVIET THREAT AND US SUPERIORITY

With the end of WWII, the administration did not think that the Soviet Union posed the most likely threat to the postwar balance of power. Rather, FDR believed in cooperation with the Soviet Union, and Truman continued his policy as late as fall of 1945.[209] In fact, the Truman administration proved just as eager as its predecessor to teach Churchill that the days of balance-of-power diplomacy were over. Interestingly, officials in the FDR and Truman administrations were suspicious and critical of Churchill while being favorable toward Stalin.[210] Indeed, at the time of FDR's death, Moscow was not seen as an enemy, and the US was not frightened by Soviet military power. The Soviet Union appeared as a devastated country, and compared to the US, it was weak.[211] The military estimated toward the end of WWII that there was a low Soviet threat. Thus, in 1944 intelligence estimates downplayed the likelihood of Soviet hostility even as they acknowledged the probability of its hegemony in Eurasia.[212] In 1944–45 a cautious US military was concerned with preventing or at least reducing Soviet fears, although it was determined to prevent its dominance of Eurasia due to the implications for the balance of power. At any rate, there was a relatively benign view of Soviet intentions until the end of 1945.[213] Changes in the two key independent variables (IV1 and IV2) led to a change in the grand strategy from defensive liberalism (the Four Policemen) to defensive realism (Kennan's containment by economic means and nuclear deterrence and hope to build a multipolar world).

IV1: SOVIET POWER—THE RISE OF A BIPOLAR BALANCE COMPRISED OF SOVIET AND AMERICAN POWER

The shift in the balance of power led to a transition from liberal to realist approaches. The balance of power at the end of WWII was transformed to a bipolar world composed of only two superpowers.[214] This was the key factor leading to the dominance of realist approaches (the selection of defensive or offensive approaches depends on the level of threat). Following WWII, the Soviets had an overwhelming power on the Eurasian land mass and some major territorial gains. The other powers were much weaker: Germany and Japan were defeated and occupied; France, humiliated; Great Britain, weakened; China, engulfed in a civil war.

In contrast to the weakening of these powers, the rising power of the

Soviet Union was the combined result of the following developments: Soviet dominance of East-Central Europe; superior conventional and mobile capabilities at the heart of Europe; the acquisition of the atomic bomb in August 1949; and the 1949 Chinese Revolution and China's alliance with Stalin. The combined effect of Soviet power was to preclude a rollback in Eastern Europe.[215]

THE EXPLANATION OF CHANGE I—FROM DEFENSIVE LIBERALISM TO DEFENSIVE REALISM

The explanation is based on the structural transition from a multipolar to a bipolar world—in contrast to individual/ideological-level explanations. At the end of WWII, as indicated above, the US impulse was to bring the troops home and disband the military as it did following WWI.[216] In 1945–46 Truman and Secretary of State Byrnes didn't think in structural terms of the new post-WWII world balance of power.[217] Truman thought in Wilsonian terms, namely, that the UN would settle disputes; while Byrnes believed that his own negotiating skills would secure the peace.

Both Truman and Byrnes didn't imagine that the US would have to select among grand strategies framed in light of Great Britain's decline. They were still thinking in FDR's terms of great-power cooperation; some Americans even thought in terms of the US mediating between Great Britain and the Soviet Union. Yet, there was a growing recognition by top US decision makers that the emergence of a bipolar world eliminated the chances for "the hoped-for new order" envisioned by FDR and Cordell Hull and made it an illusion.[218]

The emergence of bipolarity was based first of all on the Soviets as the dominant power in Europe: World War II had left the Soviet Union as the only great power on the continent, and neither France nor West Germany had the power to balance effectively against it on their own.[219] As the US Joint Chiefs of Staff put it, the Soviet Union was "the sole great power on the Continent—a position unique in modern history."[220] The Joint Intelligence Committee worried that "none of these [European] countries is capable singly of waging a successful defensive war against the USSR."[221]

This was not to say that observers believed an invasion was imminent. The material cost of fighting World War II and its rapid postwar demobilization meant that the Soviet Union was unlikely to attack in the foreseeable future.[222] But as historian Melvyn Leffler notes, it had the potential to dominate—it had "overwhelming power on the Eurasian land mass."[223]

A second key factor was the absence in the international system of another great power apart from the United States and the Soviet Union. A key development in the emergence of a bipolar world was the British disengagement, particularly from the Eastern Mediterranean. Following the high costs of its key role in WWII, Great Britain became too weak to play its stabilizing role.[224] The power vacuum in the Middle East/Eastern Mediterranean—due to the British weakness—led to the Truman Doctrine and containment.[225] The British withdrawal from the Greek crisis showed that only the US could carry the burden. Thus, the US couldn't do buck-passing as sometimes great powers tend to do,[226] especially when the threat is relatively far away.[227] In the bipolar world, there was no other power that could contain the Soviet Union.[228] In this sense, the US commitment was imposed by the international system reinforced by the post-WWII international developments in the three key regions for the global balance of power—Europe, the Middle East, and Asia.[229]

In Europe, no real balance emerged from the war—following the partial US withdrawal, the Soviet Union became dominant on the continent. The Central European power vacuum encouraged Soviet expansion irrespective of the ideological rivalry. The British weakness and retraction also induced Soviet expansion. The weakness of Europe and Japan necessitated US protection.

In the Middle East, the weakness of Iran, Turkey, and Saudi Arabia had led to calls for US protection. The initiative came from them, *not* the US. The US responded (notably, the Truman Doctrine of March 1947 addressed the delicate situation of Greece and Turkey) because allies were important in the East-West rivalry, even if the allies were also concerned about regional threats and even if there was the bias of the domino doctrine.[230] Finally, in East Asia the balance of power changed with the communist victory in China in October 1949.[231]

Kissinger argues that FDR's Four Policemen manifested a mismatch between an ideational approach and the logic of the balance of power.[232] If the concept were to work, the US would have to be willing to intervene wherever peace was threatened. But according to FDR, the US was unwilling to maintain the balance of power in Europe (US troops would stay only two years in Europe), and since Great Britain was unable to do it alone (and also its unilateral actions—like in Greece—were not supported by FDR and were seen as imperialist), that would mean Soviet dominance in Europe (and Asia). FDR overestimated the British capabilities to handle the defense and the reconstruction of Europe; but eventually, the logic of the balance of power won, and the US was drawn back into Europe, and Japan and Germany were restored.

The transition to bipolarity led to the collapse of defensive liberalism because of the need for each of the superpowers to focus on balancing the capabilities of the other and to contain the other's potential expansion. As Waltz
points out, in bipolarity, as opposed to multipolarity, there was no one else
to contain the Soviets.[233] The culture of US foreign policy didn't suddenly
change. Thus, it was not a cultural change that brought about the change
in grand strategy. It was rather the structural change that forced the US to
embark on the Truman Doctrine, the Marshall Plan, NATO, the Korean intervention, and the subsequent deployment of two divisions to Europe—all
within six years.

   This is related to our argument that liberal approaches (both defensive
liberalism/collective security and offensive liberalism) are more likely to work
under liberal hegemony.[234] While there were strong domestic sources for liberal approaches, there was a lack of material support for these approaches
in the international system. Thus, the structural forces (the distribution of
capabilities) brought about the dominance of realist approaches, whereas the
rising threat led to a shift from defensive realism to offensive realism.

IV2: THE GROWING THREAT LEADS TO THE CHANGE
FROM DEFENSIVE APPROACHES TO AN OFFENSIVE ONE[235]

With the end of WWII, the great imponderable was whether the Kremlin
wanted more than just security.[236] Was the Soviet Union greedy/revisionist
or security/status quo seeking?[237] The change in US position followed a rising
recognition that Soviet behavior was more greedy, aggressive, non–security
seeking, and unilateral.[238]
   With the end of WWII, the international conditions were ripe for the
emergence of a high Soviet threat: a victorious large Red Army in the middle
of Europe and socioeconomic and political instability across the continent.
The Soviet Union was a revisionist power: both capable and willing to inflict
harm on vital US interests. The more threatening the Soviet behavior became, the greater was the US willingness to invest in a defense buildup of armament and alliances. Thus, the change in the balance of power is reinforced
by IV2—the balance of threat. FDR and Truman initially tried to construct
a cooperative world. By the end of 1946, many US officials had, however,
reached the conclusion that the Soviet adversarial conduct threatened US security, and they wanted to meet the Soviet threat.[239]
   Stalin presided over Soviet expansion for creating a wide security belt so
long it did not lead to war.[240] The rise of the Soviet threat was based on Stalin's failure to keep his word from Yalta, which the US understood as holding

free elections and establishing democratic governments in Eastern Europe.[241] On top of the ideological gulf, the lack of responsiveness by Stalin to FDR's and Truman's accommodative approach reinforced the sense of the Soviet threat.[242]

The critical difference between post-WWI isolationism and post-WWII global involvement was the severity, clarity, and the focus of the threat. The Soviet Union had become the most plausible source of threat by 1947. The US empire arose primarily not from internal causes, but from a perceived external danger powerful enough to overcome American isolationism.[243]

The *willingness* component of the Soviet threat, on top of Soviet capabilities, was based on an aggressive Soviet behavior. This was manifested, first, by the "Sovietization" of Eastern Europe (imposing a hostile/threatening ideology that poses a threat to key US values), and also attempts at Finlandization of Iran and Turkey. Eastern Europe became the chief indicator, a litmus test of the behavior that could be expected of the Soviet Union in the wake of WWII.[244] Why had the Sovietization of Eastern Europe led to the fear that the Soviet Union would seek an expansion elsewhere?[245]

First, it was combined with their aggression in other places (see below). The second reason was Soviet unilateralism: Soviet unilateral actions regarding the Sovietization of Eastern Europe even though the US accepted the Soviet Union's new borders and its sphere of influence in Eastern Europe.[246] This acceptance didn't prevent rising cases of Soviet unilateralism. The third reason was the association of domestic oppression with external aggression; the Sovietization of Eastern Europe—Soviet expansion—was seen by the US both as breaching the right of self-determination and as a harbinger of more aggressive goals.[247] Fourth, the Soviet Union was apparently breaking its promises. In contrast to the promises made in Yalta, it sought not only a sphere of influence for security or foreign policy purposes, but also domestic oppression in Eastern Europe. As the military situation turned more in his favor, Stalin progressively raised his terms: in 1941, his key concern was frontiers; in 1945, regime imposition of pro-Soviet communist regimes. Soviet domination of Eastern Europe—determining the domestic regimes in their sphere of influence—led to a harder line in Congress and the public.[248]

There were other cases of unilateral Soviet behavior which increased the perception of the Soviet threat. In Iran the Soviets failed to remove their troops by the agreed-upon deadline and established a puppet regime in Northern Iran. The US forced a Soviet retreat. The Soviets also demanded bases on the Turkish Straits, and there was a communist-led insurgency in Greece.[249]

Even if one could argue that Soviet domination of Eastern Europe shouldn't have generated security fears because it could be understood as a key Soviet security interest (preventing an invasion from the west—from where Napoleon and Hitler invaded Russia in the past), the same could not be said in the other cases of Soviet unilateralism and aggression. According to Gaddis, Soviet encroachments on Greece, Turkey, and Iran couldn't be justified by security concerns, and thus they led to change in US policy.[250] In other words, the perception of threat is determined by the behavior of the adversary—whether it is guided by security or expansionist motives.

Another American concern was about not only the use of communist parties, which were loyal to the Soviet Union, to take over Eastern Europe,[251] but also the growing power of communist parties in Western Europe,[252] the Eastern Mediterranean, and China. There were also underlying systemic sources of threat related to the uncertainty under anarchy: The more fundamental problem here was the instability and uncertainty and even chaos that prevailed in the aftermath of WWII in certain regions—under international anarchy—and that could be taken advantage of by the USSR through the local communist parties.[253]

According to this systemic logic, neither Truman nor Stalin wanted a dangerous rivalry such as eventually emerged during the Cold War. It came about because conditions in the international system created risks that Truman and Stalin could not accept and opportunities they could not resist. The threat for the US was derived from chaos, socioeconomic collapse, and instability and thus the rise of communism in Europe, which was seen as a tool of the Kremlin;[254] hence, the Marshall Plan was seen as an appropriate response.[255] There was also a concern about instability in the Third World—fear that Stalin would capitalize on these conditions.[256]

A systemic account—focusing on the security dilemma, mutual fear, and action-reaction dynamics—highlights that the source of US grand strategy was not the evil character of Stalin and his regime, but the fact that the USSR could take advantage of the turmoil in Europe (and decolonization in the Third World), which provided opportunities to expand Soviet power and especially—the greatest threat—that Germany might join the Soviet Union.[257] The US feared that the economic resources of Europe would fall under Soviet control, which would pose a threat to United States' free economy and provide opportunities for Soviet expansion in the Third World.[258]

As a result, the US offensive—the Truman Doctrine, the Marshall Plan, and the rebuilding of West Germany—was a response to the anarchy in the international system, upon which the Soviet Union could capitalize. On the other hand, Stalin's view of the Marshall Plan as a threat, which would isolate the Soviet Union, led to the tightening of control over Eastern Europe, and to increasing Soviet defense expenditures.[259]

Certain post-WWII structural elements encouraged a mutual security dilemma, notably vacuums of power in Central Europe and Northeast Asia after the defeat of Germany and Japan.[260] As a result, the US became concerned that the revival of nationalism or the emergence of independent neutrality might lead to an alliance of Germany and Japan with the Soviet Union.[261] The threat to US interests—what was at stake—"if Western Europe goes beyond the Iron Curtain" might have included, among other issues, heavy economic costs and serious infringements on domestic freedoms.[262]

A comprehensive study concluded that the Soviet Union acted unilaterally and that it was unwilling to cooperate in maintaining the balance of power. Still, Truman responded cautiously to Soviet unilateralism. The US was willing to give the Soviet Union the benefit of the doubt for many months.[263] There was an accumulation, however, of indisputable evidence of Soviet unilateral expansionism.[264] The US fear of Germany under Soviet control (the Soviet Union turned down a US proposal to keep Germany united and disarmed and not under the control of any of the great powers) served to make the idea of a divided Europe and Germany more acceptable for the US.[265]

The sense that a military aspect of containment was needed was reinforced in January 1948 when Ernest Bevin, the UK foreign secretary, alerted the US to Soviet expansion and the need for the West to defend against it. This was further strengthened by the February 1948 coup in Czechoslovakia, which demonstrated that the Marshall Plan was not enough and that there was a need for an explicit military guarantee.[266]

The key point is that the policy change was a reaction to external events that brokered among the competing ideas on the desirable grand strategy. Truman and Acheson gave the Soviet Union the benefit of the doubt well into the early postwar era; Truman and other US officials updated and adjusted their beliefs in response to the facts, as any good scientists would. Truman's shifting positions were not determined by ideology—liberalism or capitalism.[267]

"Truman never self-consciously decided to transform the foreign policy content and approach he inherited from FDR. Instead, external circumstances drove the creation of the Truman administration's foreign policy."[268] The Truman Doctrine was not born as a result of ideas like Kennan's, but rather as a result of the obstinacy and adventurism of Stalin and Molotov— such as the Prague Coup and the Berlin Blockade—leading eventually to the creation of NATO in 1949.[269] Gaddis describes the fear that the Soviet Union could become superior if it took over the big industrial centers in Europe and

Asia—either by armed aggression or by political and subversive means. Such a takeover would make the Soviet Union superior, which would then threaten US security and core values.[270]

1946: The system as a broker of ideas "By February 1946, Soviet behavior seemed to confirm that the hard-liners were right. The USSR seemed to be acting in an aggressive and heavy-handed manner, not only in Eastern Europe but also in Turkey and Iran."[271] Advocates of cooperation were marginalized because of the Soviet aggressive behavior. Truman was genuinely alarmed by the threat of Soviet expansion and endorsed a hard-line approach early in 1946.[272] Despite US preference for limited liability,[273] the international pressures of the Soviet threat and weakness of Japan and Europe, especially Britain's decline (this is the meaning of bipolarity), compelled the US to take care of European and Japanese security.[274] The British decline manifested the transition to bipolarity without the possibility of buck-passing.[275] Some of the worrisome signals in Europe in the late 1940s included Iran / Turkey encroachments; rigged elections in Hungary and Poland (1947); the coup in Czechoslovakia in February 1948, which created fear in Western Europe so that most Western Europeans sought military alliance with the US, leading to the establishment of NATO;[276] the Berlin Blockade (June 1948–May 1949); and the Soviet atomic test in August 1949.

In response, Truman escalated gradually, starting with the diplomatic means and economic assistance of the 1947 Truman Doctrine and the economic means of the 1948 Marshall Plan;[277] via the forceful move of the Berlin airlift of humanitarian supplies to the besieged city, upping the ante with the extension of the US security umbrella to Western Europe in 1949;[278] and then the decision to build the H-bomb/superbomb in response to the loss of the atomic monopoly in 1949.[279] Due to its conventional inferiority in Europe and Asia, the US relied more heavily on nuclear weapons for deterrence. Thus, such a loss led to the fear that deterrence was becoming less credible to counter Soviet conventional force superiority.

The underlying concern of the Western Europeans was the Soviet Union's mobile tank division in East Germany: 175 divisions—five times as many as the US, Britain, and France combined. The Europeans felt threatened by this huge force, and this created the need for NATO.[280] This US security umbrella was what made possible European economic and political integration. The balance of power also seemed to be changing in October 1949 in East Asia with the communist victory in China. The "loss of China" made the rest of East Asia more vulnerable.[281] Such changes in the balance of power and the level of threat led to a gradual/partial shift toward offensive realism: The moves in response (notably the establishment of NATO) built "situations of strength" (Acheson) so that strength came to be viewed as an end in itself, not as a means for a larger end.[282]

EXPLAINING THE TRANSITION FROM DEFENSIVE REALISM TO OFFENSIVE REALISM—THE QUEST FOR MILITARY SUPERIORITY

The key point is that the shift to offensive realism occurred due to an external-material input: the North Korean invasion of South Korea. It was a military aggression across international boundaries, backed by the Soviet Union and China. Such aggression led to the adoption and implementation of NSC 68, which until then had been rejected.

So long as in 1949 the Cold War seemed to thaw, Truman offered the Fair Deal, which focused on domestic spending rather than defense spending. Thus, he proposed for defense only $14.3 billion for fiscal year 1950 and $13.5 billion for 1951.[283] Even after reading NSC 68 in April 1950, Truman was still committed to lowering the defense budget. The outbreak of the Korean War changed all of that, "providing the shock necessary to shift the budgetary arguments of NSC-68 from the realm of theory to that of practical necessity."[284]

NSC 68's advocates did not have to work as hard as anticipated to win support for it thanks to the unexpected help from the Soviet Union in the form of Stalin's approval of the North Korean invasion. Truman had not formally endorsed NSC 68 at the time the war erupted in Korea, and Congress was reluctant to fund it. The invasion caused both things to happen.[285]

The administration adopted NSC 68 in September 1950, only after the North Korean invasion, which also made possible congressional funding of it.[286] NSC 68 was implemented in the following months and years—this would have been much less likely in the absence of the events of June 1950. As Gaddis argues, the Korean War signals the start of global containment.[287]

The Korean War seemed to validate several of NSC 68's key conclusions: all interests had become equally vital; any shift in the balance of power could undermine the entire international structure; the attack on South Korea made this country vital, even if it was peripheral before, in order to maintain US credibility; the Soviet Union might resort to war by proxy, even in the face of US superiority (this assumption was shared by Kennan); US capabilities at the time of the North Korean invasion were insufficient—nuclear weapons did not deter lower-level aggression, conventional means necessary to cover all contingencies were absent, and there was questioning in Europe of US credibility, as capabilities were much less available there than near Korea. [288]

US strategy in Korea was consistent with NSC 68, but there were contradictions in NSC 68. There was tension between escalation avoidance (limited war) and credibility/resolve: Crossing the thirty-eighth parallel would be seen as an escalation; while not crossing it as a lack of resolve. Still, the Truman administration's action on Korea was according to NSC 68: both resist proxy aggression and avoid escalation.

Some of the effects of the Korean War included increased willingness to spend money on defense;[289] accelerated changes in US tactics;[290] and the increasing threat also prevented neoisolationism.[291] The invasion of South Korea intensified fear in Europe of Soviet invasion of Western Europe, thus leading to a demand for US ground deployment there.[292] While Truman initially rejected NSC 68 recommendation of preponderance, "as it became increasingly clear that the Soviet Union was not a status-quo power, but a global competitor, it was difficult for Truman to sustain his restrained approach."[293]

The rise of a perceived high-level threat was influenced by the combined effect of the Eastern Bloc's preceding moves (the Prague Coup, the Berlin Blockade, the communist takeover of China), but the key driver was the invasion of South Korea. Snyder correctly concludes that the Korean War was crucial in "help[ing] to solidify the 'Cold War consensus' behind a globalist strategy of containment."[294] "Nothing did more to intensify the confrontation, however, than Stalin's ill-judged Korean war."[295]

FALSIFICATION OF ALTERNATIVE EXPLANATIONS: NONSYSTEMIC LEVELS OF ANALYSIS[296]

This section will show the limitations to explanations based on the individual and domestic/ideological levels of analysis—due to the discrepancy between the expectations deduced from their logic and the selected grand strategy—though it will also indicate some of the shortcomings to a pure systemic/polarity account.

Individual/worldview   According to this level of analysis, we should expect:

(1) Decisive effects of Truman's personality and worldview on policy outcomes;
(2) Continuity in policy of the same president even facing important events and changes in the external world that disconfirm US policies.

It is noteworthy that the changes in strategy under Truman contrasted with Truman's initial preferences and thus show the limitations to the individual level: Truman continued the grand strategy of FDR until the material/

external environment refuted it.[297] This refers to the crises in Iran, Turkey and Greece, Eastern Europe, Berlin, and the Czech Coup (see above on the transition from defensive liberalism to defensive realism). Then the administration made another change following Korea (the transition from defensive realism to offensive realism discussed above).

Alternative ideational/individual-level explanations would expect the following documents or statements to exercise major influence:

- Kennan's Long Telegram of February 1946[298]
- Churchill's "Iron Curtain" speech
- NSC 68

The background to the great influence of the Long Telegram, for example, was that it provided an answer to "a question flummoxing Washington: why was the US unable to find a policy toward the Soviet Union that worked?"[299] A few competing theories explaining Soviet unilateralism emerged:

1. The linkage between the nature of the domestic regime and foreign policy: a common US belief—and of Truman (like Wilson and FDR)—that totalitarian regimes are aggressive in foreign policy.[300]
2. Ideological—communism: most Americans were concerned about Soviet communism and the vanguard of world revolution that could explain the post-WWII aggression.[301]
3. Soviet insecurity, which can be overcome by Western reassurance.

By providing a coherent and informed answer to this question, one may argue that it was the idea presented in the Long Telegram,[302] which brought about the change in US grand strategy. Kennan argued in this document that reassurance by the US will not affect the Soviet Union because autocracy and ideology lead to the treatment of the world as hostile. In Kennan's view, Soviet hostility was not a function of US policy but of Russian history and psychology reinforced by communism and the Stalinist police state. Irrespective of US behavior, the Soviet Union would try to undermine the US.[303] The telegram reinforced the growing tendency in the US to see Soviet behavior with suspicion—thus no practical difference between defensive and offensive motives.[304]

Yet, the influence of such ideational elements was limited. The Truman administration changed its policies not because of them but because changing circumstances had a compelling effect.[305] The key to the change in grand strategy is empirical: it became increasingly clear that Soviet unilateral behavior was not responsive to Western gestures of restraint and goodwill during and immediately after the war.[306]

At any rate, the Long Telegram in no sense specifically put an end to the floundering in US foreign policy.[307] Regarding NSC 68, it was not endorsed by Truman until the Korean War, as discussed above.[308]

Domestic explanations   In accordance with the logic of this level of analysis, we should see important influence of the US public with its ideational leanings in favor of the liberal approaches (either defensive liberalism or offensive liberalism) and against realist approaches.[309] On the defensive liberal side, the public was in favor of demobilization in the aftermath of WWII.[310] The public also saw the Soviets (and Stalin) positively, and there were great hopes attached to the UN. On the offensive liberal side, on the other hand, there was sympathy among parts of the public for the liberation of Eastern Europe. At any rate, the domestic level was not supportive of offensive realist approaches. Domestic politics was not conducive for major commitments overseas; Congress was hostile toward foreign aid. Indeed, until Korea, Congress was unwilling to fund NSC 68.[311] Overall, key officials in the Truman administration worried that the US might not fit the role of global leadership with intensive international responsibilities.[312]

The grand strategies during the peak of the Cold War were, however, not liberal but realist — initially defensive and later offensive. The selection of defensive realism and later offensive realism also went against ideological preferences such as the opposition to balance of power/realism by FDR and others. Global engagement (alliances, forward deployment), which took place especially after Korea, was implemented despite the opposition to entangling alliances, while rollback was not endorsed despite the support for and appeal of liberation ideas.

While we highlight systemic factors, changes within the same structure cannot be explained by bipolarity as such. One has to identify variations within the systems level that can account for the changing grand strategy. This is what we have tried to do here by integrating the effects of the balance of capabilities with the effects of the balance of threat.

THE ROLE OF DOMESTIC AND IDEOLOGICAL FACTORS: INTERVENING VARIABLES

While the systemic factors played a key role, domestic politics and ideational factors as intervening variables magnified the threat and the domestic willingness to sacrifice and to invest to reach superiority.[313] Truman acted in the international arena as he did because he feared Stalin would exploit conditions to aggrandize Soviet power, not because he felt a groundswell of public opinion demanding new foreign policy initiatives. Still, the public perceived an ideological threat: Stalin's regime was ruthless and was imposing "godless" communist regimes on Eastern European countries from where many Americans came.[314] Partly in response, the administration also posed the threat in ideological terms to secure congressional support, thus generating an unintended ideological crusade.[315] The key domestic/ideological factor as an intervening variable was anticommunism. It generated domestic constraints on negotiations with the Soviets,[316] although this opposition also had an offensive realism aspect by pointing out that such negotiations might challenge the credibility of the US commitment to contain Soviet aggression.

Decision makers' perceptions, notably Truman's Cold War belief system, including the domino theory (the belief in bandwagoning with the strongest power) aggravated the Cold War.[317] In this context it was also aggravated due to the ideological/liberal opposition to a spheres-of-influence agreement with the Soviet Union.[318] US aversion to a spheres-of-influence agreement in Europe was also due to the fear of a resurgent isolationism in the US in case of such an arrangement.[319] In contrast to Dueck's claim, this opposition to division to spheres was, however, more a matter of anticommunism than liberalism. This was the context for the antidemocratic behavior of the US in Iran and elsewhere against seemingly radical regimes (suspected of becoming potential Soviet allies). This conduct shows first of all the strength of the American anti-Soviet competitive drive but also of anticommunism rather than of a commitment to liberalism.[320]

Another manifestation of the influence of domestic politics was the use of emotional symbols. Because of domestic politics, Truman had to justify his request for aid to Turkey and Greece in terms of "freedom" against "totalitarianism" rather than in terms of the balance of power for public consumption.[321] Domestic politics influenced Truman's presentation of the containment policy, but was not sufficient to cause the US to enter a Cold War against the Soviet Union. Thus, domestic politics didn't cause the shift to Cold War policies as the democratic coalition (labor, liberals, intellectuals, internationalists) preferred continuous US-Soviet cooperation.[322]

Conclusion

The years 1945–50 turned out to be the nurturing and formative years of the Cold War. They began with the United States and the Soviet Union as allies in defeating the Axis powers in World War II. But quickly the alliance turned south and broke, thus leaving the two superpowers in a rivalry that polarized the international system and lasted until the late 1980s. Unlike several explanations for the formation and evolution of the US grand strategy in those years, this chapter shows that developments in the international system compelled the Truman administration to review its approach toward the Soviet Union despite its initial hope to reach a global modus vivendi with the Soviets. Soviet actions—mostly in Eastern Europe and in the Middle East—shook the US view of Moscow's intentions on top of its considerable military capabilities, especially the numerous armored divisions in the heart of Europe. In other words, the US saw both major power-projection capabilities and a greater threat, while the US itself was demobilizing and cutting its defense budget. The sense of emergency grew with the rapid decline in British power, which culminated in passing the Greek problem to the US in 1946. Thus, the US shifted from its initial postwar cooperative strategy to a defensive realist one, focusing essentially on diplomatic and economic balancing of the Soviet Union. But this did not seem to stop the Soviets. In early 1950, NSC 68 reviewed the strategy and suggested a much stronger response to Soviet behavior. The buildup of American forces, that is, reversing the course of the years prior to the report, was the major recommendation, which had remarkable economic consequences. But Truman did not adopt the report until shortly after the Korean War broke out in late June 1950, demonstrating—in Truman's and America's eyes—the Soviet revisionist drive to change the status quo and enlarge the territory under their control. This was proof that Paul Nitze was correct in his reading of the international situation, which led to the adoption of his NSC 68 report and to a complete reversal of the administration strategy. This change was almost imminent. It was not in the cards when Truman became president in April 1945, when he in fact tried to follow in Roosevelt's footsteps in reaching a major deal with the Soviet Union over running the postwar world. Truman held to his new post-Korean invasion offensive realist strategy for his final eighteen months in office, and his successors—Dwight Eisenhower and then John Kennedy— maintained it until the Cuban missile crisis compelled Kennedy to reconsider his understanding of the rivalry with the Soviets, Soviet intentions, the nature of the threat, and his own strategy. This shift is the subject of the next chapter.

4

From Preponderance to Détente after the Cuban Missile Crisis

The division in realism between its offensive and defensive variants has been useful in the last two decades of research in accounting for states' international behavior as either conforming to the defensive or offensive variants. But the literature discussed the key question much less: under what conditions might a state change its grand strategy from one variant to the other, particularly to the more cooperative variant—defensive realism? This is an important question for current US relations with Iran and potentially with China or Russia. This chapter identifies some of the key conditions for such a change, focusing mainly on the changing nature of the threat from intended revisionism to inadvertent escalation.

Such scenarios of inadvertent escalation are not new or unfamiliar to scholars and policy makers.[1] The major case of potentially inadvertent escalation, which could have led to a nuclear war, took place during the Cuban missile crisis.[2] This chapter argues that the acute danger of inadvertent escalation, miscalculation, and loss of control demonstrated during the crisis—as well as its peaceful resolution—caused a major change in US grand strategy toward the Soviet Union. A key argument is that a major change in grand strategy is likely to take place if the state leadership understands that the key danger is not the malign and premeditated intention of the other side to attack their country, but rather an inadvertent escalation during a crisis. In such a case, the grand strategy is likely to move away from ideas of preponderance and preventive war (which are associated with offensive realism) to defensive realist ideas of cooperation in reducing the dangers of miscalculated escalation and loss of control by establishing an effective mutual deterrence and a stable regime of arms control.

In accordance with the book's model, the chapter also asks the following questions related to changes in grand strategy: Under what conditions would grand strategy most likely change? Are these conditions related to the relative dominance of different ideas, or are they more related to material factors? And are these conditions derived from the external environment, or are they based on domestic politics and the leaders' worldviews?

These questions are raised with regard to the changes in US grand strategy following the Cuban missile crisis. Why was this crisis such a turning point in the evolution of US grand strategy? Why, following what appeared as Soviet deception and reckless behavior in deploying the missiles to Cuba, did the US endorse a relatively more moderate strategy rather than a more hawkish policy?

In this chapter we analyze the emergence of the US-Soviet détente, which prevailed in the years of 1962–79. Based on the book's theory, we explain the change in US grand strategy in this period, in relation to the peak of the Cold War era, by arguing that while there is an ideational competition over which idea will inform the grand strategy, the material international system brokers between the competing ideas and selects which one will be translated into the national security policy. We identify the four major ideas that competed for dominance in the American foreign policy establishment and then we explain—using the international system—how grand strategy was formed following the Cuban missile crisis and how this new grand strategy of détente with the Soviets continued through four consecutive administrations only to break down toward the end of a fifth administration, a total of seventeen years.

Prior to the détente era, the Cold War was at its peak, as both superpowers raced for hegemony, and for victory. The American grand strategy since the outbreak of the Korean War in 1950 focused on the pursuit of preponderance, an offensive realist idea. Twelve years later, the US did not seem to have achieved that goal, but as a result of the Cuban missile crisis, it sensed that the Soviets had become more cooperative.

The key explanation for which idea is translated into the dominant grand strategy is derived from the international environment following twelve years of attempted preponderance. Détente emerged because the international environment following the missile crisis favored the ideas of defensive realism, namely, arms control and MAD and some degree of cooperation to prevent an inadvertent escalation.

The Cuban missile crisis changed President John Kennedy's initial grand strategy that included flexible response and resolve (both were intended to enhance preponderance by correcting the flaws that Kennedy saw in President Dwight Eisenhower's policy; Kennedy wanted preponderance as much as Eisenhower) into a new grand strategy that included MAD and negotiations with the Soviets for the sake of mutual understanding and compromise to enhance international stability. After Kennedy's assassination, Lyndon Johnson followed suit and reinforced the cooperation with the Soviets. His successor, Richard Nixon—with his assistant on national security, Henry Kissinger—made this into an official policy of détente.[3] It was pursued for nearly seventeen years, although its final years (under Presidents Ford and Carter) were marked by major decline in support for détente, due to the reemerging Soviet challenge to the US, which peaked with the Soviet invasion of Afghanistan.

The change in grand strategy is best explained by changes in the balance of threat and in the balance of capabilities. Changes in the balance of threat resulted from the Soviet behavior in managing the Cuban missile crisis, which indicated a decline in the Soviet threat to the US and a change in the nature of the threat from naked aggression to a fear of unintended and uncontrollable escalation. The placement of the missiles in Cuba signaled a greater peril to the US, but the resolution of the crisis (the retreat of all missiles in mutual understandings between Kennedy and Khrushchev) signaled a reduction in the level of threat and that was what counted. The successful resolution allowed Kennedy to reach an arms control deal with the Soviets, whose material capabilities meanwhile grew. The superpowers agreed on reconnaissance flights and satellite observation and inspection for verification of the agreement. In other words, material developments in these areas made possible arms control agreements. We examine the following three propositions:

1. As the Soviet threat decreased following the peaceful end of the Cuban missile crisis, the US strategy became more cooperative.
2. As the perceived threat changed from naked aggression to a fear of an inadvertent escalation, the prospects for a defensive strategy increased.
3. As the parity in nuclear weapons increased, the focus of US strategy turned to the nuclear balance of capabilities, leading—under the conditions of the threat transformation—to arms control agreements and the dominance of the idea of MAD.

The combined effect of the greater parity in nuclear weapons and the lower threat posed by the Soviets and its changing character resulted in the dominance of defensive realism manifested by arms control and mutual deterrence.

Two Ideal Types of Major Wars

It is useful to distinguish between two ideal types of major wars: premeditated and inadvertent.[4] Some scholars are skeptical of the idea of unintended war;[5] whereas others tend to overlook the distinction between intended and unintended wars as a springboard for the construction of a theoretical model of outbreak of wars.[6] Nevertheless, this distinction is critical for considering the effects of anarchy and the security dilemma on international conflict. The difference between the two types of war is in their respective dynamics of decision making.

Premeditated wars break out as a result of a calculated decision by at least one party to resort to a massive use of force in the pursuit of its objectives, which could be outright aggression (self-aggrandizement at the expense of other states) or prevention (blocking or retarding the further rise of an adversary in order to avoid the worsening of the status quo and the risk of war under less favorable conditions).[7] Yet whatever the objectives may be, the war is intended if a state deliberately decides to initiate it when it could choose not to.

In contrast, *inadvertent* wars are usually preceded by a crisis.[8] They occur because of nonvolitional factors, that is, a given international crisis escalates because of a failure or breakdown of crisis management. The crisis might either be a direct great-power crisis from its outset or a third-party crisis or a local war that entraps the great powers at a later stage. At the outset of such a crisis, all sides have limited objectives, and neither side wants or expects a war,[9] or at least not a *major* war (involving most or all the great powers of the day).[10] Yet, at some point during the course of the crisis, one side might conclude that initiating a war has become inevitable in order to secure its objectives or avoid an unacceptable outcome.

Typically, the sides in a crisis are not faced with a single decision whether or not to go to war. Rather, they face a series of decisions at a succession of critical points as the crisis unfolds, each decision progressively narrowing their freedom of maneuver.[11] Thus, they are drawn into war due to an action-reaction process and a series of incremental decisions. It is difficult to pinpoint the crucial decision that inexorably led to war. Even if one can identify such a decision, it will likely be either based on miscalculation or misunderstanding of the consequences of one's actions, or it might be the result of a loss of control over allies or domestic pressures. In either case, it is likely to be the culmination of a process whereby the parties have maneuvered themselves into a situation where war was the only acceptable outcome.

Inadvertent wars are one of the major adverse effects of the security dilemma in the anarchic international system. This dilemma makes it hard for actors to distinguish between "defensive" and "aggressive" intentions. The security dilemma leads to the "spiral model,"[12] an action-reaction process in which each state views its own behavior as defensive, but its antagonists perceive it as aggressive. Accordingly, in an inadvertent war, it might be difficult to identify the "guilty" or "aggressive" party. Rather, these wars may erupt even between status quo powers, despite their reluctance at the outset of the crisis to go to war—or, at least, to a major war.

Scholars have identified major sequences or paths to failure in crisis management and to inadvertent war.[13] For the purposes of this study, two major sequences to inadvertent war will be distinguished: miscalculation and loss of control. *Miscalculation* might escalate into war—perhaps even major war— due to misperception of the balance of interests, a mistaken estimation of the rival's resolve and commitments or of the relative capabilities. One party in the crisis might cross the other's threshold to war because of an erroneous belief that the other will not respond violently.[14]

Loss of control during crisis as a cause of inadvertent wars can derive from three main sources: domestic pressures, loss of control by a great power over its allies, and loss of control by the political leadership over the military. In this sequence, the top decision makers are driven to an inadvertent war as a result of allied, military, or public pressures that they are powerless to resist, even though they may perceive the external situation correctly.

PREEMPTIVE VERSUS PREVENTIVE WARS

The concepts of preemption and prevention were discussed thoroughly during the Bush administration following the 9/11 attacks on the US and the consequential 2002 National Security Strategy that included the idea of preemption, which many scholars argue was actually prevention.[15] The Cuban missile crisis was the main historical event that the Bush administration referred to in justifying its new policy, which resumed the historical debate over the Kennedy administration's actions in October 1962, but also brought into debate previous events where the US considered preventive military actions.[16]

The differentiation between preventive and preemptive wars is related to the distinction between intended and inadvertent wars, in that preventive wars are one type of intended wars, while preemption based on an erroneous strategic estimate constitutes one of the paths to inadvertent war.[17] These types of war are often confused because both are based on a logic of "better now than later." Yet, in a preventive war, the initiator perceives a long-term threat based on differential rates of great-power growth and the changing balance of power in the opponent's favor, which makes a showdown more desirable at the time, before the opponent gets any stronger.[18] In contrast, the preemptor faces (or mistakenly believes that it faces) an imminent attack by the opponent. Therefore, the threat it perceives is "instant, overwhelming, leaving no choice of means and no moment for deliberation."[19]

Indeed, in this context Levy notes that preventive wars are "wanted wars" in the sense that there is no compelling reason to act militarily now, but this is the choice of the preventer who does not face an immediate military threat. It can attempt other methods to redress the situation such as new alliances, negotiated settlements, and so on, and, in the worst case, fighting a preventive war later if conditions warrant it. By contrast, a preemptor feels, even if mistakenly, highly constrained by the circumstances to resort to force *immediately*, otherwise the opponent will attack first.[20] Thus the preemptor has far less of a choice and may prefer to avoid war, whereas "the preventer basically 'wants war,' in the sense that it would demand enormous concessions by the adversary and make few (if any) of its own in order to avoid war."[21]

Premeditated and inadvertent wars are ideal types. In specific complex cases of major war, there may be controversies among historians, some of whom may regard the war as largely inadvertent and absolve all parties from responsibility, while others attribute it to the deliberate will of one side. Indeed, such controversies took place with regard to both World War I and World War II.[22] Yet, these difficulties in specific cases do not blur the general analytical distinction, which parallels, to some extent, the distinction between a premeditated murder and manslaughter in criminal law.

The Grand Strategy of Preponderance: From Eisenhower to Kennedy

The previous chapter showed how, following the North Korean invasion of the South in June 1950, NSC 68 informed American grand strategy until the Cuban missile crisis. NSC 68 viewed Soviet international behavior as aggressive and dangerous to American vital interests—and accordingly offered responding with massive rearmament and rebuilding of American military forces, alongside standing firm behind any anti-Soviet regime or movement in order to prevent the USSR from spreading its communist ideology across the globe. The view of the Soviet Union as an aggressive, revisionist power, bent on world domination, has also led to some thoughts of preventive war starting in the late 1940s and becoming more serious in the 1950s. In a note to Secretary Dulles, President Eisenhower asked whether "our duty to future generations did not require us to initiate war at the most propitious moment" and raised the issue several times at NSC meetings during 1952–54.[23]

While the Eisenhower administration avoided resorting to a preventive war, it was much keener on endorsing the philosophy of superiority that was behind NSC 68 than was the Truman administration, although Truman adjusted his policy toward the logic of NSC 68 following the compelling events of the Korean War. Eisenhower went a further step and threatened the Soviets with massive nuclear retaliation for any challenge they might pose to the US, especially if it was in the American sphere of dominance.

However, the massive retaliation doctrine was not working and lost credibility over time. Communist and allegedly communist movements, such as the Vietnamese, challenged the US constantly, and the US did not use nuclear weapons against any of them. The competition for world dominance between the two superpowers continued and intensified at times, such as when it went into space, but the grand strategy remained the same. In 1960, Senator John F. Kennedy offered a different style than that of outgoing President Eisenhower and the Republican candidate for the presidency, Vice President Richard Nixon, but Kennedy did not undermine the foundations of the grand strategy of preponderance.

One of Kennedy's most effective critiques of the Eisenhower administration in public opinion was that even with a massive investment in rearming, the US was still inferior to the USSR in intercontinental ballistic missiles ("the missile gap").[24] Only after the transition did Kennedy learn that he was actually wrong and that the US was ahead of the Soviets, but this did not prevent him from ordering a "massive buildup of nuclear weapons, missile-firing submarines, and long-range missiles to establish clear superiority over the USSR."[25] Kennedy's critique and his order for buildup show that he was thinking within the lines of the grand strategy of preponderance.

After taking office, Kennedy began revising Eisenhower's doctrines, but not the grand strategy itself. Following Secretary of Defense Robert McNamara's advice, Kennedy replaced the failing doctrine of massive retaliation with flexible response, which meant that the president no longer committed himself to a total nuclear war in response to a Soviet challenge.[26] But he also did not moderate the deterrent the US posed. Instead, he gave himself enough space to maneuver and decide what level of response would better suit the threat in a given situation. Again, this was still in line with the grand strategy of preponderance.[27]

This should be sufficient in refuting a major alternative explanation for the change in American grand strategy toward the Soviet Union, namely, that Kennedy took office with détente in mind. However, the evidence is inconclusive. There are arguments that Kennedy wanted an agreement with the Soviets from day one.[28] But it seems more appropriate to view JFK's strategy—at least until the missile crisis—as a continuation of the earlier administrations' focus on superiority. Stephen Rabe comments:

In the context of the Soviet-American confrontation, or the Cold War (1945–1989), Kennedy cannot be considered a historically significant figure. Presidents Harry S. Truman, Dwight D. Eisenhower, Nixon, and perhaps Reagan developed policies and made decisions that shaped the course, conduct, and eventual end of the Cold War. Kennedy did not conduct a fundamental reassessment of the U.S. foreign policy and remained attached to the core of Cold War thinking. . . . Like Secretaries of State [Acheson and Dulles], Kennedy believed that only a tough, determined response grounded in military superiority, could ensure the nation's survival.[29]

The Soviet capabilities improved parallel to the American ones; therefore, no victory in the Cold War was in sight. The Soviets posed a dangerous threat with the deployment of their missiles in Cuba in October 1962, but their moderate behavior and willingness to concede in order to prevent a nuclear war that was sure to destroy the world (according to the MAD logic) caused a major change in the superpower relations.

Competing Ideas under Kennedy until the Cuban Missile Crisis: Superiority versus Disarmament versus Arms Control

The key ideational competition in the early 1960s was between the ideas of offensive realism and defensive realism, namely, superiority and a focus on developing first-strike/war-fighting weapons versus arms control and MAD. There were also some defensive liberal ideas, however significantly less prominent. While the idea of superiority provides an offensive realist response to the aggressive, revisionist, or greedy state, MAD and arms control suggest a defensive realist response to the fear of inadvertent escalation.

Offensive liberalism is associated with the neoconservative ideas that dominated US grand strategy during George W. Bush's presidency. However, they are by no means a new philosophy, although in the 1960s and later they were not prominent. It was one of the competing ideas during the early stages of the Cold War—promoted mostly by John Foster Dulles under the grand strategy of rollback—but then it was defeated by the strategy of preponderance. By the time Kennedy became president, ideas such as rollback were rarely heard, therefore it can be considered absent from the contest for dominance (though, again, it did not disappear).

Ideas associated with defensive liberalism, mostly multilateralism, joint management of the international system and economic interdependence, were also rarely heard, although some of them did have advocates such as Adlai Stevenson who expressed such ideas already in the 1950s, in his presidential races,[30] and even during the Cuban missile crisis while serving as US ambassador to the UN.

Stevenson suggested appealing to the UN or the Organization of American States (OAS) for inspection of Cuba and for negotiations on removal of the missiles from both sides (i.e., from Cuba and Turkey).[31] This idea was promptly rejected (although it was eventually the basis of the crisis resolution), and no similar position seemed competitive compared to the realist options.

According to McGeorge Bundy, Eisenhower and Kennedy supported the logic of offensive realism, while Vice President Lyndon B. Johnson was somewhat less supportive.[32] However, Eisenhower and Kennedy differed in their strategies, and Kennedy's initial grand strategy, flexible response, gave him a symmetrical capacity to act in all levels of violence, an ability to respond without either escalation or humiliation.[33] This new logic increased the number of escalatory steps that could be taken prior to resorting to nuclear weapons. This brought about conventional buildup, but also nuclear buildup (even after the "missile gap" myth was exposed), because these weapons "complement each other," as McNamara insisted in 1962.[34]

The idea of arms control appeared in the late 1950s. It was defined as "the substance and process of all international negotiations concerned with regulating armaments."[35] Arms control deals with managing rather than eliminating the arms race. It signaled a shift from abolishing nuclear weapons to making their presence more tolerable. Arms control was designed to complement and strengthen deterrence by confining nuclear weapons to this role. A related objective was to guard against a surprise attack, and "to reduce all temptations to pre-empt" and to create "stable mutual deterrence" and reassurance.[36]

Defensive realists, relying on the logic of MAD, see missile defense in the nuclear age as both futile and dangerous. It is futile because technically it would not work as the scientists Jerome B. Wiesner and Herbert F. York concluded that there was no technical solution to the problems of American (or Soviet) vulnerability to a nuclear attack.[37] It is also dangerous because defensive buildup, which makes the state less vulnerable to attacks and therefore more capable of preemption, increases the opponents' security dilemma, thus leading to an arms race and greater mutual insecurity. It deprives the other side of the confidence that it has its deterrence-retaliatory ("second strike") capability secure in place and thus might give an incentive to strike first in a crisis.

Defensive liberalism vis-à-vis the Soviet Union has two dimensions: external and internal. The external dimension is divided in two:

A. Multilateralism was détente in the form of joint management of regional conflicts. This was the Soviet preference in the 1973 Arab-Israeli War and in the détente with Kissinger.[38]

B. Nuclear disarmament was an extremely external variant of multilateralism. The idea was to abolish nuclear weapons, as they were seen by the "nuclear pacifists" as the source of the problem, which might lead to a disastrous war. Holding these weapons, they argued, implied using them.[39] They claimed that the causal mechanism was like with World War I: the arms race led to political hostility and rivalry that ended in war. They said that there was no real need to fear one another since there was no underlying hostility. It was the armament that led to fear. Any plan to use nuclear weapons and the arms race itself can lead to an awful nuclear war—either by deliberate or accidental use—with catastrophic consequences for humankind. Defensive liberals do not believe in the stability of deterrence/MAD.

The domestic dimension of defensive liberalism is "nation building": "a determination to alter the internal structures of foreign societies to enable them to withstand unavoidable pressures for revolutionary change without resorting to communist solutions."[40] This could be accomplished by sociopolitical reforms and economic development. The US should provide financial and technological aid and the power of example. This view reflects an aspiration for a diverse world of independent states, that is, not dominated by the communists.

There were virtually no voices expressing the offensive liberal idea of democracy promotion in the Soviet Union or in its bloc. There were few who expressed defensive liberal or defensive realist ideas. Let's now specify the views of some of the key figures in the US government in the early years of the Kennedy administration.

President Kennedy   There was no change in the primary strategic thinking in the transition from Eisenhower to Kennedy. Kennedy's offensive realist thinking regarding national security and foreign policy toward the Soviet Union is reflected in his defense budget that increased by 10 percent in three years, from $49.6 billion in fiscal year 1961 to $54.8 billion in 1964.[41] In a special message to Congress on the defense budget on March 28, 1961, Kennedy stated that his goal was "to deter all wars, general or limited, nuclear or conventional, large or small—to convince all potential aggressors that any attack would be futile—to provide backing for the diplomatic settlement of disputes—to insure the adequacy of our bargaining power for an end to the arms race," and also that American "arms will never be used to strike the first blow in any attack." He promised never to threaten, provoke, or initiate aggression.[42]

Kennedy decided to manage foreign policy by himself. Thus, his nominees to foreign policy positions were not supposed to challenge his views or educate him in the field, but to advise him within his framework. Kennedy was not looking for diversity in ideas, but for people he could work with and control.[43] For instance, Secretary of State Dean Rusk was appointed to be "a soldier, not a general."[44] Nevertheless, due to his narrow election victory, Kennedy kept several of Eisenhower's officials (most notably, Douglas Dillon and Allen Dulles) in his administration, and added Robert McNamara. The fact that these Republicans did not offer dissident voices implies that there was a wide agreement on foreign policy, although not a consensus.

Robert McNamara   The secretary of defense worked with Kennedy to abort the massive retaliation doctrine in favor of the alternative flexible response, which went along with the formation of limited war-fighting capabilities. McNamara also enlarged the armed forces from a bit less than 2.5 million troops to a peak of 2.8 million within his first year in office.

Walt Whitman Rostow   A key figure in Kennedy's administration on foreign affairs, he "exhorted nations in the 'childhood' of modernization to learn from mature societies like the United States,"[45] which sounds like defensive liberalism. However, Rostow was also zealous for military intervention in Third World countries where communists threatened existing governments; thus Rostow was an offensive realist (not a liberal, since his zeal for intervention was to defend noncommunist governments, not necessarily democracies).[46] Nevertheless, in the draft of Basic National Security Policy of March 26, 1962, he wrote that "we should try to work over the longer run toward tacit understandings with the U.S.S.R. as to the ground rules covering our competitions"; and "if they are convinced of our capacity and will to deal with their efforts to extend power into the free community, it may become increasingly possible to make them feel that we share a common interest in the exercise of restraint,"[47] which is a defensive realist approach to the key component of the grand strategy—the relations with the key adversary in bipolarity.

Adlai Stevenson   Twice the Democrats' presidential candidate against Eisenhower, who was considered his party's prominent foreign policy figure, he was not offered a cabinet position (such as the secretary of state) and eventually accepted the UN ambassadorship. He called for a nuclear test ban already in the mid-1950s and was not very popular in the Kennedy entourage. He did not have influence on Kennedy's foreign policy, who "thought Stevenson was 'a weeper'—that is too idealistic,"[48] or a defensive liberal in the terms used here.

Paul Nitze   Assistant secretary of defense in Kennedy's administration and the leading author of NSC 68 in 1950, he advocated in December 1961 that the US should pursue a strategy of superiority because it was essential for deterrence.[49] One of Nitze's worst fears was that the Soviet Union could eventually use its intercontinental weapons to keep the US arsenal at bay while the Soviet Union made full use of advantages in geography and the regional balance of conventional forces to prevail in a political showdown.[50] During the Cuban missile crisis, Nitze favored an immediate air strike and opposed the blockade. He feared that any delay would turn a later removal of the missiles into a nuclear war. He later admitted his mistake.[51]

There were also defensive realist thoughts within Kennedy's administration: officials such as Maxwell Taylor, David Bell (budget director), and Carl Kaysen of the NSC thought that the drive for strategic superiority was dangerous and expensive and would lead to an arms race without adding to security in a world of nuclear weapons.[52]

The military   Military leaders favored pursuing overwhelming superiority, and in fact kept this opinion into the 1970s.[53] The Joint Chiefs of Staff had in mind a full-scale antiballistic missile (ABM) system, and they had a major dispute with McNamara who objected to ABM systems and preferred the logic of MAD.[54] The Joint Chiefs did not trust the Soviets and disapproved of Kennedy's deal with Khrushchev that settled the Cuban missile crisis. They warned him that the Soviets "were preparing the ground for diplomatic blackmail." Kennedy, who felt betrayed by the Soviet deployment of the missiles in Cuba after assuring him that they wouldn't deploy, confided to McNamara that he agreed with the Joint Chiefs that it might happen again.[55]

Curtis LeMay   Chief of staff of the air force (1961–65), he continued to believe that the US would be able to fight and win a strategic nuclear war as long as the government provided the required weapons. The type of weapons necessary for assured destruction by a second strike was quite insufficient for LeMay's strategy.[56] He had been the conceptual rival on strategic matters of the advocates of MAD in the administration. Unlike McNamara, who, following the Cuban missile crisis (though not before the crisis), pushed for an assured second-strike retaliation capability to stabilize the international system (the defensive realist concept of MAD), LeMay preferred denying such capabilities from the Soviets, thus reaching superiority over them.[57]

Several senators are also worth mentioning, as they participated in the ideational debate, however with little effect. Among the offensive realists, Republican Senator Barry Goldwater demanded that Kennedy "do anything . . . to get rid of that cancer. If it means war, let it mean war";[58] and Democrat Henry Jackson, a "Cold War Liberal," advocated "large defense expenditures in order to counter growing Soviet power."[59] Among the defensive realists, Senator Hubert Humphrey, Kennedy's major opponent in the 1960 Democratic primaries, continuously called for arms control and a nuclear test ban.[60] Democrat Senator J. William Fulbright, chairman of the Senate Foreign Relations Committee (1959–74), urged the US to abandon the concept of ideological war with the Soviets and opposed offensive liberal thoughts of changing the Soviet system. During the Cuban missile crisis, he objected to the blockade fearing direct confrontation between Soviet and American soldiers, and preferred invading Cuba.[61] A defensive liberal, Senator George McGovern—a leading critic of American foreign policy since his election in 1962—voted regularly to reduce defense appropriations and expenditures on new weapons systems.[62]

In sum, the Kennedy administration—and Congress—believed it was necessary to gain the upper hand in the Cold War (already indicated in Kennedy's harsh but erroneous criticism of Eisenhower during the campaign for presumably allowing the Soviets to possess more intercontinental ballistic missiles [ICBMs] than the US). All this changed with the Cuban missile crisis.

From Preponderance to Détente: The Aftermath of the Cuban Missile Crisis

When the US found out about the missiles in Cuba, Kennedy asked, "If it doesn't increase very much their strategic strength, why is it—can any Russian expert tell us—why they . . . ? After all Khrushchev demonstrated a sense of caution over Laos, Berlin, he's been cautious."[63] And later he added, "I don't know enough about the Soviet Union, but if anyone can tell me any other time since the Berlin blockade where the Russians have given us so clear a provocation, I don't know when it's been. Because they've been awfully cautious, really."[64] This is a surprising statement by Kennedy because until then the Soviets were considered reckless (to an extent), rather than cautious.

The story of the Cuban missile crisis itself is fairly well known and overwhelmingly documented.[65] During the initial stages of the crisis, Kennedy behaved according to offensive realist logic of maintaining US superiority by trying to deny the Soviet attempt of reaching a greater balance with the US through the placement of the missiles in Cuba.[66] US policy makers seriously considered a preventive air strike against the missile sites.[67] While the administration selected the naval quarantine option, it conveyed (on October 27) a clear threat of an air strike to the Soviets, and Kennedy was probably planning to resort to an air strike by October 30 if the missiles were not removed.[68]

But toward the end of the crisis, Kennedy moved to a more accommodative defensive realist approach, which led to the deal that terminated the crisis. The bargain included a Soviet agreement to remove the missiles in exchange for an American commitment not to invade Cuba and to tacitly assure the Soviets that the Jupiter missiles in Turkey would be removed within several months.[69] The changing balance of threat was crucial for this change in US strategy during the crisis as it was a key for the gradual transformation in the grand strategy following the crisis.

The constant competition among the three ideas for promoting security was taking place also after the crisis was over, but in a different environment. The Cuban missile crisis had profoundly changed the US view of the international environment and especially its perception of the threats it faced.[70] The grand strategy changed from preponderance (offensive realism) to détente and arms control under the logic of MAD (defensive realism). This shift could only have occurred when the US sensed a relatively more benign environment, partly related to the changing character of the threat, but the US also accepted that there was parity in the system. Parity was the result of a successful Soviet effort to possess capabilities that assured mutual destruction, which created a more equal balance between the two superpowers.[71]

The level of threat in the international system declined following the end of the Cuban missile crisis with Khrushchev's public capitulation. Shortly afterward, Khrushchev and Kennedy exchanged letters that indicated mutual determination to reach understandings that would prevent a similar scenario from evolving again.[72] Defeated Khrushchev was more forthcoming and anxious than triumphant Kennedy on this. Nevertheless, both leaders understood the need for assurances, and in November 1962 they exchanged such measures by implementing the understandings regarding the Cuban missile crisis; first by Soviet dismantling of the missiles and removing the light bombers from Cuba, and then by American lifting of the blockade.[73]

Kennedy changed his perception after receiving Khrushchev's messages that proved how shaken the Soviet leader was by the crisis. Khrushchev was eager to reach understandings that would decrease the possibility of another such crisis, which might inadvertently escalate into nuclear exchanges.[74] This signaled the Soviet rationality and willingness to compromise. In essence, as

Blight and Lang put it, the crisis had "transformed [Khrushchev] from a bitter enemy of America into Jack's partner in searching for a way through the
missile crisis and the Cold War."[75]

Following the Cuban missile crisis, McNamara's position changed significantly, from offensive realism to defensive realism, from counterforce—
the "no-cities" doctrine (briefly maintained in 1962) to countervalue/MAD,
namely, that both superpowers should possess assured-destruction capability
of a second strike.[76] He came to believe in the concept of mutual assured
destruction and preferred deploying nuclear missiles over ABM systems.[77]
When Kennedy announced the lift of the quarantine on Cuba on November 20, 1962, he remarked that progress in fulfilling the mutual commitments
of October 27–28 was made and "the completion of the commitment on both
sides and the achievement of a peaceful solution to the Cuban crisis might
well open the door to the solution of other outstanding problems."[78]

Kennedy perceived the Soviet threat after the crisis in very moderate
terms. In a press conference on February 7, 1963, he replied to a question on
Soviet military presence in Cuba that "we ought to keep a sense of proportion about the size of force we are talking about." He estimated that there
were "about 6,000 men. Obviously, those forces cannot be used to invade
another country."[79] To another question concerning Komar boats in Cuba,
Kennedy said,

> If the Soviet Union is prepared to begin a major war, which will result in
> hundreds of millions of casualties by the time it is finished, then we all face a
> situation which is extremely grave. I do not believe that that is what the Soviet
> Union wants, because I think they have other interests. I think they wish to
> seize power, but I don't think they wish to do so by a war. I therefore doubt
> if a Komar torpedo boat is going to attack the United States very soon. It is
> possible—it is possible—everything is possible. After our experience last fall,
> we operate on the assumption while hoping for the best, we expect the worst.[80]

On April 19, 1963, Kennedy told the Annual Convention of American Society
of Newspaper Editors that "in part, as the result of last October's events, there
is today more widespread assurance that both peace and freedom can prevail
in the world."[81]

In his speech at American University on June 10, 1963, Kennedy declared
that he was not seeking Pax Americana,[82] which signaled his relinquishment
of preponderance. He based his call for peace on the assumption that the
Cuban crisis fortified the American strategic position, and pressed for a test
ban treaty, which was criticized by the Republicans as a "grave" mistake.[83]
The speech was drafted secretly by Kennedy and few advisors. The State De-

partment was kept in the dark, and this took place eight months after the Cuban missile crisis. This indicates that it took Kennedy a long time and many efforts to change the strategic concepts of his administration.[84] As William Hyland pointed out, "One should date the advent of 'détente' from the American University speech of President Kennedy in 1963. . . . The basic idea after the Cuban crisis was that there could be gains in stability through the consolidation of overlapping interests, especially in economics and in arms control."[85] The term "détente" was common in 1963, expressing the strategic change in the grand strategy. Yet, for tactical electoral considerations, Kennedy did not want to be associated with it during the 1964 campaign, while Nixon and Goldwater—the leading Republican candidates—were accusing him of being weak.[86]

With the demise of the Cuban affair, Germany once again was considered the greatest problem between the superpowers (as was at the beginning of Kennedy's presidency). Llewellyn Thompson, the State Department's leading Soviet expert, told Kennedy that the prospects of East and West Germany to "liquidate" each other's social system were "sheer fantasy" that could not be done without war. Therefore, he suggested to "record situation as it existed now (in Germany)," and work for peace.[87] Soviet Ambassador to Washington Anatoly Dobrynin told Kennedy that Khrushchev feared an inadvertent escalation of the US-Soviet confrontation due to East German–West German tensions; hence he offered a nonaggression pact that would accept the status quo of divided Germany.[88] Thus, it appears that after the Cuban missile crisis, both superpowers feared an inadvertent war, which led them to think of easing tensions around the world in order to decrease the probability of unintended escalation of local or regional conflicts into superpower confrontation. Gradually, within a decade, the superpowers ratified the status quo of a divided Berlin and Germany.[89]

Still, the aftermath of the Cuban missile crisis signaled a period of relative stability in superpower relations.[90] Kennedy's address at American University indicated a change from his initial focus on thwarting communist advances in the Third World to a focus on achieving peace.[91] Similarly, the focus of the grand strategy shifted from resolve in crises to a quest for negotiations with the Soviet Union to work out the ground rules of the competition.[92]

Kennedy began implementing the grand strategy of détente by establishing the hot line with Moscow (June–July 1963)—a move directly related to the frustration over the cumbersome communication methods used during the crisis.[93] Kennedy also signed the Limited Test Ban Treaty (August 1963),[94] similarly intended to ease tensions and build trust.[95] The treaty banned all but underground nuclear tests,[96] without linkage to Soviet cooperation in Cuba and Laos, in contrast to Rostow's advice.[97] Speaking at the UN on September 20, 1963, Kennedy also suggested exploring space together and "keeping weapons of mass destruction out of outer space."[98]

The Limited Test Ban Treaty was a major arms control advance that pointed the way toward the 1968 Nuclear Non-Proliferation Treaty and also aggravated the Sino-Soviet split as China condemned superpower collusion.[99] According to Gordon Barrass, Kennedy's first major step to ease tensions was when he withdrew the Jupiter missiles from Turkey (and Italy) in March 1963.[100]

The Cuban missile crisis also stabilized the status quo in Europe. Since neither party wanted a similar crisis along the heavily armed Iron Curtain in Europe, within a decade the superpowers ratified the status quo of a divided Berlin and Germany.[101] Kennedy remarked in January 1963, "We now have a hostage in this hemisphere just as the Russians have had one in Berlin for several years."[102] Coleman notes that Kennedy never made this comparison public in order not to inflame tensions.[103] Post–Cuban missile crisis US-Soviet competition became stable, even predictable—what later was called "the long peace." Neither party would ever again initiate direct challenges to the other's sphere of influence.[104]

Explaining the Policy Change toward Détente

The transition from preponderance to détente is explained by the combination of two factors: changes in the balance of threat (the declining perceived threat from the Soviet Union and its changing character—both changes took place since the Cuban missile crisis) and changes in the balance of capabilities (the greater parity with the Soviets). The termination of the Cuban missile crisis proved to the Americans that the Soviets were willing to compromise; therefore, the Soviet threat to the US was declining. However, their material capabilities were growing into parity with the American capabilities; hence, the US concluded that it could not gain preponderance. While the Soviet capabilities were growing, the two superpowers were willing to approve reconnaissance measures and satellite surveillance to verify arms control due to their mutual understanding that otherwise they might face one another again in a nuclear conflict with good chances for inadvertent escalation.[105]

Three propositions are in place here, and their combination forms the explanation to the shift from preponderance to détente:

1. The lower the Soviet threat after the Cuban missile crisis, the more cooperative the US strategy would be.

2. The likelihood of cooperation increases when the nature of the threat changes from an outright aggression by the opponent to an inadvertent escalation. This was another effect of the Cuban missile crisis.

3. As nuclear weapons parity grows, the realist approaches to security prevail. This leads to a greater focus on nuclear balance of capabilities that ends up in an arms race when the level of threat is high but ends up in arms control when the level of threat is low.

The combined effect of greater parity, lower threat, and changing character of the threat increased the tendency toward a defensive realist grand strategy, in this case, arms control and mutual deterrence under the logic of MAD.

DECLINING THREAT

The Cuban missile crisis was the closest event in history to the destruction of the entire world. Both Kennedy and Khrushchev understood how serious it was, and the Soviet leader was much more willing than before the crisis to compromise in order to prevent its repetition. Kennedy understood that compromise demanded changing his grand strategy and gaining some trust where no trust existed (he accused Khrushchev of lying to him by sneaking the missiles into Cuba contrary to his specific promise shortly before the missiles were discovered).[106] In other words, the negotiations after the Cuban missile crisis were more the result of changes in Soviet policies than in American policies.[107] However, Kennedy also made concessions (at the end of the Cuban crisis) to permit progress: the public promise not to invade Cuba and the tacit assurance to remove the Jupiter missiles from Turkey. Many years later it was revealed that Kennedy was even willing to publicly accept a deal that UN Secretary General U Thant would offer to remove missiles from Cuba and Turkey.[108]

Several days after the Cuban missile crisis was over, Carl Kaysen of the NSC sent a memo to McGeorge Bundy stating, "The only way to test the assumption that the events of the last week have created the potential for a major change in U.S.-Soviet relations and consequently in the international political scene is to act on it. We can act in two directions—Berlin and disarmament. There is reason to believe that these are complementary not competing possibilities."[109] Preparing a Berlin summit properly had advantages: "This argument points up in turn another condition of a successful summit, that we view our situation in relation to the Soviets as symmetrical; namely, that recent events have enabled us both to see with greater clarity where our joint interests lie and how it is in our joint interest to limit occasions of conflict and direct confrontation between us and to reduce the potentiality for any remaining occasions to escalate into general war."[110] Khrushchev's letters to Kennedy indicated that the Soviet position concerning the test ban negotiations (that started long before the Cuban missile crisis) was changing.

There were obviously still concerns about the Soviets. Thus, for example, Sherman Kent, chairman of the Board of National Estimates, wrote to CIA Director McCone that "the chances for an early move toward genuine détente seem even lower. Soviet bargaining power is at low ebb, and they would conclude that, when the West was under little pressure to make concessions, general settlements could only be at the expense of Soviet interests in such matters as Berlin and disarmament. They will almost certainly wish, as a general principle, to repair the present disarray and find means to restore an image of strength before they are ready to consider any real diplomatic give-and-take."[111]

Yet, overall, following the Cuban missile crisis, Kennedy saw the Soviet Union more as a status quo power than as a revisionist one and called for a test ban treaty in his American University address on June 10, 1963.[112] Khrushchev responded positively on July 2, and on July 25 the "hot line" was established.[113]

THE CHANGING CHARACTER OF THE
THREAT: FROM AN INTENTIONAL WAR OF
AGGRESSION TO AN INADVERTENT WAR

During the Cuban missile crisis, particularly during its most dangerous point on October 27, Kennedy feared that he was losing control, that his efforts at managing the crisis to avoid resorting to force were handicapped by unfavorable developments, and that he might soon face overwhelming pressure to authorize air strikes against missile sites in Cuba, which might lead to a Soviet military retaliation.[114] Such a frightening stage of the crisis led to the realization that an inadvertent escalation was the major threat for both superpowers and thus they should cooperate to avoid it.

Indeed, a recent review of the research on the Cuban missile crisis suggests that "the peril of *intentional escalation* was less acute than once formerly believed."[115] As the crisis reached its climax, Khrushchev and Kennedy strived toward compromise rather than belligerence. Both leaders increasingly realized their joint, ultimate interest in avoiding war. The risk of inadvertent escalation seems to have been even greater. There were a number of scenarios of potential escalation and loss of control by both the US and the Soviet Union, especially regarding Soviet nuclear weapons in and around Cuba other than the strategic missiles:[116]

- The tactical nuclear weapons that local commanders could have used regardless of Moscow's instructions.
- With Soviet nuclear-armed submarines maneuvering around the quarantine, even a limited collision posed a risk of escalation because any use of nuclear weapons against US forces would have provoked an automatic nuclear retaliation. At least one Soviet submarine commander, harassed by US forces during the quarantine and without communication with Moscow, is reported to have concluded that war had begun and considered firing his nuclear torpedo against US ships. He had to be dissuaded by his subordinates from using the torpedo.
- A high-level US military alert (DEFCON-2) given in the open communications system, possibly presaging to a wary Soviet Union a likely US first strike.[117]
- A test launch in California of a US ICBM that might have been interpreted by Soviet agents as the beginning of a US first strike.[118]

A number of actual incidents could have escalated:[119]

- A U-2 was downed over Cuba by a Soviet air-defense unit without Khrushchev's authorization. This could have led to an escalation, but Kennedy avoided retaliation. Soviet troops in Cuba also targeted Guantanamo with tactical nuclear weapons.
- Another U-2 blundered over the Soviet Union without Kennedy's knowledge. A weather-sampling mission by the U-2 strayed over Siberia leading to scramble by Soviet planes, while US planes armed with nuclear weapons rushed aloft to help but fortunately there was no shoot-out in the air. Kennedy then uttered: "There's always some sonofabitch that doesn't get the word." This expression indicates Kennedy's realization of the great danger of inadvertent escalation during the Cuban missile crisis. His nightmare was that a small incident would bring about a major escalation with millions of deaths.[120]
- NATO aircraft with Turkish pilots loaded nuclear bombs and advanced to an alert status in which individual pilots could have chosen to take off, fly to Moscow, and drop a bomb.[121]
- On the whole, many of Kennedy's messages were misinterpreted by the Soviet Union.[122]

By rejecting the air strike option during the crisis to avoid the mistakes of 1914,[123] Kennedy indicated his growing awareness of the danger of inadvertent escalation. This indicated a changing focus from the "lessons of Munich"[124] of avoiding weakness or appearing weak, informing offensive realism, to the "lessons of Sarajevo," highlighted by defensive realism—namely, the greatest fear is an inadvertent escalation or loss of control. In this spirit, Kennedy said in an interview on December 17, 1962, that the crisis was a result of "misjudg-

ments of the intentions of others" that had pulled nations into war throughout the century.[125]

One could argue that the individual level is important here as Kennedy
was reported to be influenced from reading Barbara Tuchman's *The Guns
of August*.[126] Yet, the key point here is that the change in grand strategy was
in response to cautious Soviet behavior and the desire to avoid war, and the
fear of both sides about unintended escalation that led them to overcome
this danger by arms control and confidence-building measures. The hot
line (July 1963) and the Limited Test Ban Treaty (August 1963) were the immediate fruits of the new strategy.

Following the Cuban missile crisis, both Kennedy and Khrushchev understood that a nuclear war would be a "disaster" and that "they had come
so near the precipice that there was a real chance of slipping over it. Their
choices were much affected by that understanding." The key meaning of the
Cuban missile crisis was "that having come so close to the edge, the leaders
of both superpowers have since taken care to keep away from the cliff."[127]
Nuclear war had come to be seen in the US as a threat in itself, greater in
magnitude than most provocations that could conceivably have justified
resort to it.[128]

The Soviet Union shared this fear of nuclear war (in contrast to China).
Kennedy was impressed by the extent to which mutual misperceptions had
caused the Cuban missile crisis similarly to what they caused in 1914, 1939, and
1950.[129] While it reinforced the credibility of nuclear deterrence, the Cuban
missile crisis showed that a miscalculation on either side could have resulted
in a devastating war.[130] Thus the most powerful influence of the crisis was that
"neither side want[ed] to run such risk again."[131] As a result, both sides realized their strategic interdependence—security cannot be achieved only by
unilateral moves but must involve some level of coordination and cooperation with the other side to avoid disaster, especially an inadvertent escalation,
which almost happened in the missile crisis several times. Moreover, superiority—as has been maintained by the US until the missile crisis—does not
guarantee security and cannot prevent inadvertent escalation; it rather might
even encourage the other side to resort to dangerous moves—as a balancing
act—like the Soviet nuclear deployment in Cuba.

How to prevent an inadvertent escalation resulting from misperception
fits nicely with the logic and prescriptions of defensive realism. This approach
suggests various measures to avoid such situations, most notably mutual deterrence, arms control, and confidence-building measures as initially manifested in the hot line and the limited test ban. Another manifestation was

the focus on the danger of nuclear weapons and proliferation that appeared in Kennedy's address to the UN General Assembly on September 20, 1963.[132]

MATERIAL FACTOR—GROWING SOVIET CAPABILITIES LEAD TO THE RISE OF MAD AND ARMS CONTROL

The Cuban missile crisis marked a turning point in the debate over whether or not nuclear war was winnable. It became clear that even "victory" over the Soviet Union would lead to millions of American casualties, and thus the idea of a first strike or preventive war lost its attraction.[133]

The massive Soviet buildup following the Cuban missile crisis convinced the US that achieving superiority and using such preponderant capabilities for strategic purposes was illusive, costly, and dangerous. This buildup made irrelevant Eisenhower's 1959 guidance that nuclear planning should ensure that the US should "prevail and survive" after a war. Both Kennedy and Johnson realized that nuclear superiority was fading, and nuclear weapons could be used only for deterrence, not for preemption or war-fighting.[134]

The US realized that it had to embark on arms control negotiations in order to curb the Soviet buildup of strategic nuclear weapons that were on the verge of overtaking their own.[135] By the end of 1966, McNamara realized that any mutual restraint would have to be negotiated.[136] There was no achievable level of force that would allow a satisfactory degree of "destruction of the enemy's military forces." The Soviet Union could always construct additional survivable forces sufficient to destroy the US in retaliation.[137] Thus McNamara moved away from a position favoring counterforce/war-fighting (the "no-cities" doctrine)[138] to MAD as a result of the character of nuclear weapons and the capabilities of both superpowers (related to their priorities). He suggested in March 1963: "The increasing numbers of survivable missiles in the hands of both the U.S. and Soviet Union are a fact of life. Neither side today possesses a force which can save its country from severe damage in a nuclear exchange";[139] thus the US will be unable to develop first strike because the Soviet Union will deploy more and better protected missiles.[140] As Walter Lippmann wrote: "In the age of nuclear parity there is no alternative to coexistence."[141]

A key consideration in moving to a focus on MAD was the recognition in the futility of defense in the nuclear age. In this context came McNamara's abandonment of defense (shelters) in favor of deterrence in 1965:[142] it became clear that most defensive measures could be neutralized by the adversary relatively cheaply in relation to the defense (three times more expensive than the offense for each level of damage). The scientific opposition to the feasibility of missile defense was augmented by the high costs and local opposition to deployment in their area.[143]

In December 1964, McNamara told President Johnson that there was no combination of damage-limiting measures that the Soviets could not overcome. Assured destruction became the key criterion rather than damage limitation, though he procured a bit more for political reasons.[144] Three years later McNamara told the Soviet premier Aleksey Kosygin that missile defense would only intensify offensive deployments on both sides.[145]

Since both superpowers understood that missile defense would only intensify offensive buildup, they endorsed the ABM Treaty of 1972, which accepted MAD as a state of nuclear parity.[146] The Soviets also realized that no matter who fired first, neither side could win a nuclear war and thus moved away from preemption (first strike) to retaliation (second strike).[147] It is noteworthy that the opposition to missile defense signified a major change from the initial preferences of Johnson and Nixon.[148]

The preference of McNamara's ideas over those of LeMay was not because of the power of McNamara's personality or his bureaucratic standing, "but the realities of thermonuclear warheads, that made victory a mirage." The underlying problem was the unavoidable and growing Soviet capacity for a devastating reply to even the strongest preemptive strike." During the years 1965–75, LeMay's strategy was overtaken by the massive Soviet deployment of strategic missiles. It became clear that victory was impossible.[149]

A material development which facilitated the selection of the idea of arms control was the production of satellite reconnaissance (the first Russian reconnaissance satellite went into orbit in April 1962). But what made possible the emergence of a reconnaissance regime was the Cuban missile crisis, which developed some sense of mutual interest in stabilizing the arms race. Thus, the Cuban missile crisis should be taken into account in explaining the Soviet toleration of satellite reconnaissance.[150] The regime of satellite reconnaissance instituted a certain degree of transparency that reduced the danger of a surprise attack and enabled verification of arms control agreements (such as the Limited Test Ban Treaty).[151]

In later years the Nuclear Non-Proliferation Treaty that Johnson signed (1968) and the ABM and Strategic Arms Limitation Talks (SALT I) Treaties that Nixon signed (1972) solidified the new strategy and the relations with the Soviets. These agreements—by nature—turned the early logic of the superpower competition on its head. The US and the USSR were no longer engaged in an arms race for superiority (an offensive realist approach) that became materially impossible. However, these treaties did not go so far as disarmament and joint management (a defensive liberal approach). The treaties only froze the status quo, made the presence of nuclear weapons (now under some restrictions) tolerable, and permitted the superpowers to engage in some cooperation while continuing their competition, especially in regional conflicts. Yet, the rise of MAD has made the likelihood of superpower war extremely low. Gaddis states that détente in the late 1960s and later was designed as a set of rules to continue the Cold War competition with one mutual interest—avoiding a nuclear holocaust.[152]

ALTERNATIVE EXPLANATIONS TO THE MATERIAL/ EXTERNAL ACCOUNT PRESENTED HERE

1. *Domestic level*: Domestic pressures to change course in referring to the Soviet Union and abandon the strategy of preponderance were very weak. Kennedy, as we demonstrated, was not far from Eisenhower in his strategic thought. There was no strong opposition in either the Senate or the House of Representatives to Kennedy's initial preponderant conduct, and this did not seem to change during or after the crisis. It is fair to argue that the American government—both the executive and the legislative—was entirely supportive of preponderance. The change toward détente was not obvious and was eventually a result of the president's decision in response to events and dangers in the external environment.

2. *Individual level*: On this level of analysis, one might argue that Kennedy entered the White House with the idea of détente in mind. Trachtenberg argues that Kennedy wanted from the beginning of his term to reach an agreement with the Soviets.[153] However, Kennedy's words and actions suggest otherwise. He would not consent to Soviet demands and did not attempt to reach agreements on core issues such as Berlin while he believed the US was inferior to the Soviets. All this changed after the Cuban missile crisis, and Kennedy pushed for forming a basis of agreement with the Soviets in order to prevent such crises from reoccurring. In other words, an external event, which changed the level and the nature of the balance of threat, led to a major change in Kennedy's initial positions from an offensive realist to a defensive realist.

3. *A key alternative explanation of arms control*[154]—*an ideational account*: Emmanuel Adler developed a constructivist-ideational explanation of the rise of arms control as a dominant pattern in superpower relations. He argued that

> the idea of nuclear arms control spurred the interest of the Eisenhower administration, but did not affect American policy until many members of the arms control community went to work for President Kennedy. Once on the inside, they promoted their arms control ideas, created public and private arms control institutions. . . . and persuaded key

political actors, such as . . . McNamara, who provided political support. They also generated the technical knowledge needed to implement arms control agreements, helped think through the bargaining positions to be adopted by American negotiators, and contributed to the formulation of norms and rules.[155]

Adler adds that the ideas and activities of these experts led to arms control accords and to the habitual practice of arms control becoming rooted in the US bureaucracy, media, and the public. Their impact culminated with the dissemination of arms control ideas and practice to the Soviet Union. Thus, in Adler's view, Gorbachev's ideas (and also those of his advisors) echoed McNamara's ideas of MAD twenty years earlier.[156] While one cannot overlook the influence of the scientists on McNamara's thinking, it seems that the secretary of defense himself changed his position from counterforce/war-fighting/damage limitation to deterrence/countervalue (MAD),[157] taking into account, first of all, the material context of Soviet capabilities and the material character of nuclear weapons and, as noted, the influence of the Cuban missile crisis.

Gorbachev, for his part, came up with the arms control idea when the Soviet Union was already unable to endure the contest with the US, especially for material/economic reasons.[158] When Gorbachev was in power, advancing arms control was endorsed by the Soviet Union due to the urgent economic needs to cut defense expenditures (which, in turn, also necessitated better relations with the US expressed by arms control agreements).

Arms control was preferred over disarmament because the latter was seen as based on oversimplified theorizing and certain ignorance as to the strategic facts of life,[159] since there was conflict of interest and hostility between the superpowers while mutual deterrence could be potentially stabilizing. The key reasons for the failure of the idea of disarmament were closely related to the overall argument advanced here with regard to the rise of defensive realist ideas following the missile crisis:[160]

1. The successful management of the Cuban missile crisis;
2. Nuclear deterrence as a practical solution;
3. The rise of arms control with the Test Ban Treaty and of détente.

Adler argues that the change occurred once people with strong convictions against the nuclear arms race entered government with Kennedy's administration and brought their ideas of arms control into official policy debates.[161] Timing is a critical aspect in examining the validity of this explanation. First of all, their ideas were known even before 1960 but could not compete with the offensive realist ones under the conditions preceding the missile crisis, notably the widespread view of the Soviet Union as a revisionist power and the insufficient realization that the key danger is of an inadvertent escalation during a crisis—rather than a premeditated attack—as became clear during the missile crisis.

But more important, even if he was open enough to have supporters and promoters of arms control in his administration, Kennedy did not support the idea at the beginning of his presidency. He preferred preponderance. It wasn't until the Cuban missile crisis that the alternative ideas materialized. It was only after the Cuban missile crisis that Kennedy changed his mind. The change—even if it emerged from the concepts advocated by these devotees—occurred only due to the external changes that followed the Cuban missile crisis. In fact, Adler demonstrates that it took several years after the Cuban crisis and many efforts by McNamara to materialize the arms control that might not have survived a transition in 1964–65.

Conclusion

The shift from offensive realism to defensive realism during the 1960s began with the Cuban missile crisis and continued with the détente policy in the late 1960s. It began when the US understood that the strategy that it held during the Eisenhower administration and the early Kennedy administration was ineffective and brought the two superpowers closer than ever to a nuclear war. President Kennedy replaced the doctrine of massive retaliation with flexible response, but following the dramatic and traumatic events of October 1962, Kennedy shifted to a more moderate strategy. The international system was much less threatening after Khrushchev proved he was not willing to risk a general nuclear war that might have destroyed the world. The Soviets, then, stopped challenging the US in its own backyard in exchange for an American promise not to invade Cuba.

Miscalculation, loss of control, and an inadvertent escalation became the main sources of danger, rather than outright aggression. For such a challenge, defensive realism offers a menu of potentially useful mechanisms, notably mutual deterrence, arms control, and confidence-building measures.

After twelve years (1950–62) of intense efforts to achieve preponderance over the Soviet Union, the US shifted course and sought to achieve a modus vivendi with its global rival. It began when both superpowers realized that their arsenals and strategies might lead to devastating consequences, and that there can be no victory in the course they were on. The Soviet capitulation was a signal to the US that the Soviet leadership was rational and willing to compromise.

This episode was a peak in international tensions, following two dramatic years that included the Bay of Pigs fiasco and the construction of the Berlin Wall, with the Vienna Summit in between. The US seemed to project weakness toward the Soviet Union.[162] The Cuban missile crisis produced the exact opposite impression, and then the Soviets moderated their positions and the US followed with its own moderation. The grand strategy of détente evolved slowly under Kennedy and Johnson, and flourished under Nixon, with the climax of success in 1972. But since then, détente lost support (especially under Ford and then Carter), as signs that the Soviets were starting to challenge the détente arrangements mounted, raising again the level of threat in the international system. As the next chapter discusses, détente collapsed with the 1979 Soviet invasion of Afghanistan that forced President Carter to change course, contrary to his initial beliefs, and return to a more offensive realist Cold War strategy despite his liberal tendency.

Several ideational approaches to promoting security are in constant competition for dominance in the US. As we demonstrated here, the shift from preponderance to détente—from offensive to defensive realism—was made possible only when the adversary achieved nuclear parity that clarified that no victory was foreseeable, but also was much less threatening than before, and proved it was willing to cooperate. As long as these two issues were not challenged (i.e., the Soviets were not clearly stepping up their attempt to break parity in their favor or increase threats to the US), the détente grand strategy was dominant.

POSSIBLE IMPLICATIONS FOR A
POTENTIAL NUCLEAR CRISIS

What are the lessons of the missile crisis with regard to the utility of the competing grand strategies in a potential nuclear crisis? The crisis shows the great dangers inherent in offensive approaches, particularly offensive realism. A focus on superiority by one of the parties might lead to dangerous moves by the other side. Such moves could lead to an inadvertent escalation triggered either by miscalculation or loss of control (over allies or the military) or both. Both defensive liberalism and defensive realism offer useful prescriptions. The defensive liberal strategy offers engagement and negotiations in order to reach a far-reaching, comprehensive, and multilateral agreement, which might include some elements of disarmament.

Defensive realism offers a more modest arrangement, which includes confidence-building and arms control measures reached through unilateral or multilateral steps of the parties based on a certain nuclear balance, preferably MAD. This was the type of arrangement reached between the two superpowers following the Cuban missile crisis. Indeed, the theoretical model presented here expects that under great-power parity and low threat, as was the case in the aftermath of the missile crisis, a defensive realist strategy would emerge.

Epilogue: Does the Vietnam War Challenge the Conception of the US Grand Strategy as a Realist One?

Many realists—such as Morgenthau, Waltz, Mearsheimer, Walt, and others—see the US interventions on the periphery of the Third World during the Cold War, most notably the Vietnam War, as nonrealist. Some might see these wars, notably Vietnam, even as "liberal wars." Indeed, from a realist point of view, the Vietnam War was an unnecessary "war of choice." First, the weakness of Vietnam meant that even if it fell to the communists, it would not have any effect on the global balance of power and would not pose any serious danger to US security.

Second, the fear of falling dominos if South Vietnam fell to communist hands was seen by realists as unjustified because of the expectation that balancing rather than bandwagoning is the dominant dynamic in international relations.[163] Thus, the realist expectation was that following the occupation (or liberation, in the eyes of Vietnamese nationalists) of South Vietnam by the North in 1975, a balancing coalition would emerge in the region against Vietnam. Indeed, although two marginal and weak neighboring states—Cambodia and Laos—also became communist, most of the Southeast Asian states formed ASEAN already in 1967 as an anticommunist organization designed to prevent communist expansion into their countries. Moreover, rather than the communist countries uniting against the West, Vietnam went to war with Cambodia in 1978 and became engaged in war with China a year later. Third, some realists even see the war as a "liberal" one since the component of the anticommunist "crusade" was so salient in this US intervention and that is something that obviously the realists oppose very strongly as it is unrelated to national security.

We argue, however, that even though these points are valid, this doesn't challenge the core point of US grand strategy during the Cold War as a realist one, including defensive realist during the détente period as suggested in this chapter, because of the following three reasons. First, the key focus of the grand strategy during the Cold War was the strategy toward the Soviet Union. Until the Cuban missile crisis, the key component—as chapter 3 shows—was to maximize power and achieve superiority and dominance vis-à-vis the Soviets in order to deter them from initiating an attack, most notably, on Western Europe but also all over the globe and eventually to bring about "peace through strength." Following the Cuban missile crisis, as this chapter discusses, the grand strategy vis-à-vis the USSR started to include the notable defensive realist elements of arms control, confidence-building measures, and deterrence through MAD/parity rather than superiority. This approach culminated with the defensive realist strategy of Nixon-Kissinger. As Hal Brands suggests, they believed that "a more equitable distribution of power . . . could facilitate great-power negotiations and lessen the danger of nuclear war."[164] A limited war on the periphery such as Vietnam, which the US worked hard to contain as much as possible so that it would not involve the Soviets or the Chinese, didn't challenge fundamentally the realist logic of the strategy vis-à-vis the Soviets.

Second, even if the interventions in the Third World were attempts to help anticommunists, it is somewhat ironic to call the Vietnam War and other interventions on the periphery "liberal," while the US protected in these interventions very illiberal/authoritarian/military regimes. Not only did these wars avoid democracy promotion but in quite a few notable cases, as noted in chapters 1 and 3, the US has committed democracy removal, such as in Iran in 1953, Guatemala in 1954, and Chile in 1973, while maintaining close strategic and economic relations with numerous despotic regimes in the Third World like Saudi Arabia and Iran under the Shah and many authoritarian Latin American and Asian regimes. This type of behavior can't be viewed as liberalism by any stretch of the imagination.

Third, these wars had some realpolitik reasoning, notably in the eyes of the administrations—even if the reasoning was mistaken in some cases.[165] The wars were, first of all, against what were perceived by the US to be proxies of the Soviet Union and the Eastern Bloc. The objective of these wars was to prevent what seemed to be an expansion of Soviet power. A related goal was—even if mistakenly—to maintain the credibility of the American commitments and US resolve so as to deter what was viewed in Washington as attempts at further Soviet aggression against American allies or clients.[166]

Overall, those who call Vietnam and the other related wars "liberal wars" are committing a conceptual overstretching of liberalism, while doing a bit of "understretching" of realism. In other words, they broaden slightly too much the concept of liberalism to include the protection of illiberal regimes, while they discount completely the realpolitik elements of such interventions. If Vietnam and the other interventions are liberal wars, how could we distinguish these wars from the liberal wars of the post–Cold War era that indeed focused on liberal causes (even if they didn't succeed in many cases in advancing them)? This might cause a serious, and certainly unnecessary, conceptual confusion. To further clarify this confusion, we discuss the post–Cold War liberal wars in chapters 7 and 8.

5

From Détente to the "Second Cold War": From Kennedy to Carter

Introduction

The previous chapter explained the shift from the grand strategy of preponderance to that of détente following the Cuban missile crisis of 1962. The grand strategy of détente persisted for seventeen years, until 1979, which means that it dominated the foreign policy of five presidents, three Democrats, and two Republicans. Under one of them, President Nixon, it was least controversial. But Nixon's foreign policy of détente is not to be confused with the grand strategy of détente. It went by the same name, but the grand strategy was already in place, and sometimes also by its name. Nevertheless, détente was not only during Nixon's term.

The following analysis will take off from Kennedy's assassination and the beginning of Lyndon B. Johnson's administration. It will then briefly overview the eight years of Republican presidents Richard Nixon and Gerald Ford during which détente was at its peak (orchestrated by the dominant national security advisor and secretary of state, Henry Kissinger) but also began to decline. The chapter will focus on the Carter administration, which began as a strong supporter of détente—although on a completely different basis than the previous administrations, emphasizing liberal factors instead of realist ones—but ended with a totally different view of the Soviet Union, which in turn was reflected in a hard-line foreign and defense policy and culminated in the Carter Doctrine and the intensification of the Cold War into the 1980s. The discussion of Carter's policy will outline the initial policy that was based on the worldviews of the key policy makers in Carter's administration; then we'll address the key alternative strategies; the persistence of the grand strategy of détente despite domestic opposition; the rise of the Soviet threat; and then the change in Carter's view and consequently his strategy.

We argue that during the mid- and late 1970s, Soviet moves were identified as breaching the foundations of détente and as security risks that needed
a tougher American response. In turn, the defensive liberal view that dominated Carter's administration and his personal views was replaced by an offensive realist view. The shift back to offensive realism occurred because of
events external to the US in the international system (i.e., alarming Soviet
moves), and not because of domestic pressures such as Ronald Reagan's offensive realist challenge to Carter as the 1980 elections were nearing or the
intrabureaucratic struggle between the State Department and the National
Security Council that took opposite views.

Détente under Johnson, Nixon, and Ford

Kennedy was assassinated while a lively debate was taking place among his
chief advisors over détente. "Rostow warned that a relaxation of tensions
with Moscow would legitimize Communism and induce people in the West
to let down their guard. Rusk, however, believed that détente with the Soviets
'was bound to work in favor of the West.'"[1] The debate was soon over, as the
grand strategy of détente gained ground under President Johnson. The reason for this result was that it suited Johnson's political needs, as he was taking
over from his slain predecessor.

Kennedy's assassination made no difference to the new strategic track.
Khrushchev sent President Johnson messages that indicated his wish to continue what he already started establishing with Kennedy. Johnson's political
priorities—promoting his domestic agenda and getting elected in 1964—
were clear to his aides and to the Soviets. These priorities came down to favoring peace, but "détente was not going to get in the way of his election."[2]
However, Johnson had no idea what to offer the Soviets as content of peace;
therefore he relied on his top aides, all of whom were Kennedy's appointees.[3]
Johnson wanted to win in Vietnam, and détente was not the way.[4] He believed
in the domino theory and told Henry Cabot Lodge, the ambassador to South
Vietnam, shortly after Kennedy's assassination, "I am not going to lose Vietnam. I am not going to be the President who saw Southeast Asia go the way
of China."[5]

Johnson—loyal to Kennedy's legacy and to his own domestic agenda—
continued his efforts to ease tensions with the Soviets. In fact, there were
no major confrontations between the superpowers during his presidency.
But the Soviets grew stronger militarily despite a slowing economy, secured
nuclear parity, and even built a blue-water navy. Johnson wished for an agree-

ment to head off an ABM race that might shatter deterrence under the MAD principle. Costigliola attributes Johnson's ability to promote détente to the stabilization of Germany.[6]

In early 1965, Leffler reports, "the qualitative and quantitative superiority of the U.S. over the Soviet Union was so great, Secretary of Defense Mc-Namara acknowledged, that he sometimes wondered, 'why there has not been a Congressional investigation of why we have so much military strength.'"[7] Until late 1967 McNamara was against ballistic missile defense because he didn't see it as a feasible possibility (while the Soviets did, as they were building their ABM systems), but technology improved and with the Joint Chiefs of Staff recommending an ABM system, McNamara acceded, though he presented the development as designed vis-à-vis China.[8]

Concerning the Soviets, however, given the growing parity in nuclear power, McNamara advocated simple deterrence, including the destruction of cities, which both superpowers were capable of doing. This would be deterrence emerging from the MAD principle, that is, the ability of both superpowers to absorb a surprise nuclear attack and still inflict an unacceptable damage to the attacker by resorting to their survivable second-strike capability. Based on MAD, both sides could reduce their nuclear forces. Johnson liked the idea, as it promoted arms control.[9]

During his final year in office, Johnson signed the Nuclear Non-Proliferation Treaty.[10] This was his most significant contribution to the process, which lay the ground for Nixon and Kissinger to proceed and sign the SALT I Treaty. Nixon and Kissinger promoted and deepened détente (and accordingly labeled their policy) in realization that the US power was relatively in decline vis-à-vis Europe and Japan (economically) and the Soviet Union (militarily).[11] Trachtenberg goes even further saying that the West was at a disadvantage at that point since the US would not start a nuclear war with the USSR in the event of a European war. In other words, the nuclear deterrent "was a sham."[12] In fact, the West was content to live the status quo, and it was up to the Soviets to decide whether or not to keep it.[13] Trachtenberg concludes that Nixon and Kissinger did not plan to build a "global structure of peace" on cooperation with the Soviets, but rather on keeping the Soviets "in line by making sure they had to worry about a strong China on their Asian border."[14]

Bundy argues that Nixon realized what both Kennedy and (especially) Johnson didn't: strategic superiority was unreachable. Therefore, a week after taking office, Nixon said that his administration was seeking sufficiency and not superiority.[15] In 1972, the policy of détente seemed successful as it brought the two superpowers to sign the SALT I Treaty.

Détente proved profitable for the United States on the regional level, as the Soviet influence in the Middle East declined and culminated in the decision of Egypt's President Sadat in 1972 to dismiss and expel all the Soviet military advisors and technicians. Only after the Yom Kippur War of 1973, during which the Soviets still backed and armed Egypt, Sadat officially detached from the Soviet orbit and made Egypt an American client,[16] but the expelling of the Soviet advisors and technicians in 1972 signaled that the Soviets were losing a major stronghold in the Middle East. This region was a major scene in the superpower Cold War political confrontation. Even though there was no direct military confrontation, the probability could not be disregarded, especially at the end of the October 1973 Arab-Israeli War. Under the Johnson and Nixon administrations, the US gained a significant advantage over the Soviet Union with Israel's military victories that were perceived as major blows to Soviet prestige, and later with the Egyptian alignment with the US. The American dominance in the Middle East was significant in the superpower competition due to the central role of the Middle East in world politics as a major global energy source. The Middle East was a major scene in world politics, attracting the attention of all great powers. Not surprisingly, the Middle East was the region over which détente ended at the end of the 1970s.

Under President Ford, Kissinger promoted the SALT II negotiations with the Soviets. However, the negotiations lingered and ended only in 1979, although in November 1974 Ford met with Brezhnev in Vladivostok and their joint statement—while not bringing the superpowers to a positive conclusion of the negotiations—provided terms of reference for later phases of the negotiations, well into Carter's term. But Carter did not think these understandings were ambitious enough, as the Soviets learned shortly after he became president. This added much mistrust and tension into the delicate relations between the superpowers.

Critics of détente argued in the mid-1970s that the strategy and policy of détente were counterproductive in the sense that they permitted the Soviets to make several moves that undermined the American leading position in the system, while the United States was limited in its ability to react properly, due to the restrictions that détente imposed.[17] Apparently convincing evidence for this notion eroded the support for détente toward the end of the Ford administration. But Ford and Kissinger tended to maintain détente, which was one of the reasons that former California governor Ronald Reagan—the leader of the right wing of the Republican Party—challenged Ford for the Republican nomination in 1976.

Ford won the party's nomination narrowly, but lost to Democrat Jimmy Carter. This was a competition between a defensive realist incumbent president and a defensive liberal challenger. Despite the different reasoning each of the candidates brought to the public, they in fact wanted détente to persist. It is true, though, that the Republicans eliminated the term "détente" from their election campaign in 1976 due to its unpopularity because of the Soviet intervention in Angola that seemed to undermine détente; but both Ford and Carter wanted the SALT II framework to end in agreement. Ford and (especially) Kissinger wished to maintain the agreements with the Soviets at the level they were discussing, whereas Carter pursued a much more radical agreement that would dismantle missiles.

The Initial Worldview of the Key Decision Makers in the Carter Administration

Jimmy Carter came to the White House with a liberal agenda of human rights that was not restricted to the United States but was global in its reach and intent.[18] He also wanted a complete nuclear disarmament, and once in office, he tried—through Vance—to make this the goal of the SALT II negotiations, an ambitious goal that was very far from the Vladivostok understandings of 1974 that the Ford administration left for him.

During the campaign, Carter argued that the defense budget was too large and should be reduced, and stated that the Ford administration's defense spending could be cut by $15 billion. This figure was later cut by half, although the initial statement haunted Carter during the final part of the campaign.[19] In any case, Carter believed that the defense budget could be cut significantly and wanted the public to know this.[20] Carter repeated many times the need for "a legitimate foreign policy," clearly challenging the Nixon/ Ford–Kissinger policy.[21]

When discussing needed and possible cuts, Carter was referring to what he saw as too many troops stationed abroad, too many overseas bases, overly long training and too many training staff, an excessive bureaucracy, unnecessary weapons systems, and so on. Carter was a nuclear abolitionist.[22] He called for reduction of nuclear weapons—in the course of abolishing them eventually—and not for arms limitation.[23] This was the basis of his disappointment with the Vladivostok understandings between Brezhnev and Ford.[24] The framework allowed the superpowers to maintain an "unnecessarily and immorally high numbers of nuclear weapons."[25] Carter was against the ceiling of 1,320 MIRVs that was set in Vladivostok, since the US had only eight hundred MIRVs at the time, which meant an agreed arms race.[26]

Carter also considered during the campaign withdrawing American troops from South Korea, Taiwan, and Japan if there were equivalent measures for these allies' defense.[27] He discussed the need to review strategies of NATO that were outdated, and also argued that while the US was busy in Vietnam, the Soviets were improving their blue-water navy to an extent that could challenge American naval dominance.

Carter, in brief, was not considering escalating the confrontation with the Soviet Union and did not seem to sense an acute threat from it. He did sense that the weapons both superpowers possessed were dangerous to all mankind and therefore wished to abolish them. Nevertheless, Stuart Eizenstat who served as Carter's chief advisor on domestic affairs points out that Carter in fact increased defense expenses because the Soviet Union "came closer to matching the US in strategic power than it had in any other period,"[28] and that it was Carter who ordered the development of new Pershing and cruise missiles in 1979, which were deployed only in 1983.[29]

Betty Glad provides a different view, that in his campaign in the South, Carter echoed Reagan and criticized Ford and Kissinger and claimed that he "had no illusions about Russia's intentions." And in the foreign policy debate with Ford, he said that the Soviet Union knows what it wants in détente while the US does not.[30] Glad argues that "Carter was vulnerable because he did not have a well-developed strategic vision." This made him dependent on his chief advisors, Cyrus Vance and Zbigniew Brzezinski. While Vance was wholeheartedly supportive of Carter's idealistic causes, Brzezinski was much more suspicious of the Soviet Union and succeeded during Carter's presidency to gain control over the China policy and "tilted it in an anti-Soviet direction."[31]

According to Glad, Vance believed that the Soviet Union was "a state that the United States could deal with on the basis of their complementary interests in matters such as the limitation of the arms race," while Brzezinski "saw the Soviet Union as a megalomaniac state bent on world domination." Vance saw the limitations of the American military power, whereas Brzezinski "viewed U.S. military power and the threat that it might actually be utilized as the most important factors in shaping Soviet policies."[32]

Vance testifies that "strategically, our main problem as the administration came to power was to contain Soviet expansion while reinvigorating the long-term American effort to moderate U.S.-Soviet tensions. . . . The backbone of our policy would be the maintenance of strong American defenses and alliances so that we could manage our relationship with the Soviet Union from a position of equivalent strength."[33] He does not indicate any parting from Carter's policy objectives, including human rights, but does indicate that he preferred quiet diplomacy over publicity, except in rare cases,[34] which means that he only differed on the methods to achieve the same goals. On arms limitation and reduction, Vance testifies that he agreed with the goal of deep cuts in nuclear arms that others promoted but preferred taking a more moderate path by securing SALT II as it was forming at the time and waiting for SALT III for the dramatic cuts.[35] He in fact reports that he objected to Carter's decision to try skipping SALT II but eventually yielded.[36]

The Initial Grand Strategy

Carter introduced the human rights issue into American foreign policy as soon as he assumed office. Human rights are a liberal cause, but Carter did not attempt to force them on the Soviet Union (not to mention that even his minor gestures and pleads on this matter were promptly rejected by Moscow), but rather he tried promoting them through negotiations and in a co-operative spirit. This is a defensive approach.

Carter was in contact with Soviet dissidents who wrote or appealed to him, and took special care for Soviet "seruvniks" (Jewish activists whose applications for a visa to emigrate to Israel were refused), especially Nathan Sharansky. Carter made human rights not only an issue in American foreign policy but a central issue that determined relations with various regimes. For instance, his administration sanctioned Pakistan—a longtime ally of the United States—for nearly his entire term due to its nuclear weapons program but also because of its poor human rights record. This later became a major problem for Carter, when the US needed Pakistan to cooperate in supplying the mujahideen in Afghanistan following the Soviet invasion in December 1979.

However defensive in nature, this policy was a major source of confrontation between the superpowers. Whereas Nixon, Ford, and Kissinger were careful not to make this an issue in their policy toward the Soviet Union (as defensive realists who accept that domestic policies are not an issue between the superpowers), Carter insisted on criticizing the Soviets on their record of human rights. This created many tensions between the two leaderships and became an obstacle for promoting the SALT deal.

Brzezinski told Carter in early 1977 that the Soviets needed détente (implied, more than the US?) due to their economic situation, the rising dissident groups, the rivalry with China, and the disquiet in Eastern Europe that would only increase with détente. The "basic fact is that the West in general, and the US in particular, has the power to greatly aggravate the Soviet dilemma."[37]

Carter, unlike Nixon and Ford, thought when he took office that the SALT II negotiations were not ambitious enough. He wanted to reduce nuclear weapons, not merely to restrain them.[38] But he also came with a liberal agenda of human rights that became a major factor in his administration's foreign policy. This issue soured relations with the Soviet Union throughout Carter's term, as he would issue démarches on human rights in the Soviet Union and would make it an issue in the negotiations over SALT and other matters. In other words, Carter linked the strategic and material issues with ideational ones. However, he did not aim at changing the Soviet regime, but merely its practice of human rights. At no point was Carter willing to try forcing his human rights policy, but rather he was constantly seeking cooperation on the strategic issues. Nevertheless, the pressure he put on Moscow over human rights made the Soviets very suspicious of Carter.[39]

Gati writes that when Carter instructed Vance to reach for the ambitious goal of massive cuts of arms in Moscow in March 1977, Brzezinski considered siding with Vance, only to change his mind later into thinking it would be easier to get that from the Soviets only after US-China relations were normalized.[40] Gati also writes that Carter might have favored Brzezinski over Vance due to his confrontational approach in order to quiet the Republicans that constantly accused the Democrats of being weak on national defense.[41]

Carter and his administration advocated cooperation with the Soviet Union and were even willing to allow the Soviets back into the Middle East after the years that they were virtually kept out of that region following Egypt's defection to the American camp after the Yom Kippur War of October 1973. This was a scheme led by President Anwar Sadat in full consultation and cooperation with Secretary of State Henry Kissinger under President Nixon. After Egypt became an American protégé, Kissinger was able to promote reconciliatory steps between Egypt and Israel through shuttle diplomacy missions during which he hammered out two interim agreements on the Sinai Peninsula, in 1974 and 1975 (as well as separation of forces between Israel and Syria in 1974). But even as the Soviet Union was pushed out of the Middle East (not fully, as it retained its strong connections with Syria), the strategy of détente did not seem to change.

Carter's cooperative approach included the efforts to reignite the Middle East peace process, nuclear proliferation, and most importantly the bilateral strategic relations, especially arms control. Discussions were frank and "businesslike," a term the Soviets used very often, but also very formal, except during Dobrynin's meetings in Washington, which seemed more casual. The Soviet involvement in Africa—denied tirelessly by the Soviets—was an alarming sign for the Carter administration. However, the Soviets accused the US of going behind the Soviet Union's back in the Middle East, deserting the Geneva Conference track that both superpowers were to cochair, and preferring the direct Egypt-Israel talks that came to fruition in the Camp

David Accords of September 1978. Dobrynin once told Vance that the Soviets were unsupportive of Sadat's visit to Jerusalem in November 1977 because it came just as the Soviets obtained—so they claimed—Syria's agreement to go to Geneva.[42] Sadat's visit to Israel foiled this Soviet effort for the convening of the Geneva Conference in which they would have a major role.

The Soviets were constantly complaining about America's intervention in their domestic affairs with the human rights agenda and the American demand to release dissidents or cancel or postpone their trials. This was especially evident in the case of Jewish dissidents such as Nathan Sharansky. At one of the peaks of tension between the two superpowers, in late 1978, Dobrynin suggested passing a personal message from Carter to Brezhnev after a long period of disconnection, as he was heading to Moscow for consultations. Carter wrote on the margins of the memo in which Dobrynin's suggestion was mentioned: "Yes—release Sharansky!"[43]

In his first letter to Brezhnev on January 26, 1977, Carter introduced his view on the US-Soviet relations that he wished to establish. He wanted "to improve relations . . . on the basis of reciprocity, mutual respect and benefit." Carter interpreted Brezhnev's speech at Tula on January 18 as saying that the Soviets "will not seek superiority in arms, will oppose the concept, and will require only a defense sufficient to deter any potential adversary. The United States seeks nothing more or less for itself."[44] Carter thought that this could lead to avoiding a new armaments race, and also to eliminating all nuclear weapons. The first step was, according to Carter, reaching a SALT II agreement without delay. He hoped to agree on "an adequately verified comprehensive ban on all nuclear tests." Carter added that the two superpowers should renew negotiations for a "balanced reduction of forces in Central Europe."[45]

On February 4, 1977, Brezhnev sent a congratulatory letter to Carter on assuming the presidency and suggested moving forward with arms control, including implementing the treaties "on the limitation of underground nuclear weapon tests and the explosions for peaceful purposes." He added that the Soviet Union wanted to cooperate with the US in reaching "complete and general cessation of nuclear weapon tests and the prevention of proliferation of such weapons. We are in favor of achieving a progress in the Vienna negotiations on the reduction of armed forces and armament in Central Europe. We would like the new US government to regard with attention the proposals submitted there by the Warsaw Treaty countries last year."[46] Brezhnev continued that the Soviet Union felt compelled to secure itself and its allies as long as "the arms race in the world has not yet been stopped," but that the defensive capabilities "should be sufficient so that no one would dare to launch an attack on us or to threaten us with an attack. . . . However, I would like to stress once again very definitely that the Soviet Union does not seek superiority in arms."[47]

Carter's reply ten days later emphasized the need to collaborate on efforts, especially in nuclear arms limitations, and to exercise "self-restraint in regard to those trouble spots in the world which could produce a direct confrontation between us."[48] Carter welcomed Brezhnev's "desire for increased cooperation looking toward an ending of the arms race and the achievement, without delay, of specific disarmament agreements."[49] Carter wished to push forward on arms control, saying that "obviously, we must be mutually secure from successful attack" and that the US and the Soviet Union should take advantage of their "roles as the most powerful nations to initiate substantive reduction in the level of conventional and nuclear armaments."[50]

In late March, Vance went for the first time to Moscow to negotiate. During their meeting on March 28, Brezhnev told Vance that "détente implied a certain degree of trust and a willingness to take into account each other's legitimate interests."[51] Vance, under instructions from Carter that he disliked but accepted, tried unsuccessfully to convince the Soviets to alter the goal of the SALT II negotiations from the Vladivostok-based arms control to reduction of arms. Nancy Mitchell explains Vance's failure on this trip: "Carter was not interested in arms control as therapy. He wanted deep cuts." Vance traveled to Moscow in March 1977 with the administration's revised SALT II proposals. He "sought dramatic cuts in existing weapons systems and a ban on the testing and deployment of several future systems." Carter, Mitchell writes, "considered the proposals an impressive step toward the elimination of nuclear weapons." But the Soviets viewed them as "reneging on promises the Kremlin believed had been made at Vladivostok." They also saw that the "cuts eviscerated the heart of their nuclear force, their large ICBMs, while leaving the US force, more reliant on bombers, largely in place."[52] Eizenstat writes that Carter sent Vance with two alternatives for the Soviets to choose from: "either agree to extending Vladivostok with slightly lower limits on nuclear weapons of about 10 percent on each side, or begin negotiating deeper cuts," while informing the Soviets that Carter preferred the deeper-cuts option.[53]

In his memoirs, Brzezinski elaborated on the policy goals as of 1977. The fourth point concerned the Soviet Union: "To push U.S.-Soviet strategic arms *limitation* talks into strategic arms *reduction* talks, using the foregoing as an entering wedge for a more stable U.S.-Soviet relationship." At the same time, he added, they "wanted to rebuff Soviet incursions both by supporting our friends and by ameliorating the sources of conflict which the Soviets exploit."

The idea was "to match Soviet ideological expansion by a more affirmative American posture on global human rights, while seeking consistently to make détente both more comprehensive and more reciprocal."[54] In other words, the administration wanted to mend détente.

Brzezinski contended that at first there was general agreement in the foreign policy establishment and specifically between him and Vance that "détente had been oversold to the American public." He maintains that he and Vance believed that "a better agreement than the original SALT I could be obtained." However, their reasoning was different. "Vance hoped that a new SALT agreement would pave the way for a wider U.S.-Soviet accommodation, while I saw in it an opportunity to halt or reduce the momentum of the Soviet military buildup."[55] He explained that the Soviets were gaining strategic parity and became "more daring" in the Third World. "The sustained Soviet strategic and conventional buildup posed the threat that by 1985 Moscow might attain military superiority over the United States—notwithstanding Mr. Kissinger's casual dismissal in 1972 of the importance of such superiority."[56]

Brzezinski identified Vance with the "liberal establishment" of the Democratic Party that still supported détente;[57] yet "Carter would be the first to admit that he came to the White House without a detailed plan for managing U.S.-Soviet relations. He was, however, determined to move on SALT, and he firmly supported the concept of détente."[58] Carter, mentored by Brzezinski in international affairs, said during the 1976 campaign that détente had to involve both cooperation and competition and would have to be more comprehensive and reciprocal. Brzezinski recalled that later—when the Carter administration was in office—Vance and State objected to the use of these two last terms and would cross them out of drafts of Carter's speeches, only to have them reinserted by Brzezinski. "In any case, in early 1977 Carter was determined to achieve greater stability in the U.S.-Soviet relationship primarily through progress in arms control negotiations."[59]

Carter was consistent in this goal, as he wrote to Brezhnev on November 4, 1977, that the United States' "major goal in seeking an agreement is to achieve the sharpest mutual reductions and to insure balanced forces, with adequate verification of compliance with agreements."[60] Indicative of Carter's profound desire for cooperation with the Soviet Union is Brzezinski's report in his memoirs that on April 25, 1977, there was a meeting of the American team in which they agreed on a new position for the SALT II negotiations. He commented in his journal that there was such an eagerness for an agreement that they would change the American proposals until the Soviets would be willing to consider them.[61] He and Hamilton Jordan agreed that the new position should not be changed in order not to weaken the president politically in the US and that he should reject the more conciliatory approach of Vance and Paul Warnke.[62] This account refers both to domestic politics and to the international arena. Politically, Carter was vulnerable for what appeared as a weak stand with the Soviets, and in the negotiations themselves, Vance—in Carter's name—appeared conciliatory, that is, weak.

Despite a few alternative views,[63] it seems that Carter's initial view of the relations with the Soviet Union was generally cooperative. In the Middle East, it was made candid by his administration's insistence on cochairmanship of the Geneva Conference that was planned for late 1977. The conference was first cochaired by the US and the USSR just weeks after the Yom Kippur War ended. Reconvening it—at least on protocol grounds—required repeating the cochairmanship arrangement. However, once the Soviets lost any effective role in Egypt's political considerations, it seemed obscure to both Israel and Egypt that Carter insisted on a role for the Soviets. The Americans explained that they thought this was the best way to prevent the Soviets from obstructing the peace conference. "The Secretary said the difficulty with the Soviets is that they are concerned about being left out. We have to give them a role that gets them off their insistence on functional negotiations. The Soviets want functional negotiations because they feel it gives them a role. If we can assure them that they will have a role in non-functional working groups they will feel good."[64]

But Israel and Egypt were not convinced. On October 1, 1977, the US and the USSR issued a joint statement toward the presumed conference in Geneva at the end of 1977. While Israel rejected it on the basis of the participation of the PLO, Sadat saw no merit in the Soviet participation. Shortly after, and once Israel and the US issued another statement that in fact voided the US-Soviet statement, Sadat decided to desert the Geneva track and preferred a direct dialogue with Israel, starting with a stunning visit to Jerusalem in November 1977. This visit transformed the Israeli-Egyptian peace process. This initially left the Americans stunned for a while—until Israel and Egypt asked the US to provide its good offices and its leverage to their negotiations—and the Soviets angry, but out of the cycle. Thus, the US became the sole broker of the peace process, and the Soviets were excluded from it.[65]

Brzezinski describes the disagreement within the administration over Presidential Directive (PD) 18 of August 24, 1977,[66] which was based on Presidential Review Memorandum (PRM) 10. PD 18 "directed that we maintain a strategic posture of 'essential equivalence'; that we reaffirm our NATO strategy, namely a forward defense in Europe, and the maintaining of a 'deployment force of light divisions with strategic mobility' for global contingencies, particularly in the Persian Gulf region and Korea." He adds that "the interagency debate over the PD-18 draft revealed a sharp dispute within the Administration about the implications of PRM-10," where one side wanted to limit the US strategic forces to the minimum needed to assure destruction and considered reducing forces in Europe and Korea, whereas Brzezinski himself and others emphasized "the momentum of the oil-rich region around the Persian Gulf, and the growing Soviet projection of power in Africa, Southeast Asia, and possibly even the Caribbean. The final version of the PD reflected NSC/Defense preferences for NATO and Korea, the NSC initiative for a Rapid Deployment Force, and a stalemate on the strategic forces issue. It left open the final policy decision on nuclear employment doctrine, subject to later analysis and study."[67]

Documents show that Vance had not always been very supportive of cooperation with the Soviets. Vance told Brezhnev and Gromyko on April 22, 1978, that Carter's foreign policy objectives were "a more peaceful world based on the reduction and control of arms; a deeper understanding with the Soviet Union; a resolution of regional conflicts; and restraint on the part of the major powers."[68] Nevertheless, Vance told Gromyko on May 31, 1978, in response to the latter's complaint that there is a sudden "anti-Soviet propaganda" in the US, that there was "very deep concern . . . over the fact that during the last several years the Soviet Union had been building up its military forces." The concern was that the buildup in Europe was beyond the needs of deterrence. Vance told Gromyko that Soviet military expenditures were rising consistently during the previous decade while the American expenses were stable.[69]

Gromyko denied any Soviet buildup and asked what the US wanted. Vance replied that the US "did not want to return to a period of tensions and confrontations." He specified that the US sought progress on SALT, MBFR (Mutual and Balanced Force Reductions), and other arms limitations, reaching "a better understanding that détente had to be a two-way street," and improving cultural, scientific, and trade exchanges.[70]

Carter's initial strategy as described above is defensive liberal, emphasizing liberal causes like human rights but not attempting to promote them forcefully; while the policy focuses on cooperation and multilateral actions. Secretary Vance supported this and served as its prominent advocate. National Security Advisor Brzezinski was his opponent. Vance tried to negotiate a comprehensive arms control deal that Carter desired, but the Soviets rejected it, only to accept a more phased method of reaching a more comprehensive deal a few months later.[71]

The Alternative Grand Strategies

While Carter and Vance were promoting their defensive liberal strategy of cooperation in the management of the international system and an attempt to reach an agreement on reducing nuclear weapons, there were at least two alternatives in foreign policy cycles. Both appear to derive from the same source: distrust in the Soviets. Unlike Carter and Vance who thought that the Soviet Union could be convinced to join their call for nuclear weapons reductions, Brzezinski was offering a realist reading of the Soviets, by which they were not expected to cooperate at all. He played the role of the "devil's advocate," increasingly countering Vance's advice with offensive realist advice of his own to reignite American defense expenses. Brzezinski's opinion was in minority throughout the first three years of the administration.

Outside the administration the Republicans were divided into two camps, both realists: one was of the previous administration, led by former Secretary of State Henry Kissinger, former presidents Nixon and Ford, and George H. W. Bush, at the time former head of the CIA who would compete against Ronald Reagan in the 1980 primaries and serve as his vice president before succeeding him in 1989. This camp, which was the establishment of the party during the 1970s, was defensive realist (see the reference above). Kissinger, more than others, was a very active player—as a consultant—and was critical of the Carter administration on their conduct of SALT and the peace negotiations in the Middle East.

The other camp within the Republican Party was led unquestionably by former California governor and future president Ronald Reagan. They called for more assertiveness in the strategy toward the Soviet Union. Reagan criticized Ford during the latter's presidency and challenged him in 1976. He denounced the Helsinki Accords that obligated the Soviets to respect human rights in the Soviet Union and its Eastern European satellites because the accords also recognized the reality of communism controlling Eastern Europe.[72] When Ford lost the election, Reagan became the front-runner for the Republicans. He criticized the SALT I and SALT II Treaties because he did not trust the Soviets to uphold them. He thought that the US could convince the Soviets to negotiate "a legitimate reduction of nuclear weapons on both sides to the point that neither country represented a threat to the other," he wrote a supporter in July 1980.[73] Reagan said when he announced that he was running for president, on November 13, 1979, that "during a time when the Soviet Union may enjoy nuclear superiority over this country, we must never waiver in our commitment to our allies nor accept any negotiation which is not clearly in the national interest."[74]

There were two distinct philosophies regarding the Soviet Union when Carter was president. One was led by the Committee on the Present Danger (CPD), which argued that the Soviet Union was pursuing military superiority. Paul Nitze, Richard Pipes, Paul Wolfowitz, and others (called Team B, established by President Ford to take another look at evidence that conservatives argued that the CIA was underestimating) asserted that "the Soviet Union was seeking military superiority and indeed global hegemony and was exploiting détente to that end." Based on Team B's report, the CPD demanded a massive defense buildup (similar to the NSC 68 conclusions in 1950 that the CPD was established to promote back then), which would give the United States an "absolute military superiority."[75]

The opposite view was provided by the Trilateral Commission founded in 1973 by David Rockefeller. Business executives, academics, and government officials from the US, Western Europe, and Japan made up this informal network and argued that "the age of US supremacy was over" and a new era of "complex interdependency" was under way. They claimed that the Soviets had many internal problems and an outdated ideology, and that Nixon and Kissinger focused on a too narrow issue—American-Soviet relations—leaving out more important matters.[76] They argued that the Western powers needed to cooperate to promote human rights and help Third World countries meet their economic needs. This would shift the strategic view from East-West to North-South.[77]

As more and more Americans lost their faith in détente, the general adherence to détente drifted away and other views became more vocal. However, and although many of these voices were heard even before Carter assumed the presidency, he persisted with the defensive liberal grand strategy.

The Persistence of the Defensive Liberal Strategy

It is important to clarify again that the defensive liberal strategy did not come instead of détente. It changed some of the substance of SALT II, but within the framework of détente. However, this was only from the American side, whereas the Soviets persisted with the same line they had with Ford, although Carter's new issues—especially human rights—made the Soviets wary and suspicious of Carter's real intentions. Although he gave no indication that he was trying to impose his moral stance on the Soviet Union, they did not believe that he did not have this in mind. This changed the Soviet approach to the deliberations.

Vance recommended to Carter—probably in late May 1978—to accept Secretary of Defense Harold Brown's recommendation to "undertake a prudent increase in our defense spending and continue our efforts to strengthen NATO to preserve the military balance." This was to be complemented by concluding the SALT II agreement "to stabilize the strategic competition."[78] He also recommended reviewing the application of the human rights policy on the Soviet Union since he comprehended that this was counterproductive, and not "to play China off against the Soviets."[79] Vance suggested also not to link Soviet behavior in Africa to SALT that was critical to the US. This latter recommendation is significant. Vance preferred viewing any sign of Soviet offensive acts as an isolated or regional matter but not as an indication of a global strategy that required a more robust American strategy.

According to Vance, Carter had received opposite advice from Brzezinski, and combined the two lines of thought, which did not work well. Vance describes further meetings with Gromyko in which no progress was made due to human rights violations in the Soviet Union.[80] Vance attributes the Soviet hardening of positions just when it seemed that the SALT II agreement was around the corner to the normalization of the US-China relations that came in mid-December 1978, just a few days before a crucial Vance-Gromyko meeting took place in Geneva.[81] Vance specifically referred to the US-China statement on the normalization of their relations. This statement mentioned their objection to hegemony, which he explained was the Chinese code for the Soviet aspirations in Asia.

The Rising Soviet Threat

During Carter's term, in several cases, there were suspicions of Soviet buildup in Cuba, especially the placing of MiG-23 airplanes with nuclear capability. The Soviets assured the US in November 1978 that the MiG-23s were not nuclear, hence the Soviets did not break the promise from 1962.[82]

The SALT II agreement was signed in May 1979. The capability to verify that the Soviets were not violating the agreement was, however, compromised by the loss of two CIA stations in Iran with the revolution in early 1979. The administration's assurances that the recovery of these capabilities was possible long before the Soviets could conduct tests that violate the agreement were not convincing to many.[83] Then, while the Senate was discussing SALT, a Soviet brigade was discovered in Cuba.[84] SALT II was brought to a vote only after the Soviet brigade affair abated, but in late 1979, it fell victim—as Vance puts it—to an external event, the Soviet invasion of Afghanistan.[85]

In sharp contrast to Vance's attitude, Brzezinski had been much more suspicious of the Soviets and never connected to the human rights agenda in foreign policy that Carter and Vance promoted. Brzezinski argued—on the basis of the situation in Africa—that the Soviets were seeking a "selective détente" in which they would cooperate with the US where they can "cement parity relationship with the US." He assessed that the Soviets wanted to make things difficult for the US in the Third World and recommended to increase the cost of such Soviet moves.[86]

Brzezinski argues—by quoting from his journal in March 1980—that the US-Soviet relations were derailed over the Soviet/Cuban intervention in Africa which received underreaction (Carter accepted Vance and Brown's argument against sending aircraft carriers to the Horn of Africa), followed by overreaction over the Soviet brigade in Cuba. That derailed SALT and the momentum it gained, and the last nail in the coffin was the Soviet invasion of Afghanistan.[87]

The "Arc of Crisis" and the Change of Grand Strategy to Offensive Realism

Nancy Mitchell argues that Carter's problem was not that he didn't take sides with Vance or Brzezinski but that he took both sides simultaneously.[88] Vance and Brzezinski appear to support this critique of the president. But indecision of this type could last only so long as there was no hard evidence to unequivocally support either approach. All three—Carter, Vance, and Brzezinski—seem to agree that the Soviet invasion of Afghanistan was that piece of evidence that tilted the scales in Brzezinski's favor.[89] However, there is sufficient evidence that Carter's mind might have changed earlier.

Keren Yarhi-Milo analyzes the shift in Carter's grand strategy that began in 1978 with an interbureaucratic conflicting understanding of the Soviet actions. In this conflict, Secretary of State Cyrus Vance was moderate and unalarmed by the Soviet's actions, while National Security Advisor Zbigniew Brzezinski was much more alarmed and hawkish. They competed for Carter's ear in order to have him set a foreign policy that corresponded with their conflicting arguments. Carter did not take sides for quite a while, which meant that he remained loyal to the détente strategy until the Soviet invasion of Afghanistan that indicated that Brzezinski was correct.[90]

"My opinion of the Russians," Carter announced days after the invasion, "has changed most drastically in the last week [more] than even in the previous two and a half years before that."[91] Carter's foreword in an analytical edited volume of Brzezinski's worldview states that "some critics at the time [of Carter's presidency] and afterward have blamed Zbig for a revival of the cold war during this period. While it is true he was the most skeptical among my advisors regarding the conduct of the Soviet Union, I reject the idea that he somehow convinced me to retreat from détente. The actions of the Soviet

Union clearly had to be addressed."[92] Vance resigned from his position as secretary of state in late April 1980 in protest of Operation Eagle Claw, which attempted to rescue the hostages in Iran by force and that signaled his defeat to Brzezinski in foreign policy management.

The common explanation corresponds with this statement by Carter on the effect of the Soviet invasion of Afghanistan in changing his policy. But knowing that the ingredients of the tougher policy toward the Soviet Union were already in place long before the invasion, this incident appears circumstantial. We argue that the reason for the change in Carter's policy was changes in the international system, which means in this case that the US faced a new threatening environment. An alternative explanation emerges from domestic politics and highlights the political pressure on Carter from the Republican Party's right wing and its leader, Ronald Reagan. Reagan challenged incumbent President Ford in 1976 and toward 1980 was a leading presidential candidate within the party. His positions became more and more influential and pushed Carter to show more resolve than he perhaps planned to show. Hence, Carter was pushed to become tougher in order to prevent Reagan from taking over the national defense discourse. Brian Auten presents several common explanations for Carter's "conversion" (of the defense policy): The Vance-Brzezinski split (over how to read reality), an electoral gambit, and an executive-legislative bargain (in which Carter wooed prodefense legislators with harder defense policy lines in exchange for their support of his policies and preferences).[93]

Perhaps surprisingly early on, there were indications that Carter had suspicions of the Soviet intent. Carter's instructions to Vance for his trip to Moscow, April 14, 1978, were:

> It is in the interest of both countries that SALT succeed. However, I am concerned that Soviet strategy is to focus attention on SALT as proof of progress in U.S.-Soviet relations while the Soviet Union pursues its political objectives elsewhere by military means. Therefore, you should begin the discussions with a broad review of U.S.-Soviet relations, emphasizing that the U.S. seeks a détente that is increasingly comprehensive and genuinely reciprocal. Unless this happens, some of the central factors of our relationship, including SALT, will be adversely affected by the consequent deterioration in the political environment. It is for this reason that you should stress that détente cannot be compartmentalized and that mutual restraint lies at the core of a détente relationship.[94]

A sense of the deep Soviet distrust of Carter was delivered approximately at the same time, in April 1978, in a memo from CIA Director Stansfield Turner to Brzezinski: "Kirilenko [Andrei Kirilenko, member of the Politburo and

secretariat of the Communist Party of the Soviet Union] insisted [to whom is
unclear] that the Soviet Government does not trust any of the statements or
declarations made to them privately or publicly by President Carter, largely
because of the influence of Brzezinski. The Kremlin simply does not believe
anything Carter says and has no confidence in whatever negotiations the US
might enter into vis-à-vis the USSR."[95]

Similar to the argument made by Auten in *Carter's Conversion*, we do not
accept the common arguments that Carter changed his policy toward the
Soviet Union due to the gradual victory of Brzezinski over Vance (which was
based on different philosophies, institutional competition, or closeness to
Carter), or that it occurred due to public opinion pressures following the rise
of the conservative right.[96] Another possibility is that Carter made a bargain
with legislators, which included strengthening the defense policy in return
for support for SALT II.[97] The international systemic explanation for Carter's
conversion is the "geopolitical shocks" of 1979 (Iran and Afghanistan, Angola, the Horn of Africa), though Auten claims that the conversion came before the "shocks," not as their consequence.[98]

Secretary of Defense Harold Brown explained to reporters in the first
week of Carter's term that the US and USSR were in "rough parity." However,
intelligence assessments varied widely on Soviet future programs.[99] Auten
explains that while Carter cut the nuclear armament budget significantly in
1977, he increased the investment in conventional forces, especially NATO
forces. In winter 1977–78, many referred to the 1979 budget as the "NATO
budget."[100]

During the first half of 1979, two budget packages were discussed, one was
the FY1980 budget (submitted in January 1979) and the other was a supple-
mental to FY1979. Both were prepared by the Carter administration, and both
contained a request for additional money for strategic and theater nuclear
systems.[101] Auten maintains that the conversion came to fruition once the
two budgets were assessed. He further demonstrates that the actual conversion, from the winter of 1978–79 to June 1979, was made by the hardening of
the administration's existing defense stance. This happened because of shifts
in strategic thought, allied cooperation in theater nuclear forces (TNF) and
the end of the SALT II process and the beginning of the SALT III process.[102]

The defense establishment, according to Yarhi-Milo, was worried about
the rapid improvement in the Soviet nuclear counterforce capability. "In
mid-1979, the National Security Council (NSC) cautioned that the strategic
nuclear balance was deteriorating faster than the United States had expected
two years earlier, and would get worse into the early 1980s."[103] Soviet behavior
indicated that they were becoming aggressive. On the one hand, the Sovi-

ets signed the SALT II Treaty in June 1979 that put a limit of 2,250 delivery vehicles of strategic forces, but it also intervened in twenty-six crises in the world during 1975–80. These interventions were not only by proxy (still most of the interventions) but also direct use of force, namely, in Ethiopia and Afghanistan.[104]

In February–March 1978, the clash between Brzezinski and Vance on the interpretation of the Soviet moves in Ethiopia and elsewhere was at a peak. Brzezinski argued that the Soviets had a "larger design" in mind,[105] while Vance saw the Soviet actions in Africa as merely opportunism.[106] When Carter appeared to lean toward Brzezinski's view, Vance requested a formal review of the policy to the USSR.

Things seemed to cool down for a while, but the invasion of Afghanistan ultimately convinced Carter that Brzezinski was correct. He saw the move as a betrayal of his trust and of promises that Brezhnev gave him in Vienna in June that year. He indicated that the Soviet aggression was putting détente into question, made it impossible to pass the SALT II Treaty through Senate, and signaled that the Soviets "were not to be trusted."[107] Vance never accepted this view of the Soviets. Yarhi-Milo argues that the improving Soviet capabilities are not mentioned at all in records as the reason to the change in the view of the Soviets, and that the Soviet behavior in the Horn of Africa and in Afghanistan created very different reactions from Carter himself, while Vance and Brzezinski held consistent and opposite views.[108]

Brzezinski assessed at a National Security Council meeting with Carter, Brown, and Vance that the Soviets were getting stronger than the Americans due to their increased investment in military power. He and Brown argued that the Soviets would have the lead in the early 1980s. Brown said that "by 1985 the Soviets would have greater strength in almost every military category," no matter what the US would do.[109]

On May 29, 1979, Brzezinski wrote in a memo to Carter titled "Summit Strategy" (before the summit with Brezhnev) that "despite the successful completion of SALT II, U.S.-Soviet relations are clearly strained by a number of conflicting interests." He mentioned that "the United States is increasingly skeptical of Soviet intentions because of the momentum of its military programs and its intervention in the Third World."[110] He made the point that previously Soviet capabilities were limited therefore the US could discount the intentions, whereas at that point (1979) their capabilities were such that even benign intentions were suspicious.[111] This seems critical to the explanation of the shift from defensive liberalism to offensive realism. As long as the Carter administration did not perceive the Soviet capabilities as threatening to alter the balance between the superpowers, the shift was not imminent. But once they were perceived as threatening to allow the Soviets to forcefully change the balance (while the US either lacked counterforce or was developing one), the strategy toward the Soviet Union had to change. While the new strategy could have been more defensive (that is, focusing on deterring the Soviets from altering the balance by force), the administration preferred a more ambitious goal of obtaining capabilities that would resume its advantage.

Brzezinski admitted that the mistrust was mutual, specifically since the SALT II Treaty ratification in the Senate was uncertain. It seems that the sources of distrust were very different: the Americans were increasingly concerned with the improving Soviet capabilities, whereas the Soviets were worried about Carter's political capability to pass the treaty in the legislature.

Brzezinski suggested telling the Soviets during the summit that the US wishes to join with the Soviets "in containing the nuclear arms race through further cuts in SALT II and more ambitious cuts in SALT III" and to see the USSR as a partner in dealing with emerging global problems. However, the American delegates should warn that Soviet "insensitivity" to American interests in the Middle East, Southern Africa, Vietnam, and Cuba will produce a strong American reaction. He added, "Soviet military buildup, both strategic and conventional, has gone beyond the point of legitimate defense needs, and is generating a genuine threat to the United States and its principal Allies—and unless the Soviet side shows restraint, the West, with the United States in the lead, will undertake major, comprehensive, and matching efforts."[112] Means of verification were vital to SALT II, and as in the past, the Soviets refused to permit the verification systems the US insisted on. The National Security Council decided to develop the maximum missile that was allowed under the SALT II Treaty.

After the Vienna Summit, as the administration was pushing for Senate ratification of the SALT II Treaty, it also wanted to increase defense expenses. According to Brzezinski, Carter was favorable to this effort based on the experience of dealing with the Soviets and the growing suspicion of their intentions and the threat they posed by their rising military capabilities and greater global presence. Brzezinski's own pressure via memorandums and NSC meetings also had some influence.[113] Meanwhile, Brzezinski reports, the Soviets continued building up their military presence in Vietnam and increased their support of Vietnam's aggression against Cambodia.[114]

And yet, it was the Soviet invasion of Afghanistan that served as the watershed, according to Brzezinski. He emphasizes the fact that Carter now saw the wide implications of the crisis, unlike the Soviet brigade in Cuba from the previous year that Carter saw as an isolated event.[115] The invasion was indeed the first time the Soviets used force outside the sphere of influence the Americans recognized in the late 1940s.

Following the invasion to Afghanistan, on December 29, 1979, Carter sent Brezhnev a message through the hotline and in a cable that Warren Christopher (acting secretary of state) sent to the embassy in Moscow. Carter's message was clear: "I want to insure you that you have fully weighed the ramifications of the Soviet actions in Afghanistan, which we regard as a clear threat to the peace. You should understand that these actions could mark a fundamental and long-lasting turning point in our relations."[116]

Leffler accuses Brezhnev of the termination of détente. He writes that until the invasion of Afghanistan both he and Carter were expressing their interest in détente, but that Brezhnev's decision to invade Afghanistan was the end of these decade-long relations. Carter wrote to Brezhnev on December 28, 1979, that the invasion breached international peace, violated the principles of détente, and flouted "all the accepted norms of international conduct." Carter was specific in saying that intervening in a nonaligned nation "represents an unsettling, dangerous and new stage in your use of military forces. . . . Unless you draw back from your present course of action, this will inevitably jeopardize the course of U.S.-Soviet relations throughout the world."[117] Brezhnev asked to continue détente and argued that the Soviet troops were in Afghanistan only temporarily. Carter—knowing that the Senate would not vote in favor of SALT II—asked the Senate to suspend the procedure of ratifying it. He also reduced diplomatic connections, cut trade, placed an embargo on grain sales, and limited Soviet fishing rights off US shores. A while later he also decided to boycott the Summer Olympic Games in Moscow. In addition, he boosted defense appropriations and accelerated the development of the rapid deployment force (RDF). Based on the fear that Brzezinski expressed that the Soviet invasion of Afghanistan would permit them to invade Pakistan and access blue water, Carter increased military assistance to Pakistan.[118] However, the Carter administration never regained Pakistan's trust after years of sanctions over Islamabad's poor human rights record and the nuclear program.

The China card was played as early as December 1978. The normalization of relations—with the price tag of eliminating any formal relations with Taiwan and canceling the defense alliance with it—was important to China and the US. It was a major blow to the Soviets, although China was already not aligned to it. Apparently, Carter was pushed by Reagan and other Republican leaders who denounced the abandonment of Taiwan and was eventually forced (in April 1979) to sign the Taiwan Relations Act, which was passed with an overwhelming majority in Congress. The act was actually a modified version of the Mutual Defense Treaty that Carter canceled.[119]

Brzezinski argued that there was an "arc of crisis" from North Africa to South Asia, which the Soviets were attempting to bring into their orbit by taking advantage of political and social circumstances. At the center of the "arc" was the Middle East with its oil reserves that were second to none in material significance. These oil reserves made the Middle East crucial for the global balance of power. Most of the crises that brought down the détente were within the "arc," as Carter would eventually understand.[120]

The crises in the Horn of Africa, Iran, and Afghanistan—all across the "arc"—pushed Carter to accept Brzezinski's arguments instead of those provided by Vance (who saw the crisis in the Horn of Africa as a regional problem, not a part of the superpower conflict). The Soviet invasion of Afghanistan was the end of détente for the US. In January 1980 the Carter Doctrine was in place, even though the president did not like the label. The doctrine was formed for a single most important region—the Middle East—which seemed under growing Soviet pressure, which jeopardized the flow of oil to the west, but also appeared to give the Soviets a greater opening to the Indian Ocean and blue water in general. The doctrine was spelled out this way: "Let our position be absolutely clear: An attempt by any outside force to gain control of the Persian Gulf region will be regarded as an assault on the vital interests of the United States of America, and such an assault will be repelled by any means necessary, including military force."[121] Commerce with the Soviet Union was reduced, the Summer Olympic Games were boycotted, the SALT II Treaty was withdrawn from the Senate, the reinforcement of the US military forces that began in 1979 was intensified, and the US renewed (or actually tried to renew) its alliance with Pakistan. The change in America's grand strategy was "the result of a prudent (albeit late) change in the assessment of the Soviet Union's military power, and of its power-projection capabilities and potential possession of strategic geography relative to that of the United States."[122]

Surprisingly, Secretary of State Edmund Muskie told Andrei Gromyko in New York on September 25, 1980, that the administration would seek ratification of SALT II "early next year or before; it was a long shot but worth the effort."[123] He added, "On the question of equality or equivalence, the US is committed to it. We can't have Arms Control on any other basis. This is common sense—though not to all. Some believe in superiority but this is impossible."[124] This seems very different from the distrustful statements of Moscow from Washington in the previous year, but it is evident that superiority was impossible. Hence, the US was perhaps seeking a more defensive realist approach than it sought at the beginning of 1980.

Presidential Directive 59, "Nuclear Weapons Employment Policy," was issued on July 25, 1980. Gromyko expressed concern over it, as it seemed to indicate that "the Americans are beginning to think about the acceptability—or the inevitability—of nuclear war. There is a military fever with civilians scaring the military and the military scaring the Administration. This really worries the Soviet Union and we cannot fail to reach the conclusion that the US is preparing for the first strike. If the Soviet Union did the same thing, nuclear war would become inevitable."[125]

Muskie agreed the question was legitimate and stated that "the US had no intention of acquiring a first-strike capability and didn't believe the Soviets did either. In any event, strategic capabilities are determined by weapons, not by doctrine alone." "The purpose of the new US doctrine," he added, "was to cover the full range of deterrents. PD 59 succeeds NSDM 242 issued at the end of the Ford Administration. It reflects an evolutionary change from this doctrine, not a sharp departure."[126]

Conclusion

Carter's change of attitude from his initial defensive liberalism to offensive realism was the result of his understanding that the Soviets were attempting to change the status quo. This understanding was not merely perceptual, but was based on an understanding that the Soviets had possessed material power that allowed them to be more robust than before. The military aspects of changing the grand strategy began in 1978, and the change of the grand strategy itself came through once the Soviets invaded Afghanistan. This was dramatic because it was the first time that the Soviets invaded a non–Warsaw Pact country in full force, understood as an attempt to break out of its sphere of influence/dominance. The change in grand strategy was due to material changes that the US identified. This was reflected in the domestic arena with Carter's shift toward Brzezinski at the expense of Vance. It does not seem that domestic politics—most important, the rise of the conservative right, led by Ronald Reagan—was the reason for the change, however. The change in grand strategy was a response to a rising threat—manifested most dramatically in the invasion of Afghanistan—posed by a seemingly more militarily capable Soviet Union, which showed its readiness to cross an internationally recognized boundary. As noted in chapter 2, crossing offensively international boundaries signals a high level of threat even if it happens in remote regions.

Moreover, changes in the international system can influence not only the changes in grand strategy but also domestic politics Thus, the outcome of the 1980 election seems to be at least partly affected by this changing external

environment. Reagan, a wholeheartedly offensive realist—unlike Carter—
defeated him in 1980 and continued and even enhanced Carter's new strategy
during his first term. Offensive realism seemed to be better aligned for at least
a while with the international system. Only when this system changed in the
mid-1980s did Reagan change his strategy, from offensive to defensive realism. This change will be discussed in the next chapter.

6

Reagan's Turn to the Second Détente

This chapter highlights the changes in American grand strategy in relation to changes in the international environment in the second term of President Ronald Reagan. We'll start with a short discussion of the 1980 election of Reagan as a reflection of how the international system may affect domestic debates. Reagan was elected as a well-known hawk—in accordance with the perception of a high-threat environment in that period, which supposedly called for an offensive realist administration.

Later in his presidency, Reagan's strategy would change in response to changes in the international environment—this time in a more defensive realist direction following the 1985 rise of the moderate Gorbachev and accordingly the declining threat to the US. Thus, in both the cases of Carter and Reagan, US grand strategy changed during the presidential term itself—even if in opposite directions—in response to major systemic changes. The initial offensive realist strategy was easy for Reagan and his team to continue and intensify. In contrast, the shift back to a defensive realist strategy ("the second détente") under Reagan's second term was apparently uneasy for his administration and raised internal tensions to the surface.

In this chapter, we discuss Reagan's initial view of the Soviet Union that informed his administration's grand strategy and its alteration in his second term. We begin with a brief overview of key actors in his administration who influenced his views, some more than others, and we detect their clashes as their relative weight in the administration changed. Some of these figures certainly fit Reagan's initial views but not his changed views, while others were somewhat less in line with the initial strategy and later played a more constructive role when Reagan moderated.

We demonstrate how Reagan's strategy changed due to his understanding that the Soviet Union was no longer posing a major threat to the United States. This happened when Mikhail Gorbachev became the leader of the Soviet Union in 1985, although there are strong indications that Reagan's thinking began changing earlier. In any case, the major change in the US-Soviet relations came with the Intermediate-Range Nuclear Forces (INF) Agreement in 1987, but this was merely the fruit of the moderate strategy that sought such an agreement since 1985.

The 1980 Election

A key selector among the contending approaches, especially in a democracy, is elections. Our model allows for presidents to come to office with their own set of beliefs (like President Carter with his moderate idealistic-liberal views), especially when no dramatic changes took place internationally before the elections. In the case of Carter's election, the more dramatic events were related to domestic politics—the Watergate affair and its aftermath. In the case of Carter, the change in grand strategy occurred in response to systemic changes during his term in office. Election outcomes might, however, be affected by major changes in the international system and bring to office a president whose views are more consistent with the international changes—such as the election of Reagan following the major international changes in the late 1970s.[1]

With the Iran hostage crisis exactly one year old on election day and about eleven months since the Soviet invasion of Afghanistan, Carter was viewed by many as weak on foreign policy. Carter's emphasis on strengthening security and spending more on defense was in line with the public sentiment, Mason notes, but "many believed that he did not—exemplifying the depth of the perception that he was weak on defense."[2] A New York Times exit poll "found that a majority of respondents favored a tougher line against the Soviet Union, even if increasing the risk of war; of this group, 70 percent voted for Ronald Reagan, while Carter had a 64 percent share of the minority that disagreed."[3]

As a well-known offensive realist, the 1980 election of Reagan seemed very appropriate in relation to the rising threat posed by the Soviet Union, especially following the 1979 invasion of Afghanistan. Given his hard-line views, Reagan's election to president in a time that the US pursued preponderance in response to the growing external threat (a policy that started under Carter) seemed to better fit the external circumstances than a second term of Jimmy Carter who changed his strategic view into an offensive realist only late in the game. Reagan seemed to be the more "original" offensive realist and thus seemed to better fit the changing environment.

Accordingly, a key causal mechanism refers to the "second image reversed," namely, the effects of the international system on domestic politics.[4] In this case, we mean that external systemic conditions affect the results of internal struggles among the supporters of the various security approaches. The external environment brokers the debates among the competing perspectives and decides the winner.

REAGAN'S TEAM

Reagan's team during his two terms was not coherent. Vice President George H. W. Bush was a defensive realist like his former bosses, Presidents Nixon and Ford, as well as Kissinger and Brent Scowcroft. Bush was part of the Republican Party's establishment, strikingly different from Reagan himself and the secretaries of state and defense, Alexander Haig and Caspar Weinberger, all three offensive realists. This difference would show very clearly when Bush replaced Reagan in 1989, although by then the differences between them narrowed following the change in Reagan's position. But while serving as vice president, he was loyal but also quite marginal in the strategy formation process.

Reagan's two secretaries of state, Alexander Haig in the first eighteen months and after that George Shultz, were complete opposites. General Haig was an offensive realist who supported wholeheartedly Reagan's hard-line stance toward the Soviets and divided the world between friends and foes. Dr. Shultz, an economist, was more moderate and in some respects, closer to Bush in his worldview, after serving himself in the administrations of Nixon and Ford, though with minimum contact with foreign affairs. Haig's replacement with Shultz was quite early and apparently had nothing to do with the shift in Reagan's strategy toward the Soviet Union.[5] Nevertheless, Shultz was the secretary of state when the shift occurred, and he had significant influence on the president, and had Reagan's confidence.

Reagan also had two secretaries of defense. Caspar Weinberger was a friend of Reagan and served for the first six years, until he resigned and was replaced by Frank Carlucci.[6] Weinberger, like Haig, fully accepted Reagan's initial offensive realist view and in fact oversaw a major part of it—the military buildup. Once Haig was replaced, Weinberger was the senior advisor to Reagan, until Shultz settled in. However, Weinberger never changed his view and remained an adamant hard-liner while Reagan himself changed his view and approach. At that time, and due to the changing strategy, Weinberger lost most of his influence to Shultz. Toward the end of Reagan's first term, Weinberger tried to push Shultz out of office, and Shultz indeed offered to resign several times due to his ongoing conflict with Weinberger. Shultz was in favor of forceful intervention, although he was accommodative and even conciliatory toward the Soviet Union. In contrast, Weinberger was against military interventions such as in Lebanon but was a hard-liner toward the Soviets. But Reagan actually supported Shultz and forced Weinberger to play along, telling him (and writing in his diary) that Shultz was implementing his policy correctly. Carlucci's short term came long after the alteration of policy, therefore his role will not be discussed.

The third side in the foreign policy advisory team is the national security advisor, sitting at the White House. Unlike his predecessors Nixon, Ford, and Carter, Reagan did not manage to keep a dominant national security advisor. In fact, he had six advisors, on average one every sixteen months, which implies that each one had limited and short-lived influence on Reagan's policies, especially compared with the dominant and veteran secretaries of state and defense. This is true even though several of them were close to Reagan, such as Richard Allen and his successor William ("Judge") Clark. Therefore, if in Carter's administration the conflicting worldviews were of Secretary Vance and National Security Advisor Brzezinski (while Secretary of Defense Harold Brown was clearly a secondary figure), in Reagan's administration the major rivals were Weinberger and Shultz. Reagan began in seeming harmony with Weinberger's views, but the new strategy that Reagan pursued caused a rift between them and Reagan worked more closely with Shultz.

Reagan's Approach

While it is clear that Reagan ordered a massive military buildup in order to counterbalance the apparent Soviet advantage,[7] it is also important to bear in mind that Reagan wanted to strike a deal with the Soviet Union. He wanted to negotiate with them on arms reductions (he rejected the logic of SALT, and in fact he was a nuclear abolitionist no less than Carter)[8] but from a position of strength, which meant that before negotiating, the US had to retake the lead and in fact have a decisive advantage.[9]

In 1982, Reagan wrote in his diary critically against those who "don't think any approach should be made to the Soviets. I think I'm hard-line & will never appease but I do want to try & let them see there is a better world if they'll show *by deed* they want to get along with the free world."[10] Hal Brands makes the point that from the start Reagan increased defense spending while also calling for negotiations on arms reductions. However, Brands also points out that Reagan wanted the agreement to favor American interests—hence his willingness to negotiate was incomplete—and that could be advanced if the US already came with a strategic advantage.[11] Francis Marlo specifies three core elements in the dialogue with the Soviets: arms control, human rights, and Soviet international behavior.[12] For Reagan, "arms control agreements could not be an end in themselves but a single component of a much broader effort to enhance U.S. security."[13] The human rights aspect was part of the US strategy, but it never blocked the chances of reaching power-based understandings with the Soviets.

As Brands demonstrates, Reagan's strategy worked only partly. He seemed credible to the Soviets with his military buildup (he did not conceal that it was structured to break the Soviet Union's economic back) to the point they expressed fear that the US might succeed at gaining superiority. Nonetheless, Reagan was unsuccessful in credibly passing to the other side his interest in sincere negotiations on arms reduction.[14] In order to fix that and build trust with Moscow, Reagan toned down his rhetoric regarding the Soviet Union.[15] In his second term, Reagan tried to convince Gorbachev that it was both nec- essary *and* desirable to reach an accommodation.[16] Reagan wrote: "We must always remember our main goal and [Gorbachev's] need to show his strength to the Soviet gang back in the Kremlin."[17]

Barbara Farnham connects this change in Reagan's approach to his strik- ing understanding in November 1983—after Able Archer 83—that the Soviet Union might perceive *American* moves as threatening; ever since, he took that into consideration.[18] However, she attributes the change not to Reagan's altered perception of the Soviet Union, which did not happen so early, but to his view of the nuclear threat that became real in his mind due to a se- ries of incidents at that time.[19] This is similar to Kennedy's realization after the Cuban missile crisis that an inadvertent nuclear war is a common threat to the USSR and the US. This might have been a necessary condition for a change in the grand strategy toward reaching arms control agreements, but it was not sufficient for a major change in the strategy without also a major change in the Kremlin leadership. In other words, Reagan's perception of the Soviet threat might have begun changing even before Gorbachev took power in Moscow. The latter event, however, reinforced Reagan's perception, while also adding credibility to it.

Lawrence Freedman points out that the Soviet invasion of Afghanistan that was the turning point for Carter, was only a "propaganda point, dem- onstrating Soviet ruthlessness" for Reagan and his administration.[20] Rea- gan merely followed Carter's policy on Afghanistan, but it seems to have

informed his view of the Soviets, at least publicly. The ongoing Soviet occupation of Afghanistan overshadowed perhaps other signals that Reagan could
lean on to alter his initial strategy, namely, the relative nuclear stability in the
early 1980s and the moderate Soviet response to the crisis in Poland in 1981.[21]
Nevertheless, the moderate response to the crisis in Poland was probably a
result of a warning that Secretary of State Haig issued as soon as he took
office in a letter to his Soviet counterpart.[22]

The Strategy Change

The important question is *when* did the strategy change? There are several
possible dates in the literature. The earliest is 1983. According to Don Oberdorfer, the policy toward the Soviet Union began changing as early as February 1983, when Reagan told Shultz that he wanted to visit the Soviet Union
while eventually he accepted a secret meeting with Dobrynin in the White
House, in which he challenged the Soviet ambassador on a humanitarian issue (Pentecostals that took refuge in the American embassy in Moscow since
1978), on which the Soviets eventually agreed to look favorably (and allowed
them to leave the Soviet Union).[23]

Others point to early 1984 as Reagan's turning point. Jack Matlock, who
was in Reagan's White House the NSC senior director for European and Soviet affairs (1983–86) and then ambassador to Moscow (1987–91), pinpoints
Reagan's speech in January 1984 as the most definite outlining of his strategy
toward the Soviet Union (which for the first time laid out the whole concept
of negotiations with the Soviets to the public). He also emphasizes that while
many of Reagan's critics—some of whom also criticized Shultz and wanted
him to be replaced—thought that the speech was merely a reelection campaign gimmick, after being reelected, Reagan instructed Shultz to put the
plan for negotiations in motion with full speed.[24] The same position is offered
by Beth A. Fischer,[25] and by Norman A. Graebner, Richard Dean Burns, and
Joseph M. Siracusa, who point to several conciliatory statements that Reagan
made toward the Soviets. In the State of the Union Address, he mentioned
that Americans and Soviets never faced each other in war, "and if we Americans have our way, they never will." On April 6, at Georgetown, he said that
the American military buildup granted the US the capacity to negotiate successfully.[26] Brands quotes Reagan from late 1984 telling the National Security
Planning Group that "we can build on the Soviet preoccupation with defending the homeland by making clear that we have no intention of starting a
nuclear war." And in connection with SDI he said, "We have no objections to
their having defenses, but we have to look at defenses for ourselves."[27]

In his meeting with Soviet Foreign Minister Andrei Gromyko at the White House in September 1984, Reagan stated that the United States respected the Soviet Union's status as a "superpower" and had no wish to change its social system; it did not seek military superiority over the Soviet Union but wanted to deal with Moscow as an equal.[28] Regarding arms control, Reagan continued, he wanted to resume the talks and promised to be flexible if the Soviets returned to the table.[29] This statement suits a defensive realist strategy, but until Mikhail Gorbachev took over in Moscow, Reagan could not seriously implement it. Reagan said sarcastically after Konstantin Chernenko's death, the third chairman of the Communist Party to die in three years, "How am I supposed to get anyplace with the Russians if they keep dying on me?"[30]

The Gorbachev Effect

It seems that Reagan had changed the strategy and sought negotiations on arms reduction with the Soviets long before Gorbachev became the Soviet leader, and it so happened that until Gorbachev assumed the leadership in March 1985, Reagan found no partner. What Gorbachev's rise to power really did was to reduce the sense of threat the Soviet Union posed to the US. This made the actual change of the American grand strategy possible. More specifically, the realization that there was a real partner in the Kremlin enabled the shift in the strategy.

Thus, Farnham concludes that Reagan understood that American behavior can help change Soviet behavior. For instance, his conciliatory policies allowed Gorbachev to gain the Politburo's support for his own initiatives, while if Reagan would retain the previous approach, the Politburo would prevent Gorbachev from promoting his own conciliatory policies.[31] In other words, Reagan understood that Gorbachev also had a domestic struggle to conduct against the old-guard establishment and that by toning down the public hostility he could facilitate a change in the Soviet policy toward a more accommodative position as was his objective. The Soviet Union's "black box" opened up with Gorbachev who may have been a devoted communist but was different from any other previous leader the Soviets had. Reagan already received indications about his different nature from British Prime Minister Margaret Thatcher and Secretary Shultz.[32]

Matlock notes that the cooling down of the tensions began in early 1985 with the Shultz-Gromyko talks in Geneva, before Gorbachev came to power in Moscow.[33] But, he emphasizes, the Soviet policies had not changed until Gorbachev came to power. The Soviets were eager to discuss arms control but not much more. The US, for its part, was eager to get back to negotiations.[34] Matlock argues that when Chernenko died and Gorbachev replaced him, the US had four components for its policy framework: the arms race, the use of arms in Third World countries, protecting human rights, and raising the Iron Curtain. The latter two were direct challenges to the Soviet system.[35]

Since assuming chairmanship of the Soviet Communist Party, Gorbachev argued that the two superpowers needed to accept the idea of strategic parity, and the result would be that they could reach an understanding on the amount of arms each of them believed sufficient for relative security.[36] Shultz and Alexander Bessmertnykh (who held several senior positions in the Soviet foreign ministry and eventually replaced Shevardnadze in 1991 as foreign minister) said in an interview in 1993 that the Geneva Summit began the new relationship because Reagan and Gorbachev said that the two superpowers would not seek superiority over one another.[37] The leaders accepted strategic parity, and apparently, although there were still many obstacles, the superpowers were on a track of restabilizing their relations.

On September 17, 1985, Reagan stated: "In spite of some of the misinformation that has been spread around, the United States is still well behind the Soviet Union in literally every kind of offensive weapon, both conventional and in the strategic weapons."[38] Reagan said this while he was already engaging the new Soviet leader Gorbachev to restart negotiations for removing the nuclear threat. Reagan and Gorbachev shared the desire to rid the world of this mortal danger.

On September 27, 1985, Soviet Foreign Minister Shevardnadze proposed to Reagan a reduction of long-range nuclear arsenals by both superpowers by 50 percent. Kennan raised this proposal in a speech in 1981, but at that time it was unrealistic. Four years later, once put on the table in Gorbachev's letter to Reagan that Shevardnadze carried, it became the shared goal of the two superpowers.[39] Nevertheless, when implemented, the arsenals were reduced by much less than 50 percent. The initial Soviet proposal included a definition of strategic arms that put the US at a disadvantage, but the greater problem was Gorbachev's condition that Reagan would accept a total ban on "space attack weapons," which referred to the SDI.[40] In October 1985, while visiting in Paris, Gorbachev stated a change in the Soviet foreign policy, speaking of "reasonable sufficiency" in armaments, instead of Brezhnev's "equal security," meaning that the Soviets would be as powerful as all their potential rivals combined. He also made the point that he sought "peaceful coexistence."[41]

The Geneva Summit of November 1985 ended in a joint statement that included an agreement that "a nuclear war cannot be won and must never be fought," that war should never break out between the US and the Soviet Union, and that "they will not seek to achieve military superiority."[42] Matlock points out that at Geneva "Gorbachev had agreed to a 50 percent reduction of strategic nuclear weapons, a prime American goal," and compared it to Gromyko's prompt rejection of Vance's proposal in 1977 for 'deep cuts' that amounted to 35 percent.[43] This was a significant change in Soviet strategy, which opened the way for the United States to change its own strategy.

Reagan, who consistently objected to all arms control agreements with the Soviets since the 1950s, endorsed the idea of an arms control treaty once he met Gorbachev.[44] For his part, Gorbachev concluded that with all the domestic and international troubles the Soviet Union faced, it was best to reduce or even eliminate the nuclear arsenal.[45] He knew that the Soviets would never gain nuclear supremacy while the effort would demand greater costs—human and material—than the Soviets could afford.[46]

Gorbachev proposed on January 15, 1986, to reduce the nuclear arsenals by 50 percent by the year 2000. Reagan and Shultz welcomed the proposal, and unlike previous Soviet statements on the issue that were rejected as propaganda, this statement appeared serious with its detailed phases, the first of which was to eliminate all American and Soviet intermediate-range missiles in Europe. Unlike past statements, Gorbachev's plan excluded British and French missiles, leaving a Western advantage intact. Moreover, Oberdorfer emphasizes, Gorbachev did not demand that the US halt the research of the SDI (but he did mention development, testing, and deployment).[47]

The Chernobyl disaster of April 26, 1986, led Gorbachev to push even harder on reducing nuclear weapons and concluded that the Soviet Union had enough nuclear weapons and should not produce any more. Although a summit was scheduled for 1987 in the US, Gorbachev pleaded for an earlier meeting in Europe. His letter to Reagan from September 15, 1986, included many concessions: he offered to restrict the SDI research to laboratories for fifteen years, would consider American on-site inspections in the Soviet Union, and would not include the British and French nuclear forces in the agreement.[48] Shultz recommended that Reagan accepted the invitation to a summit.

According to Matlock, Reagan came to the Reykjavik Summit in October 1986 with a clear idea of what he wanted: "an understanding regarding one or two major agreements that would permit Gorbachev to come to the United States for a full-fledged summit. He had concluded that INF (Intermediate Nuclear Forces) presented the most likely subject for an arms control agreement and was willing to accept several variants of a compromise as the first step toward eliminating this class of weapons. He also hoped to settle on a framework for a strategic arms agreement if Gorbachev dropped the linkage with SDI and agreed to reduce his heavy ICBMs by 50 percent. In addition, he came with a radical proposal, already mentioned in his correspondence, to eliminate and ban all offensive ballistic missiles before strategic defenses, if found feasible, could be deployed."[49]

In Reykjavik, Gorbachev accepted Reagan's offer to eliminate all nuclear warheads by the year 2000, which surprised the Americans. But the condition was that Reagan would agree to limit the SDI research to "laboratories" for at least five years. Reagan refused and left.[50] But one significant concession that Gorbachev made did not go unnoticed: he accepted for the first time on-site inspections that were one of the major sources of suspicion and distrust in previous agreements.[51] This Soviet concession became problematic for the US itself when the implementation required on-site inspections also in the US.[52] Brands noted regarding the Reykjavik Summit that although there was no agreement, both leaders noticed how close they actually were to cutting a significant deal, and that opened the way for actual success in the remaining time Reagan and Gorbachev were their countries' leaders.[53]

Matlock reports that in April 1987, just days before he became the US ambassador to Moscow, Gorbachev announced that he decided to drop the linkage between the INF agreement and the SDI.[54] He attributes the change in Gorbachev's position to Margaret Thatcher's visit to Moscow in March 1987 during which she explained that the West still saw the Soviets as a military threat due to its commitment to the Brezhnev Doctrine.[55]

The most significant milestone of Reagan's conversion into a defensive realist was the INF treaty he signed with Gorbachev in Washington on December 8, 1987, which replaced the language of "arms control" with "arms reduction," as Reagan emphasized.[56] Although the treaty covered only 4 percent of the superpowers' nuclear power, it "launched the process of arms reductions."[57] Whereas this agreement did not change Reagan's insistence on the SDI program, Gorbachev signed it and in fact conceded more missiles and far more warheads that would be dismantled than Reagan did.[58] Archie Brown makes the point that

> it is not so much the hard-line policies of Reagan's first term that ended the Cold War, but his willingness to enter into serious negotiations and treat the Soviet leader more as a partner than an enemy (the Reagan of 1985–1988) that played a crucial part in bringing the Cold War to a relatively peaceful conclusion. That Reagan did this was partly a result of his own abhorrence of nuclear weapons and partly a consequence of his being persuaded [by Thatcher, Shultz and Matlock] that Gorbachev was a different kind of Soviet leader from his predecessors, one with whom you could do business.[59]

Marlo argues that Reagan never changed his view of the Soviet Union, even after signing the INF treaty. "In 1986 he noted that the Soviet Union 'is bent on an expansionist policy in an effort to make the whole world into a single Communist state.' Even after the signing of the INF Treaty (which many saw as 'proof' that the Soviets had changed), Reagan continued to re-assure his supporters that 'I'm still the same Ronald Reagan I was and the evil empire is still just that.'"[60] Marlo emphasizes that Reagan understood the potential improvement in East-West relations based on Gorbachev's re-forms, but never lost sight of the ideological struggle that was at the core of the Cold War.[61] Nevertheless, we argue, regardless of Reagan's continued animosity toward the Soviet Union, that the agreement he signed with Gor-bachev indicated his understanding that the Soviet Union under Gorbachev posed a much lower threat than before Gorbachev and thus he could reach a verifiable agreement with it.

Toward the end of Reagan's second term, the Soviets were willing to lib-eralize domestically in an unprecedented manner. Apparently, Gorbachev understood that by complying with American demands to make *perestroika* real the Soviet Union would be rewarded significantly, that there would be a payoff.[62] At the UN in late 1988, Gorbachev announced a major reduction in the Soviet armed forces and that the Soviets were moving "from the economy of armaments to the economy of disarmament."[63]

Conclusion

There is some evidence for several potential turning points in Reagan's strategy toward the Soviet Union. It appears that even though Reagan had been will-ing to negotiate with the Soviets from 1983—presumably, the US was by then already strong enough to negotiate from a position of strength—nothing could really come to fruition until the Soviets began changing, signaling that they were no longer threatening the US. Only following the rise of Gorbachev to power in 1985—after most of the old-guard leadership had perished—was the Soviet leadership able to read the reality correctly and ceased to seek pri-macy; however, it was also crucial to deliver the message to the US in order to prevent the Americans from continuing their rearmament, which the Soviets could no longer keep up with. Gorbachev's message at the Geneva Summit was the first signal that he no longer sought to win the confrontation. It was also the first time that Reagan saw a Soviet leader that seemed in control and that could deliver his own promises. Reagan attempted after that to promote the arms reduction that Gorbachev offered. Gorbachev's concessions indi-cated a profound change in the Soviet worldview. This change became real to America once Gorbachev committed himself publicly to it and by deeds proved that the Soviet Union no longer posed a strategic threat to the United

States. This change made it possible for Reagan, who was critical of arms control for many years, to end his term with treaties with the Soviet Union (INF and START [Strategic Arms Reduction Treaty]).

Vice President Bush—a defensive realist—ran for president when the Cold War was in many respects ending, if not over. Bush would preside over the collapse of the Soviet Union, which made the United States a sole superpower by the end of his one-term presidency, in many respects against his wish. The next chapter will analyze the consequent shift in grand strategy, from defensive realism to defensive liberalism, where the US emphasized multilateral actions and launched a humanitarian intervention in Somalia.

7

Making the World in Its Own Image: The Post–Cold War Grand Strategy

The 1991–2001 Decade: The Emergence of Defensive Liberalism

This chapter discusses the grand strategy that the US had adopted as the new global hegemon in the 1990s. We discuss why this strategy was chosen and to what extent it accorded with the expectations of the book's theoretical model. The strategy focused on liberalizing former opponents—China, Russia, and others—and the rise of humanitarian interventions.

The strategy adopted by the US in the first post–Cold War decade largely accords with defensive liberalism as described in chapter 1. Both the Bush Sr. administration—toward the end of his term—and the Clinton administration showed a commitment to a liberal agenda. Thus, in January 1993, just before the end of his term in office, Bush Sr. outlined a defensive liberal doctrine in which "in the wake of the cold war, in a world where we are the only superpower," the United States, "act[ing] in concert" with other powers and with international sanction, should take the lead in promoting "less than vital interests" and a "democratic peace."[1] According to Russett, "by 1992 . . . both Bush [Sr.] and [Secretary of State] Baker . . . accepted the principle of democratic peace—and explicitly discarded the principle that power relationships alone matter, or even matter most. . . . A very unrealist position."[2]

By the time the Clinton administration came to power, the major transformations in the international system—especially the rise of unipolarity and the absence of major strategic threats—became much clearer. Thus, the focus of all the earlier postwar administrations (the Soviet Union) disappeared, while it became increasingly obvious that its successor (Russia) was far weaker than the Soviet Union, despite supposedly maintaining the same military capabilities. Frankly, Russia could barely count as a great power. Under these new systemic conditions, the Clinton administration, inspired by the democratic peace theory, adopted the doctrine of "enlargement," designed to enlarge the world's "community of market democracies."[3] Clinton explicitly asserted that this strategy serves US interests because "democracies rarely wage war on one another."[4] The Clinton administration also sought to promote free trade and economic interdependence, as manifested in its "engagement" policy with China.[5] The administration also tried to help in the democratization of Russia.[6]

During the Cold War, the US grand strategy focused on the competition with the Soviet Union, employing realist strategies. While encouraging the democratization of some key countries, notably West Germany and Japan, the US was willing to overlook the domestic character of many of its authoritarian partners. Thus, the post-1970s rapprochement with China ignored the major human rights violations committed by the regime, especially under Mao. In this spirit, Nixon stated to the Chinese leadership in 1972: "What brings us together is a recognition on our part that what is important is not a nation's internal philosophy."[7]

The end of the Cold War, culminating with the collapse of the Soviet Union, transformed the US strategy. The global changes made it possible for Washington to address much more seriously the domestic nature of its former two key rivals—China and Russia—and other unstable countries. Thus, the focus of US grand strategy shifted from the balance of power (armament and alliances) and arms control with its rivals to issues related to domestic politics and economic policies: democratization, globalization, and economic engagement and humanitarian interventions. In other words, the US aimed at liberal transformation—or convergence—of key states, as well as some fragile ones.[8] Even if ideas of (liberal) ideology-promotion played some role, it should be emphasized that we do not argue that this shift was done only for altruistic reasons. This shift, and particularly the focus on the domestic nature of Russia and China, was beneficial to the US worldview and world order—liberal, capitalist, globalized, and democratic. The US viewed such world order as not only profitable economically (enhancing free trade), but also beneficial for its national security (specifically the argument that democracies would not go to war against other democracies and also that economic interdependence reduces the likelihood of conflicts). Even if the balance of power changes sometime in the future, according to the liberal belief, these liberalized states would supposedly not pose a threat to the US.

More specifically, the US used a number of convergence strategies:[9]

- Economic—convergence to market economies and joining international economic institutions;

• Humanitarian interventions—stabilize conflict-prone states by removing violators of liberal norms;

- Democratization—regime change of the target countries, which may be done peacefully and gradually (defensive liberalism) or by the use of force (offensive liberalism discussed in the next chapter);

- Highlighting common transnational threats faced by the great powers, which arguably are more relevant than traditional security issues such as territorial disputes and great-power competition. These transnational threats include nuclear proliferation, massive terrorism, climate change, the malfunctioning of the world economy, regional instability, and pandemic diseases.

In contrast, the "new world order" promoted by the Bush administration during the Gulf crisis of 1990–91 was still in essence a Westphalian concept, namely, focusing on state sovereignty, sanctity of boundaries, and noninterference in the domestic affairs of other states.[10] The major US military intervention in the Gulf War can be viewed in this Westphalian perspective. In this way one can also see the reluctance of the Bush administration to intervene in the civil war in the former Yugoslavia and its unwillingness to impose severe economic sanction on China after the violent suppression of the prodemocracy demonstrations in Tiananmen. The administration behaved cautiously and effectively toward the dramatic transformation of 1989–91: the collapse of communist rule in Eastern Europe and German unification and eventually the collapse of the Soviet Union itself. At the same time, the US didn't intervene in the domestic affairs of all these states, which, at any rate, seemed to be moving in a favorable direction from the American perspective.[11]

Yet, toward the end of his term in office and with the Soviet Union no longer there, Bush—the defensive realist in his basic inclinations[12]—adopted a defensive liberal strategy, culminating in the endorsement of the innovative idea of humanitarian intervention as manifested in the Somalia intervention discussed below. According to this liberal view, the US should "win the democratic peace for people the world over." At the same time, Bush underlined the defensive (liberal) character of the expected interventions by saying that the US "should not seek to be the world's policeman . . . it must not go running off on reckless, expensive crusades."[13]

Bill Clinton came to power focusing on domestic affairs and the economy and without much background or interest in foreign affairs. His intention to be a domestic affairs president was based on the assumption that the termination of the Cold War would release resources for the renewal of the American economy.[14] There was no threat on the horizon, and "by any measure— economic, political, or military—[the US] reigned supreme."[15] Nonetheless,

"One of Clinton's greatest challenges," writes James Boys, "was in defining exactly where US interests lay in the absence of a single, formidable foe and his efforts to reconfigure the economy or the armed forces remained impeded by an inability to do so."[16] But Clinton saw that the end of the Cold War brought "unfamiliar threats, not the absence of danger."[17] He identified old forces—ethnicity and religion—as the new-old sources of violence that the US needed to cope with. Still, these were not major strategic threats such as the nuclear weapons of the Soviet Union posed during the Cold War. In a period in which the Soviet Union didn't exist anymore, the Clinton administration, inspired by the democratic peace theory, adopted the doctrine of "enlargement." A key expression of the new strategy was articulated by Clinton's national security advisor, W. Anthony Lake. On September 21, 1993, he declared that "the successor to a doctrine of containment must be a strategy of enlargement—enlargement of the world's community of market democracies."[18] In addition, the Clinton administration also sought to promote free trade and economic interdependence, as manifested most notably in its engagement policy with China.[19]

China

Partly under the influence of the harsh suppression by the Chinese government of prodemocracy students in Tiananmen Square, the Democratic Party adopted a position in favor of linking an extension of trade benefits to China (the renewal of the status of most favored nation to China) with major improvements in its human rights policies. This position was endorsed in an executive order by Clinton when he came to power in 1993.[20] Thus, the US demanded major changes in China's domestic character, notably during Secretary of State Warren Christopher's visit to China in March 1994. Yet, the Chinese turned down the US demands, and the administration abandoned this policy. This abandonment was due to the higher stakes the Chinese leadership had in this issue, related to their political control of the country. The business community in the US also opposed the conditioning of trade on human rights behavior because of the growing economic opportunities in China.

The Clinton administration reversed its policy and focused instead on economic engagement with China, awarding it with an open-ended most-favored-nation status (rather than one year at a time), thus opening US markets to Chinese goods and encouraging its World Trade Organization (WTO) membership. Such an economic engagement through trade and investment became more broadly a cornerstone of US foreign policy toward the world under Clinton.

The Clinton administration focused on integrating China to the US-led liberal international order based on the huge benefits it is gaining from globalization and from this international order. The American expectation was that China would become "a responsible stakeholder," in the words of Robert Zoellick, the deputy secretary of state in the George W. Bush administration.[21] Thus, the US was very helpful in 2001 in facilitating the membership of China in the WTO—the leading international institution in charge of international trade.[22] The US also welcomed Chinese participation in other leading institutions and cooperating with it on global governance and regional security (including by developing confidence-building measures). Based on this logic, the US has granted China most-favored-trading status in the 1990s (and later established a high-level economic dialogue in 2006 and negotiated a bilateral investment treaty under Obama).[23]

The administration believed that such economic engagement would generate domestic liberalization in China—economic and then political. Economic growth and increasing ties with the world—including people-to-people interactions such as through tourism and the admission of many thousands of Chinese students to American universities—were expected to lead to domestic transformation. Presumably a rising middle class in a Chinese market economy will demand political rights—as took place following the industrial revolution in Europe.[24] The Chinese would also probably realize that in the information age a free society is essential for economic success.[25] The more democratic China becomes, the more peaceful it will be in its external behavior.[26] At the very least the expectation was that intensive engagement and integration would make China committed to the current international order, turning it a "responsible stakeholder."[27]

These developments didn't take place as the US expected based on its liberal beliefs. That is, China got richer due to its economic engagement, especially with the US, which only reinforced the power of the governing communist elite, but the level of political repression has remained very high in order to forestall potential domestic threats to the regime.[28] We do not elaborate on this subject here as our focus is more on the sources of US behavior rather than on its effects.

Russia

Managing the transition from a bipolar world to a unipolar one, the Bush Sr. administration focused on security issues and the balance of power with the Soviet Union and later Russia but avoided intervention in their domestic affairs.[29] In contrast, Clinton, coming to power in a unipolar system, invested quite a bit in helping the Russian president, Boris Yeltsin, in his efforts to transform Russia into a free-market democracy.[30] Even if initially Clinton didn't think of or wish to focus on foreign affairs, after a few months in power the administration realized that the domestic developments in Russia bore huge importance for US security and economic interests.[31] The administration saw an investment in Russian domestic development as a key policy for preserving the US-led liberal post–Cold War order. Russia was an authoritarian country both under the czars and communism, so it could easily fail to democratize. Yeltsin was seen as the best person to liberalize Russia. Russia had nuclear weapons and could potentially pose a major danger to the West, thus making it "too nuclear to fail."[32] This provided a major national security incentive for the US to assist in the liberalization of Russia, thus presumably turning it to much less of a security threat. If that happened, the US could reduce defense spending and invest in the domestic programs that Clinton cherished.[33]

The implementation of this new agenda took place most forcefully under the Clinton administration. The US engaged the Russian economic reform program by providing technical expertise, and direct grants and International Monetary Fund (IMF) loans, although the American financial support was limited.[34] To help the internal transformation of Russia, the administration also offered diplomatic support and integration into the West. Thus, Clinton supported the admission of Russia to the G-7—the exclusive club of the Western industrialized economies—making it the G-8, despite the great economic weakness of Russia and the huge corruption in its economy. The idea behind this policy was that it would bolster Russia's democracy and free market and integrate it to the global economy.

Clinton also provided some financial assistance for democracy promotion, though—despite the commitment in principle and the rhetoric—it was quite limited in general and in relation to assistance for economic reform in particular. The latter reform was prioritized and received the lion's share of the funding, while only 2.3 percent, or $130 million, of the $5.45 billion in direct US assistance to Russia went to programs related directly to democratic reforms.[35] Moreover, as opposed the economic reforms, which were viewed as preconditions for democracy, the administration didn't have in hand a blueprint for how to promote democracy in Russia.[36]

By the end of the twentieth century, the Clinton administration strategy to liberalize Russia resulted in an uphill battle for transition to democracy and free market in the country, though the transition was quite partial and very fragile.[37] The widespread discontent from this problematic transition reinforced negative Russian views of the US,[38] which were accelerated during the reign of Yeltsin's successor, Vladimir Putin, in the 2000s.

In the security field, the Bush Sr. administration succeeded to promote common security in Europe through arms control agreements based on transparency and defense dominance. Nuclear weapons were removed from three former Soviet republics to Russia, while the Nunn-Lugar initiative helped to establish a tighter control over nukes in Russia.[39] These security accomplishments were challenged by the expansion of NATO to include Eastern European countries, former members of the Warsaw Pact and a few former Soviet republics. Russia opposed very forcefully this expansion from which it was excluded, while seemingly aiming at potential future Russian aggression. In Russian eyes, NATO expansion was a provocative anti-Russian move, which indeed alienated it and harmed democratization in Russia.[40]

The Clinton administration, for its part, justified the expansion in post–Cold War liberalization missionary terms, namely, as a means for democracy promotion in Eastern Europe. While domestic politics (Eastern European lobbies, competition with the Republican Party) contributed to the decision to expand, what made it possible were international structural changes following the end of bipolarity and the Cold War.[41] In addition to NATO expansion, another Clinton policy which worsened relations with Russia was the novel pursuit of humanitarian interventions, particularly twice in the Balkans. A key point for our explanation is that the Clinton administration followed these policies, which a decade earlier could have led to a major superpower conflict, because it was "emboldened" by the realization by the late 1990s "that Russia had little capacity to influence American foreign policy even in traditional spheres of Russian influence such as the Balkans."[42]

The Rise of Humanitarian Intervention

The newfound US commitment to liberal values in the 1991–2001 decade was not limited only to rhetoric or even to diplomatic and economic steps. It was manifested most of all in the repeated US willingness to undertake humanitarian interventions, primarily in Somalia in 1992–93 (which was started by Bush Sr.), in Haiti in 1994, and in the Balkans—Bosnia in 1995 and Kosovo in 1999. These interventions were undertaken in response not to particularistic material American interests such as strategic and economic interests. Thus, all of the interventions took place in areas with marginal importance to the global distribution of capabilities and to US standing as the unipole. Rather the interventions were designed to protect liberal values, often seen by liber-

als as universal values. These were foremost to prevent humanitarian disasters and atrocities—mass starvation in Somalia and ethnic warfare and mass
killings in the Balkans.[43]

CASES OF HUMANITARIAN INTERVENTIONS[44]

Somalia, 1992–94

The intervention in Somalia started in early December 1992. Although around
twenty-five thousand troops were deployed in Somalia by mid-January 1993
(close to Clinton's inauguration), less than three months later US force levels
had declined by half. An indication of the declining US commitment to Somalia can be found in the Security Council decision to replace most of the
American force by a twenty-five-thousand-strong UN peacekeeping force in
early May 1993. Only around 1,700 US combat troops remained in Somalia.
After the killing of eighteen US servicemen in early October 1993 in Mogadishu, President Clinton stated that the US would increase its military presence
in and around Somalia by over five thousand troops, but only for a period of
less than six months, at the end of which time the US forces would disengage
from Somalia. Indeed, by the end of March 1994, the US disengagement was
completed.[45]

The main motive for the American intervention in Somalia, an area seen
by the Bush Sr. administration as having a marginal importance at best to US
material interests, was clearly humanitarian, the intervention being described
by one researcher as "an act of 'idealism.'"[46] According to a biography of
Bush, "The civil struggle had created a humanitarian crisis, and Bush saw
an opportunity to put American power to work to save, in his words, 'thousands of innocents.' 'There is a feeling that we won't help black nations, so
that would be a peripheral benefit showing that the United States does care,'
he told his diary in Monday, November 30. 'There is a feeling in the Muslim
world that we don't care about Muslims. A large U.S. humanitarian effort
backed by force would help in that category.'"[47]

Under Clinton there was, however, some "mission creep" toward establishing law and order in the country by fighting the Somali armed clans,
which created anarchy there. Yet, the US military mission against the militias
in October 1993 went astray. The killing of eighteen US servicemen in that
mission led to US disengagement from Somalia, and the country remains a
failed state in the present.

Shortly after the withdrawal from Somalia, the Clinton administration issued Presidential Decision Directive 25 (PDD 25). It looked like the directive

was putting major limits on humanitarian interventions in the framework of calling for a retreat from "assertive multilateralism." The directive called for authorizing interventions only when they are linked to vital US national security interests and when the intervening force had sufficient force and a clear goal.[48] Yet, as DiPrizio shows in his comprehensive book on the humanitarian interventions:

> Presidential Decision Directive 25 seems to have been more of a politically expedient sop to Congress than it was an articulation of the principles that would guide Clinton's humanitarian-intervention decisions. Although PDD25 was cited as the rationale for keeping the US out of Rwanda, the Clinton administration's later interventions in Haiti, Bosnia and Kosovo are difficult to justify based on its criteria.[49]

PDD 25 (as well as the earlier and somewhat similar Weinberger-Powell Doctrine) did not inform the motivations for the post–Cold War humanitarian interventions. Looking closely at each of the post-Gulf 1990s interventions shows that the key factors driving them are not easily accounted for by these two related doctrines.[50]

Haiti, 1994

In fall 1994, an American intervention of about twenty thousand troops took place in Haiti. In this case there was no need to resort to violence due to an agreement reached at the last minute with the military rulers of Haiti under a very credible threat of an imminent US invasion. While a realpolitik (and domestic political) reason was to stem illegal immigration from the island to the US, the intervention was an implementation of the administration's idea of "enlargement" of the democratic community of nations. Yet, the attempt to transform Haiti into a prosperous democracy didn't work out, and it has continued to be a failed state.[51]

Bosnia, 1995; and Kosovo, 1999

In Bosnia the nonintervention pattern had been the dominant one until fall 1995, US diplomatic involvement in the dispute and its limited use of air-power notwithstanding.[52] Yet, following some major humanitarian crimes committed by the Bosnian Serbs, NATO under US leadership carried out air bombardments against them in late August into September 1995 that were much more effective than previous air raids. In the aftermath of the establishment of a cease-fire in Bosnia, the initialing of a peace agreement by the leaders of Serbia, Croatia, and Bosnia in Dayton, Ohio, in November 1995, and the signing of the agreement in Paris during the following month, the Clinton administration decided to deploy twenty thousand US troops in Bosnia (as part of a NATO peacekeeping force of up to sixty thousand soldiers).

The KLA (Kosovo Liberation Army) revolted in the late 1990s against the Serb control of the Muslim-majority province of Kosovo. The Serbs responded with a brutal campaign of ethnic cleansing against the Albanian Kosovars. Following the failure of diplomatic negotiations, the US led a seventy-eight-day massive bombing campaign by NATO against the Serbs in spring 1999 to convince them to accept the international proposal they turned down earlier.[53] Once the Serbs withdrew from Kosovo, the US and NATO deployed a fifty-thousand-person multinational peacekeeping force on the ground there.

The military interventions in the Balkans—similarly to other humanitarian interventions—took place despite the region's limited strategic and economic value to the US. Both the Bush Sr. and the Clinton administrations had a shared view of low intrinsic US interests in the former Yugoslavia.[54] Despite the absence of compelling realpolitik interests, however, the US eventually implemented a limited intervention in Bosnia in 1995 and in Kosovo in 1999, based on the humanitarian considerations of putting an end to ethnic cleansing and mass killings.[55] Then secretary of state Madeleine Albright, for example, stated that the atrocities in the Balkans were "horrors of biblical proportions."[56]

Two matters stand out in this case: one is the US intervention came after the EU—which didn't and doesn't have an army—proved ineffective in dealing with this ongoing crisis. Second, this humanitarian intervention had a different approach than the intervention in Somalia. In Somalia, the military was sent in the first place to provide humanitarian aid. In the Balkans, the intervention was conducted as brute force to stop the atrocities. Moreover, the Clinton administration's intervention in Bosnia was also motivated by the liberal value of preserving the supposedly "pluralist" character of the multiethnic Bosnian society even if this was at least partly a myth rather than reflecting the beliefs of many Bosnians from all three communities there.[57]

Shortly before the end of the 1990s, the US managed to bring about the termination of hostilities and the killings in Bosnia and Kosovo. In Bosnia it also presided over the Dayton peace agreement among the local parties even if the accord has led to a de facto partition of Bosnia to highly autonomous and homogenous units, based on the division to the ethnonational groups. At any rate, the US failed to transform Bosnia into what the administration hoped for it to become: a unified multiethnic democracy; rather, it remained a malfunctioning state.[58] Since Kosovo was an integral part of Serbia, the US-led NATO intervention clearly violated the Westphalian norms of sovereignty and nonintervention in domestic affairs. In other words, the liberal norms of human rights overcame the traditional norms of state rights, which constitute a fundamental pillar of world order.[59] This was also reflected in the domestic support for the Kosovo War. Liberals supported the war; conservatives opposed it.[60] At the same time, the US didn't transform Kosovo—like the other places where the US conducted humanitarian interventions—into a liberal democracy despite the rhetoric in this direction.

The Defensive Nature of the Liberal Strategy

It should be noted that while liberal in nature, the US strategy in the first post–Cold War decade was defensive rather than offensive. Its defensive character was manifested, first, in a strong US emphasis on multilateralism. Namely, in its resort to force in the 1991–2001 decade the US consistently acted in a multilateral framework and with international sanction: UN sanction in the 1990–91 Gulf War, in Somalia, and in Bosnia; and NATO sanction in Kosovo (since UN Security Council authorization was unavailable due to Russian and Chinese opposition). The US adhered to multilateralism even though collaboration with other powers was unnecessary for these interventions from a purely military point of view (and may even have been counterproductive).

In addition, in its military interventions, the US pursued limited humanitarian goals of putting an end to atrocities and gross violations of human rights and refrained from any serious investment in state building, and in ideological crusades for regime change and democratization. The absence of such major allocation of resources may at least partly—on top of the huge difficulties involved anyway in such missions, especially in poor and fragile states—explain the failure to democratize and to build the states where the humanitarian interventions took place.[61]

During the 1990s the idea of democratization and regime change did emerge once in the form of the Iraqi Freedom Act of 1998, which the Clinton administration committed to. However, Clinton did not attempt to remove Saddam, and in fact, the use of force against Iraq, particularly Desert Fox in 1998, was not intended to do so, and Clinton stopped it despite all of his senior advisors' advice.

The US also maintained friendly relations with autocratic Arab regimes, while overlooking their lack of democratization. Thus, following its victory in the first Gulf War of 1990–91, the US did not pursue regime change or promote democratization in either Iraq or Kuwait. At the end of the war, the

US committed only a minimal invasion of Iraqi territory for tactical military purposes but restored the Iraqi territorial integrity with its borders intact following the war. Moreover, even when it had the chance to carry out democratization in liberated Kuwait, the US did not take it, and instead preferred to adhere to the traditional norms of sovereignty and noninterference in other states' domestic affairs. Thus, it presided over the restoration of the Sabach family to power in Kuwait without insisting on any major domestic reforms such as granting voting rights to women, let alone full-blown democratization. Even when a regime change toward democratization occurred as a result of the US use of force, as in Serbia in 2000, it was as a by-product of an intervention undertaken for humanitarian goals, that is, limited and defensive liberal reasons, rather than offensive liberal ones.

Post–Cold War Sources of Humanitarian Interventions: Realist Factors and Liberal Values

Two key changes in the aftermath of the end of the Cold War and the collapse of the Soviet Union have led to the rise of the idea and practice of humanitarian intervention.[62] From an international systemic perspective, the key change was in the balance of power, more precisely, the transition from bipolarity to unipolarity. This new power structure meant that the US remained the sole superpower without a countervailing coalition arrayed against it. This change—producing US hegemony and Western power superiority in the international system—has made possible humanitarian interventions because of the declining external constraints on US-led/Western interventions. The 1991 Gulf War has already shown the formidable US power-projection capacity to far-flung areas of the world. In short, realist factors provided the *opportunity* for humanitarian interventions.

The transformation of the balance of power in favor of the West was closely related to the emerging dominance of Western liberal ideas such as democracy and free markets. More specifically, post–Cold War US decision makers—similarly to their predecessors—believed in the universality of American liberal values and institutions and that it was the role of the US to spread them globally, especially while unipolarity seemingly made it possible. In addition to the ideological fulfillment, the spread of liberalism could contribute to the US economically through the globalization of free markets. Liberalization of other great powers could also contribute to US national security as liberal states are not expected to fight each other according to the democratic peace theory. Thus, even when the balance of power changes and unipolarity declines, supposedly these rising powers are unlikely to pose a security threat to the US.

A key value of liberalism is the relative centrality of universal human rights versus state rights. These latter rights are mostly associated with the Westphalia international order based on the norm of nonintervention in the domestic affairs of other states. Thus, liberalism provided the *motivation* for humanitarian interventions related to the idea that the international community should be committed to protect human rights everywhere in the world, even if that might mean—at least in extreme cases of violations of human rights—an external intervention in the domestic affairs of sovereign states.

More specifically, the material factors provide the explanation and the conditions for the capacity to intervene worldwide:

- *Balance of Power I*: The presence of a hegemon under unipolarity reduces drastically the chances for the formation of a balancing coalition, which could constrain the hegemon's capacity to intervene.
- *Balance of Power II*: Yet, when a balancing coalition emerges, the likelihood of interventions declines drastically. This might explain the variation between the humanitarian intervention in Libya in 2011 and the lack of an intervention in Syria in the following years despite the major human rights abuses there, including well over five hundred thousand people being killed. Such a nonintervention can be explained at least partly by the balancing and strong opposition by Russia and Iran to any Western intervention in Syria (on the Libyan and Syrian cases, see chapter 9).
- *Balance of Threat*: The absence of a major strategic threat following the collapse of the Soviet Union has made considerable military forces potentially available for Western, especially American, nonstrategic interventions, notably humanitarian ones.

WHAT ARE THE IMPLICATIONS OF THE MATERIAL FACTORS FOR HUMANITARIAN INTERVENTIONS?

The material/systemic/realist logic would lead us to expect that a cost-benefit balance would provide some of the key conditions for when humanitarian interventions will take place and at what level. These conditions would include expected limited material benefits (otherwise it would be considered a "national interest" type of intervention, namely, strategically or economically based intervention) and also expected low costs in terms of "blood and treasure"—that is, casualties to the intervening forces and the financial costs of the intervention.

If strategic interests are engaged, then it is not a humanitarian intervention. When strategic interests are at stake, there will always be a suspicion that the realpolitik interests are hiding behind the humanitarian rhetoric. A truly humanitarian intervention usually takes place in areas without great strategic and/or economic importance such as Africa, the Balkans, and the Caribbean. If there are expected high costs, however, no humanitarian intervention is likely to take place. Thus, no humanitarian intervention took place in Darfur, the Democratic Republic of Congo, and post-2011 Syria despite the large-scale human rights violations in all these places.

In sum, humanitarian interventions are likely in areas with low material interests and expected low costs, such as the US intervention in Somalia in 1992 and also in the Balkans and Haiti. Indeed, there is a proportionality between national interests and the willingness to sacrifice. States—and societies—are much more willing to sacrifice—both blood and treasure—when key national security interests seem to be at stake (even if sometimes mistakenly so, due to political manipulation or misperceptions) than for universal goals such as protection of human rights in foreign countries.

Thus, both realist logic and the domestic politics of tolerance for costs would lead us to expect that states which engage in a humanitarian intervention will do their utmost to avoid even minimal casualties—even if that might jeopardize the success and the effectiveness of the mission itself. Thus, the conduct of humanitarian interventions is often reflected in the following features:

- The use mainly of air power rather than ground troops—for example, the interventions in the Balkans in the 1990s (Bosnia in 1995 and Kosovo in 1999) were by air power even if "boots on the ground" could have been very useful for the success of the mission for stopping the killing.[63]
- The use of air power is from fifteen thousand feet and above.
- Avoidance of the use of helicopters even if they are most useful for the type of mission typical of humanitarian interventions.
- Since the willingness to tolerate casualties is very low, the forces are going to be withdrawn if the casualties are even minimally higher than expected. A notable example is Somalia, where shortly after eighteen US servicemen were killed in Mogadishu in October 1993, the US forces disengaged from the humanitarian intervention there.
- Deployment on the ground takes place only following the establishment of peace. Thus, only following the achievement of the 1995 US-brokered Dayton peace agreements settling the Bosnia conflict were the US and NATO willing to contribute ground troops to a peacekeeping force.

"SOFT SECURITY" INTERESTS IN THE
HUMANITARIAN INTERVENTIONS

In addition to the humanitarian motivations, "soft" security concerns played an important role in some of the interventions.[64] In Haiti, it was the Clinton administration's concern about the flow of Haitian refugees to American shores caused by the turmoil of the military coup. In Bosnia and Kosovo, the administration was worried about the spread of the conflict and jointly with waves of refugees would produce regional instability in Europe.[65] While the absence of such soft security interests didn't prevent the Somalia intervention, it did preclude an intervention in Rwanda in 1994 despite the huge humanitarian disaster there in 1994. But by that time there was also concern about potential casualties—a concern that was missing before the Somalia intervention, but the issue of casualties was learned the hard way in Mogadishu.

It is worth emphasizing that humanitarian intervention is not necessarily the supply of humanitarian aid to the victims, as was the initial mission of the intervention in Somalia. Humanitarian intervention may certainly be conducted by using considerable force against the oppressor in order to halt or stop its assault on the victim. And supplies of humanitarian aid may be delayed until the hostilities on the ground cease.

IMPLICATIONS OF LIBERALISM FOR THE
HUMANITARIAN INTERVENTIONS

The dominance of liberal ideas in the 1990s brings about a preference for multilateral interventions: the best case would be if it could be sanctioned by the UNSC; if not, at least by a multilateral organization such as NATO. The prevalence of a multilateral coalition means that there are institutional constraints on the freedom of military action of the hegemon, which has to gain the support of the other members for its military plans. In case of the 1999 Kosovo intervention, the UNSC didn't authorize the NATO humanitarian intervention there,[66] but at least in most of the West, the support of NATO in the intervention provided a sufficient multilateral legitimacy rather than being seen as a unilateral US intervention. This is because in NATO there is a need to reach a consensus with its allies.[67]

Another implication of liberalism is the tendency to protect people irrespective of race, gender, nationality, religion, ethnicity, or civilization but rather based on universal human values.[68] Since these are the intervention's objectives, the classical material/realpolitik interests behind military interventions do not constitute important considerations. Thus, interventions are likely to take place in any country that violates human rights on a massive scale even if it is poor and weak and lacks any strategic or economic significance. Realist logic would suggest that these places are likely targets of interventions because of the limited constraints they pose, though they are also unlikely to attract interventions as they do not offer much in the form of material interests. Yet, in accordance with the liberal logic, interventions took place in poor and weak countries that are not significant for the world balance of power. Moreover, quite a few of the interventions were designed to protect Muslims (Somalia, Bosnia, and Kosovo), thus fitting the universalist liberal conception of protecting people irrespective of their belonging to "our" group in the sense of a nation or religion.

Finally, in the postconflict stage, under liberalism there are likely to be attempts to build democracy and free markets in the aftermath of the intervention (which might be seen as "mission creep"). Indeed, while intervening initially to protect persecuted people or to prevent starvation, over time, the objective of the interventions expanded through a "mission creep" to "nation building" or more accurately "state building," namely, to construct effective, well-functioning and democratic institutions. Such institutions were fragile or completely absent in the states where the humanitarian interventions took place. Building such institutions, the administration expected, would prevent the occurrence of the disasters that led to the interventions in the first place. Here the success was usually quite limited in most cases.[69]

Both the realist and liberal logics challenge the logic of Westphalia, which imposes constraints on intervention in the domestic affairs of sovereign states. The realist challenge is based on the logic of the balance of power, which enables military interventions by powerful states in weak states, though it limits the likelihood of such interventions in strong states. This excludes the possibility of liberal military interventions in the domestic affairs of strong states such as China and Russia and their immediate neighborhoods.

Liberalism, for its part, elevates the prominence of human rights at the expense of state rights as they are manifested in the Westphalian norms. Even if they oppose liberal interventions because of realpolitik reasons, such as an opposition to American hegemony (and also to liberal values), authoritarian powers may use the Westphalian norms in order to oppose liberal interventions such as the strong Russian opposition to NATO intervention in Kosovo. Together with NATO expansion, liberal interventions reinforce Russian fears that the West is engaged in democracy promotion and regime change, which might eventually also endanger their own regime.

Explaining the Rise of Defensive Liberalism in the 1991–2001 Era

Domestic politics did not lead to the rise of humanitarian interventions as the majority of the American public didn't press for such interventions and was unwilling to pay in a single American life even if it didn't oppose the interventions in principle.[70] The rise of defensive liberalism in US grand strategy in the 1990s was made possible and encouraged by the combined effects of the changes that took place in the aftermath of the Cold War in both systemic parameters highlighted by the model: the balance of capabilities and the balance of threat. The systemic changes stimulated the US to advance its liberal ideas and domestic identity abroad.

As a result of the collapse of the Soviet Union, a unipolar or hegemonic world has emerged since the early 1990s, due to the US dominance in overall power resources, especially in the military sphere, including a unique global power-projection capability.[71] This structural change makes possible for the US to shift to a liberal strategy due to its hegemony and the overall superiority of the US and its allies.[72] In 1994, US allies commanded roughly 47 percent of global gross domestic product (GDP) and 36 percent of global defense spending, in addition to America's own 24 percent and 38 percent, respectively. And after the United States, America's closest allies—France, Germany, Japan, and the United Kingdom—rounded out the top five in both of these categories. Moreover, Russian power was in free fall during the early 1990s, and other US competitors (or potential competitors) possessed mere fractions of global wealth and power, and this situation created great benefits for US policy. China still didn't have the capabilities to challenge the regional order in East Asia and the American dominance there.

Thus, the rise of liberalism at the expense of realism was the result of the collapse of the Soviet Union, which had posed the major constraint on US overseas intervention and resort to force during the Cold War. In the absence of the former constraints posed by Soviet power, the unconstrained hegemon could afford to pursue a liberal agenda in accordance with its ideological and cultural preferences, as the costs of pursuing such an agenda declined sharply with the disappearance of the Soviet countervailing force. According to Halper and Clarke, "as growing American power enabled a more robust emphasis on values, so the liberal Wilsonian strain came to prominence."[73] The Balkans are a good example of a region where the United States could use force much more freely in the post-Soviet era than during the Cold War.

Especially noteworthy is the fact that the shift from realism to liberalism in US grand strategy was not the result of a change from a realist to a liberal administration. While the Clinton administration was indeed liberal in its ideological preferences, the shift to a liberal strategy began already under the Bush Sr. administration that was initially realist oriented. Once the US became a global hegemon and gained an unprecedented freedom of action, however, even such an administration began thinking in defensive liberal terms. Thus, as noted, it was the Bush Sr. administration that initiated the military intervention in Somalia in 1992 (with president-elect Clinton's blessing). Behavior that is contrary to previous foreign policy preferences testifies to the importance of systemic factors that compel the decision makers to change their initial inclinations. Still the Somalia intervention under Bush was more modest in its objectives than under Clinton (Bush stated that it was not a "nation-building" mission).[74] The Bush administration was also reluctant to intervene in Bosnia, although it also took quite a bit of time for Clinton to decide on the intervention there. The US-led NATO intervention came only after it became evident that the European forces in Bosnia could not deal with the crisis, and it was getting out of control both in the scope of the humanitarian crisis,[75] and in the rising challenge to the soft security interests noted above.[76]

At the same time, the other key systemic development was the decline of the major threat to the US—that is, the Soviet Union—which had brought about the massive American global engagement in different regions during the Cold War. With the collapse of Soviet power and the absence of any major power both willing and able to threaten the US, the international system became very benign for US security. This made it possible to focus on domestic and economic issues, as Clinton intended to do.[77] The decline of security issues in the post–Cold War era allowed the emergence of free market and globalization, therefore prosperity became the key issue.[78] This new setting, which certainly brought liberal ideas to the forefront as the dominant ideas in the international system (certainly while the competing idea, communism, virtually disappeared), combined with the US dominance of the system at the time, made the 1990s a decade of multilateralism and promotion of liberal values, with a relatively minimal use of force. These liberal values included democracy and even more so free markets as political legitimacy seemed to depend on economic growth, which in the liberal view is closely related to the expansion of trade and globalization.

On the one hand, the dramatic decline in the level of external threat allowed the US the luxury to advance its liberal preferences, but on the other hand, with the disappearance of the main threat to its security, the US did not have a strong enough incentive to do so, at least with regard to the use of force. The offensive liberal approach, which calls for a major resort to force to promote regime change and democratization, could not have much of an appeal under these benign circumstances. Thus, the nonthreatening character of the international environment gave rise to a defensive rather than an offensive liberal strategy.

As a result, despite its apparent commitment to humanitarian intervention, in practice the US was quite cautious and hesitant with regard to the resort to force in the 1991–2001 period. While the disappearance of the Soviet countervailing force has made US military intervention in the Balkans much more feasible and less costly than during the Cold War, the US intervened both in Bosnia and in Kosovo only after considerable hesitation and the incompetence shown by its allies. Thus, the intervention in Bosnia took place more than three years after the outbreak of the ethnic violence and the humanitarian crisis there. In addition, the US exhibited a very limited willingness to incur casualties, manifested in avoiding combat ground operations, limiting its interventions to air power, and even refraining from the use of helicopters, an effective weapon in this kind of low-intensity warfare.[79]

The unwillingness to sacrifice for the sake of humanitarian considerations was also manifested in the hasty US disengagement from Somalia, following the loss of just eighteen US servicemen, killed in Mogadishu in October 1993.[80] It also resulted in a very selective commitment to pursue humanitarian intervention—notably the nonintervention in Rwanda, where the greatest humanitarian catastrophe in the post–Cold War era took place.[81]

To sum up, as the model leads us to expect, the combination of US power preponderance and a low-threat environment in the 1990s gave rise to a defensive liberal strategy, manifested notably in attempts to promote democracy and free markets and in the multilateral, cautious, and qualified US approach to humanitarian intervention. This benign international system would change dramatically with the terror attacks of September 11, 2001, and the next chapter will deal with the strategy that emerged out of these events.

1990s = Defensive liberalism

Promotion of democracy, humanitarianism, free markets + multi lateralism

8

The Post-9/11 Period: The Emergence of Offensive Liberalism

Introduction

While in the 1990s the US acted largely in accordance with defensive liberalism, in the aftermath of 9/11 major changes once again took place in its grand strategy, which again raises the question of what security approach the US adopted and why. This chapter focuses on the argument that the combined effect of US hegemony and the post-9/11 rising threat led to a major change in the grand strategy. The change was from the defensive liberalism of the 1990s and then the realist strategy of the early (pre-9/11) George W. Bush administration to the post-9/11 offensive liberalism. This strategy focused on the democratization of Iraq as a critical step toward the spread of democracy all over the Middle East. Offensive liberals expect that such a regime change—even if done unilaterally by hegemonic resort to force—will supposedly take care of the security threats of large-scale terrorism and the proliferation of weapons of mass destruction (WMD). The chapter—in accordance with the focus of the book—analyzes the sources of the strategy change, while discussing only very briefly its consequences, including the effects of the Iraq intervention.[1]

George W. Bush came to power with an intent to reduce the US involvement in humanitarian interventions, nation building, and democracy promotion. In his winning campaign for president, he criticized the Clinton administration for its involvement in too many overseas affairs. This was particularly evident in the Middle East, where Clinton invested time, effort, and political capital—and his presidential prestige—in the failing Israel-Palestinian Oslo peace process as well as the futile Israel-Syria peace process. Bush was determined to reduce the US involvement in this region, especially since there seemed to be no place for optimism with the outburst of the second intifada in late September 2000. The investment seemed not only not to pay off but also counterproductive because it drew American attention away from other matters and cost the US credibility as a sole hegemon who appeared impotent to move relatively weak players to settle their differences. These players include Israel, a regional client that depended on the US; Syria, which had just lost its Soviet patron; and the very weak Palestinian Authority.

The defensive liberal approach that dominated the US foreign policy establishment during the Clinton years, with the high profile of humanitarian operations in Africa, the Balkans, and the Caribbean, seemed by the end of the 1990s too costly without concrete benefits. Thus, George W. Bush wanted to end it and reinstall a realist worldview that would, for instance, include increasing the investment in the armed forces. The liberal order that had emerged with the fall of the Soviet Union and was stabilized—at least so it seemed—in the following decade seemed to work. The US, Bush argued, had domestic issues to deal with but also rising challenges that the US had to consider more seriously, such as China.

Once in office, Bush reduced the American involvement in the Middle East but also in other regions. This policy held for merely eight months, until the 9/11 attacks. We do not argue that if the US had not partly retrenched, the attacks would not have occurred. But the violent nonstate actors were not taken in full seriousness before al-Qaeda hit the heart of Manhattan and the Pentagon. The al-Qaeda terror attacks in New York (the World Trade Center), Washington, DC (the Pentagon), and Pennsylvania (the plane that crashed on its way to strike in Washington) changed instantly the strategy of the Bush administration. The distancing from Middle Eastern affairs was abruptly shattered. In the aftermath of the 9/11 attacks, the Bush administration launched two wars to alter the region. One war was in Afghanistan, which is on the margins of the Middle East, geographically speaking, but is partly related to the Middle East culturally and ethnically. This war was launched several weeks after the attacks. The international community broadly supported the war because the attacks on US soil were masterminded and directed by al-Qaeda leader Osama bin Laden and his headquarters, which found refuge in Afghanistan under Taliban control. The US-led coalition invaded Afghanistan in order to remove the Taliban and eliminate Afghanistan as a terror refuge by installing a new Western-friendly regime. The war also received broad domestic support, and this seems to persist—even if there is a significantly gradual erosion and indications of opposition to the continuation of the war—as the US presence in Afghanistan is by now nearly nineteen years long.[2]

The other war was on Iraq, launched a year and a half after the 9/11 attacks. Its purpose was more ambitious because it was not directly related to the 9/11 attacks—allegations of Iraq involvement in 9/11 were aired but re-futed. Democratizing Iraq by force was intended to remove Saddam Hussein's regime, which was hostile to the United States and its allies—particularly Saudi Arabia, Egypt, and Israel, but also Kuwait and the other Persian Gulf countries—and had produced weapons of mass destruction in the past. The allegation that Iraq resumed the production of such weapons was used as an explanation for launching war but was refuted in the following years. In any case, the logic of democratizing by force (the ultimate end of offensive liberalism) was to install a democratic regime that would refrain—due to its democratic nature—from getting involved in such activities as well as in terror sponsorship, which Saddam Hussein's regime was known to have done for many years.

The idea of democratizing by force is the most distinctive policy under offensive liberalism. It sees security threats even under a global military and political-ideological hegemony (i.e., there is no competition to liberal de-mocracy as communism was) and operates to remove such threats by force-ful regime change. This idea did not suddenly emerge after 9/11. Chapter 1 elaborates on some of the older origins of this school. In the pre-9/11 Bush Jr. administration, this approach had only a few advocates—and not at the top echelons. Their ranks mostly included officials in the Pentagon planning di-vision, led by Deputy Secretary of Defense Paul Wolfowitz, and in the vice president's office, led by Lewis "Scooter" Libby. The 9/11 attacks changed all of that by converting the views of top officials, notably Vice President Rich-ard (Dick) Cheney and Secretary of Defense Donald Rumsfeld who became advocates of offensive liberalism at the cabinet level. This chapter argues that and demonstrates how 9/11 changed the worldview of these key officials and thus shifted the grand strategy from realism to offensive liberalism.

The ideas of the offensive liberals—commonly labeled neoconservatives (neocons)—were suppressed within the administration until 9/11, as the president intended to take a low-key path in the world, especially with re-gard to the business of "nation building," humanitarian interventions, and democracy promotion, instead focusing on domestic issues. The first eight months saw a major shift away from the interventionist activism of the Clinton administration. The 9/11 events changed that instantly, be-cause the threat perception became suddenly high. The 9/11 attacks were the first time since the War of 1812 that US sovereign soil—moreover, the main-land—was attacked.[3]

It is noteworthy that the change in the US strategy after 9/11 was demon-strated more dramatically in the Iraq War than in the Afghanistan War. The United States launched war in Afghanistan (with the support of the Northern Alliance that operated from within Afghanistan) as a defensive measure against an enemy that resided there—al-Qaeda and the hosting regime of Taliban. There was no immediate Iraqi provocation that justified a war. In a nutshell, while the war in Afghanistan was triggered by security threats and democratization was a welcome by-product, in Iraq, war was planned to remove Saddam Hussein's regime in order to enhance security. In other words, the connection between the democratization of both countries and US or international security was opposite. The reasoning for war was very different: Afghanistan—defense; Iraq—democracy promotion.

Colin Dueck argues that the international structural pressures explain very little in cases of shifts in grand strategy, while ideas explain much more. Bush replaced Clinton's liberal internationalism with realism, and after 9/11 the realist strategy was replaced by American primacy.[4] In our terms, it seems, Dueck says that Bush changed the strategy from defensive liberalism to defensive realism and then to offensive realism. We argue, however, that the changing external threat (and US hegemony) led to offensive liberalism, manifested by the focus on the democratization of Iraq, which became the defining foreign policy of the Bush administration.

Daniel Deudney and John Ikenberry argue that the Iraq War was not for liberal reasons but for "the pursuit of American hegemonic primacy."[5] They correctly suggest that the top architects of the war were Vice President Cheney and Secretary of Defense Rumsfeld and his deputy Wolfowitz, and that this troika was certainly not "liberal-internationalist." However, Deudney and Ikenberry err in seeing Cheney and Rumsfeld, on the one hand, and Wolfowitz, on the other hand, as the same.[6] Wolfowitz, we will show, was a prominent offensive liberal or neoconservative. His liberalism was indeed not internationalist à la the Clinton administration, that is, a defensive liberal approach, but he was an advocate of democratization by force, which is not a realist strategy but an offensive liberal one. Cheney and Rumsfeld indeed were realists, but we will show that after 9/11 they accepted the neoconservative argument that changing the Iraqi regime to a democracy would work in favor of the security of the US and its allies, that is, they were converted to offensive liberalism.

Concerning democratization, Deudney and Ikenberry argue that it was "a solution proffered by the Bush administration to simultaneously sustain public support for the war and provide a template for post-war Iraqi reconstruction. Democracy was not the core objective; it emerged both as a means to legitimize the war and as a program for making Iraq into a new pillar of the hegemonic American order in the region."[7] We demonstrate, through available evidence, that this argument is incorrect. Democracy promotion was a key goal of the Iraq War, although under the offensive liberal belief that democratization (initially of Iraq and later of the whole Middle East) would enhance US national security. Yet, it was too controversial (in the public sphere and the diplomatic one) to put up front, thus the administration emphasized the WMD issue.

The Rise of Offensive Liberalism

Three main changes took place in the US approach to security after 9/11. We will show that their combined effect was to bring US grand strategy in line with the offensive liberal perspective as described in chapters 1 and 2. This grand strategy has been applied most fully in the case of the 2003 Iraq War. Even though it is a single case of offensive liberalism discussed here, the Iraq War became a key issue for US foreign and security policy with major international, regional, and domestic implications.[8] Thus its importance for US grand strategy goes far beyond a single case. More specifically, three key changes in US conduct followed 9/11 in relation to the defensive liberalism of the 1990s: (1) the United States replaced multilateralism with hegemonic unilateralism; (2) the defensive strategy of the use of force was replaced by an offensive one; (3) peaceful democracy promotion was replaced with forceful regime change and imposed democratization. The following section explains each of these.

FROM MULTILATERALISM TO
HEGEMONIC UNILATERALISM

In the domain of diplomacy, the United States switched from its previous defensive liberal tendency to act in multilateral coalitions and with international sanction to a much greater reliance on unilateral hegemonic behavior, in which allies are in the backseat, with only very limited, if any, capacity to limit or block actions that the United States decided on. According to the new strategy, the United States should not compromise its national security and the life of its citizens by accepting multilateral obligations and committing itself to submit to the decisions of international institutions that might constrain its freedom of action, especially when 9/11 dramatically demonstrated that security dangers to the United States are acute. Rather, when international institutions put unnecessary obstacles in its path that prevent it from taking care of its security needs, the United States should use the opportunities provided by its global superiority and be ready to act unilaterally or to lead informal ad hoc "coalitions of the willing" (that is, states that are willing to follow the US lead), especially as, according to this approach, due to its superior liberal-moral character, its actions will also contribute to international freedom and peace.[9]

Thus, the "coalition of the willing" that the United States formed was structured to give it wide international support by allies who were indeed willing—that is, willing to be led. The United States decided to lead an ad hoc coalition, which included quite a few members—forty-nine. This coalition sounds similar to the coalition assembled for the Gulf War in 1990–91, but that coalition operated under clear UN Security Council authority, while in 2003 the coalition had no UNSC mandate. In 2001 the United States was acting in self-defense when it invaded Afghanistan, thus it did not need the same authorization as it needed for striking Iraq in 2003, or for that matter, in 1991. Afghanistan was the country from where the strike against the United States was masterminded and directed. Thus, the United States had the international legitimacy to act unilaterally there under any international circumstances.

The United States decided to make the most of its global superiority and not abide by the constraints established by international institutions, which raised suspicion in Washington that they reflected the interests of potential rivals. Such an attitude can be understood toward the UN Security Council, where four other countries have the veto power, and only one—the United Kingdom—was undoubtedly on the United States' side. Despite the expected increase in expenses and burden, the unilateral alternative was attractive because of the freedom of action it provided. The United States could cherry-pick its partners for the ad hoc alliances that might be needed. But the United States also believed that its liberal nature and the democracy that it would promote and enforce would make the world safer and more peaceful. This was the reason for toppling Saddam Hussein and making Iraq a democracy—overnight, if the plan would have worked out—instead of replacing Hussein with another dictator who could have been more cooperative.

The Iraq War was the major manifestation of the shift to a unilateral approach in US grand strategy. It is true that the Bush administration tried multilateralism first by approaching the UN Security Council to convince it to enforce the numerous Security Council resolutions passed on Iraq over the preceding twelve years. Yet, the administration was committed from the outset of the Iraq crisis to go to war with or without endorsement by the UN or by its major allies.[10] Indeed, the prewar debate over Iraq demonstrated the new US willingness to ignore the UN Security Council, the Europeans, the Russians, and the Chinese when its perceived key security interests were at stake.

It may be argued that the difference between Bush Jr., on the one hand, and Bush Sr. and Clinton, on the other, with regard to multilateralism (marked by UNSC blessing) is overstated. After all, Bush Sr. was determined to liberate Kuwait, with or without the UNSC. Clinton would have liked to have UNSC blessing for the US intervention in Kosovo, but knew he would not get it, and thus did not ask. Hence, they were supposedly as willing to forgo multilateralism and to act unilaterally as Bush Jr. was in Iraq. Our response is based on the above definition of multilateralism as the extent of institutional constraints on the freedom of action of the most powerful member of the coalition.[11] Thus, the multilateral coalition that Bush Sr. built for the Gulf War did constrain the United States from going to Baghdad after its overwhelming military victory and the liberation of Kuwait in 1991.[12] Especially notable was the opposition of two key coalition members: Saudi Arabia and Turkey, who strongly opposed regime change in Iraq with its potential destabilizing effects on their regional security environment.

In the case of Kosovo, Clinton did indeed bypass the UNSC due to the expected opposition of two permanent members, Russia and China. But, on the other hand, he did subordinate the United States to the institutional constraints of NATO during the Kosovo intervention. As a result, "decisions on everything from timing to targets were harder to make through an alliance than if the United States had been operating alone, because consensus needed to be reached among nineteen allies." Even though the United States dominated all the military operations, "each decision required painstaking negotiation . . . that cost . . . somewhat in terms of military efficacy." Allies were able to impose limits on US freedom of action by, for example, vetoing bombing targets in Serbia preferred by the US military leadership. Thus, for many US military leaders the lessons of Kosovo were to avoid multilateral military actions in the future because of the costs and the constraints due to the necessity of seeking consensus with allies during such sensitive operations.[13] Thus, even though the United States could have led a multilateral military operation in Afghanistan based on the universal political legitimacy of its operation there, it preferred, at least in the first stage, to intervene unilaterally in Afghanistan. In Iraq, obviously, there was not such a multilateral military option available because there was strong political opposition to the US intervention there—both in the UNSC and in NATO; still, the United States overlooked such opposition and acted unilaterally.

FROM A DEFENSIVE TO AN OFFENSIVE-PREVENTIVE
STRATEGY WITH REGARD TO THE USE OF FORCE

In the strategic-military field a shift occurred from a defensive strategy based on retaliation, deterrence, and use of force proportional to the threat, to an offensive approach in the form of preventive war. In the 2002 US National Security Strategy (NSS; the "Bush Doctrine"), this policy was called "preemption," a term that refers to a strike to preempt an imminent attack by the adversary. Yet, in fact, it is a preventive strategy, as the focus is on a resort to war against "rogue states" that do not necessarily threaten the US at present but might pose a threat a few years down the road if they are not stopped. As Bush himself defined it in a letter accompanying the NSS, the US must act "against . . . emerging threats before they are fully formed."[14]

FROM PEACEFUL DEMOCRACY PROMOTION TO FORCIBLE REGIME CHANGE AND IMPOSED DEMOCRATIZATION

The post-9/11 US grand strategy is liberal in its strong belief that a state's domestic regime is the source of its international behavior,[15] and therefore the nature of other states' regimes is important both to US national security and to global security. Yet, in contrast to the 1990s, when the United States was content to coexist with illiberal regimes and promote democracy by peaceful, softer means as a long-term goal, following 9/11 it adopted an offensive liberal approach, at least in extreme cases of anti-US "rogue states," which constituted a threat to its national security by sponsoring terrorism, developing weapons of mass destruction, or both. In such cases the offensive liberal approach calls on the United States to change the tyrannical regimes in these states by the use of force and install democratic (and therefore more peaceful) regimes. Forcibly removing dangerous despotic regimes is a much more ambitious undertaking than the limited humanitarian interventions that the United States pursued in the defensive liberal 1990s.

Thus, the 2002 NSS commits the United States to "champion the cause of human dignity and oppose those who resist it" by creating "a balance of power that favors human freedom." According to this approach, democratization is feasible everywhere because, as the Bush Doctrine suggests, "no people on earth yearn to be oppressed, aspire to servitude, or eagerly await the midnight knock of the secret police."[16] As Bush argues, "values of freedom are right and true for every person, in every society."[17] Offensive liberals believe that once a people is liberated from tyranny, it will automatically and universally endorse democracy irrespective of regional, religious, national, or cultural variations, because liberty is what people everywhere aspire to achieve.

Still, in practice this approach has focused mostly on the Middle East, as a region particularly dangerous to US national security—the region where the 9/11 terrorists came from and where their radical Islamic anti-US ideology developed. Accordingly, the strategy of regime change was manifested most clearly in Iraq (even though it was applied first in Afghanistan). As a result, the objectives of the 2003 Iraq War were much more ambitious and far-reaching than in the first Gulf War. In 1990–91, the United States was a status quo power, restoring the status quo ante that revisionist Iraq had violated. This time, in accordance with the offensive liberal rationale, the United States was the revisionist power that aimed to transform the Iraqi regime and potentially other regimes in the region. The objective of the Iraq War was not only to prevent Saddam Hussein from acquiring weapons of mass destruction or handing them to bin Laden (an unlikely option in the first place), but more fundamentally, to remove his regime from power in order to install a democratic one, and thus to spread democracy into the heart of the Middle East and the Islamic world.[18] Bush argued in 2002 that "liberty for the Iraqi people is a great moral cause and a great strategic goal."[19] He also said that "stable and free nations do no breed the ideologies of murder. They encourage the peaceful pursuit of a better life."[20] Thus, according to Bush, the United States has "a responsibility to promote freedom that is as solemn as the responsibility to protect the American people, because the two go hand-in-hand."[21]

Offensive liberals expect that through "domino" or bandwagoning dynamics, enforced regime change (such as in Iraq) will promote democratization in general, or at least in the neighboring countries. Such an undertaking, if successful, will strengthen the US reputation for resolve in opposing tyranny, and will lead to an imbalance of power in favor of liberal change. Successful regime change and democratization will show that dictators are not an inevitable feature of life and are not invulnerable, and that democracy is preferable to tyranny, and thus will inspire and encourage other peoples in the region to topple their own dictators and establish democratic regimes.[22]

According to offensive liberals, such a change in the Middle East in the direction of democratization would not only be beneficial for the cause of human freedom, but would also provide the most fundamental resolution of the terrorism problem, because terrorism and dictators are seen as two sides of the same coin. Tyranny creates discontent, and the lack of avenues of political expression in despotic Middle Eastern regimes breeds extreme anti-Western Islamic ideologies with a penchant for violence. In addition, anti-US dictators such as Saddam may also cooperate directly with terrorists. As then national security advisor Condoleezza Rice defined it in 2002, tyrants and terrorism "are different faces of the same evil. Terrorists need a place to plot, train and organize. Tyrants allied with terrorists can greatly extend the reach of their deadly mischief. Terrorists allied with tyrants can acquire technologies allowing them to murder on an ever-larger scale. Each threat magnifies the dangers of the other. And the only path to safety is to effectively confront both terrorists and tyrants."[23]

Explaining the Rise of Offensive Liberalism in the Post-9/11 Era

BUSH'S FOREIGN POLICY BEFORE 9/11

For our purposes, it is significant that Bush did not come to power with a preconceived offensive liberal agenda or with any enthusiasm for democracy promotion, and neither did his closest advisors and the top members of his cabinet. According to the model, when an administration comes to power, it is initially influenced by the beliefs of the key players. However, changing systemic conditions may compel it to accept new ideas and to change its grand strategy. Indeed, in contrast to Clinton's defensive liberal approach, both during the 2000 election campaign and in his first eight months in office, Bush's initial foreign policy approach could be described as tending toward defensive realism, with some offensive realist (unilateralist) elements.[24] This approach was more influenced by the worldviews of his administration's key decision makers than by the systemic factors, which should have led at that stage to a defensive liberal strategy. Thus, in an article published before the 2000 elections, Rice (then a close confidant of Bush and his chief foreign policy mentor) outlined a generally defensive realist line for the new administration, focusing on strengthening the US military and on great-power politics—that is, managing US relations and competition with other great powers such as China and Russia. Rogue regimes, proliferation of weapons of mass destruction, and terrorism were listed last on its list of priorities. Moreover, Rice explicitly attacked "the echoes of Wilsonian thought" in the Clinton administration and expressed a strenuous objection to humanitarian interventions.[25] Bush himself explicitly and repeatedly objected during the election campaign to the use of the US military in open-ended nation-building missions, a characteristic of the Clinton administration. Indeed, the new Bush administration seemed to replace the defensive liberal strategy of humanitarian interventions with a more "humble" defensive realist approach to intervention in others' domestic affairs.[26]

In addition to Rice, the other key members of the new Bush administration, notably Vice President Richard Cheney, Defense Secretary Donald Rumsfeld, and Secretary of State Colin Powell, were also far from supporting offensive liberal doctrines such as forcible regime change and democratization prior to 9/11.[27] Thus, during the 2000 election campaign, Cheney

̗ressed his support of the Clinton administration's containment policy toward Iraq and argued that the United States should not act as though "we were an imperialist power, willy-nilly moving into capitals in that part of the world, taking down governments."[28]

While several prominent offensive liberals were appointed to senior positions in the Bush administration (in the vice president's office, the Pentagon, the National Security Council, and the Defense Policy Board),[29] the key members of the administration—Cheney, Rumsfeld, Powell, and Rice—could be described as "traditional hard line conservatives far more interested in using American military power to defeat threats to US security than to remake the world in America's image," and "deeply skeptical of nation-building, especially when it involved the US military, and scornful that American power could create what others were unable to build for themselves,"[30] that is, realists rather than liberals. All—except for Rumsfeld—served under George H. W. Bush. Cheney and Powell were the leading defense figures who fully supported the limited goals of the Gulf War. The highest-ranking person in the new Bush administration who had held offensive liberal views (including support for forcible regime change in Iraq) long before 9/11 was Deputy Secretary of Defense Paul Wolfowitz, but given the realist views of all the other top members of the administration, he was unable to shape US grand strategy in an offensive liberal direction at that time.[31]

Indeed, while criticizing Clinton during the 2000 election campaign for not removing Saddam, once in power Bush initially maintained a containment strategy vis-à-vis Iraq and did not show much interest in regime change or in any significant military action against Saddam, and neither did Rumsfeld, Cheney, Powell, or Rice.[32] Among the top administration decision makers, the "war party" on Iraq before 9/11 consisted of Wolfowitz alone.[33] According to Immerman, Wolfowitz's view was that "to ensure liberty for all, America must destroy liberty's enemies. . . . Wolfowitz had identified Saddam Hussein as liberty's number one enemy."[34]

The policy option that seemed to be prevailing within the administration with regard to Iraq in summer 2001 was the one championed by Powell—"smart" sanctions, which focused on preventing Iraq from acquiring military materiel while relaxing limitations on civilian goods.[35] Bush later noted that prior to 9/11 "we were discussing smart sanctions . . . my vision shifted dramatically after September 11, because I now realize the stakes, I realize the world has changed."[36] As Daalder and Lindsay suggest, "had terrorists not attacked America on September 11, Iraq would likely have remained a secondary issue in American foreign policy."[37] Indeed, there is no indication that the Bush administration made any operational plan to remove Saddam from power prior to 9/11.

To sum up, prior to 9/11 neither Bush nor his closest advisors and top cabinet members showed any inclination to offensive liberalism in general and with regard to Iraq in particular. Despite the hawkish offensive realist tendencies of such key members of his cabinet as Cheney and Rumsfeld, the ideas of imposed regime change were absent from their agenda. These ideas came to the fore only in the aftermath of 9/11.

THE EFFECTS OF 9/11: THE RISING THREAT

The 9/11 attacks, in which about 2,900 Americans lost their lives, constituted the first significant attack on the continental United States since the end of the 1812 war, and the bloodiest day in US history since the end of the American Civil War in 1865. This event shattered US complacency and provided a traumatic demonstration that the international environment was much more dangerous than the US government and public previously imagined. As Bush defined it in his speech to Congress on September 20, 2001, "tonight, we are a country awakened to danger."[38] The attacks of 9/11 proved that the United States was threatened by a dangerous and undeterrable enemy with offensive capabilities—Islamic terrorism in general and al-Qaeda in particular—who demonstrated conclusively that it is not only willing but also capable of striking at the heart of its major cities and inflicting heavy damage to important US values. Al-Qaeda seemed committed to further terrorist attacks against the United States. Thus, a few months after 9/11, Cheney famously argued that it was not a matter of whether, but when, the terrorists would strike again.[39]

A particularly severe threat raised by 9/11 was that such militant Islamic terrorists might acquire WMD.[40] This connected the threat of terrorism with the issue of anti-US "rogue states" such as Iraq that might potentially provide the terrorists with such weapons.[41] Even if the rogues and the terrorists did not trust each other, they could conceivably form an alliance based on their common hostility toward the United States. In the case of Iraq, both Bush and Cheney became concerned that Saddam might use WMD to threaten US interests in the Middle East or provide them to anti-US terrorists.[42] Bush argued that this threat changed his attitude toward "Saddam Hussein's ability to create harm . . . all of his terrible features became much more threatening. Keeping Saddam in a box looked less and less feasible to me."[43] On September 12, 2001, Bush instructed Richard Clarke, the National Security Council's counterterrorism expert, to reexamine all evidence and see if Saddam Hus-

sein had anything to do with the al-Qaeda attacks.[44] This was three days before Wolfowitz's attempt to push for war with Iraq, which Bush rejected. This
indicates that Bush needed no more than a push to fix his sight on Iraq. This
also shows that Bush viewed regime change in Iraq in national security terms.
He envisioned the possible link of the Iraqi regime with terrorist organizations that, for their part, aimed to inflict severe damage on the United States;
thus, regime change in Iraq would help American security.

Mandelbaum claims that 9/11 made Saddam Hussein and the terrorists
indirectly connected in the minds of the senior officials of the Bush administration, and "made the removal of Saddam from power seem urgently necessary."[45] The 9/11 attacks changed the world for the administration in the sense
that Islamic terror appeared to be a global threat that would be worse once
the terrorist laid hands on WMD; therefore, the United States had to check
this threat by signaling to any perpetrator or sponsors of such attacks that this
would incur severe punishment.[46]

"According to those attending National Security Council meetings in the
days after September 11, 'The primary impetus for invading Iraq . . . was to
make an example of [Saddam] Hussein, to create a demonstration model to
guide the behavior of anyone with the temerity to acquire destructive weapons or, in any way, flout the authority of the United States.'"[47] Mandelbaum
writes that "uprooting the Baathist regime in Baghdad served that purpose in
a way that ousting the Taliban did not."[48] Despite the fact that Saddam Hussein did not aid al-Qaeda or have WMD, he was the type of leader who *would*
do such things given the proper opportunity. "In the wake of the September
11 attacks, and because of the September 11 attacks, not only what Saddam had
done but also what he might do seemed to the Bush administration a pressing
consideration."[49]

Due to the 9/11 attacks, the United States reevaluated the threats and considered which ones needed to get more attention so that they weren't surprises
like al-Qaeda's attack was. And based on the administration's knowledge of
Saddam Hussein, he became a plausible answer to this.[50] The United States
could easily assume that allowing Saddam to remain in power could allow
him to acquire WMD and threaten Iraq's neighbors and thus damage American interests. This was plausible enough for the administration to decide it
was too risky and it was better to remove him. In this sense, Mandelbaum
claims, the war on Iraq was a preventive war.[51] Bush explained in a speech to
the nation shortly before the war began: "We are now acting because the risks
of inaction would be far greater. In one year, or five years, the power of Iraq
to inflict harm on all free nations would be multiplied many times over."[52]

Tommy Franks quotes Bush from their December 28, 2001, meeting: "We should remain optimistic that diplomacy and international pressure will succeed in disarming the regime. But if this approach isn't successful, we have to have other options. That's why I asked Secretary Rumsfeld and Tommy to work on this concept. The worst thing that could happen to America would be a combination of WMD and terrorism. . . . I will not allow that to happen."[53]

The rising threat of terrorism and its potential connection to "rogue states" seemed to discredit three of the possible grand strategies—defensive and offensive realism as well as defensive liberalism—because they did not seem to offer an effective response to this type of threat. The realist strategy seemed less relevant to a nonstate threat. More specifically, the focus of defensive realism on deterrence was undermined by the phenomenon of the undeterrable suicide bombers.[54] Offensive realism's notion of preventive attack could potentially deal with the rogues' WMD, but it was put into question by the suspicion that even if a rogue's WMD infrastructure is destroyed, the hostile regime will make every effort to rebuild it, including by covert means, so long as this regime itself is not removed. The defensive liberal advocacy of multilateral diplomacy to advance nonproliferation seemed misplaced with regard to regimes that are likely to cheat about their WMD programs.[55] Still, it is doubtful that these considerations would have been sufficient on their own to bring about the war against Iraq. Here an intervening domestic-ideational variable came into play—namely, the rising influence of the neoconservative school.[56]

THE RISE OF THE OFFENSIVE LIBERAL/
NEOCONSERVATIVE APPROACH

As has been widely acknowledged, the post-9/11 strategy of the Bush administration was heavily influenced by the ideas of the neoconservatives. The neoconservatives are an intellectual movement that has existed since the 1960s–70s and has been a part of the US domestic debates on foreign policy throughout the 1990s. They are an informal group or network composed primarily of prominent intellectuals, former and current officials, analysts, journalists, and pundits, who are associated with such think tanks as the American Enterprise Institute and especially the Project for the New American Century.[57] Despite its misleading name, this school in fact epitomizes the offensive liberal approach to US foreign policy as defined in this volume: a combination of a liberal belief in democracy and its pacifying effects with the offensive willingness to employ massive force for regime change (and a distrust of international institutions as ineffective and constraining US policy). Leading neoconservatives have described themselves as "hard Wilsonians" and "liberal hawks"—that is, advocates of the use of US power to enforce US-style liberalism, and they have also been called by their critics "liberal imperialists."[58]

The neoconservatives have argued that "with the decline of communism, the advancement of democracy should become the touchstone of a new ideological American foreign policy," because "the more democratic the world becomes, the more likely it is to be both peaceful and friendly to America." This school exhibits a staunch belief in liberal democracy as the best form of government that is suited to all peoples irrespective of culture or religion. As all human beings are entitled to democracy, the United States has both a right and an obligation to help them achieve it, including by the use of force.[59]

The Middle East as the Prime Target

Despite these sweeping formulations, in practice the neoconservatives did not advocate a global democratic crusade by the United States in the 1990s, but rather have focused primarily on one region—the Middle East, due to its strategic importance to the United States, and especially because of two new security threats that they saw as emanating from this region—weapons of mass destruction and Islamic fundamentalist terrorism. Indeed, they perceived the main danger to the United States in the wake of the Cold War to be "rogue" or "backlash" states, in other words "future Iraqs—lawless, renegade states in possession of modern weapons, including those capable of mass destruction, and dedicated to the pursuit of aggressive, even terrorist, ends."[60] Apart from Iraq itself, most other "future Iraqs" were also located in the Middle East: Iran, Syria, Libya, Algeria.

The other emerging threat was the threat of Islamic fundamentalist terrorism emanating from the region. According to the neoconservatives, these twin threats were interrelated, and both stemmed from the tyrannical nature of Middle Eastern regimes. In their view, militant anti-US groups emerged in the Arab/Islamic world because of the authoritarian nature of the regimes there, which effectively silenced dissent. This lack of political space pushed the frustrated people to embrace radical ideologies and use violent means, while the regimes encouraged this tendency by following a diversionary or "scapegoat" strategy of diverting the peoples' attention away from the local oppressors toward the alleged external enemies of Arabism and Islam—the United States (the "Great Satan") and Israel (the "Little Satan").[61]

Accordingly, as a solution to the twin threats of terrorism and WMD in the Middle East, the neoconservatives advocated an offensive liberal strategy, focused not only on changing the capabilities of rogue regimes, namely, destroying their WMD and preventing them from acquiring more, but also (and primarily) on changing their ideological character by transforming the nature of their political system—namely, enforced democratization. In their eyes, the liberalization of Arab/Muslim regimes would not only reduce their incentives to acquire WMD and the danger that they might provide these weapons to anti-US terrorist organizations but would also "drain the swamp" in which such anti-US terrorists thrive. Given avenues for political expression, domestic support for radical Islamic ideologies would decline, and liberal regimes would no longer encourage them. Liberal regimes in the Middle East would not pose a security threat to the United States, a fellow democracy. Thus, a democratic transformation of the Middle East would ensure US security and energy supplies. This strategy was perceived not only as necessary for US security, but also as feasible, since democracy would be welcomed by the oppressed Middle Eastern peoples if only they were helped to get rid of their oppressors.[62]

The neoconservatives called to begin the enforced democratization of the Middle East with Iraq, due to its problematic record with regard to violations of Security Council resolutions and Saddam's hostility toward the United States. Moreover, because of its relatively sophisticated and secular urban middle-class population, Iraq was seen as the ripest for democracy among the regional states. In addition, the Iraqi people had suffered much under Saddam's tyrannical regime and consequently yearned for freedom and would welcome his overthrow. The expectation of the neoconservatives was that a successful regime change in Iraq would have bandwagoning effects on the other states and would thus trigger democratization across the Middle East. Namely, a democratic regime in a prosperous and stable oil-rich Iraq would serve as a model and a beacon for other Arab and Islamic societies that would compel their governments to democratize.[63]

FROM THE IRAQ FREEDOM ACT TO PRACTICE

Freedman makes the point that although there was a law from 1998 that the Clinton administration supported and there were attempts to back anti-Saddam organizations, the administration had not taken any major push in that direction. In the 2000 campaign, Gore seemed more aggressive on this issue than Bush, and Rice's *Foreign Affairs* article demonstrates that the Republicans' foreign policy would tolerate Saddam in power. In August 2001, there was a State Department memo, "A Liberation Strategy," but it wasn't ready for presentation.[64] "The change came with 9/11. Bush later observed that prior to this day, "we were discussing smart sanctions. . . . After September 11, the doctrine of containment just doesn't hold any water. . . . My vision shifted dramatically after September 11, because I now realize the stakes, I realize the world has changed."[65]

Gideon Rose offers the following causal chain to Bush's "regime change." He suggests that the administration wanted to get rid of Saddam without getting stuck in Iraq. Assuming that the Iraqi people would welcome the overthrow of Saddam, they would cooperate with the United States and run the country as liberated and free of oppression. Thus, a long-term occupation would not be necessary. Rose suggests that "the correct historical precedent to rely on, the argument ran, was not post–World War II Germany or Japan, but post–World War II France, which had not required a lengthy or invasive foreign presence in order to flourish once the fighting stopped."[66]

In his memoirs, Bush refers to the Freedom Agenda, which was the offensive liberal component of the Bush Doctrine. He wrote that it was "[advancing] liberty and hope as an alternative to the enemy's ideology of repression and fear."[67] Bush wrote that the Freedom Agenda was "both idealistic and realistic. It was idealistic in that freedom is a universal gift from Almighty God. It was realistic because freedom is the most practical way to protect our country in the long run."[68] This is a very optimistic worldview, however misinformed concerning the weakness of a common identity among the key ethnic/sectarian groups in Iraq and about their fragile loyalty to the Iraqi state—if they do not control it—and thus their inability to tolerate a peaceful transfer of power, the cornerstone of a democracy. We'll not elaborate on this crucial issue as our focus here is on the causes of the intervention, rather than its effects.[69]

Thus, the neoconservatives consistently advocated a US military action to overthrow Saddam Hussein for over a decade, since the 1991 Gulf War (which, in their opinion, ended prematurely, short of invading Iraq). Leading neoconservatives addressed open letters to President Clinton in 1996 and 1998 calling for Saddam's removal by US force.[70] However, despite their best efforts to persuade the Clinton administration and Congress that the enforced democratization of Iraq was central for US security, the Clinton administration repeatedly rejected their recommendations, and support for removing Saddam in the 1990s remained limited.[71] In the benign low-threat environment of the 1990s, the vast offensive liberal project of the democratic transformation of the Middle East beginning with Iraq had no chance of being adopted, and the neoconservatives remained on the fringes of the policy debate.[72] Moreover, despite the fact that some prominent neoconservatives were appointed to senior positions in the new Bush administration, they failed to influence its policy in its first eight months in office.[73] Indeed, in a

2000 publication of the Project for the New American Century, leading neo-conservatives acknowledged that the US government and society would be unlikely to assume the burden of the offensive liberal program "absent some catastrophic and catalyzing event like a new Pearl Harbor."[74]

The Effects of 9/11

The traumatic attacks of 9/11 provided precisely the "new Pearl Harbor" envisaged by the neoconservatives as a prerequisite for redefining US grand strategy.[75] Following 9/11, at the crucial juncture when the Bush administration was frantically searching for an appropriate new grand strategy to deal with the rising threat of Islamic terrorism, the neoconservatives were the only ones ready with a detailed plan, based on their long-standing agenda with regard to Iraq and the Middle East. They were able to present it as the "right" response to 9/11, including an explanation of the sources of terrorism (the Middle Eastern tyrannies as a breeding ground for discontent and radical Islamic anti-US ideology), as well as a solution and a plan for action (forcible regime change in the Middle East, starting with Iraq, as a way to remove the root cause of terrorism and also to eliminate hostile regimes that might provide WMD to terrorists).[76] "Suddenly, the neo-conservatives' long-desired goal of regime change in Baghdad coincided with the president's political need for a powerful response."[77]

Targeting Iraq

This sudden understanding of Iraq's potential WMD threat delivered by unorthodox means is reflected in the memoirs of President Bush and then national security advisor Rice. Bush writes that until 9/11 he focused on tightening the sanctions, but "then 9/11 hit, and we had to take a fresh look at every threat in the world." Bush notes that there were states that sponsored terror; states that were "sworn enemies"; states whose governments were hostile and threatened their neighbors; nations that violated international demands; repressive dictators; and regimes with WMD. "Iraq combined all threats."[78] Bush adds, "Before 9/11, Saddam was a problem America might have been able to manage. Through the lens of the post-9/11 world, my view changed. . . . The lesson of 9/11 was that if we waited for a danger to fully materialize, we would have waited too long. I reached a decision: We would confront the threat from Iraq, one way or another."[79]

In an interview in April 2002, Bush stated: "I made up my mind that Saddam needs to go. . . . The policy of my government is that he goes. This is not an issue of inspectors. . . . This is an issue of Saddam upholding his word that he would not develop weapons of mass destruction."[80] The fact that Iraq was not under inspection since 1998 became a source of concern after 9/11. Wolfowitz made the connection between bin Laden and Iraq as follows: "Containment was a very costly strategy. It costs us billions of dollars—estimates are around $30 billion. It costs us American lives. In some ways, the real price is much higher than that. The real price was giving Osama bin Laden his principal talking point . . . his big complaint is that we have American troops on the holy soil of Saudi Arabia and that we're bombing Iraq. That was his big recruiting device, his big claim against us."[81] Thus, by removing American bases from Saudi soil (since they no longer would be needed to deter Iraq), a major grievance of bin Laden would be removed.[82]

Condoleezza Rice admits that "we'd failed to connect the dots in September 10 and had never imagined the use of civilian airliners as missiles against the World Trade Center and the Pentagon; that an unconstrained Saddam might aid a terrorist in an attack in the United States did not seem far-fetched."[83] She adds that Saddam had a proven history of recklessness and "when coupling his proclivity towards miscalculation with his past support for terrorist activity, it was not unreasonable to suspect that he might supply extremists with a weapon that could be detonated in an American city. And in any case, it was a chance we were not willing to take."[84]

The idea of invading Iraq as an immediate response to 9/11 (forcefully advocated by Wolfowitz and other neoconservatives both within and outside the administration) was initially rejected in favor of Afghanistan.[85] However, as the war in Afghanistan wound down, the neoconservatives were provided with a golden opportunity to shape US policy. Seen through the prism of 9/11, the long-standing neoconservative program seemed much more plausible than before. With deterrence seemingly obsolete, 9/11 provided an opening to the neoconservatives supporting an invasion of Iraq by giving greater credibility to their claims that Iraq posed far more of a danger than previously believed.[86] "After the attacks, many in the administration became more open to arguments about the need to move swiftly against Saddam's regime."[87]

OFFENSIVE LIBERALISM AT THE HELM

This situation allowed the neoconservatives to move from the fringes of the policy debate to center stage, and to gain an unprecedented access to, and influence on, the highest levels of the Bush administration. Indeed, due to the availability and the seeming plausibility of the neoconservative approach, most key members of the Bush administration (Cheney, Rumsfeld, Rice, and most importantly, Bush himself)[88] became converts to it in the months after 9/11.[89] The trauma of 9/11 seems to have effected a transformation in the views of the key officials in the Bush administration who had not been offensive liberals before.[90] Bush himself seemed to have turned virtually overnight from a "humble" realist into a democratic crusader.[91] As even two leading critics of the Iraq War acknowledge: "there is no evidence in the public record showing that Bush and Cheney were seriously contemplating war against Iraq before 9/11."[92] George Packer cites Robert Kagan to the same effect: "September 11 is the turning point. Not anything else. This is not what Bush was on September 10."[93]

Thus, offensive liberalism became more and more dominant within the administration over the next months, and indeed informed both Bush's "Axis of Evil" address of January 2002 and the new Bush Doctrine of September 2002—called by one neoconservative "a quintessential neo-conservative document."[94] As a result, Iraq was perceived not just as a much more significant threat than previously, but also as a strategic opportunity for putting the doctrine into practice. The president became convinced by the offensive liberal argument that the United States can turn Iraq into a showcase of democracy, which will then inspire other Middle Eastern states to democratize and will help undercut the roots of Islamic extremism in the region.[95] As one administration official put it at the time, "the road to the entire Middle East goes through Baghdad."[96] Bush himself stated that "a liberated Iraq can show the power of freedom to transform that vital region, by bringing hope and progress into the lives of millions."[97] As a result, the neoconservative recommendation to make Iraq the next target of regime change was wholeheartedly accepted by the Bush administration.

Dueck writes that "Cheney and Rumsfeld joined longtime true believers in arguing for immediate 'regime change' in Iraq."[98] Their reasons included Cheney's argument that if Saddam maintained or developed WMD, he might use them to threaten US interests in the Middle East; the possibility that these WMD might be provided to terrorists; a defeated Iraq could be democratized and begin a regional process of democratization; and post-Saddam Iraq might be the future base for the US forces instead of Saudi Arabia. This latter reason was based on the fact that al-Qaeda recruited many people by inflaming them against American presence in Saudi Arabia.[99] The neocons' democratization reasons—in Dueck's view—were only secondary to the geopolitical reasons, although they had an effect on Bush.[100] Nevertheless, Dueck points out, at some point early in 2002, Bush "internalized the idea of regime change," as an official said, and decided to confront Iraq.[101]

Rice indicates that it was Cheney and his staff who "were absolutely con-

vinced that Saddam was somehow culpable" of colluding with al-Qaeda to
orchestrate 9/11 despite no evidence that the CIA could find.[102] Cheney convinced Bush to hear out Lewis "Scooter" Libby who presented to Bush and
Rice the evidence for the connection as he saw it, but Bush remained un-
convinced. As Rice puts it, "He [Bush] believed that the problem was not
a connection between Saddam and September 11 but rather a potential link
between Iraq's WMD and terrorism going forward."[103] In September 2002, a
National Security Council meeting ended with Bush saying, "Either he [Sad-
dam] will come clean about his weapons, or there will be war."[104]

Cheney recalls that the question of democratization was often raised in
the administration debates, and that he "believed we had no alternative. Any
provisional government would have to agree to early, free, and fair elections. . . . If the United States took military action and removed Saddam from
power, we had an obligation to ensure that what followed reflected our values
and belief in freedom and democracy."[105] In his State of the Union Address
on January 28, 2003, Bush said: "I have a message for the brave and oppressed
people of Iraq: Your enemy is not surrounding your country; your enemy is
ruling your country. And the day he and his regime are removed from power
will be the day of your liberation."[106] Robert Jervis writes: "That Bush did
believe in the importance and possibility of making Iraq democratic is further indicated by the fact that he twice vetoed proposals from Rumsfeld and
Cheney that he install Ahmed Chalabi in power and that he jettisoned the
original plan for leaving Iraq before extensive democratizing reforms were
carried out."[107]

In addition to influencing key members of the administration, the effects
of 9/11 made it possible for the neoconservatives to mobilize congressional
and domestic support for their views, which had enjoyed only a limited support before, and thus made the offensive liberal strategy politically feasible.
The public was now ready to support an offensive strategy to deal with the
rising threat.[108] Thus, in October 2002 the Senate authorized the use of force
against Iraq, by a margin of three to one.[109] Many leading Democrats supported the intervention in Iraq, the press was generally uncritical, and the
American people were strongly supportive of the war.[110]

Was This a Genuine Agenda?

Many observers were skeptical with regard to the sincerity of the Bush administration's commitment to democracy in Iraq. Critics noted that during
the domestic and international debate preceding the Iraq War, the administration was inconsistent in its arguments and put forth a shifting rationale

for the war (Iraqi WMD versus democratic liberation) to the Congress, the American people, the US allies, and the UN. Some critics viewed both motives as a smokescreen for more sinister corporate interests. We believe, however, that the Bush administration's conversion to offensive liberalism was perfectly genuine (while, of course, the US fiasco in Iraq shows that this does not mean that the neoconservative program itself was correct).[111]

The sincerity of the Bush administration with regard to its offensive liberal doctrine is demonstrated in the fact that it was put forth in classified documents, and not only in public pronouncements, and also that it informed the actual planning (or lack thereof) for the war and its aftermath. Thus, in August 2002, a top-secret memorandum on the goals of the coming war with Iraq (signed by Bush) defined the broader war objective. After ending the Iraqi threat to develop WMD (which was discovered later as false), the goal was to liberate the Iraqi people from Saddam Hussein's tyranny and help them "build a society based on moderation, pluralism and democracy." Accordingly, the United States planned to work with Iraqi opposition groups in order to demonstrate that the American attack was an act of liberation and not an invasion. The document defined the US commitment to Iraq as not ending in the act of bringing down Saddam, but also including a significant postwar role in building "a pluralistic and democratic Iraq."[112]

THE BELIEF IN DEMOCRATIZATION

As for the war planning, one of the puzzles of the US intervention (and one of the reasons for its failure) was the deployment of a relatively small force for the occupation of Iraq, despite the opinion of top army officers in favor of a much larger force. It seems that this decision stemmed from the offensive liberal core belief that once a people is liberated from tyranny, it will automatically endorse democracy irrespective of regional, religious, and cultural variations, because liberty is a universal aspiration. As a result, the administration expected that the US troops would be welcomed as liberators by an Iraqi population joyous at their deliverance from the clutches of Saddam's regime, and that resistance would be minimal. More pessimistic assessments of the difficulties and costs of democratization, and of the number of US troops that would be necessary to police the country during the transition to democracy, which in hindsight were more realistic, were confidently brushed aside.

Similarly, one explanation for the poor postwar planning for "the day after" in Iraq is also related to the belief that once a tyrant is removed from power, democracy will spontaneously emerge, because it was only the despot who denied the people the gift of freedom. Thus, the United States expected that once Saddam was removed from power, the Iraqis would automatically endorse democracy as any other nation, and thus there was no perceived need for detailed planning. A US military victory over Saddam was expected by the administration to be the equivalent of democratization.[113] Another argument that may demonstrate the sincerity of the Bush administration's commitment to democracy promotion is that the United States disbanded the Iraqi army and took pains to arrange for a constitution and for free elections in Iraq, rather than preferring the time-honored offensive realist option of installing a pro-American military dictator or strongman.[114]

As for the administration's inconsistency in advancing the democracy motive in the domestic and the international debate prior to the Iraq War, this need not imply that it was insincere in its commitment to democracy in Iraq. Rather, while regime change was a major part of the administration's plan all along, it may have deliberately downplayed this motive and emphasized the WMD issue (which it grossly exaggerated) for tactical reasons—that is, in the belief that a focus on WMD (rather than the more ambitious and controversial idea of regime change) would be more effective in mobilizing support for the war both domestically and internationally.[115] The fact that the administration was completely misled to believe that Iraq was manufacturing and stockpiling WMD is less important, according to Mandelbaum, but selling the falsehood to the administration was easy because of Iraq's history with WMD. The administration's projection of this falsehood to the public and the world then becomes an honest mistake.[116] Indeed, Wolfowitz later admitted that the administration emphasized the WMD issue "because it was the one reason everyone could agree on."[117] By "everyone" Wolfowitz probably included Secretary of State Colin Powell who was the most important skeptic of the war. Moreover, democracy promotion was a more abstract and complex argument than the security threat posed by WMD, which made it "much harder to sell to the public."[118]

To sum up, the transition in US grand strategy following 9/11 was the result of a systemic change in the balance of threat. The shift in grand strategy took place only when a new systemic factor arose—a major security threat that emerged after 9/11 and was added to the superior US capabilities (which have already existed since the collapse of the Soviet Union). Thus, the new grand strategy was crucially dependent on the combined effects of the two systemic parameters highlighted by the model: US preponderance of power (which remained unchanged) and the rising threat of Islamic terrorism. According to the model, such a combination of liberal hegemony and a high external threat is conducive to the emergence of offensive liberalism. While the US power preponderance made this strategy possible, it was the post-

9/11 high-threat environment that provided the incentive for its adoption. Indeed, the new US strategy adopted after 9/11 was broadly consistent with the offensive liberal approach.

Neoconservatism as an Intervening Variable

The influence of the neoconservatives on the US grand strategy, while unquestionably important, was not a major independent cause for the rise of offensive liberalism, but rather an intervening variable. As noted, neoconservative thinkers consistently advanced similar ideas during the decade before 9/11, but in the benign environment of the 1990s they could not find considerable domestic support for them. "It was 9/11 that provided the political context in which the thinking of the neo-conservatives could be turned into operational policy."[119] Namely, it was only in the aftermath of the terrorist attacks of 9/11 that domestic support for these ideas became dramatically stronger, at least initially. Only the traumatic experience of 9/11 and its effect on American society was able to provide a powerful enough incentive for the United States to pursue regime change by a massive use of force—an incentive that was manifestly lacking since the end of the Cold War. As a result, "the terrorist attacks of September 2001 brought neo-conservatives in from the cold. In the wake of that national trauma they and the belligerent mindset associated with them gained a prominence and influence that they had been striving for, mostly with only moderate success, for over thirty years."[120]

Most importantly, it was as a result of 9/11 that Bush and most key members of his administration, who had not been offensive liberals before, became converts to the neoconservative cause, and this approach became paramount in US grand strategy. Thus, it was 9/11 that changed "'humble' candidate Bush to a President whose administration's policy was based on unilateral preemption and millenarian nation building."[121] Since Bush had no previous ideological predisposition to offensive liberalism, his adoption of the offensive liberal strategy was a case of a decision maker overriding his initial inclinations, accepting new ideas, and adopting a new security approach to fit an emerging external situation. Nevertheless, not everyone accepted the neocons' views. The most prominent such figure within the administration was Secretary of State Colin Powell. But this cost him the president's ear, and although he kept his job until January 2005, he lost most of his influence.

Objection to the war from outside the administration was significant, although always a minority. Noteworthy was the ad and then article of political scientists John Mearsheimer and Stephen Walt, "An Unnecessary War,"[122] but even more hurtful for the administration's position was the op-ed by

General Brent Scowcroft, national security advisor to Presidents Ford and Bush Sr. and Condoleezza Rice's mentor, in August 2002, in the *Wall Street Journal*.[123] Several weeks after the article was published, Scowcroft and Rice met at a social occasion, and Rice said she wanted to bring democracy to Iraq. Scowcroft recalled replying, "Condi, it's just not going to happen. You can't build democracy that way"; and she replied, "Oh yes you can." Rice added, "The world's a mess and someone's got to clean it up." Scowcroft later told friends he was bewildered by her "evangelical tone."[124]

DECIDING ON WAR

Mandelbaum shows that the decision to go to war with Iraq "happened," that is, there was no point in time where the decision was made or communicated from Bush down to his administration. Nevertheless, in summer 2002 it was clear to the British intelligence that the United States had already made up its mind on war. Richard Haass, who was then director of policy planning at the State Department, noted "it's not a decision that was made so much as it 'happened.'"[125] Mandelbaum indicates that Bush's memoirs do not clarify this question and points out that "in general the administration lacked an orderly approach to decision-making, at least for foreign and security policy, which frustrated Secretary of State Powell."[126]

Rice writes that the United States went to war because it felt that it ran out of other options. But "we did not go to Iraq to bring democracy more than Roosevelt went to war against Hitler to democratize Germany, though that became American policy once the Nazis were defeated. We went to war because we saw a threat to our national security and that of our allies. But if we *did* have to overthrow Saddam, the United States had to have a view of what would come next." Rice recalls that in the NSC discussions, Rumsfeld and others argued that the US did not have an obligation to democratize Iraq and any alternative to Saddam would be fine. But, she writes, Bush thought that the US had to democratize Iraq and inject hope into the region.[127]

Even analysts who believe that the idea of replacing the regime in Iraq was not a mistake still suggest that the administration miscalculated how hard it would be to install a new regime to their liking.[128] This miscalculation is, however, closely related to the offensive liberal core beliefs. Thus, there was no plan for postwar Iraq, assuming—with no practical basis—that the Iraqis would welcome the Americans and that there would immediately be an Iraqi bureaucracy that would run the country under American direction, while oil revenues would pay for the recovery of the country.[129] What is important to our argument, however, is that even if the optimistic scenario was completely mistaken, as indicated above, it fits nicely with the offensive liberal perspective. The offensive liberals strongly believe in the universal acceptance of democracy. Thus, people in every culture and region are expected, according to this perspective, to welcome the installment of a democratic regime even if it is initiated under a foreign occupation. If the occupiers democratize the state, they will be seen as liberators.

The significant changes in the opinions of Bush and other key US decision makers in the aftermath of 9/11 pose a major challenge to Monten's otherwise useful model for explaining the Bush Doctrine,[130] based on the combined effects of unipolarity and "vindicationist" liberal ideology (what we call offensive liberalism). This explanation can account neither for the pre-9/11 behavior of the Bush administration nor for the dramatic change in strategy following 9/11. Indeed, we have shown that only when a high level of external threat was added to US hegemony did the administration change its initial realist inclination to an offensive liberal strategy. Table 8.1 summarizes the application of the two causal chains proposed in the model to the post-9/11 change in US grand strategy: As a result of the changing level of threat, both causal chains jointly brought about the transition to the offensive liberal grand strategy, which produced the war in Iraq.

The mounting difficulties and costs of democratizing Iraq have reduced the US appetite for additional endeavors of regime change. Even in the absence of such additional endeavors, however, the Iraq intervention and occupation are a far-reaching event in the evolution of US security policy, which lasted for eight years and is still an ongoing project that the United States is responsible for. Moreover, the offensive liberalism of the Bush administration was not limited to Iraq alone. According to a congressional report, "The Bush Administration has been heavily invested in promoting democracy to other countries. A theme in Secretary Rice's Transformational Diplomacy,

TABLE 8.1. Post-9/11 application of the two causal chains

Causal chains	Independent variables	Intervening variables	Dependent variables
Chain I	9/11 and the rising level of threat	Changing perceptions of top Bush administration officials: adopting offensive liberal views	Changing grand strategy: from initial defensive/ offensive realist inclinations to offensive liberalism, leading to the Iraq War
Chain II	9/11 and the rising level of threat	A changing balance of influence in the domestic battles on grand strategy: the rising influence of the neoconservatives	Changing grand strategy: from initial defensive/ offensive realist inclinations to offensive liberalism, leading to the Iraq War

announced in January 2006, was her plan to reform US diplomacy and foreign assistance activities with a key objective of promoting democracy in
other countries."[131] In the Middle East, in particular, democracy promotion
affected US policy not only in Afghanistan and Iraq but also in Lebanon,
Egypt, and, probably most importantly, in the Palestinian Authority. The
Bush administration insisted on holding elections in the Palestinian terri-
tories in January 2006 even though its allies in the region, particularly the
Israeli government and the moderate leadership of the Palestinian Authority
opposed it because of their fear of the rise of the radical Hamas movement.
Indeed, to the great surprise of the Bush administration, Hamas won, resulting in its later violent takeover of the Gaza Strip and growing violence
toward both Israel and moderate Palestinians. Thus, for better or worse, democracy promotion continued well beyond Iraq (and Afghanistan) as part of
the post-9/11 offensive liberal Bush Doctrine and has exercised major effects
on regional security in the Middle East and beyond.

HOW WOULD HAVE PRESIDENT AL GORE RESPONDED?

Given the systemic conditions of unipolarity and high threat and the appeal
of the offensive liberal ideas in a liberal democracy such as the US in the early
2000s, it is likely that another administration would have also decided on invading Iraq, although an alternative administration might have handled the
aftermath of the war differently.[132]

Our argument is supported by a major counterfactual analysis that concluded that were he president, Al Gore would have acted the same way as Bush
had, following 9/11.[133] Frank Harvey's counterfactual shows that the events
that followed 9/11 did not depend on the presence of neocons in the administration. Having neocons in the Bush administration did not mean that the
administration was offensive liberal. Only after 9/11 did Bush and most of
his senior advisors adopt the offensive liberal agenda. The same could have
happened under a Gore administration, even if the neocons would not have
been included in the administration but would have operated as an advocacy
group in the public sphere. As Harvey puts it, the more evidence that Gore
and his team would have faced the same amount of public pressure to act
forcefully toward Iraq, the less important is neoconservatism to the story.[134]
In our conception, the neocons had a role as an intervening variable, as the
domestic political support for their ideas and advocacy was strengthened by
9/11, in turn, affecting the US strategy. The change in the international environment that the 9/11 attacks caused would have had a similar effect under a

possible Gore administration, reinforcing offensive liberal views, thus Gore would go down a similar road to that of Bush.

The counterfactual on President Gore going to war reinforces our argument that changes in the international environment change domestic opinion and perceptions and as a result change the grand strategy. Harvey writes that "it is entirely conceivable (indeed highly probable) that the 2003 Iraq war would not have happened in either a Bush or Gore administration had the 9/11 attacks been prevented," adding that "in the context of 9/11, Gore's team would have been more inclined to make the same decisions on the path to war."[135]

In his analysis, Harvey provides evidence from Gore's speeches and interviews as vice president, as the Democrats' nominee for president in 2000, and after the elections, up to the Iraq War, proving that Gore was in favor of regime change. For instance, in his speech to the Council of Foreign Relations on February 12, 2002, he referred to his crossing of the party lines in 1991 and supporting the use of force against Iraq but added that Saddam survived the military defeat "as a result of a calculation we all had reason to deeply regret for the ensuing decade. And we still do. So this time, if we resort to force, we must absolutely get it right. . . . Failure cannot be an option."[136]

Harvey claims that Gore would have adopted the same policy as Bush—trying initially to deploy UN inspections back in Iraq, which, once rejected by Baghdad, would have likely led to war. Gore would also have rejected the status quo of failing sanctions and containment of Iraq, alongside the need to do more *after 9/11* against the presumed Iraqi WMD programs that supposedly threatened the US and its allies.[137] Such a view of the threat posed by the presumed Iraqi WMD was widely shared in the political and public arenas as well as among the permanent members of the UNSC.[138] Gore also shared the almost consensus view of Iraq's WMD threat. This is one of the bases for Harvey's counterfactual argument that if Gore had been elected, he would have also eventually led the US to war against Iraq once Saddam rejected the UNSC resolution on the deployment of UN inspections.[139] For our emphasis on the offensive liberal ideas leading to war, it is noteworthy—for the counterfactual exercise on Gore going to war—that he also supported the policy of "regime change" and believed in the relationship between democratization and US security.[140]

Interestingly, Harvey cites sources that suggested that Paul Wolfowitz was a potential candidate for secretary of defense in Gore's administration.[141] But perhaps even without Wolfowitz, regime change would have been a major goal, assuming that Richard Holbrooke would become secretary of state, which was very likely. He wrote in the *Guardian* on August 29, 2002, that "this [Bush] administration has (rightly) called for regime change. . . . If military action against Baghdad begins, it will soon become evident that it is impossible to eliminate weapons of mass destruction without a change in regime."[142]

Conclusion: The Fall of Offensive Liberalism

The rise of US hegemony after the end of the Cold War led to the dominance of liberal approaches over realist ones, because the decline in international constraints with the disappearance of the Soviet power enabled the US to promote its ideological preferences. So long as the international environment continued to be benign, as in the 1990s, the dominant liberal strategy of the US (implemented by the Bush Sr. and the Clinton administrations) was a defensive one. The 9/11 attacks gave an impetus to the emergence of an offensive liberal strategy, manifested by the new Bush Doctrine and its implementation in the war against Iraq. The three key components of the strategy include hegemonic unilateralism, the preventive use of force, and regime change or democratization, including by the use of force.

Can the model explain the decline of offensive liberalism since its heyday leading to the Iraq War? On top of the numerous failures of the Iraq War,[143] the fall of offensive liberalism could be explained as the result of a change in one of the key systemic independent variables presented here. While the US power preponderance didn't immediately change in the aftermath of the Iraq War, a more likely explanation is the decline in the degree of threat against the US homeland. As the US moved further away from the traumatic memories of 9/11, and since no major new terrorist attack took place against the US and the al-Qaeda terrorist network seemed to be in eclipse, the US threat perception declined accordingly. Until the rise of ISIS around 2014, there has also emerged a growing disassociation between the security threat to the US (posed by al-Qaeda) and the US struggle to stabilize Iraq, and the offensive liberal Bush administration found itself vulnerable to allegations by the US public that it entangled the US in an unnecessary war that was irrelevant to the main security threat posed to the US by global terrorism. Thus, there was no support for additional major military interventions for democracy promotion.[144] Indeed, the election of Barack Obama for president in 2008 was partly the result of the US disillusionment with the Iraq War and of the decline in the perception of external threat. Even if in a completely different political context and definitely not the only or major reason for the election outcome, still the election of Donald Trump in 2016 was also a reflection of the rejection of the offensive liberal agenda.

Even if offensive liberalism declined, democratization in the Middle East remained part of US foreign policy, although as a much more modest element in an overall defensive liberal approach. So long as the US remained the global hegemon, which did not have to confront major great-power challenges, it was likely to accept and act on the liberal insight that its national security depends on democratic reforms in the region. With the decline in the level of threat, however, the Obama administration, as discussed in the next chapter, reverted to a defensive liberal strategy of promoting democracy in the region by peaceful means and multilaterally (with the Europeans, NATO, and the UN—as was reflected in the 2011 Libya intervention), and by advancing economic development and conflict resolution of the Israeli-Palestinian dispute. Thus, the initial inclinations of the Obama administration were defensive liberal ones, in tune with the systemic factors (US preponderance and a declining level of threat). Chapter 9 also addresses the changes in the Obama strategy once the systemic conditions yet again had changed.

Obama: From Defensive Liberalism to Defensive Realism — Systemic Changes Lead to the End of the Liberalization Project

President Barack Obama came to office with strong defensive liberal prefer-ences—based both on his views formed during a young age and the effects of the post-9/11 era, especially the Iraq War experience. Yet, following some notable changes in the external environment later in his administration, es-pecially in the second term, Obama moved more toward some defensive real-ist positions. At any rate, the systemic changes have diminished the focus on liberalizing the world, defensively or offensively.

The Initial Defensive Liberal Views[1]

Obama's priority was to focus on "nation-building at home" rather than do-ing it in foreign countries.[2] A key implication was to minimize military com-mitments and interventions in general, including for democracy promotion. The US should pursue a light footprint and instead of focusing on regime change should change the United States' reputation in the world and focus on weakening anti-Americanism by adopting much more moderate and ac-commodating policies. This applied particularly to the Arab and Muslim worlds as was manifested in Obama's Cairo address of June 4, 2009.[3] Obama believed in the utility of accommodating rivals such as Russia and China by offering some concessions, expecting reciprocity and compromise, while en-gaging even with rogue states on their nuclear development (notably Iran and North Korea).

As a defensive liberal, Obama subscribed to the idea that while it is pref-erable to avoid the use of force, if intervention has to take place, it should be multilateral. On the whole, he rejected the realist balance-of-power ap-proach as irrelevant for the twenty-first century. Thus, defense spending has to be cut and nuclear weapons should be eventually abolished. While the US should pursue military retrenchment from different parts of the world, it should focus on diplomacy, international institutions and global governance, economic engagement and globalization, and soft power. There should be a turn away from what realists consider "high politics"—national military security—to the supposedly "low politics" of fighting poverty, disease, and climate change, while advancing economic development and women's issues. Based on all of this, the US ought to lead by example (or soft power) rather than by coercion (or hard power).[4] Even more specifically, Obama believed in the force of his own personality, and his special life story, to transform the relations between the US and other states.[5]

The Defensive Liberal Policies

These views were reflected in some of Obama's key policies. He pursued a re-set with Russia, focusing on more cooperative relations, notably a new arms control accord and trying to reduce tensions, including by managing competition in the post-Soviet sphere.[6] The administration followed reassurance and cooperation with China. When Obama came to power in 2009 and the administration started to focus on global challenges—nuclear proliferation, climate change, and financial instability—it planned to make China the key partner in tackling these transnational issues (the idea of a G-2).[7] The administration also engaged with the rogues, notably Iran and North Korea, aiming to reach an agreement to end their nuclear programs. The administration pushed a diplomatic solution to the Israeli-Palestinian conflict in the form of the "two-state solution," while opposing Jewish settlements in the West Bank.

Notably, Obama pursued a disengagement from the Iraq and Afghanistan Wars. Yet, while he opposed the Iraq War well before it started, he saw Afghanistan as the "good" defensive war in response to an unprovoked attack. Obama favored a tough counterterrorism against al-Qaeda there (and, if necessary by using drones even in other countries where anti-US terrorists found refuge such as Somalia and Yemen). Thus, Obama initially increased the number of soldiers in Afghanistan (from thirty-eight thousand to sixty-eight thousand), even if aiming to disengage later on, thus limiting the military presence until July 2011 and deciding against nation building. But then the president delayed the full departure of soldiers until the end of 2016, and in 2015 decided to keep some military presence beyond 2016.[8]

As a defensive liberal, Obama was sympathetic to the urgent need for major political and economic reforms in the many malfunctioning states in the Middle East.[9] In light of the great difficulties, however, of pursuing such reforms in this chaotic region, his administration had not done much to promote changes in the region, while trying to lessen US engagement there. Obama didn't pursue regime change, although he demonstrated some support for democracy promotion. Most notably during the uprisings of the Arab Spring, which erupted in 2011, Obama indeed abandoned the old US authoritarian ally President Hosni Mubarak of Egypt.[10] At the same time, Obama didn't act against the democracy-suppression intervention of another US ally—the Saudis—in Bahrain. Still, he developed working relations with the democratically elected Muslim Brotherhood despite the ideological gulf between their respective worldviews, although the administration imposed only minimal sanctions on the military that removed the government of the Muslim Brotherhood in Egypt in July 2013. The US did take part in the 2011 humanitarian intervention in Libya, which became, in fact, a regime-change endeavor.[11] But the US was "leading from behind," and its intervention was by European request, authorized by the UN Security Council under Responsibility to Protect (R2P).[12] Moreover, it discontinued the intervention as soon as Gaddafi was removed from power. With regard to the massive killings in Syria during the civil war, Obama did not do much apart from bombing the Islamic State and some very limited training and arming of relatively moderate insurgents. Most infamously, Obama did not pursue his stated "red line" against the use of chemical weapons even after a major gas attack by the Assad regime on Syrian civilians.[13]

The Post-2014 Adaption of the Grand Strategy: Toward Defensive Realism?

During the second term, especially in its second half, the Obama administration adopted some elements of defensive realism vis-à-vis the revisionist great powers, namely, some components of balance-of-power strategy, though the response was fairly moderate and defensive. While not reversing completely his grand strategy, Obama adopted elements of defensive realism against Russia and China. The realist dimension is, first of all, the focus on the rising great powers. The defensive element refers to the limited steps of balancing and containment toward Moscow and Beijing.

China   The Chinese revisionism, on top of its traditional claim toward Taiwan, has been growing in the second decade of the twenty-first century by more assertive, or even aggressive, behavior in its maritime disputes with neighboring states in the East and South China Seas and also the border conflict with India.[14] In response, the Obama administration revised the initial focus on accommodation and integration in the framework of economic globalization and international institutions with a more muscular strategy of "rebalancing" or "pivot to Asia."[15] This strategy, initiated in 2011, included several elements of containment based on US military posture in Asia, starting with a small military deployment in Australia, but expecting to deploy in the region 60 percent of US naval and air capabilities.[16] Strengthening US regional alliances was also an important part of the strategy: formally with Japan, South Korea, and the Philippines; a growing partnership with India; and also informally with Vietnam. There was also an economic component, notably the Trans-Pacific Partnership, a huge trade deal linking twelve countries, including the US, but excluding China. Thus, this deal also had strategic importance as a "soft" balancing of China.[17]

The new strategy might also be interpreted as "offshore balancing," namely, buck-passing the responsibility of balancing to the regional powers so that they'll balance the aspiring regional hegemon. If they fail to balance, however, the US would be involved directly in balancing. While the post–Cold War relations with China involved both competition and cooperation, by 2014 it became more rivalry than partnership[18]—a radical change in US policy in relation to the much more integrative policies of the Bush Sr. and Clinton administrations.[19] Their administrations believed that China would be willing to join the US-led liberal order based on its successful integration to the global economy.

Even though the Obama administration initially sought to further enhance cooperation with China on a more equal footing ("G-2"), it gradually realized that China would not accept cooperation in the post–Cold War framework of the US-led liberal international order. Specifically, the revisionist Chinese conduct in East Asia demonstrated to the administration that it was aiming to establish a sphere of influence there, while removing US dominance in the region. The administration realized that China viewed its collaborative behavior as weakness and that it had to take into account the balance of power and use more assertive diplomacy. The administration deserted its initial accommodation and the idea of a "G-2," instead setting up an informal containment of Chinese expansion.[20] Thus, the Obama administration challenged the claims of China to control the South China Sea based on the freedom of navigation norm. In this context, in 2010 the administration tried to organize resistance of ASEAN countries to the Chinese claims. This move led to heavy criticism of the US by China but support from most of the ASEAN members.[21] At the very least, the US and its Asian allies started following a strategy of hedging—namely, while aiming to continue collaboration with China, they prepared to defend their interests in case China posed an even more severe threat to them. This included a new military doctrine for the Western Pacific—the so-called Air Sea Battle, intended to consider rising Chinese naval capabilities.[22]

It became clear to the administration that the defensive liberal optimistic assumptions about the benign effects of economic globalization of China were not materializing.[23] The remarkable economic growth of China produced neither a democracy at home nor peaceful behavior abroad. This realization led the strategy toward China to be based more on defensive realist power politics even if not aiming to produce a full-blown confrontational policy toward such a huge trade partner. While the administration sought to focus on East Asia, with its rising economic and strategic centrality in the global balance of power, the Arab Spring turmoil in the Middle East pulled it back to the region, while the revisionist Russian behavior also attracted attention to the escalating crisis in Ukraine.

Russia   There was also a shift in Obama's strategy toward Russia even if not as radical as some analysts hoped for.[24] Still, the policy changed from the reset of a conciliatory policy of accommodation,[25] to imposing economic sanctions following the annexation of Crimea and the intervention in favor of the separatists in eastern Ukraine in early 2014.[26] It was significant that the sanctions were imposed in concert with the EU, whose trade with Russia was fifteen times larger than that of the US.[27] The sanctions severely limited Western business with key sectors of the Russian economy: energy, engineering, defense and high-tech, and metals and mining. The US and the EU also froze the assets of and denied visas to dozens of Putin's cronies and shut down credit markets to all of the major banks in Russia apart from short-term loans.[28]

The administration also focused on reassuring European allies by raising US-led NATO deployments to front-line states in Eastern Europe, prepositioning military equipment there, conducting joint NATO exercises, and increasing political, economic, and security assistance to Ukraine. Still, critics argued that Obama had not done enough to counter Russian aggression and that the initial reset signaled weakness, which together with the lack of military response to the violation of the "red line" in Syria, encouraged Putin's aggression in Ukraine and later his military intervention in Syria.[29]

Obama's response to the annexation of Crimea did convey a growing resolve to deter Russian aggression and a shift from the initial liberal approach to a more realist one.[30] The response remained, however, well within the framework of defensive realism. The defensive nature of the strategy was manifested by the great emphasis on avoiding escalation with Russia.[31] Obama clearly understood that the balance of motivation favors Russia, which had more at stake than the US in proximate Ukraine and no American president would be willing to go to war for Ukraine.[32] The defensive character of Obama's grand strategy can also be seen in the area of arms control with Russia (the New START Treaty, which reduced US and Russian arsenals to 1,550 nuclear warheads and seven hundred delivery vehicles each), although the arms race with Russia was not terminated.[33]

Nuclear proliferation   Especially notable is the multilateral great-power agreement with Iran (P5+1) in July 2015 on blocking its path toward acquiring nuclear weapons (at least for the next ten to fifteen years) in exchange for ending the heavy sanctions imposed on Iran because of its nuclear program. The defensive liberal vision of nuclear abolition was not accomplished, but the defensive realist element of arms control made some progress even if acrimonious debates have continued regarding the effectiveness of the Iran accord in stopping its nuclear plans and also Tehran's aggressive regional behavior in a number of Arab states.[34] The Obama administration inflicted very painful sanctions on Iran—in multilateral collaboration with the other powers—which led to the Iranian acceptance of the nuclear deal. At the same time, the administration avoided the offensive realist option of a preventive war against Iran despite pressures from its allies in the region, notably Israel and Saudi Arabia, to pursue such an option.[35] At the same time, there was no success in the effort to stop the nuclear development of North Korea, so the administration embarked on the defensive realist policy of deterrence and containment toward Pyongyang.[36]

Terrorism   With regard to violent nonstate actors, Obama escalated US involvement a few years after the disengagement from Iraq at the end of 2011. In June 2014 ISIS surprised the world by occupying the second largest city in Iraq—Mosul—and formed the so-called Islamic Caliphate on a large territory in northwest Iraq and northeast Syria. In response shortly afterward, four thousand US ground troops returned to Iraq (and some special forces deployed to Syria) to fight ISIS along with a bombing campaign against the terrorist organization in Iraq and Syria. This was a modest escalation more or less in proportion to the terrorist threat also posed to Americans by ISIS. The administration moved away from the ambitious offensive liberal agenda of nation building, regime change, and democracy promotion despite the initial defensive liberal sympathy to these ideas in the administration. It became completely clear that the US didn't have the power and the willing-ness to promote such polices in the Middle East. Rather, the administration focused on a more modest counterterrorism strategy, already before the rise of ISIS—including by aggressive moves such as the killing of bin Laden in Pakistan and the resort to targeted killings by drones in a few countries such as Afghanistan, Pakistan, Somalia, and Yemen.[37]

The Explanation: Changes in the Balance of Power and the Balance of Threat

Changes in the external environment brought about some significant revi-sions in the grand strategy so that it approximated more a defensive realist grand strategy. During the second half of Obama's second term, the inter-national environment became more competitive on the great-power level. There was also an escalation in the conflict with violent nonstate actors. More specifically, changes in the *distribution of power* brought about the end of the liberalization strategy.

The US was still the dominant global power, but the balance of power had changed in key regions.[38] One key factor was the rise of others—the BRICS (Brazil, Russia, India, China, and South Africa), notably China—economi-cally and militarily in some regions. Some of the economically emerging powers translated their growing resources into rising military spending in contrast to post-WWII economic powerhouses such as Japan and West Ger-many. In East Asia, over twenty years of Chinese armament, based on its huge economic growth, have increased the costs of US ability to project power into the region in times of crisis, involving Taiwan and other partners.[39] Especially in proximity to China's coastline, the combined effect of adverse geography and much upgraded Chinese air-defense and air-superiority capabilities con-siderably constrained American aerial dominance in the region. Rising oil prices in the early 2000s made possible Russian military modernization. Such growing military capabilities made it more difficult for the US to intervene on behalf of its allies in Eastern Europe.[40]

In the second decade of the twenty-first century, the US had started to simultaneously confront a growing number of regional challenges in the Middle East, East Asia, and the post-Soviet sphere. The spread of advanced capabilities such as precision weapons, integrated air-defense systems, and others undermined US dominance, particularly in the air. This increased considerably the constraints on US freedom of action in case of armed con-flicts. This had adverse effects on US alliances, while tempting opponents to pursue their revisionist goals.[41]

The military buildup was made possible by the major economic growth of both China and Russia. Between 2000 and 2010, the Chinese economy expanded fivefold from $1.2 trillion to over $6 trillion; at the same time, the Russian economy grew almost tenfold from $259 billion in 2000 to more than $2.2 trillion in 2013.[42] Becoming more powerful economically and militarily has made it possible for China and Russia to resist more forcefully US hegemony—and its liberalization efforts—and to initiate some revisionist endeavors in their respective regions.

There was also some relative weakening of the West (composed of two major pillars—the US and Europe) following the 2008 financial crisis in the US (and the 2010 Euro crisis). The Great Recession undermined US global power and lowered the global standing of the US.[43] The very heavy economic costs to the US weakened its ability to lead the international order.[44] Due to the crisis, Europe also became less capable to pursue international engagement.[45] At the same time, the ability and motivation of China and Russia to challenge the weaker US-led order by following their respective territorial ambitions increased, while the rogue states (North Korea and Iran) enhanced their quest to acquire nuclear weapons. The limits to US power were demonstrated by the wars in Iraq and Afghanistan, and together with the economic crisis, they weakened the US public's willingness for international engagement.

These changes seem to indicate the start of a potential transition to multipolarity; more specifically, they made possible the return of great-power competition as was expressed in several crises in 2014. The changing distribution of capabilities meant that the freedom of action of the US to promote the liberal agenda by changing the domestic character of other states became much more constrained. At the same time, there was an increase in the ability of the great powers that possessed growing military power—China and Russia—to challenge US hegemony, at least in their respective regions. Under these conditions, the realist strategy reemerged again, as before the rise of unipolarity, as the most appropriate strategy for dealing with the growing great-power competition. In other words, the changes in the external environment compelled a transition from a liberal grand strategy to a realist one. The emerging international system forced again a focus on great-power rivalry.

The balance of threat   The extent of the rising threat and who poses the greatest threat became more debatable. While there was some rise in the level of threat because of the more aggressive behavior of Russia and China, the level of threat to the US and its key allies still remained low overall.[46] This was true even after the key threatening event of the Russian seizure of the

Crimean Peninsula in early 2014 and then its covert intervention in favor of the separatist insurgents in eastern Ukraine. While challenging the key international norm of territorial integrity and posing a threat to some of the post-Soviet neighbors, the Russian behavior as such posed a very low direct threat to the US or even to its key European allies.[47]

China also began to behave more assertively during Obama's second term, especially with regard to the maritime disputes with the Philippines and Vietnam, among other Southeast Asian countries. Notably, China accelerated building artificial islands in the South China Sea with some military infrastructure and installations on them. China also behaved assertively against the Japanese control of the Diaoyu/Senkaku Islands in the East China Sea. The potential threat posed by China was quite considerable, but more for the medium or longer run. Moreover, the challenge was mostly regional, while China showed a willingness to cooperate on global issues. Thus the potential Chinese threat was partly ameliorated by areas of cooperation, including in the last years of the Obama administration, notably the 2015 Paris Climate accord signed, most notably, by both China and the US among dozens of other countries and the nuclear deal with Iran in which both China and the US were among the six powers (P5+1) that negotiated the deal with Iran. China also demonstrated cooperation on the global economy and counterterrorism.[48]

The rogue states—Iran (at least until the 2015 deal) and North Korea—although not as powerful as the great powers, China and Russia, still have become more dangerous with their nuclear buildup. Following the 2015 nuclear deal with Iran, precluding its capacity to acquire a nuclear bomb, at least for ten to fifteen years, the key threat remained North Korea. Still, based on US nuclear deterrence and by 2016—still lacking the ability to reach US shores—the North Korean threat seemed manageable. Finally, the direct threat to the US posed by violent nonstate actors such as al-Qaeda and the Islamic State was not only weaker than the potential threat posed by the rival great powers, but homeland security improved considerably since 9/11 and that further minimized the threat posed by the terrorist organizations.

Conclusion

In 2014, the challenges that the Obama administration faced had mounted to such an extent that they compelled the administration to reconsider its initial assumptions of defensive liberal means. The administration ended up countering the challenges with a defensive realist strategy.

The key explanation of the strategy change refers to the rising challenge posed by the revisionist powers—China and Russia, which became more militarily powerful as well as more assertive in their respective spheres of influence. Realist grand strategy seemed to be the most appropriate for the emerging great-power competition. The level of the competition and the related threat to US national security still seemed manageable in the framework of defensive realism without escalating to a more offensive approach.

America First: The Trump Grand Strategy in a Comparative Perspective

The previous chapters show that in the post-1945 period four major competing ideas have struggled over the dominance of American grand strategy: defensive realism, offensive realism, defensive liberalism, and offensive liberalism. This ideational competition was brokered by the international system, more specifically according to variations in the global balance of power and the balance of threat confronting the US (see the tables in appendixes 1 and 2 summarizing the changes in the grand strategies of the administrations from Truman to Obama).

The puzzle addressed in this chapter is the following: what happened in 2016, and in preceding years, which led to the election of a candidate— Donald J. Trump—who strongly opposed the liberal strategies that dominated US strategy since the end of the Cold War? Moreover, despite some supposed resemblance to realist grand strategies, especially defensive realism, this chapter will also show some marked differences between realism and Trumpism (see table 10.1 below).

Thus, the question we'll explore here refers to the influence of systemic causal factors, highlighted in this book, on the selection of such an approach that differs markedly from all its predecessors even if some of the elements of this approach are not translated into actual behavior. This lack of a full translation is at least partly because of the external constraints highlighted in this study as causing differences between the initial views and the actual strategy.

Can changes in the balances of power and threat explain the rise of Trumpism? Obviously in the 2016 elections domestic factors (both economic and cultural) played a key role. But still foreign policy issues played some role in the elections—whether directly or especially indirectly—and the fact that such a markedly different orientation could be selected calls for an investigation also of the effects of the international factors.

We argue that periods in which there is a lack of clarity and consensus on the balance of power and the balance of threat may lead to the emergence of ideas about grand strategy that are markedly different from the previously mainstream ones. Such ideas might also tend to have some confused, extreme, and incoherent elements. This is taking place at least partly because in the second decade of the twenty-first century, some changes are gradually taking place with regard to the two key causal factors we discuss in this book—the balance of capabilities and the balance of threat.

While the US still has a unique combination of military, economic, scientific, and technological capabilities, some level of relative decline in US power has taken place, which weakens the post-1991 unipolarity. Such a power transition—even if a relative and a controversial one—decreases the ability and willingness of the US to advance the liberal grand strategies it has been promoting in the post–Cold War era, as discussed in chapters 7–9. At the same time, the lack of clarity about the balance of threat—with different groups highlighting different sources of threat—weakens the appeal of the realist grand strategies, which tend to be especially attractive when there is a consensus on the key threat, as was the case during the Cold War about the Soviet threat (discussed in chapters 3–6).

The disagreements in the American polity (and also among experts) over the two key balances and their rising lack of clarity increase the likelihood of the rise of an incoherent and confused grand strategy, which might also have some different ideas than the previously dominant realist and liberal grand strategies. This chapter argues that this is the international context for the rise of Trumpism/offensive illiberalism in 2016, even if factors on the domestic and personal levels play a key role in making possible the rise of Trumpism and in shaping its specific character.

The first section of this chapter analyzes some of the key differences between Trumpism/America First grand strategy and the realist and liberal strategies. The second section explains the rise of Trumpism under the conditions of a power transition and a major disagreement over threats. This is a current manifestation of the overall argument in this book that variations in power and threat can account for key changes in grand strategy over time. The third part discusses some of the details of the inconsistent and incoherent foreign policy of the Trump administration in recent years.

America First versus Liberal and Realist Approaches

It is quite obvious that Trumpism, or more generally offensive illiberalism, nationalism, or—as labeled by Trump—America First, whatever its precise content, is dramatically different from the liberal strategies—either defensive or offensive—and it challenges in some major ways the key pillars of the US-led international liberal order (on these challenges, see table 10.2).[1] America First/nationalism shares with realism—in contrast to the liberals—a focus on the material world, which includes the global balance of power (the key for realists), and also relative material gains, which are key for America First, and are also important for the realists, though their focus is less on short-term gains than the Trumpists.[2] Despite this similarity to realism in turning down key elements of international liberalism and the international liberal order, there are also important differences with realism as well, as we can see in table 10.1.

OFFENSIVE ILLIBERALISM/AMERICA FIRST VERSUS LIBERALISM

Trumpists reject the three major liberal mechanisms of democracy promotion/protection of human rights;[3] free trade and economic interdependence/globalization; and multilateralism/international institutions (the latter one

TABLE 10.1. Major competing American grand strategies in the age of Trump: The differences between offensive illiberalism/America First/nationalism and the liberal and realist strategies

	Means	
Objectives	Offensive/unilateral	Defensive/multilateral
Material focus	Offensive illiberalism/nationalism/America First	Defensive realism
	Maximize unilateral/short-term material relative gains and preserving maximal US freedom of action—militarily and economically	Restraint Offshore balancing Arms control Minimal deterrence
Ideational focus	Offensive liberalism	Defensive liberalism
	Imposed democracy and "open door" policy	−Peaceful democracy promotion −Strengthening economic interdependence and international institutions −Integrate rising powers to the liberal international order

Note: See appendix 3 for a detailed comparison of the four approaches with regard to specific policy issues.

TABLE 10.2. Nationalist/America First challenges to the liberal international order

Pillars of the liberal order in the post–Cold War era	Rising nationalist challenges
US global engagement	Retrenchment
Security umbrella to allies	Less commitment to allies
Foreign aid as an important instrument of diplomacy	Unfavorable attitude to foreign aid
Diplomacy as a key tool of statecraft	Military means more central in the grand strategy
The liberal content of the international order: democracy and human rights	No democracy promotion and marginalization of human rights as a foreign policy concern
Liberal consensus in the West	Illiberal challenges in the West: populist-nationalism in quite a few American allies in Europe and the rise of Trump in the US
Rising globalization/trade	Growing opposition to globalization in the US, esp. to multilateral trade agreements, e.g., Trump's withdrawal from the trade treaty of the Pacific—the TPP
Free trade	Growing protectionism/mercantilism, most notably a trade war with China
Growing immigration to the West	Rising opposition to immigration, esp. if it comes from non-European states
Growing power of international institutions and multilateralism	Nationalists strive to weaken these institutions, while protecting state sovereignty as a key value; e.g., Trump's withdrawal from the Paris climate agreement
Systemic explanation: 1. Balance of power—US superiority	Rise of China and the other BRICS—the US and the West less dominant
2. Balance of threat: no great-power threat, at most violent nonstate actors	Lack of a consensus on the key threat; many see a great-power threat (China or Russia); some nationalists see a multiplicity of great-power and violent nonstate threats

is a defensive liberal mechanism; the former two are common to all liberals even if they differ on the means to accomplish them). Nationalists are unwilling to invest resources in democracy promotion and defense of human rights, including humanitarian interventions (see table 10.2).[4]

Realists are also skeptical about such policies and highlight both their potential dangers and their low utility for the national interest. Both realists and nationalists reject the universality of liberal ideals and thus do not share the liberal belief in the United States' ability to spread liberal values.[5] Trumpists/offensive illiberals are also open to warming relations with authoritarian leaders, especially if they come from the same "civilization," namely, white Christians like Putin of Russia who supposedly share similarly traditional "values" related to church, country, and family.[6] Populists might be quite comfortable with other nationalist leaders even if they rule authoritarian regimes and might even prefer the latter to liberal leaders. We see this tendency not only with Trump but also with other nationalists who were elected (or reelected) in 2018—such as politicians in Austria, Italy, and Hungary—who aspire to enhance their countries' relations with Putin, while being very critical of the liberal EU. Realists will only consider alliances with authoritarian states if this is useful for national security, namely, against shared geopolitical threats.

Based on their nationalist perspective and their focus on preserving state sovereignty, nationalists oppose allowing any meaningful limitations to states' freedom of action by international institutions such as the UN in the political domain. Thus, the Trump administration indicated that it would cut its financial support for the UN and its agencies, which is likely to also harm its peacekeeping operations.[7]

To Trumpists, the very idea of international cooperation is anathema. Trump views every relationship, whether on the personal level or on the interstate level, in zero-sum terms. Either the US is the winner or the loser, and if it's not obvious that it is the winner, then it must be the loser or the sucker. That's why he sees it as such a brilliant accomplishment that he pulled the US out of a number of international agreements: the Trans-Pacific Partnership— the trade deal of a group of East Asian and South American states; the Paris Climate Accord; and the Iran nuclear deal. Because of his focus on relative gains, Trump opposes these deals because they were based on absolute gains of all the participants, namely, everyone could emerge better off. That's something that Trump totally rejects.[8]

ECONOMIC NATIONALISM

Based on their narrow transactional and nationalist view, America Firsters also oppose limits to states' economic freedom of action posed by the WTO (World Trade Organization) in the economic field. Nationalists prefer economic nationalism or mercantilism and bilateral trade accords to multilateral free-trade agreements, economic interdependence, and globalization. They expect that it will be easier for the US—as the most powerful party—to reach unilateral gains in bilateral deals, using its superior military and economic power to pressure the other side for major concessions in America's favor.[9]

Realists highlight the limited effects of international institutions under international anarchy as a matter of fact, while recognizing that trade might also produce conflicts between trading states rather than only cooperation as the liberals expect, though they do not necessarily advocate the protection-ism favored by the nationalists. While the realist view is empirically based, the nationalists have also a normative element in their positive view of sov-ereignty: "The nation-state remains the true foundation of happiness and harmony," Trump has stated, while "the false song of globalism" will lead America to ruin.[10]

ALLIANCES

Nationalists are furious about what they view as the disproportionate—and unjustified—US contribution to the distribution of collective goods (see table 10.3 below). In their view, other states, particularly US allies, are taking advantage of the US goodwill both in the security and the economic fields. Thus, America Firsters are very critical of US commitments to its allies, viewing them as free-riding on the generous US security umbrella and tak-ing advantage of it rather than paying their fair share. During the campaign Trump called for the allies to pay the US for their defense—and if not, the US must be prepared to allow these states to protect themselves, including by acquiring nuclear weapons. Even after he came to office—for example, in the May 2017 NATO Summit in Brussels—Trump conditioned the continu-ation of the security umbrella for the allies on reimbursing the US public for its spending on their defense. He also didn't mention Article 5—the cor-nerstone of NATO's collective defense—even though he acknowledged the article two months later.

Trump further escalated his criticism of the NATO allies in the July 2018 summit. Using very aggressive language, he demanded in an extremely sharp tone, an increase in defense spending of the allies, at the very least an immedi-ate fulfillment of the commitment to allocate 2 percent of the GDP to defense by each member rather than only implementing it by 2024 as the original NATO resolution called for. In the eyes of America Firsters, it is supposedly cost free to pressure the liberal allies because they are heavily dependent on the US security umbrella and they don't have a credible realignment option and thus have no much choice but to comply with US demands.

In contrast, liberals advocate the persistence of the worldwide US alliances and military deployments, creating a credible security umbrella for the inter-national liberal order based primarily on the US commitment to NATO and the American bilateral alliances with Japan and South Korea. Thus, liberals oppose the reduction of the US commitment, especially when it involves the key democratic allies in Europe and East Asia. Realists share the Trumpist concern about allied free-riding on the US that provides them with a blank

TABLE 10.3. Competing positions on military interventions and alliances

	Means of interventions	
Objectives of interventions	*Offensive/unilateral*	*Defensive/multilateral*
Material focus	**Offensive illiberalism/ America First** Maximize military power and its use against direct threats to the US homeland, but lesser/ ambiguous commitment to liberal allies	**Defensive realism** Minimizing the use of force; only against powerful aspirants for hegemony in key regions who could pose a threat to the US; allies must do their utmost to defend themselves
Ideational focus	**Offensive liberalism** Massive use of force for regime change; strong commitment to allies, esp. democracies	**Defensive liberalism** Humanitarian interventions: Limited use of force with minimal tolerance of casualties; security commitment to allies

check. Realists also demand a more equitable burden sharing, although they are less likely to abandon allies that are materially crucial to US security from the perspective of the global balance of power, especially against rising revisionist powers. In this context, it is imperative for the realists to prevent China from dominating East Asia—a region with high rates of growth in recent decades, which is critical for the world balance of power. Since the countries in this region are not powerful enough to contain a rising China, the US has to continue its engagement there, including militarily, and to prevent the rise of Chinese hegemony there.[11]

AMERICA FIRST VERSUS REALISM

Despite some shared beliefs with some realists, there are also quite a few fundamental differences between realism and Trumpist America First. Defensive realists, who advocate restraint, are very selective about the importance of allies and the willingness to defend them since they see the US as very secure—surrounded by two vast oceans and bordering two weak and friendly countries—and protected by a big nuclear arsenal with a second-strike capacity.[12] This view is dramatically different from the nationalist view of a high-threat environment confronting the US on many fronts and thus necessitating high defense spending.[13] As for a greater allied contribution to burden sharing, one defensive realist idea—based on Posen's "restraint" grand strategy[14]—is that the rich European allies will be able by themselves to balance and deter Russia, while the US will take care of the global commons: the sea, the air, and space.[15] In contrast to the nationalists' willingness to use massive force against a great variety of threats to the US that they see in the world, defensive realists are very cautious about the use of force. They highlight the counterproductive elements of a massive resort to force because of the destabilizing effects of the security dilemma, the counterbalancing by other great powers, and the nationalist opposition of other states against the offensive behavior of a bully.

IDENTITY

For realists the key commitment is to protect the national security of the state as a unitary actor based on material considerations. In Trumpism there is a strong element of an ethnonational/racial/religious identity.[16] Such nationalist populism is based on ethnic considerations with a strong commitment to white Christians, while being critical or exclusionary or both of five major constituencies.[17] These critical attitudes to the following groups also have foreign policy implications.

First, the *liberal elites* who are viewed as having cosmopolitan commitments rather than caring for the "authentic" nation of their own state. The liberal elites also advance globalization despite its supposed economic and other costs to the "real people." The elites include the mainstream media, intellectuals, a great variety of experts, judges, and the academy. The allegation that the elites are "cosmopolitan" expresses the nationalist attitude of Trumpism and the opposition to any limit on national sovereignty by international institutions and multilateral arrangements.

Second, the so-called *deep state* includes the courts and the permanent civil service. In the domain of foreign policy, the "deep state" includes, notably in the case of Trump, the intelligence services, the diplomatic corps, and occasionally even some top generals. Together with the elites, the "deep state" is viewed by Trumpists as unnecessarily constraining, and even obstructing, the ability of the elected commander-in-chief and his executive branch to govern effectively, thus supposedly interfering with the real aspirations of the "people," who elected the president.

This attitude reflects the contempt toward the foreign policy elite and experts and their supposed commitment to "globalism" and "internationalism" rather than to the national interests of "America First" and of the "real people." A key allegation in this context is that the elites and the experts brought about the disasters of the unnecessary and costly (in blood and treasure) post–Cold War US military interventions and the "endless wars" in the Middle East.

Third, ethnic/racial *minorities* have different identities from the supposedly "truly authentic" people, which usually means white Christians. Thus,
these minorities do not seem to fully belong to the "authentic" nation even
though they are fellow citizens. This also has implications for a critical attitude toward some non-European countries, which supposedly belong to
"other civilizations."

Fourth, the preceding point leads to opposition to *migrants* from different
"civilizations," who ethnically, racially, religiously, or culturally differ from
the nativists/nationalists. For American populists it refers to Hispanics in
addition to Muslims. Populists fear that immigrants from these groups—
supported by the liberal/globalist elites—challenge their national identity,
take away their jobs, and pose a security threat because of their supposed
disproportionate involvement in terrorism and crime. Thus, Trumpists tend
to oppose migration of people from these groups.

Fifth, *foreigners* who are allegedly taking advantage of the nation and are
blamed for all the state's troubles. This is a recurrent Trumpist claim and he
blames previous administrations for letting that happen and allowing foreigners to take advantage of the US.

In contrast to the nationalist view, liberals believe that many of the components of the liberal order signify a decline in the appeal of ethnic nationalism
and its power of attraction in relation to a more inclusive civic nationalism,
universal values, and cosmopolitan or regional identities and attachments. In
the nationalist perspective, there is, however, an element of a "Clash of Civilizations." The original Huntingtonian "clash" focused on the clash between
the liberal West and the illiberal civilizations, notably Islam and Confucius/
China, who are supposedly unwilling to adhere to liberal norms. In contrast,
in the populist view, white Christians might be on the same side against those
who do not share their race and religion—irrespective of their attitude toward liberalism. Thus, the US might ally with Putin's Russia against militant
Islam despite Putin's authoritarian tendencies. Realists might agree that an
alliance with Russia could be desirable but not mainly against the Islamic
threat, which is seen by realists as a relatively minor nuisance. Rather the
alliance with Russia should focus on a rising China. Such an alliance should
be based on material balance-of-power elements, including the geographical
proximity between Russia and China, which might make them a threat to
each other. For defensive realists, such an alliance would be more for creating a stable balance and deterrence; while for offensive ones, for preserving
US superiority. At any rate, realists do not share the nationalist support for
immigration restriction based on identity—religion, race, ethnicity, or the
hostility toward the elites and ethnic minorities.

THREATS

On the whole, realists, especially the defensive ones, see the world as a much less dangerous place for the US than what nationalists see. For realists the geostrategic location of the US—separated by two vast oceans from the other great powers—makes it quite a safe place, particularly in the absence of any great-power competitor in the post–Cold War era, at least until recently. The nationalists, on the other hand, see numerous threats, including immigration, most notably of Muslims; terrorism, especially of radical Islamists; China—both as a security and economic threat; Iran; North Korea; and bad economic deals with multiple economic partners, including US allies, supposedly taking advantage of US generosity. In contrast, liberals would hesitate about a close alliance with illiberal Russia, while trying to engage China economically and institutionally (defensive liberalism), hoping that this would eventually also change the Chinese regime toward greater respect for human rights and democracy (the offensive liberals' prerequisite for lasting cooperation with China).

The Explanation

THE INTERNATIONAL SYSTEMIC EXPLANATION FOR THE RISE OF NATIONALISM: THE BALANCE OF CAPABILITIES AND THE BALANCE OF THREAT

Table 10.4 accounts for the relative dominance of each of the four approaches discussed in the book. With regard to the recent rise of nationalism, the key explained phenomenon—and puzzle—in the table is the surprise victory of the nationalist agenda in the 2016 elections. Even though Hillary Clinton got almost 3 million votes more than Trump, the unexpected victory of a candidate such as Trump—completely out of the mainstream in numerous personal and policy senses—is so sensational and dramatic that it calls for an explanation. The key challenge here is to show the utility of an international explanation even though such an explanation does not capture the considerable portions of the variance that are addressed by a variety of domestic factors.[18]

How could the combined effect of the systemic independent variables of our model—the balance of power and the balance of threat—account for the rise of Trumpism/America First as a new grand strategy even if not all of its components are translated into policy? As table 10.4 shows, both the balance of power and the balance of threat have become less clear-cut as the

TABLE 10.4. Explaining the relative dominance of the competing American grand strategies in the age of Trump

	Global distribution of capabilities	
	---	---
Level of external threat	Great-power parity (1950–91) or power transition (gradually during the second decade of the twenty-first century)[1]	Unipolarity (1992–2013)
High	Offensive realism 1950–62; 1979–85	Offensive liberalism 9/11/2001–2008
Or (highly disputed) multiplicity of threats (emerging during the second decade of the twenty-first century)[2]	Nationalism/ America First/offensive illiberalism (2017–19)	
Low	Defensive realism 1963–79; 1985–91 2014–16	Defensive liberalism 1992–2001 2009–13

1. Measured by purchasing power parity, the Chinese economy overtook the American economy in 2014. Citations in Christopher Layne, "The US-Chinese Power Shift and the End of Pax Americana," *International Affairs* 94, no. 1 (2018): 95.

2. In 2014 three major potential threats escalated: Russia invaded Ukraine; China escalated its maritime disputes in the East and South China Seas; and ISIS occupied Mosul—the second largest city in Iraq—and declared the reestablishment of the "Islamic Caliphate."

second decade of the twenty-first century advanced in contrast to the earlier post-1945 period. Such a declining clarity in these two key balances didn't guarantee the rise of the Trumpist grand strategy, but it does provide some international/systemic context for the rise of such of a grand strategy. More specifically, the changes in the balance of capabilities—leading to some level of power transition—can explain the rising reluctance in the US to continue to play the leadership role in the international system, notably the promotion of the international liberal agenda. The rising perception among some sectors of American society of a new type of threats explains some of the substance of Trumpism/nationalism. The absence of agreement on the two balances and their declining clarity might explain, at least partly, the incoherent and inconsistent nature of the new strategy. Specifically, the lack of a major clear-cut source of threat reduces, particularly, the appeal of realist grand strategies.

THE BALANCE OF CAPABILITIES: GRADUAL CHANGES IN
THE SECOND DECADE OF THE TWENTY-FIRST CENTURY

In the post-1945 period, the balance of power was either bipolarity until the collapse of the Soviet Union or unipolarity in the post–Cold War era. In contrast, there is some level of power transition in the second decade of the twenty-first century as the emerging economies, notably the BRICS powers, have been rising in the recent decade. This is especially, however, relevant for China,[19] which also translates its growing economy into increasing defense spending.[20] The West, and especially the US, are still very powerful and technologically advanced.[21] Still, the 2008 financial crisis in the West—the Great Recession—and the American military failures (at least in the aftermath of the initial military successes) in Iraq, Afghanistan, and Libya undermined the confidence of many Americans in the capacity of the US—under its internationalist-oriented liberal elites—to act effectively and competently both at home and abroad and to lead the world order.[22]

Yet, the US margin of superiority also declined objectively, though its extent of decline is heavily disputed between the "primacists" and the "declinists."[23] This is precisely the point here: the key factor of the balance of power and its direction are heavily disputed in recent years. Militarily, it is most notable vis-à-vis the more assertive/revisionist resurgent Russia and rising China in their respective neighborhoods in Eastern Europe and East Asia.[24] Both American rivals have undertaken major military modernization programs, which threaten US capacity to project power into these regions. The US dominance in the Persian Gulf is also challenged by the proliferation of precision-strike and other advanced capabilities to a range of hostile actors, notably Iran—as it demonstrated with its precise strike on the Saudi oil installations in mid-September 2019.

Key US allies were very powerful militarily and economically in the early post–Cold War era but have lost quite a bit of their relative power since then and until 2015: from 47 percent of global GDP to 39 percent, and their share in global military spending from 35 percent to 25 percent.[25] This weakening happened while Russia (militarily) and, even more significantly, China (economically and militarily) got considerably stronger. Thus, while in 1990 the size of the Chinese economy was only 6 percent of the US economy, by 2011 it was 50 percent. Measured by purchasing power parity, the catch-up is even more dramatic as the Chinese economy reached 80 percent of the American one by 2012,[26] and surpassed it by 2014, while being predicted to also overtake the US by the mid-2020s in GDP measured by market exchange rate.[27] The American GDP was 30.4 percent of the world's GDP in the year 2000, while the Chinese share was 3.6 percent in that year. By 2018 the US share declined to 23.3 percent, while the Chinese increased to 16.1 percent.[28] In addition, by 2016 China produced 20 percent of global manufacturing, contributing 35 percent of global growth and engaging in 11 percent of global trade.[29]

More generally, while the developed countries of the West accounted for 62 percent of the world GDP in 1990, they accounted for less than half by 2011, while growth in Asia accounted for most of the rest of the world economy and the predictions are that the Asian share will continue to grow. The Chinese economic growth allowed the country to increase its defense spending from $26 billion in 1995 to $226 billion in 2016. According to some security experts, American military dominance in East Asia, where China aims to establish its sphere of influence, is significantly eroding, and the region is on the verge of a power transition.[30]

As Brands et al. comment, such changes in the balance of power "bodes ill for a post–Cold War order that has rested on a degree of Western overmatch that no longer seems so impressive today."[31] In this new international systemic context, the rising illiberal / Trumpist challenge to the US-led liberal international order might be better understood, particularly the Trumpist opposition to the role of the US as the key provider of collective goods to the international system, notably in the security and the economic domains. During an era of power transition (even if somewhat disputed), there is a declining willingness to pay disproportionate costs for maintaining the international order and even to protect allies as was the case in the bipolar and the unipolar eras.

THE BALANCE OF THREAT: DECLINING CLARITY IN THE SECOND DECADE OF THE TWENTY-FIRST CENTURY

Changes in clarity of the balance of threat have also made the ground more fertile for the emergence of an illiberal/nationalist challenge. Until recently the key threat to US security could be easily identified even if there was not a full consensus about the extent of the threat and its immediacy. During the Cold War, the threat perception naturally focused on the Soviet Union even if there had been changes in the severity of the threat in different periods of the Cold War as we noted in chapters 3–6. Following the collapse of the Soviet Union, the consensus in the 1990s was that the US didn't face a major threat, but only limited ones, while the key arenas of Europe and East Asia became secure. In the aftermath of 9/11, there was almost a consensus that the key threat was jihadist terrorism, especially if it got hold of weapons of mass destruction.[32]

In recent years, however, the key threat is not as clear-cut, while a growing cleavage emerged with regard to the identity of the major threat to US security, especially since 2014.[33] Liberals focus on the threat posed by illiberal Russia and its disruptive behavior, culminating in the 2014 annexation of Crimea and intervention in eastern Ukraine—violating a key norm of the liberal international order—states' territorial integrity; on top of that also came the

Russians' forceful intervention in Syria in fall 2015, with its indiscriminate bombing against the opposition to the Assad regime, killing numerous innocent civilians. Finally, the Russians allegedly intervened in the 2016 US elections; many liberals believe that this intervention—even if without collusion with the Trump campaign—helped Trump to win the elections.

Realists, on the other hand, focus on the threat posed by the key rising power—China, which is seen as aiming to establish its own sphere of influence in the rapidly growing region of East Asia, while displacing the US from the region.[34] Such a change could affect the global balance of power and potentially pose a threat later on to the US itself. Realists see Russia, in contrast, as a much weaker actor, which might even under certain circumstances ally with the US against the common threat posed by the jihadists and a potentially common threat posed by the rising Russia's neighbor—China.

In contrast to realists and liberals, ethnonationalists/Trumpists view the key threat as posed by militant Islam and its terrorism, which in their eyes also makes migration from Muslim-majority countries a dangerous threat.[35] While terrorism is much weaker than either Russia or China, the supposed threat terrorists pose is more immediate and concrete for considerable parts of the public,[36] magnified by fears of migrants from Islamic countries and their supposed connections to terrorism even if these connections are hugely exaggerated by the nationalists.[37] Thus, one of the first steps of the Trump administration when it came to power was to ban migration from some Muslim-majority countries because of its supposed security threat. But there is also a nationalist cultural element as the America Firsters/populists see the Muslim—and sometimes other nonwhite Christian, notably Hispanic— migrants as being from an "alien" and "backward" civilization, which in their eyes poses a "cultural threat" to white Christian civilization and its "traditional values" (the traditional family, church, and the "nation").[38] Indeed, the attitudes to migration reflect key issues of national identity and the conception of who should be included in the nation and who shouldn't belong.[39]

This type of migration/terrorism threat captures the imagination of many Trump supporters as globalization has increased migration, while terrorism was also globalized in the post-9/11 period. At the same time, nationalists see the liberal elites as globalists who open the gates to migration from all over the world—in addition to the support of these elites for ethnic/racial minorities in the US. Together these migrant and minorities pose a threat to the dominance of the white Christians.

In this context, Russia can be considered to be a potential ally against the common Islamic threat despite its authoritarian regime (or at most illiberal democracy). On the whole, Trumpists show a friendly attitude toward authoritarian regimes that are American allies—or can be seen by them as potential allies—while criticizing only authoritarian regimes that are hostile to Washington and which the Trumpists see as a threat, notably Iran, North Korea, and Venezuela. (Trump changed the attitude to North Korea, however, following what he considered as his very successful summit with the North Korean dictator in June 2018.) At the same time, the attitude of Trump to liberal allies can be sometimes a bit lukewarm, if not hostile as he demonstrated in the G-7 meeting in Quebec, just before the summit with the North Korean ruler, and in the NATO Summit in Brussels in July 2018, on the eve of his Helsinki Summit with Putin.

The rising perception of new identity threats—related to terrorism and migration (and the supposed connections between them and also with crime)—explain some of the substance of the Trumpist grand strategy. At the same time, the lack of basic agreement in the US on the nature of the key threat (or its absence) might explain, at least partly, the incoherence and inconsistency of the strategy and of Trump's foreign policy.

Trump's Inconsistent Foreign Policy

Trump provides a difficult case for the theory presented in this book. Being so dramatically different—in his personality, style, and substance—from all of his predecessors, we should expect a completely different presidency with important implications also for foreign policy. After about three years in office (at the time of writing), it is a bit premature to reach a final verdict for such an incoherent presidency, as Trump's behavior in many respects is unique. But how does he respond to the external environment? We identify a few—but quite inconsistent—patterns.

WITHDRAWING FROM THE LIBERAL INTERNATIONAL ORDER

In general, Trump maintains quite a few of his core beliefs, challenging and criticizing traditional American policy, especially the post–Cold War "liberal hegemony."[40] Trump sees such hegemony as the US playing the "sucker," which tolerates numerous free-riders in both the security and economic fields. Thus, he weakened the three pillars of the US-led international liberalism: international institutions, economic interdependence, and democracy promotion. For example, he has abandoned both the large trade treaty of the Pacific—the TPP—and the Paris Climate agreement. He weakened the credibility of the US as the security provider to its allies in Europe and East

Asia, and the US under his leadership withdrew from the multilateral Iran nuclear deal. Trump also ended the policies of democracy promotion and the protection of human rights, while being friendly with authoritarian leaders and very critical of Western liberal allies such as Canada and Germany. In addition, President Trump has initiated trade wars when, in his eyes, trade harms the US economy.

PARTIAL AND INCONSISTENT CONTINUITY IN AMERICAN INTERNATIONAL COMMITMENTS

At the same time, Trump did restrain some of his more extreme ideas to change American foreign behavior.[41] Although some of the key restraining factors are domestic (Congress and what populists would call the "deep state"), international constraints are also relevant in creating some gap between Trump's initial views and his actual behavior in office. For example, he moderated the challenge to American alliance commitments in East Asia and to NATO. After hesitating for a while to explicitly cite Article 5—the core component of the trans-Atlantic alliance's collective defense commitment—he acknowledged this commitment. He even increased US funding for improved defense in Eastern Europe, including new stockpiles of US equipment in Europe sufficient to equip a US armored division in case of emergency.[42] Despite Trump's very heavy criticism of NATO and essentially seeing it as a "bad deal," the US continued—and even enhanced—military activities designed to reassure vulnerable NATO members like the three Baltic states and Poland, which the alliance would defend against potential Russian aggression. Notably, during 2017–18 the US and NATO allies deployed about 4,500 troops in these states and have positioned a few thousand other armored soldiers mostly in Eastern Europe as a deterrent against Russian aggression.[43] Moreover, even though Trump was extremely critical of the allies' defense spending at the July 2018 summit, and even hinted at a potential unilateral US steps if his demands were not met with compliance, the leaders, including Trump, had signed on to a statement that highlighted agreement on a plan to improve the readiness and mobility of the armed forces across the continent and to make progress on issues like cybersecurity. And they agreed on tough language aimed at Moscow, especially regarding Russia's annexation of Crimea.[44] This kind of behavior gives room for liberals to argue that "setting aside Trump's threats of complete withdrawal and his chaotic and impulsive style, his renegotiations of trade deals and security alliances can be seen as part of an ongoing and necessary, if sometimes ugly, equilibration of the arrangements underlying the institutions of the liberal world order."[45]

Trump also has not—so far—reinstated the clearly illiberal policy of torture and the killing of suspected terrorists' families.

On the other hand, a key policy area where Trump implements his nation-alist/mercantilist agenda is the economic field. Thus, he defied opposition from his own party and protests from overseas while imposing stiff and sweeping new tariffs on imported steel and aluminum from key US allies. He also imposed considerable tariffs on huge imports from China.[46] Trump claims that the tariffs are intended to force the US trade partners to negoti-ate new terms that will tilt the trade balance in favor of the US. The tariffs were imposed in mid-2018 and seemingly started a trade war between the US and its trade partners—most significantly, China, Canada, Mexico, and the EU—mutually imposing tariffs on their major imports from each other.[47] Economists have argued that the tariffs will only harm the US economy (or at best will have little to no effect on improving the US economy—falsifying Trump's expectations).[48] By July 2018, the US government started paying US farmers a compensation package of $12 billion to cover for their losses due to the tariffs.[49] Moreover, and consistent with other aspects of Trump's for-eign policy, the tariffs, particularly on steel (25 percent tariff) and alumi-num (10 percent tariff), primarily harm US allies like Canada, which supplies 16 percent of US steel, and not its adversaries, like China, supplying only 2 percent,[50] although quite severe tariffs were also imposed on imports from China.[51] By early September 2019, the average tariffs on Chinese imports reached 21.2 percent, up from 3.1 percent when Trump came into office.[52]

Despite quite a few complimentary comments on President Putin and at-tempts to improve relations, Trump has not initiated, at least not until the beginning of 2020, a major diplomatic breakthrough with Russia and the economic sanctions imposed after the annexation of Crimea were even made more severe by Congress. The president also didn't order by early 2020 a withdrawal from Afghanistan nor replace the US soldiers with mercenaries, but rather modestly raised troop levels despite his earlier opposition to the war (and thus far the ineffective US campaign there).[53] While initially sup-porting the idea of Assad as a partner in the war on terror, he ordered two

missile strikes—in 2017 and 2018—on Syrian military sites after the Syrian regime used chemical weapons against civilians, fulfilling the Obama's
red line against their use. Trump continued the policy of his predecessors
of nonproliferation, including by the threat of use of force, as he threatened
North Korea and almost reached the threshold of escalation to war with it.
Such threats fit nicely with America First—the focus on direct threats to the
homeland—as North Korea seemed to achieve the capacity of firing intercontinental ballistic missiles that might reach US shores. However, it supposedly also shows an enduring commitment to protect US allies in East Asia
who are most threatened by North Korean nukes—South Korea and Japan.

Yet, when the North Korean ruler supposedly showed signs of reconciliation and willingness to reach an agreement on "denuclearization," Trump
immediately agreed to meet him in an unprecedented summit. This response
presumably also demonstrated a commitment to the East Asian allies even if
the atmosphere around the summit was dominated by the unique attributes
of Trump's personality and the major focus on his ego. By the beginning of
2020, Trump seemed to be overlooking the firing of short-range missiles,
which especially threaten the East Asian allies, while continuing to praise
his "friend"—the dictator Kim. Thus, some doubt Trump's commitment to
the allies.

At the same time, Trump escalated the conflict with Iran, challenging the
reliability of the six powers' nuclear agreement with it.[54] In May 2018 he withdrew from the accord despite the lack of evidence that Iran was violating
the agreement. Thus, he committed a dramatic step of unilateralism and a
complete disregard for an international system based on rules, international
cooperation, and multilateral agreements. In addition, Trump initiated a
"maximum pressure" campaign of imposing biting sanctions on Iran.[55] At
the same time, thus far the Iran case shows Trump's disinclination to be entangled in what he calls "the endless wars" in the Middle East—even if he is
doing it in a very incoherent, unpredictable, and inconsistent manner without following common procedures of decision making and consultations
with the relevant bureaucracies and aides. Thus, we can never be sure what
might be the next step and if it will not be in the opposite direction.

At least thus far, Trump shows great interest—like in the North Korean
case—in reaching a new deal with Iran, which will supposedly be better than
the one reached by his predecessor. He also avoided a military response to
the downing of the unmanned American intelligence drone and even more
dramatically avoided the resort to force when Iran destroyed the two Saudi
oil installations in mid-September 2019 despite the seven-decade US security
umbrella over the Saudis.

The pattern of military disengagement from the Middle East continued in October 2019 when Trump also withdrew the small US force deployed with the Kurdish militias in northern Syria along the border with Turkey. Trump decided to do it after a conversation with another strongman—Turkey's President Erdogan—who wants to establish a "security zone" deep into northern Syria and thus to undermine the Kurdish enclaves in the area. Trump's critics argue that by ordering this withdrawal not only did he desert the Kurdish militias, who were key US allies in the fight against the terrorists of the Islamic State, but he also strengthened the position of other US opponents—the dictator Assad and his patrons—Iran and Russia. Yet, in a seeming reversal of the disengagement from the "endless wars" in the Middle East, he later—on January 3, 2020—ordered the targeted assassination of Qasem Soleimani, the key commander orchestrating the Iranian-led Shiite militias deployed in the Middle East. Maybe in some consistency with "America First," this killing was ordered in response to the killing of an American contractor by one of these militias in Iraq (and also the attack of the militia on the US embassy in Baghdad), thus supposedly showing the commitment of the president to the lives of Americans in contrast to the willingness to abandon foreigners (even if they are allies). When no US troop was killed in the Iranian attack in response to the assassination a few days later (though some were injured), the US did not retaliate for the attack.

Offensive Illiberalism

On the whole, Trump continues the offensive realist mode of maximizing US power and preserving its superiority by increasing defense spending and persisting—and in some places even reinforcing—forward deployment in East Asia, Europe, and the Persian Gulf. Thus, he markedly differs from defensive realism despite the supposed resemblance with the limited disengagement from the Middle East. The power maximization is done without the liberal content—thus he completely departs from the liberal approaches, in fact, pursuing offensive illiberalism. The policy to maintain US primacy is manifested by rising defense spending. Key manifestations of growing armament include the modernization of the nuclear triad and the over 40 percent rise in the acquisition of war-fighting equipment such as precision-guided munitions. The offensive behavior—with major inconsistencies and self-contradictions—has included a growing willingness to resort to force against the Taliban (but also to negotiate with it on a peace deal), Syria (but abrupt withdrawal from its northern part), and the Islamic States (which Trump declared as completely defeated, though not all agree about that); a more confrontational behavior toward Iran, culminating with the killing of Soleimani, although avoiding the use of force against it in response to some Iranian provocations against US allies, notably the Saudis; and the initial military threats against North Korean nukes—in contrast to the campaign rhetoric about Japan and South Korea developing their own nuclear capacity—but later focusing on a diplomatic deal with it.

DOES THE "DEEP STATE" RESTRAIN TRUMP?

It might be possible to distinguish between the individual expressions of the president, quite a few of them—notably in his Twitter account—in the Trumpist mode of "America First," and the policy directions led by his bureaucracy and the key foreign and security policy assistants (supposedly part of the so-called deep state) as reflected in the White House's National Security Strategy and the Pentagon's National Defense Strategy.[56] A key issue here is great-power conflict. Trump continues to show his respect for authoritarian leaders, including those of China and more so his admiration of Russia's Vladimir Putin. He continues to downplay the emergence of great-power conflict. In contrast, the administration's National Defense Strategy highlights a shift from a focus on counterterrorism, rogue states, and nation building to great-power competition.

One reason for this gap between the president's America First views and his key professional aides was that there were not sufficient America Firsters among foreign policy professionals so Trump had to nominate to key positions people who did not fully share his nationalist views,[57] although more recently he compensated for that by nominating two hawkish hard-liners to top policy positions: John Bolton as national security advisor (who resigned or was fired later on) and Mike Pompeo as the secretary of state. At any rate, while sharing with Trump a major focus on the "rogue states"—North Korea and Iran and the terrorist threat—these new officials were likely to join the growing focus on great-power conflict. Indeed, after the cozy summit with Putin, the gap between Trump's friendly Russia policy and the hawkish policy of the administration's security agencies became especially remarkable.[58] Such a gap between Trump's foreign policy statements and the more hawkish foreign policy of his national security team and bureaucracy in key policy issues—not only Russia, but also with regard to Iran and North Korea—led the New York Times to conclude: "There's Trump's Foreign Policy and Then There's His Administration's."[59] On the whole, while Trump's foreign policy might reflect his personality and worldview, his bureaucracy seems to be more attuned to the "real" external world.

Thus, some observers argue that the combined influence of the "deep state" of the foreign/security policy establishment together with the checks and balances of the American liberal democratic system—free media, independent courts, energized opposition and civil society, and state and local authorities—might minimize the translation of Trump's illiberal views into foreign policy that would destroy the liberal world order.[60] This view is in complete contrast to other analysts who think that Trump is already wreaking an irreparable damage to the liberal order,[61] or to the long-term credibility and leadership of America.[62] At any rate, it seems that the restraining power of the "deep state" or the "adults in the room" seemed to be weakening more recently, especially with the resignation in late 2018 of Secretary of Defense Jim Mattis, who represented most forcefully US global commitments, most significantly, to its allies.[63]

Summary

The chapter discussed some of the major differences between the Trumpist grand strategy and the four grand strategies that rotated in guiding US strategy in different periods in the post-1945 period according to variations in the balance of capabilities and the balance of threat. A key point in the chapter was to show that such variations in the two key causal factors of our model still provide a useful explanation of a grand strategy change. In the Trumpist case, however, it refers to the growing unclarity with regard to the two balances and the absence of an agreement over them. Such a lack of clarity and consensus provided an international context for the rise of Trumpism, although causal factors on the domestic and individual levels of analysis played a major role in causing this rise. More specifically, the relative—even if limited—decline in US power undermines the support for the liberal international strategies. The absence of an agreed-upon major external threat weakens the support for realist strategies. Thus, our expectation—discussed briefly in the final chapter—is that the potential rise of such a major threat in the context of a reemerging great-power competition, especially with China, increases the likelihood of a return to some version of a realist grand strategy. The future level of the threat posed by China to the US is likely to affect—in accordance with our model—whether this realist grand strategy will have a defensive or an offensive character.

The Past, Present, and Future of American Grand Strategy: Some Final Observations

From Cold War Realism via Post–Cold War Liberalism and the Present Trumpism: Back to Realism?

We argue that since the end of WWII there has been an ongoing ideational competition in the foreign policy community among four major approaches: offensive realism, defensive realism, defensive liberalism, and offensive liberalism. This competition is brokered by external/systemic forces, notably the distribution of capabilities and the balance of threat. A key indicator that systemic forces shape the grand strategy is provided by the variations between the initial views in the White House about the grand strategy and the eventual major changes that take place in this strategy.

In the following sections, we review briefly the past (Cold War realism and post–Cold War liberalism), present ("America First"), and potential future (return of realism?) of US grand strategy. At the end we introduce three appendixes as tables summarizing some of the key points of the book. Appendix 1 exposes the variations in grand strategy as addressed in the book. Appendix 2 summarizes the key changes in the various administrations and their explanations. Appendix 3 overviews some of the major policy differences among four current approaches to grand strategy.

The Past

More specifically, the book addresses the two key puzzles presented at the beginning of the book: why—and when—does a liberal power endorse a realist strategy? And how could realist factors explain the selection of liberal strategies? For the first puzzle, a liberal power will endorse realist strategies once it is engaged in a keen competition with peer great powers. Under such an international structure, the focus on ideology promotion is a costly and dangerous enterprise that is also unlikely to be very successful. Instead the focus is either on trying to have superior capabilities in relation to the other powers according to the logic of offensive realism or to balance and deter the other powers and even to reach confidence-building measures and certain arms control accords with them based on the logic of defensive realism. The choice between these two strategies is affected by the balance of threat. In a high-threatening environment, the preference will be given to a power-maximization strategy based on the logic of offensive realist strategy. This was the choice during the peak of the Cold War—between the Korean War and the Cuban missile crisis. The Truman administration endorsed the offensive realism of NSC 68 only after the growing Soviet threat culminated with the North Korean invasion of South Korea in 1950. Offensive realism also dominated the second round of the Cold War from 1979 to 1985. This dominance started well before the hawkish Reagan came to power in 1981. Rather, the strategy change was initiated by a dovish president—Jimmy Carter—under the influence of the growing Soviet threat, culminating with the 1979 invasion of Afghanistan.

In contrast, when the international system is viewed as relatively benign, it is likely that the defensive realist logic of power moderation and some international cooperation will be selected. Such a grand strategy dominated the détente period following the 1962 Cuban missile crisis—when it became clear that both superpowers wanted to avoid WWIII, which might have taken place as a result of an inadvertent escalation to a nuclear war. Because both powers shared the common threat of an unintended war, they were willing to make considerable concessions for avoiding such a war. Defensive realism was also selected after Gorbachev came to power in 1985 with a much more benign Soviet foreign policy. This second case of détente shows how an initially hawkish president—such as Ronald Reagan—can revise his strategy once the systemic conditions change markedly even if there is domestic opposition among the president's conservative base.[1]

In the post–Cold War era, the US selected liberal strategies. What made possible such a selection was the dramatic transformation in the international system following the collapse of the Soviet Union in 1991. The changing distribution of capabilities, which meant declining constraints on its freedom of action, made it possible for the US to try to promote its liberal ideology by changing the domestic character of other states. If Russia was democratized and China was globalized economically and would later go through democratization, the world would become much more peaceful, prosperous, and cooperative in the liberal American view. It seemed to be a relatively affordable strategy with far-reaching benefits once it succeeded—which for a liberal power seemed to be a very high probability, believing in the universality of the liberal ideas. The balance of threat again played the key role in selecting whether it would be a defensive or offensive liberal strategy. In the benign 1990s, in the absence of a major threat to US security, defensive liberal strategy dominated. Only in the more threatening post-9/11 environment, offensive liberalism dominated the agenda, culminating in the 2003 invasion of Iraq and the major attempt to transform the Middle East—including by the use of force—into a democratic region, thus supposedly taking care of the problem of massive terrorism. This strategy was based on the liberal belief that in a democracy people will be busy with the numerous opportunities for political and economic mobility rather than with initiating and supporting large-scale violence in general and against the US in particular. The decline in the 9/11-type terrorist threat allowed the return of defensive liberalism early in the Obama administration. The rise of other powers has, however, encouraged Obama's move later on from its initially defensive liberal inclinations toward defensive realism.

One short way to overview the differences among the grand strategies, as discussed in chapter 1, is to look briefly at the key issue of the regime-change policy of each of the grand strategies and what were the conducive systemic conditions for the emergence of the grand strategy. The offensive realist approach, especially at the peak of the Cold War, tolerated—or even occasionally encouraged—democracy removal, for realpolitik considerations related to the Cold War. Examples include Iran in 1953 and Guatemala in 1954. The conducive systemic conditions were a bipolar system and high level of the external threat of Soviet expansion.

Following the Cuban missile crisis and during the détente period, the key threat shifted from a fear of WWIII initiated by a revisionist/aggressive Soviet Union to an inadvertent escalation that might have led to mutual destruction. Thus, a strategy of nonintervention—in accordance with the cautious logic of defensive realism—seemed appropriate. An example is the nonintervention when the Soviets crushed the Prague Spring of 1968, although the US also avoided intervention earlier when it engaged direct Soviet interests in its proximate sphere of influence—in Hungary in 1956. Moreover, guided by Cold War considerations, the US also intervened against legitimately elected leaders in the 1970s and 1980s in Chile and Nicaragua—in its own sphere of influence.

Following the end of the bipolar competition, the US moved to a more liberal strategy of supporting democracy promotion and less forceful intervention against legitimately elected officials. When the system was transformed to unipolarity and with a low-threatening environment in the 1990s, the US embarked on the defensive liberal strategy of a gradual/peaceful democracy promotion, including by pursuing humanitarian interventions such as in Somalia (initiated in 1992 by the George H. W. Bush administration despite its clearly realist orientation until then), and in the Balkans—Bosnia in 1995 and Kosovo in 1999 (see chapter 7). When the threat became more powerful in the aftermath of 9/11, the George W. Bush administration moved from an initial realist orientation to select the offensive liberal strategy of an imposed democracy in Iraq in order to fundamentally counter the terrorist threat coming from the Middle East (see chapter 8)

The Present Trumpist Age

The rising uncertainty about the distribution of power in the international system and with regard to the balance of threat confronting the US and the lack of a consensus about these factors reduced the likelihood of the selection of realist or liberal strategies. This uncertainty and the major disagreements paved the way for the rise of the incoherent and inconsistent Trumpism with its various nationalist/America First positions. By the middle of the second decade of the twenty-first century, the appeal of international liberalism was already in decline, while realism still did not capture the imagination of the public and policy makers. This is because the selection of a realist strategy is less likely in the absence of an overwhelming—and agreed-upon—external threat as was the case during the Cold War with the Soviet threat. At the same time, in a period of power transition in the international system, it is less likely that the US will engage in the liberal policies of democracy promotion and humanitarian interventions and that the American public will support them, especially following the costly failures in Iraq, Afghanistan, and Libya.

Thus one source of support for the nationalist/America First Trump strategy is that it opposes the liberal American interventions in the Islamic world. In the nationalist view, Islamist radicalism—whether Sunni (the Islamic State) or Shiite (Iran and its Shiite militias deployed in various Arab states)—is a major threat. But it is futile to address this threat through an imposed democratization of the Islamic world. Such a democratization is not only very costly in American blood and treasure, but at any rate it is unlikely to succeed in the foreseeable future in the "Islamic civilization," which is fundamentally different from Western civilization.[2] Even though not a major threat from a realpolitik viewpoint, from an "America First" perspective, the "Islamist threat" has major implications for immigration and its supposed association with terrorism, especially Islamic terrorism. More generally, immigration from non-European countries potentially poses a "cultural, identity and demographic threat" to the conception of a white/Christian Western civilization in addition to the supposedly high levels of crime it generates in the eyes of the nationalists.

The perceived Islamist threat also affected the rising conflict with Iran manifested by the withdrawal from the nuclear deal and the "maximum pressure" campaign against its supposedly malign regional behavior. Trump's hard-line resulted in growing Iranian aggressiveness leading to increased regional tensions. But based on the logic of avoiding costly interventions in the Middle East, the other side of Trumpism is the dual attempt to avoid the resort to force and to reach a deal with Iran—despite the "fire and fury" type of rhetoric.

Trump also pursues trade wars aiming at maximizing unilateral American relative gains in contrast to the liberal focus on free trade, globalization, multilateralism, and strengthening international institutions that deal with international trade and the global economy. In the name of "national sovereignty," Trumpism also tries to undermine the other international institutions that address real threats to the whole of humankind such as climate change or nuclear proliferation (abandoning the multilateral accord on climate and on Iran's nukes).

The Future of US Grand Strategy: The Return of Realism?

The systemic explanation for the expected gradual shift to a rising focus on great-power competition is based on the material changes that have been taking place in recent years in the international system. One key change is in the distribution of capabilities manifested by the rising power of China (economically and militarily) and Russia (militarily) and potentially in the longer run of India and maybe also others (Brazil?). The second is in the balance of threat: the more assertive—if not aggressive—behavior of China in its maritime disputes in East Asia (the South China and the East China Seas and also a potential escalation with Taiwan on top of its aggressive/nationalist trade and economic/technological policy) and of Russia in Ukraine and Syria and its interference in the 2016 US presidential elections. Thus, one might expect that US grand strategy will be heavily affected by the rising great-power competition between the US (probably supported by other Western countries) and the revisionist/authoritarian powers—rising China and resurgent Russia.

According to this book's theory, when the world moves back to a great-power parity, we can expect that the US will return to a realist grand strategy. In the near future, it looks like the structure of the great-power parity will be bipolarity—US and China as the two superpowers, much more powerful than all the other powers.[3] Russia modernized its military and uses hybrid warfare effectively.[4] Yet, as you can see in table 11.1, its economy is much

TABLE 11.1. Comparing American, Chinese, and Russian military and economic capabilities

GDP in current prices: USA, PRC, Russia, and the world as a whole

	2000	2005	2010	2015	2018
USA	10,285	13,094	14,964	18,121	20,413
PRC	1,215	2,309	6,066	11,226	14,093
Russia	279	821	1,639	1,368	1,720
World	33,867	47,581	65,960	74,429	87,505

Source: IMF Datasets 2018, http://www.imf.org/external/datamapper/NGDPD@WEO/OEMDC/ADVEC/WEO/JPN/FRA.

Note: GDP, current prices, billions of US dollars.

GDP of USA, PRC, and Russia as a percentage of the world's GDP

	2000	2005	2010	2015	2018
USA	30.4%	27.5%	22.7%	24.3%	23.3%
PRC	3.6%	4.9%	9.2%	15.1%	16.1%
Russia	0.8%	1.7%	2.5%	1.8%	2%
World	100%	100%	100%	100%	100%

Military expenditure of USA, PRC, and Russia and the general world military expenditure

	2000	2005	2010	2015	2017
USA	421	619	769	604	597
PRC	41	77	138	205	228
Russia	20	30	43	65	55
World	1,055	1,359	1,679	1,666	1,686

Source: SIPRI 2018, https://www.sipri.org/sites/default/files/4_Data%20for%20world%20regions%20from%201988%E2%80%932017.pdf.

Note: Military expenditure in constant 2016 US billion dollars.

Military expenditure of USA, PRC, and Russia as a percentage of the world military expenditure

	2000	2005	2010	2015	2017
USA	39.9%	45.5%	45.8%	36.3%	35.4%
PRC	3.9%	5.7%	8.2%	12.3%	13.5%
Russia	1.9%	2.2%	2.6%	3.9%	3.3%
World	100%	100%	100%	100%	100%

weaker than that of the US and China. Later on, the world might move to multipolarity—if other great powers are able to catch up and approach the US and Chinese military and economic capabilities.

In the unique case of the Trump presidency, however, his personal inclinations might delay or even change the expected effects of the rising conflict between the liberal West and the authoritarians on the evolution of US grand strategy. Such Trumpist inclinations include his affection toward Putin and Russia and his criticism of Western leaders and institutions (such as the European Union and also NATO). Thus, Trump's behavior during his Helsinki summit with Putin on July 16, 2018, was extremely different from the behavior of previous US presidents in appeasing Russia and its authoritarian leader, while being critical of the US intelligence services and the American law-enforcement agencies and in the preceding week being highly critical of the European democratic allies of the US. This might suggest a major change in American policy, but it is noteworthy that Trump's performance at the summit—and at the press conference in its aftermath—was heavily criticized not only by the Democrats in the opposition and the mainstream media, but also by quite a few Republican members of Congress and probably does not enjoy much support in large sectors of the "deep state"—the bureaucracy and the foreign policy elites.

It is also not clear what the consequences of these developments will be, if any, in international politics. One question refers to the European reaction—will they feel abandoned by the US and balance both the US and Russia, maybe with additional partners or bandwagon with one of them? Will Russia take advantage of the Trumpist appeasement to continue aggression in Eastern Europe? Will the US and Russia form an alliance—even if informally—against a rising China? Will the two authoritarian-revisionist powers form a Chinese-Russian alliance against the US, which they see as consistently aiming at regime change of their own political systems, or will these three powers (US, Russia, and China) divide the world into great-power spheres of influence? One problem with the latter scheme is that allowing China the dominance of East Asia might be especially problematic because of the centrality of this region to the global balance of power. Thus, Chinese attempts at dominance in East Asia might lead to US-Chinese conflict.

The Middle East is an interesting case in which the US under Trump seems (inconsistently, with ups and downs and many reversals) to concede its previous hegemonic position in the region to Russia. The latter intervened successfully to save the crumbling Assad regime in Syria since 2015 and became a de facto broker in the rising Israeli-Iranian rivalry in the region. In contrast, Trump seems to try to expedite an American disengagement from what he calls the "endless wars" in the region. A dramatic case in this direction was the abrupt abandonment in fall 2019 of American allies in the fight against the Islamic State—the Kurds in northern Syria. The way the withdrawal was carried out was quite Trumpist—following a discussion with the authoritarian leader of Turkey (Erdogan) and in the absence of a systematic decision-making process, while not asking for input from the relevant agencies in the administration.

Yet, systemic/material factors—beyond Trump—seem to play a role here. One is the relative declining importance of the oil-rich Middle East because the US has reached in recent years energy independence (even though other industrialized countries still depend on Middle Eastern oil supply). Another key factor refers to the process started under Obama—"the pivot to Asia" or "rebalancing," namely, the change in US strategic priorities from the Middle East and maybe even from Europe to East Asia because of the rise of China and the growing economic and strategic importance of the region.

Based on the model presented here—explaining changes in US grand strategy by changes in the international system—the rising Chinese power and the potential threat it might pose to the US constitute the key variables that are likely to affect potential changes in American strategy. On the whole, the ongoing changes in the distribution of capabilities should lead us to expect an emerging realist American grand strategy under a growing great-power parity (bipolarity for the foreseeable future, later evolving to multipolarity). If it becomes clear that China has limited ambitions and is unwilling to go to war, defensive realism will provide at least some of the key elements of the US strategy including cautious balancing, minimal nuclear deterrence, confidence-building mechanisms, and arms control. A key goal will be then to avoid inadvertent escalation, for example, between the American and Chinese navies in the South China Sea.

If, however, China becomes more aggressive in the key region of East Asia and shows hegemonic inclinations, while also posing a potential threat to the US sphere of influence in the Western Hemisphere, an offensive realist strategy is more probable. Under this grand strategy, the US will attempt to reach superiority over China in order to deter it by a major US armament, a major increase in defense spending, a considerable forward deployment in Asia/Pacific, and containing China by strengthening US alliances with China's neighbors, notably India, Japan, South Korea, and Australia.

Thus, the questions about the future and the depth of the changes in US grand strategy continue to depend on future developments in the international system. Particularly crucial are potential changes in the balance of capabilities and the balance of threat. Such changes will have major effects—according to this book's model—on the ongoing competition among different ideational approaches to national security in the US and on their relative appeal and domestic support and accordingly on the nature of the American grand strategy.

Appendix 1: Indicators of Grand Strategy Change

The Four Grand Strategies
DL—Defensive liberalism
OL—Offensive liberalism
DR—Defensive realism
OR—Offensive realism

In accordance with the model, a shift to offensive/defensive strategies follows the changes in the level of threat:

1. The North Korean invasion (rising threat) leads to OR
2. The Cuban missile crisis (declining threat and change of its character) leads to DR
3. The Afghanistan invasion (rising threat) leads to OR
4. The rise of Gorbachev (declining threat) leads to DR
5. The absence of threats in the 1990s (declining threat) leads to DL
6. The rise of threat following 9/11 leads to OL

A shift to either realist or liberal strategy follows changes in the distribution of capabilities. There were two key changes in this respect:

1. The rise of bipolarity after WWII—the US emerged as the only power that may balance the Soviets; leads to a shift to realist strategies
2. The rise of unipolarity after the Cold War; leads to a shift to liberal strategies with much greater freedom of action for the US

A third potential change—starting with Obama and culminating in a completely different way with the 2016 election of Trump—occurred in recent years as a result of the growing uncertainty regarding the persistence of unipolarity with the rise of other (non-Western) powers and the financial crisis in the West.

TABLE A1.1. Systemic effects on the domestic competition of ideas

Cases/presidents	Scope of change	Indicators of change	
		Timing—in relation to the changes in the international system	International systemic effects on domestic competition of ideas
Truman (1945–53)	From DL via DR to OR	Following Soviet aggression in East Europe and Mediterranean, culminating in the North Korean invasion	Initial support for US-Soviet cooperation declines following the external events; Some considerable support for OL (rollback), but it is not endorsed
Kennedy (1961–63)	From OR to DR	Following the Cuban missile crisis	Considerable domestic opposition to DR emerges only later in détente under the Nixon-Ford-Kissinger and the Carter administrations as the Soviets become more powerful and behave more aggressively in the Third World
Carter (1977–81)	From DL to OR	Following the Soviet invasion of Afghanistan	Public support—influenced by the external events
Reagan (1981–89)	From OR to DR	Following Soviet moderation under Gorbachev	Some reservations, esp. of hawkish advisors
Bush Sr. (1989–93)	From DR to DL	Following the collapse of the Soviet Union	No major opposition to the initial intervention in Somalia
Clinton (1993–2001)	From disinterest in foreign affairs to DL	Following the clarity of the unipolar system with no major threats	Strong opposition particularly when casualties occur during humanitarian interventions
Bush Jr. (2001–9)	From realism to OL	Following 9/11	Initially considerable support—the public is also influenced by 9/11
Obama (2009–17)	From DL to DR	Russia and Crimea, Chinese assertiveness, ISIS terrorism	

Note: DL, defensive liberalism; DR, defensive realism; OR, offensive realism; OL, offensive liberalism.

TABLE A1.2. Substantive changes in the grand strategy

	Type of change			
Cases	Change to an offensive strategy (realist or liberal)	Change to a defensive strategy (realist or liberal)	Changes to a realist strategy (offensive or defensive)	Changes to a liberal strategy (offensive or defensive)
Truman	Following the 1950 N. Korean invasion		Following greater Soviet aggressiveness under bipolarity (US as the only power that can balance the Soviets)	
Kennedy		Following the Cuban missile crisis—danger of an inadvertent war		
Carter	Following the Soviet invasion of Afghanistan		(The same as in the offensive column)	
Reagan		Following declining threat with the rise of Gorbachev and his moderate policies		
Bush Sr.		(The same as in the liberal column)		Following Soviet collapse
Clinton		(The same as in the liberal column)		Consolidation of unipolarity and absence of major threats
Bush Jr.	Following the rising threat on 9/11			(Same as in the offensive column)
Obama			Russian and Chinese behavior, ISIS	

Appendix 2: Summary of Major Changes in US Grand Strategy and Their Explanation

TABLE A2. From Truman to Trump—summary of major changes in US grand strategy and their explanation

Administration	Initial strategy	Ultimate strategy	Explanation
Truman	DL—cooperation with the Soviets	2 stages: 1. DR—diplomacy and economic 2. OR—search for military dominance over the Soviets	–Clarification of distribution of power—rise of bipolarity –Threat—rising following an aggressive Soviet behavior and also its client (North Korea)
Kennedy	OR—military superiority	DR—arms control	Threat—from an exclusive focus on the Soviet threat to a greater focus on common threats (fear of an inadvertent escalation)
Carter	DL—international cooperation, arms control, human rights	OR—military superiority	Threat—growing in the late 1970s, culminating with the Soviet invasion of Afghanistan
Reagan	OR—military superiority	DR—arms control	Threat—declining following Gorbachev's conciliatory moves
Bush Sr.	DR—managing the global balance of power	DL—humanitarian intervention in Somalia	Power—from bipolarity to unipolarity; threat—absent
Clinton	Focus on domestic/economic issues—disinterest in foreign policy	DL—making the world liberal in peaceful ways and humanitarian interventions	Clarity of the changes—US dominance and no major threat
Bush Jr.	Realist	OL—democracy promotion by the use of force	Threat—9/11—terrorism and the fear of WMD[1]
Obama	DL (at least in rhetoric)	DR	Financial crisis; rise of the others; Iraq quagmire
Trump	"America First"; Unilateralist; Illiberal	Incoherent and unpredictable, though a bit more international engagement than expected by the purist "America First," but still mostly unilateralist: Middle East—disengagement from Syria and from Iran's nuclear deal; withdrawal from climate accord; trade wars	Lack of clarity of power transition Disagreement over priority of threats (ISIS, Russia, China, trade) But rising threats in Middle East (Iran expansion) and North Korea (nuclear/missile tests)

Note: DL, defensive liberalism; DR, defensive realism; OR, offensive realism; OL, offensive liberalism.

1. The threat was that Al-Qaeda would get hold of weapons of mass destruction.

Appendix 3: Competing US Approaches to Grand Strategy in the Age of Trump

TABLE A3. Competing US approaches to grand strategy in the age of Trump

	Offensive liberalism	Defensive liberalism	Defensive realism	America First/offensive illiberalism
American role in the world	Global hegemony	Deep engagement	Restraint/offshore balancing	Maximizing selfish/exclusive US material gains
Strategic engagement	Regime change	Preserve the US-led liberal international order	Balancing of last resort	Only when direct/tangible US interests are engaged, though the conception of threats to them can be expanded to include broad "cultural/identity" threats
How much engagement can US power afford?	Massive, including military	Leadership and regional pacifier	Selective/cautious engagement	Depending on the level of threat to US material interests
External costs of US engagement: Anti-US sentiments	Only by the "bad guys" (despotic; pariah states), which are hostile to the US— irrespective of what the US does	Benefits higher than costs due to widespread recognition of US's crucial role in providing collective goods	Counterbalancing; entrapment in allies' conflicts; temptation to engage in unnecessary interventions	Careless about anti-US sentiments
Internal costs (blood and treasure)	Reasonable due to interests	Sustainable	Too high in the post–Cold War era	Not worth it for preserving the liberal order
Military intervention	Quite a lot	If approved by UN Security Council or NATO	Only when the regional balancing fails against a rising power in a key region	Mainly to counter direct threats against the US
Unilateralism vs. multilateralism	Unilateralism, though attempt to build "coalitions of the willing"	Multilateralism	Depends on the situation	Unilateralism
Democracy promotion	Yes	Minimal/conditional	No	No
Humanitarian interventions	Conditional	Minimal/conditional	No	No

	Offensive liberalism	Defensive liberalism	Defensive realism	America First /offensive illiberalism
Defense spending	Preserve high spending	Limited cuts	Major cuts	Increase
Forward deployment	Massive	Continuity	Major retrenchment	Depends on the level of direct threats against the US
Alliances	Mainly with democracies	Continuity of the US-led alliance system	Rich free-riders should take care of themselves	Weaken existing commitments
Rise of China	Focus on democratization and human rights	Integration to the US-led order if possible and continuous commitments to the allies	Offshore balancing— deploy only if regional balancing fails	Reduce the trade gap with it and stop its currency manipulations/ technology theft
Terror	Democracy promotion in Islamic world	Multilateral cooperation with allies against terrorists	Limited policing action	Major offensive against it and limit migration from Muslim countries
Proliferation: Iran and North Korea	Preventive strike/ regime change	1. Diplomacy 2. Multilateral sanctions 3. Security umbrella to allies	Deterrence	"Maximum pressure" (unilateral sanctions) and trying to reach a deal
Trade	Free trade; pressures to open markets— "open door"	Multilateral free-trade agreements	Free trade, but avoiding unilateral concessions	Economic nationalism, mercantilism, trade wars
International institutions	Opposition to limiting US freedom of action by them	An important contribution to the international order under US leadership	Not very significant vs. states' national material interests	Major opposition to them, esp. to any limits on US sovereignty

Notes

Introduction

1. A grand strategy refers to a set of ideas (or a "theory") informing the overall approach that a state pursues to maximize its security and protect itself against actual or potential threats to its values. It includes the prioritization of foreign policy goals, the identification of existing and potential resources, and the selection of a plan or road map that uses those resources to meet those goals. See Barry R. Posen, *The Sources of Military Doctrine* (Ithaca, NY: Cornell University Press, 1984), 7; Colin Dueck, *Reluctant Crusaders: Power, Culture, and Change in American Grand Strategy* (Princeton, NJ: Princeton University Press, 2006), 2; Robert J. Lieber, *The American Era: Power and Strategy for the 21st Century* (New York: Cambridge University Press, 2007), 41; Stephen G. Brooks and William C. Wohlforth, *America Abroad: The United States' Global Role in the 21st Century* (New York: Oxford University Press, 2016), 75; see also Nicholas Kitchen, "Systemic Pressures and Domestic Ideas: A Neoclassical Realist Model of Grand Strategy Formation," *Review of International Studies* 36, no. 1 (2010): 117–43; Colin Dueck, *The Obama Doctrine: American Grand Strategy Today* (New York: Oxford University Press, 2015), 14–25; Hal Brands, *What Good Is Grand Strategy?* (Ithaca, NY: Cornell University Press, 2014); and Nina Silove, "Beyond the Buzzword: The Three Meanings of 'Grand Strategy'," *Security Studies* 27, no. 1 (2018): 27–57.

2. Chaps. 9 and 10 will explain the grand strategy changes in the second decade of the twenty-first century, most dramatically related to the election of Donald J. Trump in 2016.

3. For realist approaches to grand strategy, see Posen, *The Sources of Military Doctrine*; Barry R. Posen, *Restraint: A New Foundation for US Grand Strategy* (Ithaca, NY: Cornell University Press, 2014); John J. Mearsheimer, *The Tragedy of Great Power Politics* (New York: Norton, 2001; 2nd ed., 2014); Robert Art, *A Grand Strategy for America* (Ithaca, NY: Cornell University Press, 2003); Fareed Zakaria, *From Wealth to Power: The Unusual Origins of America's World Role* (Princeton, NJ: Princeton University Press, 1998); Stephen M. Walt, *The Hell of Good Intentions: America's Foreign Policy Elite and the Decline of US Primacy* (New York: Farrar, Straus and Giroux, 2018); Stephen M. Walt, "US Grand Strategy after the Cold War: Can Realism Explain It? Should Realism Guide It?," *International Relations* 32, no. 1 (2018): 3–22; Christopher Layne, *The Peace of Illusions: American Grand Strategy from 1940 to the Present* (Ithaca, NY: Cornell University Press, 2006); Christopher Layne, "The US-Chinese Power Shift and the End of the Pax Americana," *International Affairs* 94, no. 1 (2018): 89–111.

4. For the constructivist approach, see Peter Katzenstein, ed., *The Culture of National Security: Norms and Identity in World Politics* (New York: Columbia University Press, 1996). See also Alexander Wendt, *Social Theory of International Politics* (Cambridge: Cambridge University Press, 1999); and Martha Finnemore, *The Purpose of Intervention: Changing Beliefs about the Use of Force* (Ithaca, NY: Cornell University Press, 2003).

5. On different variants of liberalism, see Michael W. Doyle, *Ways of War and Peace: Realism, Liberalism, and Socialism* (New York: Norton, 1997); and Bruce M. Russett and John R. Oneal, *Triangulating Peace: Democracy, Interdependence, and International Organizations* (New York: Norton, 2001); on economic liberalism, see Richard N. Rosecrance, *The Rise of the Trading State: Commerce and Conquest in the Modern World* (New York: Basic Books, 1986); on democratic liberalism, see Bruce M. Russett, *Grasping the Democratic Peace: Principles for a Post–Cold War World* (Princeton, NJ: Princeton University Press, 1993); and Tony Smith, *America's Mission: The United States and the Worldwide Struggle for Democracy* (Princeton, NJ: Princeton University Press, 1994).

6. See, for example, Jack S. Levy, "The Diversionary Theory of War: A Critique," in *Handbook of War Studies*, ed. Manus I. Midlarsky (Ann Arbor: University of Michigan Press, 1989), 259–88; and Christopher Gelpi, "Democratic Diversions: Governmental Structure and the Externalization of Domestic Conflict," *Journal of Conflict Resolution* 41 (1997): 255–82. In the case of the US, domestic political explanations address the role and effects of Congress (James M. Lindsay, *Congress and the Politics of US Foreign Policy* [Baltimore, MD: Johns Hopkins University Press, 1994]), domestic lobbies (Tony Smith, *Foreign Attachments: Ethnic Group Power and the Making of American Foreign Policy* [Cambridge, MA: Harvard University Press, 2005]; John J. Mearsheimer and Stephen M. Walt, *The Israel Lobby and US Foreign Policy* [New York: Farrar, Straus and Giroux, 2007]), and public opinion (Ole Holsti, *Public Opinion and American Foreign Policy* [Ann Arbor: University of Michigan Press, 1996]). For a variety of domestic perspectives on grand strategy, see Richard Rosecrance and Arthur Stein, eds., *The Domestic Bases of Grand Strategy* (Ithaca, NY: Cornell University Press, 1993); and Eugene R. Wittkopf and James M. McCormick, eds., *The Domestic Sources of American Foreign Policy: Insights and Evidence*, 3rd ed. (Lanham, MD: Rowman & Littlefield, 1998). Books focusing on the effects of US domestic politics and ideology on its grand strategy include Louis J. Hartz, *The Liberal Tradition in America* (New York: Harcourt Brace, 1955); Walter Russell Mead, *Special Providence: American Foreign Policy and How It Changed the World* (New York: Knopf, 2002); Michael H. Hunt, *Ideology and U.S. Foreign Policy*, 2nd ed. (New Haven, CT: Yale University Press, 2009); Peter Trubowitz, *Politics and Strategy: Partisan Ambition and American Statecraft* (Princeton, NJ: Princeton University Press, 2011); Helen V. Milner and Dustin Tingley, *Sailing the Water's Edge: The Domestic Politics of American Foreign Policy* (Princeton, NJ: Princeton University Press, 2015). On the importance of domestic identity—notably, liberal identity in the case of the US— see Tony Smith, *America's Mission: The United States and the Worldwide Struggle for Democracy in the Twentieth Century*, expanded ed. (Princeton, NJ: Princeton University Press, 2012); Tony Smith, *Why Wilson Matters: The Origins of American Liberal Internationalism and Its Crisis Today* (Princeton, NJ: Princeton University Press, 2017); Henry Nau, *At Home Abroad: Identity and Power in American Foreign Policy* (Ithaca, NY: Cornell University Press, 2002); Mark L. Haas, *The Ideological Origins of Great Power Politics, 1789–1989* (Ithaca, NY: Cornell University Press, 2005); John M. Owen IV, *The Clash of Ideas in World Politics: Transnational Networks, and Regime Change, 1510–2010* (Princeton, NJ: Princeton University Press, 2010), and Paul D. Miller, *American Power and Liberal Order: A Conservative Internationalist Grand Strategy* (Washington, DC: Georgetown University Press, 2016).

7. On the beliefs of US presidents as the key factor in shaping US intervention, see Elizabeth N. Saunders, "Transformative Choices: Leaders and the Origins of Intervention Strategy," *International Security* 34, no. 2 (Fall 2009): 119–61. On the key importance of leaders, see Daniel L. Byman and Kenneth M. Pollack, "Let Us Now Praise Great Men: Bringing the Statesman Back In," *International Security* 25, no. 4 (Spring 2001): 107–46; Giacomo Chiozza and H. E. Goemans, *Leaders and International Conflict* (Cambridge: Cambridge University Press, 2011); and Michael C. Horowitz et al., *Why Leaders Fight* (Cambridge: Cambridge University Press, 2015). The individual level of analysis underlines decision-making processes. See, for example, Graham T. Allison and Philip Zelikow, *Essence of Decision Explaining the Cuban Missile Crisis* (New York: Longman, 1999); Irving L. Janis, *Groupthink: Psychological Studies of Policy Decisions and Fiascoes* (Boston: Houghton Mifflin, 1982); Robert Jervis, *Perception and Misperception in International Politics* (Princeton, NJ: Princeton University Press, 1976); Alexander L. George, *Presidential Decisionmaking in Foreign Policy: The Effective Use of Information and Advice* (Boulder, CO: Westview Press, 1980); Yuen Foong Khong, *Analogies at War: Korea, Munich, Dien Bien Phu, and the Vietnam Decisions of 1965* (Princeton, NJ: Princeton University Press, 1992); Steve A. Yetiv, *Explaining Foreign Policy: US Decision-Making and the Persian Gulf War* (Baltimore, MD: Johns Hopkins University Press, 1997); and Emilie M. Hafner-Burton et al., "The Behavioral Revolution and International Relations," *International Organization* 71, no. S1 (2017): S1–S31. The general theme of the excellent book by Goldgeier and McFaul "is that the worldview of key decision-makers plays a central role in the making of American foreign policy." James M. Goldgeier and Michael McFaul, *Power and Purpose: US Policy toward Russia after the Cold War* (Washington, DC: Brookings, 2003).

8. See Jonathan Monten, "The Roots of the Bush Doctrine: Power, Nationalism, and Democracy Promotion in U.S. Strategy," *International Security* 29, no. 4 (Spring 2005): 112–56; Colin Dueck, *Reluctant Crusaders*; Layne, *The Peace of Illusions*; Posen, *Restraint.*

9. Posen, *Restraint*; John J. Mearsheimer, *The Great Delusion: Liberal Dreams and International Realities* (New Haven, CT: Yale University Press, 2018); and Stephen M. Walt, "The Donald versus 'The Blob,'" in *Chaos in the Liberal Order: The Trump Presidency and International Politics in the 21st Century*, ed. Robert Jervis et al. (New York: Columbia University Press, 2018); John J. Mearsheimer and Stephen W. Walt, "The Case for Off-Shore Balancing," *Foreign Affairs*, July–August 2016. See also various columns by Stephen W. Walt in *Foreign Policy*, online; for example: "Could There Be a Peace of Trumphalia?," November 14, 2016.

10. As we discuss in chap. 3, a leading academic realist, John Mearsheimer (*The Tragedy of Great Power Politics*), highlights the (defensive) realist nature of the strategy during the Cold War. (We explain in chap. 3 why we call Mearsheimer's interpretation of the US Cold War strategy defensive realist even though Mearsheimer is usually associated with the theory of offensive realism.)

11. A related point here is that there might be intense debates among realist scholars on what is the right policy even if all of them claim to be guided by realist logic and imperatives. See, for example, the debate between Posen, *Restraint*, and Brooks and Wohlforth, *America Abroad*, on the desirable US grand strategy. See also Robert Lieber, *Power and Willpower in the American Future: Why the United States Is Not Destined to Decline* (New York: Cambridge University Press, 2012).

12. The model draws on Benjamin Miller, "Explaining Changes in US Grand Strategy: 9/11, the Rise of Offensive Liberalism and the War in Iraq," *Security Studies* 19, no. 1 (March 2010): 26–65.

13. We use the term liberalism to reflect the ideology of the United States. Applying the

theory to any nonliberal great power would require replacing the term liberalism with that of a great power's ideology. Thus, in a more general theory—not focused on the United States—we would use the term ideology promotion.

14. On ideas and foreign policy, see Judith Goldstein and Robert Keohane, eds., *Ideas and Foreign Policy: Institutions and Political Change* (Ithaca, NY: Cornell University Press, 1993).

15. For various classifications of competing approaches to US grand strategy, see Barry Posen and Andrew Ross, "Competing Visions for U.S. Grand Strategy," *International Security* 21, no. 3 (Winter 1996): 5–53; Mead, *Special Providence*; Nau, *At Home Abroad*; Henry R. Nau, *Conservative Internationalism: Armed Diplomacy under Jefferson, Polk, Truman, and Reagan* (Princeton, NJ: Princeton University Press, 2013); Monten, "The Roots of the Bush Doctrine"; Dueck, *Reluctant Crusaders*; and Layne, *The Peace of Illusions*. See also Art, *A Grand Strategy for America*.

16. Such a theoretical integration can be affiliated with neoclassical realism. See Gideon Rose, "Neoclassical Realism and Theories of Foreign Policy," *World Politics* 51, no. 1 (October 1998): 144–72; and Randall Schweller, "The Progressiveness of Neoclassical Realism," in *Progress in International Relations Theory*, ed. Colin Elman and Miriam Fendius Elman (Cambridge, MA: MIT Press, 2003), 311–47; Norrin M. Ripsman, Jeffrey W. Taliaferro, and Steve E. Lobell, *Neoclassical Realist Theory of International Politics* (New York: Oxford University Press, 2016). On combining material incentives and ideas, see also Richard Herrmann and Richard Ned Lebow, *Ending the Cold War: Interpretations, Causation, and the Study of International Relations* (New York: Palgrave Macmillan, 2004), 14–15, 139–43.

17. Intervening variables are situated between the basic causal factors and the outcomes.

18. See Alexander George and Andrew Bennett, *Case Studies and Theory Development in the Social Sciences* (Cambridge, MA: MIT Press, 2005), esp. 246n27.

19. Chap. 5 explains the changes under Carter, while chap. 6 explains the shift under Reagan.

20. This mechanism might be called "the second-image reversed" (Peter Gourevich, "The Second Image Reversed: The International Sources of Domestic Politics," *International Organization* 32, no. 4 [Autumn 1978]: 881–912). The "second image" in Waltz's terms refers to the belief that the domestic character of states shapes their international behavior, in contrast to the realist "third image," according to which state behavior is shaped by the anarchic international system, and especially by the balance of capabilities. See Kenneth N. Waltz, *Man, the State and War: A Theoretical Analysis* (New York: Columbia University Press, 2001). "The second-image reversed" then is the idea that the international system may affect domestic processes.

21. On elections and foreign policy, see Andrew Johnstone and Andrew Priest, eds., *US Presidential Elections and Foreign Policy* (Lexington: University Press of Kentucky, 2017).

22. On the post-9/11 changes, see chap. 8.

Chapter One

1. These four approaches are ideal-type categories. The divisions among them are distilled, in an internally consistent way, from the fundamental, overlapping logics of authors and practitioners of IR working from within these different schools of thought. Naturally, these ideal types will seldom correspond entirely with either theoretical bodies of work of specific authors, or the specific behavior of international actors.

2. This chapter draws on Benjamin Miller, "Democracy Promotion: Offensive Liberalism vs. the Rest (of IR Theory)," Special Issue on Liberalism, *Millennium* 38, no. 3 (May 2010): 561–91.

3. On realist and liberal approaches in international relations, see Doyle, *Ways of War and Peace*; Robert Jervis, *American Foreign Policy in a New Era* (New York: Routledge, 2005), chap. 1;

and Jack Snyder, "One World, Rival Theories," *Foreign Policy* 145 (November–December 2004): 52–61.

4. On the qualification of NATO as multilateral alongside the UNSC, see Sarah E. Kreps, "Multilateral Military Interventions: Theory and Practice," *Political Science Quarterly* 123, no. 4 (2008–9): 587n39.

5. For useful overviews and citations, see Jeffery Taliaferro, "Security-Seeking under Anarchy: Defensive Realism Reconsidered," *International Security* 25, no. 3 (2000–2001): 128–61, and Layne, *The Peace of Illusions.*

6. On soft power and multilateralism, see Joseph Nye, *The Paradox of American Power: Why the World's Only Superpower Can't Go It Alone* (Oxford: Oxford University Press, 2002).

7. On the philosophical roots of this enduring debate within liberalism regarding the use of force to spread democracy, see Thomas C. Walker, "Two Faces of Liberalism: Kant, Paine, and the Question of Intervention," *International Studies Quarterly* 52, no. 3 (2008): 449–68.

8. See Walter MacDougall, *Promised Land, Crusader State: The American Encounter with the World since 1776* (New York: Houghton Mifflin, 1997).

9. Charles Glaser, "Realists as Optimists: Cooperation as Self-Help," *International Security* 19, no. 3 (1994–95): 50–90.

10. Posen, *The Sources of Military Doctrine*; Stephen M. Walt, *The Origins of Alliances* (Ithaca, NY: Cornell University Press, 1987); and Dueck, *Reluctant Crusaders.*

11. For an extended discussion—with differing opinions—on whether Bush's security policy fits Wilsonian liberalism, see G. John Ikenberry et al., *The Crisis of American Foreign Policy: Wilsonianism in the Twenty-First Century* (Princeton, NJ: Princeton University Press, 2009). On Wilsonian military intervention, see also Constance G. Anthony, "American Democratic Interventionism: Romancing the Iconic Woodrow Wilson," *International Studies Perspectives* 9 (2008): 239–53.

12. For an explicit statement with regard to deriving theories of grand strategy from structural theories, see Layne, *The Peace of Illusions,* 19. This type of a deduction is done, moreover, by many of the scholars—from all the four approaches—cited in this study.

13. Enduring, long-term or fundamental intentions or preferences should be distinguished from short-term calculations. While the former reflect, to a large extent, the character of the domestic regime and its dominant ideology, the latter can be affected also by realist strategies, based on the balance of capabilities, such as deterrence and balancing.

14. George Modelski, "The Long Cycle of Global Politics and the Nation-State," *Comparative Studies in Society and History* 20 (1978): 214–35; and Robert Gilpin, *War and Change in World Politics* (Cambridge: Cambridge University Press, 1981).

15. William C. Wohlforth, "The Stability of a Unipolar World," *International Security* 24, no. 1 (1999): 5–41; Steven G. Brooks and William C. Wohlforth, *World without Balance: International Relations and the Challenge of American Primacy* (Princeton, NJ: Princeton University Press, 2008); Brooks and Wohlforth, *America Abroad.*

16. Mearsheimer, *The Tragedy of Great Power Politics.*

17. Josef Joffe, "Europe's American Pacifier," *Foreign Policy* 50 (1984): 64–82; Benjamin Miller, *States, Nations and the Great Powers: The Sources of Regional War and Peace* (Cambridge: Cambridge University Press, 2007), chap. 8.

18. Miller, *States, Nations and the Great Powers,* chap. 5.

19. Miller, chap. 6.

20. For various presentations of competing approaches in IR, see esp. Doyle, *Ways of War and Peace*; Stephen M. Walt, "International Relations: One World, Many Theories," *Foreign*

Policy 110 (1998): 29–47; Robert Jervis, "Theories of War in an Era of Leading-Power Peace," *American Political Science Review* 96, no. 1 (2002): 1–14; and Snyder, "One World, Rival Theories." For useful contrasts of alternative approaches to US grand strategy, see Posen and Ross, "Competing Visions for U.S. Grand Strategy"; Henry R. Nau, *Conservative Internationalism: Armed Diplomacy under Jefferson, Pollack, Truman, and Reagan* (Princeton, NJ: Princeton University Press, 2013), esp. 39–60; Colin Dueck, *The Obama Doctrine* (Oxford: Oxford University Press, 2015), 14–25. Goldgeier and McFaul (*Power and Purpose,* 5–7) distinguish between "Balancers of Power" or realists and "Regime Transformers" or liberals. We think that is a very useful distinction, but there are also some major divisions inside each of these schools as we discuss here.

21. On various aspects of the realist-liberal debate, see Nye, "Neorealism and Neoliberalism," 235–51; David A. Baldwin, ed., *Neorealism and Neoliberalism: The Contemporary Debate* (New York: Columbia University Press, 1993); Charles W. Kegley, ed., *Controversies in International Relations Theory: Realism and the Neoliberal Challenge* (New York: St. Martin's Press, 1995); and Doyle, *Ways of War and Peace.*

22. Mearsheimer, *The Tragedy of Great Power Politics.*

23. Shiping Tang, "Fear in International Politics: Two Positions," *International Studies Review* 10, no. 3 (2008): 451–71.

24. Gilpin, *War and Change in World Politics,* 94–95; Zakaria, *From Wealth to Power,* 20 and 38; and Mearsheimer, *The Tragedy of Great Power Politics,* 45. These works are also surveyed by Tang, "Fear in International Politics."

25. At the same time, classical and neoclassical realists (unlike neorealists) also accept the independent role of intentions through a key distinction between revisionist and status quo states. Hans J. Morgenthau, *Politics among Nations: The Struggle for Power and Peace,* 5th ed. (New York: Knopf, 1978); Henry A. Kissinger, *A World Restored: Metternich, Castlereagh, and the Problems of Peace, 1812–22* (New York: Houghton Mifflin, 1957); Randall L. Schweller, *Deadly Imbalances: Tripolarity and Hitler's Strategy of World Conquest* (New York: Columbia University Press, 1998).

26. Michael W. Doyle, "Liberalism and World Politics," *American Political Science Review* 80, no. 4 (1986): 1151–69; Zeev Maoz and Bruce Russett, "Normative and Structural Causes of Democratic Peace, 1946–1986," *American Political Science Review* 87, no. 3 (1993): 624–38. For critiques, see Michael E. Brown, Sean M. Lynn-Jones, and Steven E. Miller, eds., *Debating the Democratic Peace* (Cambridge, MA: MIT Press, 1996).

27. On the liberal school in international relations, see Baldwin, *Neorealism and Neoliberalism;* Doyle, *Ways of War and Peace;* and Russett and Oneal, *Triangulating Peace.*

28. This view is associated with Woodrow Wilson. For a recent discussion of Wilsonianism, from different perspectives, see Ikenberry et al., *The Crisis of American Foreign Policy;* Smith, *Why Wilson Matters.*

29. This is the democratic peace theory that gained substantial empirical support (Doyle, "Liberalism and World Politics"; Maoz and Russett, "Normative and Structural Causes of Democratic Peace"), though it is still disputed by realists (Joanne Gowa, "Democratic States and International Disputes," *International Organization* 49, no. 3 [1995]: 511–22; Christopher Layne, "Kant or Cant: The Myth of Democratic Peace," *International Security* 19, no. 2 [1994]: 5–49; Mearsheimer, *The Tragedy of Great Power Politics*).

30. On the pacifying effect of the three mechanisms, see Russett and Oneal, *Triangulating Peace.*

31. For such arguments, see Michael C. Desch, "America's Liberal Illiberalism: The Ideological Origins of Overreaction in U.S. Foreign Policy," *International Security* 32, no. 3 (2007–8): 7–43; Tony Smith, *A Pact with the Devil: Washington's Bid for World Supremacy and the Betrayal of the American Promise* (New York: Routledge, 2007); Tony Smith, "Wilsonianism after Iraq," in Ikenberry et al., *The Crisis of American Foreign Policy*, 53–88; Smith, *Why Wilson Matters*; Posen, *Restraint*; and John J. Mearsheimer, *The Great Delusion: Liberal Dreams and International Realities* (New Haven: Yale University Press, 2018).

32. This includes the overwhelming majority of those scholars cited below as defensive liberals such as Nye, Russet, Ikenberry, Slaughter, and quite a few others.

33. Nye, *The Paradox of American Power*; Joseph Nye, *Soft Power: The Means to Success in World Politics* (New York: Public Affairs, 2004); G. John Ikenberry and Charles A. Kupchan, "Liberal Realism: The Foundations of a Democratic Foreign Policy," *National Interest* 77 (2004): 38–49; Anne-Marie Slaughter, "Wilsonianism in the Twenty-First Century," in Ikenberry et al., *The Crisis of American Foreign Policy*.

34. See Robert J. Lieber, *The American Era: Power and Strategy for the 21st Century* (Cambridge: Cambridge University Press, 2005); and Robert G. Kaufman, *In Defense of the Bush Doctrine* (Lexington: University Press of Kentucky, 2007), both of whom sympathize with the offensive liberal cause, while Smith, "Wilsonianism after Iraq," overviews it.

35. On this debate, see Ikenberry et al., *The Crisis of American Foreign Policy*.

36. Walker, "Two Faces of Liberalism." On such divisions inside liberalism, see also Doyle, *Ways of War and Peace*, and Beate Jahn, "Kant, Mill, and Illiberal Legacies in International Affairs," *International Organization* 59, no. 1 (2005): 177–205, although both underline the aggressive and imperialist behavior of liberal states toward illiberal ones.

37. Thomas Paine, *Rights of Man* (Baltimore, MD: Penguin, [1791] 1969), 174, cited in Walker, "Two Faces of Liberalism," 450.

38. Immanuel Kant, "Perpetual Peace," in *Kant's Political Writings*, ed. Hans Reiss (Cambridge: Cambridge University Press, [1795] 1991), 96, cited in Walker "Two Faces of Liberalism," 450.

39. Walker, "Two Faces of Liberalism," 465.

40. On neoconservatism and IR theory, see Michael C. Williams, "What Is the National Interest? The Neoconservative Challenge in IR Theory," *European Journal of International Relations* 11, no. 3 (2005): 307–37; and Aaron Rapport, "Unexpected Affinities? Neoconservatism's Place in IR Theory," *Security Studies* 17, no. 2 (2008): 257–93; recent works in IR theory, which are generally sympathetic to offensive liberalism (even if they don't necessarily share all its tenets and criticize some components of its post-9/11 implementation) include John Lewis Gaddis, "A Grand Strategy of Transformation," *Foreign Policy* 133 (2002): 50–57; Lieber, *The American Era*; Bradley A. Thayer, "The Case for the American Empire," in Christopher Layne and Bradley A. Thayer, *American Empire: A Debate* (New York: Routledge, 2007); and Kaufman, *In Defense of the Bush Doctrine*. Major neocon works include William Kristol and Robert Kagan, "Toward a Neo-Reaganite Foreign Policy," *Foreign Affairs* 75, no. 4 (1996): 18–32; and Robert Kagan and William Kristol, *Present Dangers: Crisis and Opportunity in American Foreign and Defense Policy* (San Francisco: Encounter, 2000). Three major studies of the neoconservatives are Stefan Halper and Jonathan Clarke, *America Alone: The Neo-Conservatives and the Global Order* (Cambridge: Cambridge University Press, 2004); Gary Dorrien, *Imperial Designs: Neoconservatism and the New Pax Americana* (New York: Routledge, 2004); and Jacob Heilbrunn, *They Knew They Were Right: The Rise of the Neocons* (New York: Doubleday, 2008). Another

study that emphasizes their influence on post-9/11 US foreign policy is Mel Gurtov, *Superpower on Crusade: The Bush Doctrine in US Foreign Policy* (Boulder, CO: Lynne Rienner, 2006). Key post-9/11 neoconservative works include Lawrence Kaplan and William Kristol, *The War over Iraq: Saddam's Tyranny and America's Mission* (San Francisco: Encounter, 2003); and David Frum and Richard Perle, *An End to Evil: How to Win on Terror* (New York: Random House, 2004). For a longer historical perspective, see Richard H. Immerman, *Empire for Liberty: A History of American Imperialism from Benjamin Franklin to Paul Wolfowitz* (Princeton, NJ: Princeton University Press, 2010).

41. See Ikenberry et al., *The Crisis of American Foreign Policy*, 13–14.

42. Smith, "Wilsonianism after Iraq," 59, highlights Wilson's "democratic regime change" during the US occupations of Nicaragua and the Dominican Republic; see also Ikenberry et al., *The Crisis of American Foreign Policy*, 14, and the citations in n21, esp. the reference to Lawrence E. Gelfand, "Where Ideals Confront Self-Interest: Wilsonian Foreign Policy," *Diplomatic History* 18, no. 1 (1994): 125–33; and Anthony, "American Democratic Interventionism," who underlines the interventionist inclinations of Wilson to spread democracy by the force of US arms as manifested especially in the interventions in Mexico and Haiti.

43. Michael W. Doyle, "Kant, Liberal Legacies, and Foreign Affairs," in Brown, Lynn-Jones, and Miller, *Debating the Democratic Peace*, 37.

44. J. S. Mill cited in Doyle, "Kant, Liberal Legacies, and Foreign Affairs," 37–38.

45. This distinction is developed by Doyle, *Ways of War and Peace*, 396–402.

46. Doyle, 398n17.

47. Cited in Doyle, 398n20.

48. Cited in Doyle, 399–402.

49. Nye, *The Paradox of American Power*; Nye, *Soft Power*.

50. On democracy promotion by the US, see Smith, *America's Mission*; Tony Smith, *Why Wilson Matters: The Origins of American Liberal Internationalism and Its Crisis Today* (Princeton, NJ: Princeton University Press, 2017); and Susan B. Epstein et al., *Democracy Promotion: Cornerstone of U.S. Foreign Policy?* (Congressional Research Service, 2007), 18, also available at http://fas.org/sgp/crs/row/RL34296.pdf (accessed February 7, 2009).

51. Rosecrance, *The Rise of the Trading State*; Robert O. Keohane and Joseph Nye, *Power and Interdependence: World Politics in Transition* (Boston: Little Brown, 1977). For critiques, see Norrin M. Ripsman and Jean Marc F. Blanchard, "Commercial Liberalism under Fire: Evidence from 1914 and 1936," *Security Studies* 6, no. 2 (1996–97): 5–51; and Katherine Barbieri, *The Liberal Illusion: Does Trade Promote Peace?* (Ann Arbor: University of Michigan Press, 2005). See also Dale Copeland, "Economic Interdependence and War: A Theory of Trade Expectations," *International Security* 20, no. 4 (1996): 5–41 and Dale Copeland, *Economic Interdependence and War* (Princeton, NJ: Princeton University Press, 2015).

52. Robert O. Keohane, *International Institutions and State Power: Essays in International Relations Theory* (Boulder, CO: Westview Press, 1989); Stephen Krasner, ed., *International Regimes* (Ithaca, NY: Cornell University Press, 1983). For critiques, see Mearsheimer, "The False Promise of International Institutions," *International Security* 19, no. 3 (1994–5): 5–49; and Korina Kagan, "The Myth of the European Concert: The Realist-Institutionalist Debate and Great Power Behavior in the Eastern Question, 1821–41," *Security Studies* 7, no. 2 (1997–98): 1–57.

53. Inis L. Claude, *Power and International Relations* (New York: Random House, 1962); Charles A. Kupchan and Clifford A. Kupchan, "Concerts, Collective Security, and the Future of Europe," *International Security* 16, no. 1 (1991): 114–61. For critiques, see Richard Betts, "Systems

for Peace or Causes of War? Collective Security, Arms Control, and the New Europe," *International Security* 17, no. 1 (1992): 5–43, and Kaufman, *In Defense of the Bush Doctrine*, 68–74.

54. For an overview, see Thomas G. Weiss et al., *The United Nations and Changing World Politics* (Boulder, CO: Westview Press, 1994).

55. For related themes, see Helga Haftendorn, Robert O. Keohane, and Celeste A. Wallander, *Imperfect Unions: Security Institutions over Time and Space* (Oxford: Oxford University Press, 1999).

56. Etel Solingen, *Regional Orders at Century's Dawn* (Princeton, NJ: Princeton University Press, 1998). On constructivist accounts of regional peace in different regions, see Emanuel Adler and Michael Barnett, eds., *Security Communities* (Cambridge: Cambridge University Press, 1998).

57. See, for example, Dalia Kaye, *Beyond the Handshake: Multilateral Cooperation in the Arab-Israeli Peace Process* (New York: Columbia University Press, 2001).

58. Doyle, "Kant, Liberal Legacies, and Foreign Affairs," 37.

59. On the US Open Door policy in both the political and economic realms and its influence on peace, see Layne, *The Peace of Illusions*, 30–36.

60. Smith, *America's Mission*; *A Pact with the Devil*; "Wilsonianism after Iraq"; Anthony, "American Democratic Interventionism."

61. Kristol and Kagan, "Toward a Neo-Reaganite Foreign Policy." For a powerful critique—from a defensive realist/balance-of-power perspective—of the different arguments in favor of the "benevolent" character of US hegemony, see Layne, *The Peace of Illusions*, 134–58. For a variety of views on this question, see also chapters in G. John Ikenberry, ed., *America Unrivaled: The Future of the Balance of Power* (Ithaca, NY: Cornell University Press, 2002).

62. Kaufman, *In Defense of the Bush Doctrine*, chap. 4.

63. 9/11, offensive liberalism, and the Iraq War are the focus of chapter 8 of this book.

64. On the common ground between constructivism and the neoconservatives (who are the last incarnation of offensive liberalism in the US), see Williams, "What Is the National Interest?," 327–28.

65. Adler and Barnett, eds., *Security Communities*, 59.

66. Rapport, "Unexpected Affinities?"

67. For overviews of this debate, see Sean M. Lynn-Jones and Steven E. Miller, eds., *The Perils of Anarchy: Contemporary Realism and International Security* (Cambridge, MA: MIT Press, 1995); Benjamin Frankel, "Restating the Realist Case: An Introduction," *Security Studies* 5, no. 3 (1996): xv–xviii; Benjamin Miller, "Competing Realist Perspectives on Great Power Crisis Behavior," *Security Studies* 5, no. 3 (1996): 309–57; Taliaferro, "Security-Seeking under Anarchy"; Layne, *The Peace of Illusions*, 15–25; and Tang, "Fear in International Politics."

68. Prominent offensive realists include Gilpin, *War and Change in World Politics*; Schweller, *Deadly Imbalances*; Eric J. Labs, "Beyond Victory: Offensive Realism and the Expansion of War Aims," *Security Studies* 6, no. 4 (1997): 1–49; Zakaria, *From Wealth to Power*; Mearsheimer, "Back to the Future"; Mearsheimer, "The False Promise of International Institutions"; and Mearsheimer, *The Tragedy of Great Power Politics*.

69. In contrast to most earlier offensive realists (such as Gilpin, Labs, and Zakaria), a leading offensive realist—John Mearsheimer (*The Tragedy of Great Power Politics*)—argues that because of what he calls "the stopping power of water," global hegemony is impossible to achieve and the most that can be reached by a leading great power is regional hegemony. Since the US has achieved regional hegemony in the Western Hemisphere, it has pursued outside of the

hemisphere, according to Mearsheimer, a grand strategy of offshore balancing, rather than extraregional hegemony. In other words, the US aims only to prevent the emergence of a regional hegemon in Europe or East Asia, without itself striving for hegemony there. Critics challenge Mearsheimer, however, by arguing that the US has pursued since WWII an extraregional hegemony, if not a global one (Layne, *The Peace of Illusions*). See also chap. 3.

70. Gilpin, *War and Change in World Politics*, 191; see also Dale C. Copeland, *The Origins of Major War* (Ithaca, NY: Cornell University Press, 2000).

71. Prominent defensive realists include Robert Jervis, "Cooperation under the Security Dilemma," *World Politics* 30, no. 2 (1978): 167–214; Kenneth N. Waltz, *Theory of International Politics* (Boston: McGraw-Hill, 1979); Posen, *The Sources of Military Doctrine*; Walt, *The Origins of Alliances*; Stephen M. Walt, *Taming American Power: The Global Response to US Power* (New York: Norton, 2005); Glaser, "Realists as Optimists"; and Stephen Van Evera, *The Causes of War* (Ithaca, NY: Cornell University Press, 1999). For a powerful critique of defensive realism by an offensive realist, see Fareed Zakaria, "Realism and Domestic Politics: A Review Essay," *International Security* 17, no. 1 (1992): 177–98.

72. Jervis, "Cooperation under the Security Dilemma."

73. Glaser, "Realists as Optimists."

74. This is the logic of the balance-of-threat theory of Walt, *The Origins of Alliances*, and Walt, *Taming American Power*.

75. Randall L. Schweller, "Bandwagoning for Profit: Bringing the Revisionist State Back In," *International Security* 19, no. 1 (1994): 72–107.

76. One of the leading offensive realists, Mearsheimer (*The Tragedy of Great Power Politics*) argues, however, that buck-passing rather than bandwagoning is the more prevalent pattern of behavior.

77. On the offense-defense balance as a key factor in affecting the likelihood of war in defensive realism, see Jervis, "Cooperation under the Security Dilemma"; Glaser, "Realists as Optimists"; Van Evera, *The Causes of War*; Sean M. Lynn-Jones, "Offense-Defense Theory and Its Critics," *Security Studies* 4, no. 4 (1995): 660–91; Charles Glaser and Chaim Kaufmann, "What Is the Offense-Defense Balance and How Can We Measure It?," *International Security* 22, no. 4 (1998): 44–82.

78. Jack Snyder, *Myths of Empire: Domestic Politics and International Ambition* (Ithaca, NY: Cornell University Press, 1991).

79. Jervis, "Cooperation under the Security Dilemma"; Kenneth N. Waltz, "Nuclear Myths and Political Realities," *American Political Science Review* 84, no. 3 (1990): 731–46; Glaser, "Realists as Optimists."

80. On the neoconservative (which, as noted, I see here as the latest wave of offensive liberalism in the US) critique of the materialist/pragmatic/value-free character of realism, see Williams, "What Is the National Interest?" See also the critique of both classical realism and neorealism by the offensive liberal scholar Kaufman, *In Defense of the Bush Doctrine*, chaps. 2, 3.

81. Wendt, *Social Theory of International Relations*.

82. Adler and Barnett, eds., *Security Communities*.

83. Zakaria, *From Wealth to Power*; Mearsheimer, *The Tragedy of Great Power Politics*; Layne, *The Peace of Illusions*.

84. Modelski, "The Long Cycle of Global Politics"; A. F. K. Organski and Jacek Kugler, *The War Ledger* (Chicago: University of Chicago Press, 1980); Gilpin, *War and Change in World Politics*; Wohlforth, "The Stability of a Unipolar World."

85. A. F. K. Organski, *World Politics*, 2nd ed. (New York: Knopf, 1968), 354; Modelski, "The Long Cycle of Global Politics," 217; and Gilpin, *War and Change in World Politics*, 145.

86. Mancur Olson, *The Logic of Collective Action* (Cambridge, MA: Harvard University Press, 1965).

87. Organski, *World Politics*, chap. 14, esp. 361, 366–67; and Modelski, "The Long Cycle of Global Politics," 217.

88. On Pax Britannica, see Modelski, "The Long Cycle of Global Politics"; and Gilpin, *War and Change in World Politics*.

89. Martin Wight, "The Balance of Power and International Order," in *The Bases of International Order: Essays in Honor of C.A.W. Manning*, ed. Alan James (New York: Oxford University Press, 1973), 100; Rosecrance, *The Rise of the Trading State*, 56–58.

90. Waltz, *Theory of International Politics*, 127; Walt, *The Origins of Alliances*, 18–19; Layne, *The Peace of Illusions*, 16.

91. Claude, *Power and International Relations*, 65; Arnold Wolfers, *Discord and Collaboration* (Baltimore, MD: Johns Hopkins University Press, 1962), 121; Hedley Bull, *The Anarchical Society: A Study of Order in World Politics* (New York: Columbia University Press, 1977), 110–11.

92. Posen, *The Sources of Military Doctrine*, 68–69; Van Evera, *The Causes of War*, 9; Layne, *The Peace of Illusions*.

93. Benjamin Miller, *When Opponents Cooperate: Great Power Conflict and Collaboration in World Politics* (Ann Arbor: University of Michigan Press, 2002, 2nd ed.), chap. 4.

94. Wohlforth, "The Stability of a Unipolar World"; Brooks and Wohlforth, *World without Balance*; Brooks and Wohlforth, "The Rise and Fall of the Great Powers in the Twenty-First Century: China's Rise and the Fate of America's Global Position," *International Security* 40, no. 3 (2015–16): 7–53; Brooks and Wohlforth, *America Abroad*; Lieber, *Power and Willpower in the American Future*; and Josef Joffe, *The Myth of American Decline: Politics, Economics, and a Half Century of False Prophecies* (New York: Norton, 2014).

95. Stephen Walt, "The End of the American Era," *National Interest* (November–December 2011): 6–16; John Mearsheimer, "Imperial by Design," *National Interest* (January–February 2011): 16–34; Christopher Layne, "This Time It's Real: The End of Unipolarity and the Pax Americana," *International Studies Quarterly* 56, no. 1 (2012): 203–13; Christopher Layne, "The US-Chinese Power Shift and the End of the Pax Americana," *International Affairs* 94, no. 1 (2018): 89–111; Gideon Rachman, *Easternization: Asia's Rise and America's Decline—From Obama to Trump and Beyond* (New York: Other Press, 2016). More on the changing balance of power in chaps. 10 and 11.

96. Barry R. Posen, "From Unipolarity to Multipolarity: Transition in Sight?," in *International Relations Theory and Consequences of Unipolarity*, ed. G. John Ikenberry, Michael Mastanduno, and William C. Wohlforth (Cambridge: Cambridge University Press, 2011), 317–41. See also Amitav Acharya, *The End of the American World Order* (Cambridge: Polity, 2014).

97. On the post-9/11 invasion of Iraq, see chap. 8.

98. T. V. Paul, "Soft Balancing in the Age of U.S. Primacy," *International Security* 30, no. 1 (2005), 46–71; T. V. Paul, *Restraining Great Powers: Soft Balancing from Empires to the Global Era* (New Haven, CT: Yale University Press, 2018); Robert Pape, "Soft Balancing against the U.S.," *International Security* 30, no. 1 (2005): 7–45; and Walt, *Taming American Power*.

99. Glaser, "Realists as Optimists."

100. B. K. Greener, "Liberalism and the Use of Force: Core Themes and Conceptual Tensions," *Alternatives* 32 (2007): 295–318.

101. For a comparison between the democratization of Germany and the democratization in Iraq, see Benjamin Miller, "Does Democratization Pacify the State? The Cases of Germany and Iraq," *International Studies Quarterly* 56, no. 3 (2012): 455–69.

102. On the Philippines, see Smith, *America's Mission*, 75; and Odd Arne Westad, *The Global Cold War* (Cambridge: Cambridge University Press, 2007), 23.

103. Smith, *America's Mission*, 13, 18.

104. See Robert DiPrizio, *Armed Humanitarians: U.S. Interventions from Northern Iraq to Kosovo* (Baltimore, MD: Johns Hopkins University Press, 2002).

105. Nye, *The Paradox of American Power*; Nye, *Soft Power*.

106. Dueck, *Reluctant Crusaders*, 85–86.

107. Dueck, 95–100.

108. On Iran, see Stephen Kinzer, *All the Shah's Men: An American Coup and the Roots of Middle East Terror* (Hoboken, NJ: Wiley, 2008); Westad, *The Global Cold War*, 119; on Iran and Guatemala, see Smith, *America's Mission*, 191–99. For a more detailed analysis of the Guatemala case, see Melissa Willard-Foster, *Toppling Foreign Governments: The Logic of Regime Change* (Philadelphia: University of Pennsylvania Press, 2019), 103–39; on Chile (Pinochet), see Smith, *America's Mission*, 210, and Westad, *The Global Cold War*, 201; on Chile and Guatemala, see Nick Cullather, *Secret History: The CIA's Classified Account of Its Operations in Guatemala, 1952–1954* (Stanford, CA: Stanford University Press, 1999). On US removal of several elected leaders in Latin America, see Greg Grandin, *Empire Workshop: Latin America, the United States, and the Rise of the New Imperialism* (New York: Holt Paperbacks, 2007), 41. On US support for Latin American dictators, see Alexander B. Downes and Mary Lauren Lilley, "Overt Peace, Covert War? Covert Interventions and the Democratic Peace," *Security Studies* 19, no. 2 (2010): 266–306.

Chapter Two

1. See, for example, Posen and Ross, "Competing Visions for U.S. Grand Strategy"; Dueck, *Reluctant Crusaders*; and Layne, *The Peace of Illusions*.

2. For recent books, see, for example, Seyom Brown, *Faces of Power* (New York: Columbia University Press, 2015); Nau, *Conservative Internationalism*; Keren Yarhi-Milo, *Knowing the Adversary: Leaders, Intelligence Organizations, and Assessments of Intentions in International Relations* (Princeton, NJ: Princeton University Press, 2014); Dueck, *The Obama Doctrine*.

3. However, liberal strategies were dominant in US relations with its Western liberal allies during the Cold War, since the power differentials among them made the United States the hegemonic power in the Western camp in the Cold War era.

4. Kenneth Waltz, "Structural Realism after the Cold War," in *America Unrivaled: The Future of the Balance of Power*, ed. G. John Ikenberry (Ithaca, NY: Cornell University Press, 2002), 48. For similar arguments about liberal hegemony, see John J. Mearsheimer, "Bound to Fail: The Rise and Fall of the Liberal International Order," *International Security* 43, no. 4 (2019): 13–14; and Walt, "US Grand Strategy after the Cold War."

5. On the key principles of the liberal approach, see chap. 1.

6. This factor combines two of Walt's material sources of threat: offensive military capabilities and geographical proximity. See Walt, *The Origins of Alliances*, 24–25.

7. On the effects of major formative events, see Jervis, *Perception and Misperception in International Politics*, 239–82.

8. On costly signals, see James D. Fearon, "Signaling Foreign Policy Interests: Tying Hands versus Sinking Costs," *Journal of Conflict Resolution* 41, no. 1 (1997): 68–90.

9. Mark W. Zacher, "The Territorial Integrity Norm: International Boundaries and the Use of Force," *International Organization* 55, no. 2 (2001): 215–50.

10. Barry Buzan, *People, States and Fear: An Agenda for International Security Studies in the Post–Cold War Era*, 2nd ed. (Boulder, CO: Lynne Rienner, 1991); Barry Buzan and Ole Waever, *Regions and Powers: The Structure of International Relations* (Cambridge: Cambridge University Press, 2003); Walt, *The Origins of Alliances*; and Patrick Porter, *The Global Village Myth: Distance, War, and the Limits of Power* (Washington, DC: Georgetown University Press, 2015).

11. To demonstrate the general nature of these propositions—beyond the American case—I'll cite briefly for each proposition also a few non-American examples, which are not going to be analyzed in-depth in the book. Obviously, these cases deserve full-blown studies on their own, but such studies are not going to be pursued here.

12. See Deborah Larson, *Origins of Containment: A Psychological Explanation* (Princeton, NJ: Princeton University Press, 1985), 71–76.

13. Dueck, *Reluctant Crusaders*, 93; see also 192n32.

14. See Layne, *The Peace of Illusions*, 51; see also Christopher Layne, "The 'Poster Child for Offensive Realism': America as a Global Hegemon," *Security Studies* 12, no. 2 (2002–3): 120–64, esp. 134. For other sources that interpret US Cold War policy in accordance with offensive realism as defined here, see Melvyn P. Leffler, *A Preponderance of Power: National Security, the Truman Administration, and the Cold War* (Stanford, CA: Stanford University Press, 1992), 15–19; Dale Copeland, *The Origins of Major War* (Ithaca, NY: Cornell University Press, 2001); and Robert Jervis, "Understanding the Bush Doctrine," in *American Hegemony: Preventive War, Iraq and Imposing Democracy*, ed. D. J. Caraley (New York: Academy of Political Science, 2004), 8, citations in n20.

15. P. M. H. Bell, *The World since 1945: An International History* (London: Arnold, 2001), 105, 113; see also Vladislav Zubok and Constantine Pleshakov, *Inside the Kremlin's Cold War: From Stalin to Khrushchev* (Cambridge, MA: Harvard University Press, 1996), 69.

16. Dale Copeland, *The Origins of Major War*, 56–78; Mearsheimer, *The Tragedy of Great Power Politics*, 213–16.

17. Ariel Levite, *Offense and Defense in Israeli Military Doctrine* (Boulder, CO: Westview Press, 1990).

18. On the US détente strategy, see Raymond Garthoff, *Detente and Confrontation: American-Soviet Relations from Nixon to Reagan* (Washington, DC: Brookings Institution, 1985); Henry Kissinger, *White House Years* (Boston: Little, Brown, 1979); Henry Kissinger, *Years of Upheaval* (Boston: Little, Brown, 1982); Henry Kissinger, *Years of Renewal* (New York: Simon & Schuster, 1999); Jussi M. Hanhimaki, *The Rise and Fall of Détente* (Washington, DC: Potomac Books, 2013); and Miller, *When Opponents Cooperate*, chaps. 4 and 6.

19. Hans J. Morgenthau, *Politics among Nations: The Struggle for Power and Peace*, 5th ed. (New York: Knopf, 1973); Richard Little, *The Balance of Power in International Relations* (Cambridge: Cambridge University Press, 2007).

20. On the conducive circumstances after the war for the post-1973 US mediation and for reaching mutual arrangements, see Shibley Telhami, *Power and Leadership in International Bargaining: The Path to the Camp David Accords* (New York: Columbia University Press, 1990); Benjamin Miller, *States, Nations and the Great Powers: The Sources of Regional War and Peace* (Cambridge: Cambridge University Press, 2007), 236–37.

21. Norrin M. Ripsman, "Two Stages of Transition from a Region of War to a Region of Peace: Realist Transition and Liberal Endurance," *International Studies Quarterly* 49, no. 4 (2005): 669–94; Miller, *States, Nations and the Great Powers*, chap. 8.

22. With Brexit's conclusion on January 31, 2020, there are twenty-seven members in the EU.

23. See Shimon Peres with Arye Naor, *The New Middle East* (Henry Holt & Co, 1993).

24. For a comparison between peacemaking in Europe and the Middle East, see Benjamin Miller, "Contrasting Explanations for Peace: Realism vs. Liberalism in Europe and the Middle East," *Contemporary Security Policy* 31, no. 1 (April 2010): 134–64.

25. On the post–Cold War/post–Gulf War situation as conducive for Arab-Israeli peace promotion, see William Quandt, *Peace Process: American Diplomacy and the Arab-Israeli Conflict since 1967*, rev. ed. (Berkeley: University of California Press, 2001); Miller, *States, Nations and the Great Powers*, 238–40.

26. John Owen, *The Clash of Ideas in World Politics* (Princeton, NJ: Princeton University Press, 2010).

27. Owen, 22. For an insightful analysis of foreign-imposed regime change (FIRC), see the comprehensive work on this subject by Willard-Foster, *Toppling Foreign Governments*. On pp. 249–53 Willard-Foster presents a comprehensive list of all FIRCs between 1816 and 2007. Out of a total of 178 cases, 123 were imposed by a major power, and in only eleven cases the target was a major power. Since becoming a great power in 1898, the US was involved in thirty-eight regime change attempts.

28. Owen, *The Clash*, 22, 24, 26, 179–81.

29. On the post-WWII imposition of democracy in West Germany by the US, see Benjamin Miller, "Does Democratization Pacify the State? The Cases of Germany and Iraq," *International Studies Quarterly* 56, no. 3 (2012): 455–69.

30. On the Yalta Summit of Stalin, FDR, and Churchill in February 1945, see Michael Dobbs, *Six Months in 1945—FDR, Stalin, Churchill and Truman from the World War to Cold War* (New York: Knopf, 2012).

31. On the imposition of communist regimes in by the Soviet Union in Eastern Europe during the Cold War, see Berger et al., "Do Superpower Interventions Have Short and Long Term Consequences for Democracy?," *Journal of Comparative Economics* 41, no. 1 (2013): 22–34.

32. On this regime change by the Soviets, see Willard-Foster, *Toppling Foreign Governments*, 140–74.

33. Gerald M. Steinberg and Ziv Rubinovitz, *Menachem Begin and the Israel-Egypt Peace Process: between Ideology and Political Realism* (Bloomington: Indiana University Press, 2019).

34. On the Lebanon War, see Zeev Schiff and Ehud Yaari, *Israel's Lebanon War* (New York: Simon & Schuster, 1984).

35. John Lewis Gaddis, *We Now Know: Rethinking Cold War History* (New York: Oxford University Press, 1997), 20–22, explains Soviet behavior through the tension between personality and situational explanation of the origins of the Cold War. The test is whether there was a change in attitudes with a change in situations/circumstances. The United States and Great Britain reached the conclusion, somewhat reluctantly, that the inability to cooperate/compromise with Stalin was due to his character. FDR reacted according to situations; but this was not the case with Stalin who deeply distrusted democracies continuously (in general he didn't trust anyone). In contrast, FDR didn't distrust Stalin almost until his death, while Churchill alternated. Thus, according to Gaddis, FDR and somewhat less so Churchill were more affected by

external/systemic effects than Stalin. As we'll show in chap. 3, Truman was influenced by the external systemic effects.

Chapter Three

1. We would like to thank Korina Kagan for her great help on this chapter.

2. On the president as determining US foreign policy, see Thomas Preston, *The President and His Inner Circle: Leadership Style and the Advisory Process in Foreign Affairs* (New York: Columbia University Press, 2001); Jonathan Renshon and Stanley A. Renshon, "The Theory and Practice of Foreign Policy Decision Making," *Political Psychology* 29, no. 4 (2008): 509–36; Steven L. Spiegel, *The Other Arab-Israeli Conflict: Making America's Middle East Policy, from Truman to Reagan* (Chicago: University of Chicago Press, 1985); and Spiegel, "Unnoticed Policy Makers: The President and His Crowd," paper presented at the annual meeting of the American Political Science Association, New Orleans, LA, August 29–September 1, 1985. See also Robert Dallek's various books on different presidents.

3. George F. Kennan, "Moscow Embassy Telegram no. 511: The Long Telegram, Feb. 22, 1946," in *Containment: Documents on American Policy and Strategy, 1945–1950*, ed. Thomas H. Etzold and John Lewis Gaddis (New York: Columbia University Press, 1978), 50–62; X, "The Sources of Soviet Conduct," *Foreign Affairs* 25, no. 4 (1947): 566–82.

4. Mearsheimer, *The Tragedy of Great Power Politics*; Layne, *The Peace of Illusions*; Dueck, *Reluctant Crusaders*.

5. This is Layne's correct critique of Mearsheimer (*The Peace of Illusions*, 19).

6. Mearsheimer, *The Tragedy of Great Power Politics*.

7. Layne, *The Peace of Illusions*, 28.

8. Layne, 51.

9. Mearsheimer, *The Tragedy of Great Power Politics*, chap. 2.

10. Layne, *The Peace of Illusions*, 29–30.

11. Layne, 30–33.

12. Layne, 56.

13. The revisionist school's most prominent representative is William Appleman Williams. Other leading critical scholars are Joyce and Gabriel Kolko, Gar Alperovitz, and Walter LaFeber. On the traditional-revisionist debate over the historiography of the Cold War, see Jonathan Nashel, "Cold War (1945–1991): Changing Interpretations," in *The Oxford Companion to American Military History*, ed. John Whiteclay Chambers II et al. (New York: Oxford University Press, 1999), 154–55. See also Odd Arne Westad, "The Cold War and the International History of the Twentieth Century," in *The Cambridge History of the Cold War*, vol. 1, ed. Melvyn P. Leffler and Odd Arne Westad (Cambridge: Cambridge University Press, 2010), 1–19, and the bibliographical essay on 508–10.

14. Dueck, *Reluctant Crusaders*, 88–89.

15. Dueck, 100.

16. Dueck, 89.

17. Dueck, 100–104.

18. Layne, *The Peace of Illusions*, 51.

19. For a similar argument, see, for example, the memoir of Truman's secretary of state, Dean Acheson, *Present at the Creation: My Years at the State Department* (New York: Norton, 1969), chap. 22.

20. Layne, *The Peace of Illusions*, chap. 3.

21. The founding of NATO was a European initiative to "keep the United States in, the Soviet Union out, and Germany down." This quote is attributed to NATO's first secretary, Lord Hastings Ismay. See Daniel Schorr, "With No Clear Mission, NATO Has Little Power," *NPR*, April 1, 2009, http://www.npr.org/templates/story/story.php?storyId=102618942. See also: Edward A. Kolodziej, *Security and International Relations* (Cambridge: Cambridge University Press, 2005), 132.

22. John Lewis Gaddis, *Strategies of Containment: A Critical Appraisal of American National Security Policy during the Cold War* (Oxford: Oxford University Press, 2005), 106–7; Dueck, *Reluctant Crusaders*, 100.

23. John Sakkas, *Britain and the Greek Civil War, 1944–1949: British Imperialism, Public Opinion and the Coming of the Cold War* (Wiesbaden: Harrassowitz Verlag, 2013); Thanasis D. Sfikas, "The Greek Civil War," in *Origins of the Cold War: An International History*, 2nd ed., ed. Melvyn P. Leffler and David S. Painter (New York and London: Routledge, 1994), 134–52.

24. Dueck, *Reluctant Crusaders*, 86–88; Layne, *The Peace of Illusions*, 54–57.

25. Layne, *The Peace of Illusions*, chap. 2.

26. Mearsheimer, *The Tragedy of Great Power Politics*, 256.

27. Mearsheimer, 256.

28. Mearsheimer, 256–57.

29. According to Gregory Mitrovich, *Undermining the Kremlin: America's Strategy to Subvert the Soviet Bloc, 1947–1956* (Ithaca, NY: Cornell University Press, 2000), the realist strategies were augmented by some components of offensive liberalism since 1948 and also later in 1950 (psychological warfare) as the Soviet threat grew; but growing Soviet capabilities since 1955 led to the abandonment of offensive liberalism.

30. A key source is Wilson D. Miscamble, *From Roosevelt to Truman: Potsdam, Hiroshima, and the Cold War* (Cambridge: Cambridge University Press 2007); John Lewis Gaddis, *The United States and the Origins of the Cold War, 1941–1947* (New York: Columbia University Press, 1972), 24–31; Gaddis, *The Long Peace: Inquiries into the History of the Cold War* (Oxford: Oxford University Press, 1987), 23–4; Gaddis, *Strategies of Containment*, 10 and 12; Deborah Welch Larson, *Origins of Containment: A Psychological Explanation* (Princeton, NJ: Princeton University Press, 1985), 71–76; Alexander L. George, "Domestic Constraints on Regime Change in US Foreign Policy: The Need for Policy Legitimacy," in *Change in the International System*, ed. Ole R. Holsti, Randolph M. Siverson, and Alexander L. George (Boulder, CO: Westview Press, 1980), 233–59; G. John Ikenberry, "Rethinking the Origins of American Hegemon," in *American Foreign Policy: Theoretical Essays*, ed. Ikenberry (Boston: Houghton Mifflin, 2005), 119; Henry A. Kissinger, *Diplomacy* (New York: Simon and Schuster, 1994), 395–98, 408, 411–12, 420–22, 426–27.

31. Larson, *Origins of Containment*, 3.

32. Larson, 3, 71–76.

33. George, "Domestic Constraints on Regime Change in US Foreign Policy." This obviously related to the US post-WWII demobilization and its attempt to return quickly to normal economic and civil situation. A unilateral action would have required massive military forces deployed around the globe.

34. Kissinger, *Diplomacy*, 395.

35. Gaddis, *The United States and the Origins of the Cold War, 1941–1947*, 3, 24–25.

36. Kissinger, *Diplomacy*, 400–401.

37. A major mistake in the eyes of Kissinger (*Diplomacy*, 405–8): a negotiated spheres-of-influence agreement could have prevented the emergence of satellite orbit in Eastern Europe and could have led to Finlandization of the region (that is, the Eastern Europeans could at least maintain their domestic freedoms even if their foreign policy would have been guided by Moscow).

38. Kissinger, 396, 410.

39. Larson, *Origins of Containment*, 73.

40. Gaddis, *The Long Peace*, 23–24.

41. Larson, *Origins of Containment*, 3.

42. Larson, 74–75.

43. Gaddis, *The Long Peace*, 51.

44. Gaddis, *Strategies of Containment*, 55.

45. Leffler, *A Preponderance of Power*, 372–80 passim, 448, 561, 491, 517; Leffler, *For the Soul of Mankind: The United States, the Soviet Union, and the Cold War* (New York: Hill & Wang, 2007), 99–101, 145; Gaddis *Strategies of Containment*, 153–54; Dueck, *Reluctant Crusaders*, 85–86; Laszlo Borhi, "Rollback, Liberation Containment, or Inaction? US Policy and Eastern Europe in the 1950s," *Journal of Cold War Studies* 1, no. 3 (Fall 1999): 67–110.

46. Leffler, *For the Soul of Mankind*, 99–100: "Dulles warned the Cold War would be lost if the US did not go on the offensive, if it did not seek to 'roll back' communism"; citing John Foster Dulles, *War or Peace* (New York: Macmillan, 1950), 163, also 74–78; Richard H. Immerman, *John Foster Dulles: Piety, Pragmatism and Power in U.S. Foreign Policy* (Wilmington, DE: Scholarly Resources, 1999), 1–34.

47. Ronald R. Krebs, *Dueling Visions: U.S. Strategy toward Eastern Europe under Eisenhower* (College Station: Texas A&M University Press, 2001), 16–18.

48. Krebs, 17.

49. Krebs, 18.

50. Gaddis, *Strategies of Containment*, 154.

51. Krebs, *Dueling Visions*, 14.

52. Critics of containment are summarized in Bennett Kovrig, *The Myth of Liberation: East-Central Europe in U.S. Diplomacy and Politics since 1941* (Baltimore, MD: Johns Hopkins University Press, 1973), 99–111.

53. Krebs, *Dueling Visions*, 13.

54. See Krebs, 14–15, who also cites Robert A. Tafts, *A Foreign Policy for Americans* (Garden City, NY: Doubleday, 1951), 103–13. Senator Taft was a more moderate offensive liberalism supporter rather than the rollbacker as noted in Krebs, *Dueling Visions*, and Dueck, *Reluctant Crusaders*.

55. Leffler, *A Preponderance of Power*, 372.

56. Mitrovich, *Undermining the Kremlin*.

57. See also Raymond L. Garthoff, review of Grose, *Operation Rollback*, and Mitrovich, *Undermining the Kremlin*, *Political Science Quarterly* 116, no. 1 (2001): 160–62.

58. This paragraph is based on Jerald Combs, "Introduction," in H. Diplo *Roundtable 1-6 on America and the Cold War, 1941–1991: A Realist Interpretation*, December 10, 2010. Available online: https://issforum.org/ISSF/PDF/ISSF-Roundtable-1-6.pdf (accessed February 10, 2020).

59. This ambiguity over how much intervention was enough is in part the product of a second ambiguity that permeates the view of many realists: whether realism is descriptive or prescriptive.

60. Such as, notably, Walter Lippmann, *The Cold War: A Study in U.S. Foreign Policy* (New York: Harper, 1947), summarized in Larson, *Origins of Containment*, 7. The realist views are summarized in Larson, 7–8 (citing Lippmann); Hans J. Morgenthau, *In Defense of the National Interest* (New York: Knopf, 1951), 76–78, 105–6, 108–12, 231–37; George F. Kennan, *Memoirs (1925–1950)* (Boston: Little Brown, 1967); Norman A. Graebner, *Cold War Diplomacy: American Foreign Policy, 1945–60* (New York: Van Nostrand, 1962); Louis J. Halle, *The Cold War as History* (New York: Harper & Row, 1967); Martin F. Herz, *Beginnings of the Cold War* (Bloomington: Indiana University Press, 1966). For example, Halle, *The Cold War as History*, 102–6, highlights the postwar need to develop a realist policy:

1. States should not be divided between inherently "aggressors" (Germany and Japan) versus "peace-loving" (Russia).
2. The need to reestablish a balance of power by filling the remaining power vacuums and thereby limiting the further expansion of the Russian empire.
3. Churchill (March 5, 1946) spoke of an Iron Curtain between the Soviet sphere and the free West.
4. Churchill argued that the Russians respect most military strength.

61. This analysis is largely based on the assumptions of George Kennan, according to Gaddis, *Strategies of Containment*, 24–52; Gaddis, *George F. Kennan: An American Life* (New York: Penguin, 2011). See also Wilson D. Miscamble, CSC, *George F. Kennan and the Making of American Foreign Policy, 1947–1950* (Princeton, NJ: Princeton University Press, 1992); Andres Stephanson, *Kennan and the Art of Foreign Policy* (Cambridge, MA: Harvard University Press, 1989).

62. Gaddis, *Strategies of Containment*, 55.

63. Gaddis, *Strategies of Containment*, 56. For more on Kennan's containment, see Halle, *The Cold War as History*, 106–8.

64. Gaddis, *Strategies of Containment*, 57.

65. Cited in Strobe Talbott, *The Master of the Game: Paul Nitze and the Nuclear Peace* (New York: Knopf, 1988), 43.

66. Gaddis, *Strategies of Containment*, 44.

67. Kissinger, *Diplomacy*, 395, 414.

68. Kissinger, 413; Larson, *Origins of Containment*, 107–12.

69. Dueck, *Reluctant Crusaders*, 87–88.

70. Kennan cited in Gaddis, *Strategies of Containment*, 51; see also Nicholas Thompson, *The Hawk and the Dove: Paul Nitze, George Kennan, and the History of the Cold War* (New York: Henry Holt & Co., 2009), 71.

71. Dueck, 84–85.

72. Aaron L. Friedberg, "Will Europe's Past Be Asia's Future?," *Survival* 42, no. 3 (2000): 147–59.

73. Marc Trachtenberg, *History and Strategy* (Princeton, NJ: Princeton University Press, 1991), 103–12, esp. 103–7; and Trachtenberg, "Preventive War and US Foreign Policy," *Security Studies* 16, no. 1 (2007): 1–31. See also Dueck, *Reluctant Crusaders*, 86; Jack S. Levy on "Preventive Logic in American Foreign Policy since 1945," 185–190, in his article "Preventive War and the Bush Doctrine," in *Understanding the Bush Doctrine: Psychology and Strategy in an Age of Terrorism*, ed. Stanley A. Renshon and Peter Suedfeld (New York: Routledge, 2007), 175–200; for another citation, see Krebs, *Dueling Visions*, 127n22—Russell D. Buhite and William C. Hamel, "War for Peace: The Question of an American Preventive War against the Soviet Union, 1945–

1955," *Diplomatic History* 14, no. 3 (Summer 1990): 367–84; the most comprehensive study of various administrations' debates and considerations of preventive war is Scott A. Silverstone, *Preventive War and American Democracy* (New York: Routledge, 2007).

74. Levy, "Preventive War and the Bush Doctrine," 186, citing Trachtenberg, "Preventive War and US Foreign Policy," 6.

75. Trachtenberg, *History and Strategy*, 104.

76. Trachtenberg. Bohlen: Record of the Under Secretary's Meeting, April 15, 1949, *FRUS* 1949, vol. 1, 284. Kennan: Memorandum of National Security Council Consultants' Meeting, June 29, 1950. *FRUS* 1950, vol. 1, 330.

77. Trachtenberg *History and Strategy*, 105.

78. Trachtenberg, 106.

79. Citations in Dueck, *Reluctant Crusaders*, 190n11.

80. On the differences between Kennan and Nitze, see Thompson, *The Hawk and the Dove*. The analysis here is especially informed by Gaddis, *Strategies of Containment*, 89–95. On NSC 68, see also Brands, *What Good Is Grand Strategy?*, 45–47; Stephen Sestanovich, *Maximalist: America in the World from Truman to Obama* (New York: Vintage, 2014), 46–49; Ernest R. May, *American Cold War Strategy: Interpreting NSC 68* (New York: St. Martin's Press, 1993); Ken Young, "Revisiting NSC 68," *Journal of Cold War Studies* 15, no. 1 (Winter 2013): 3–33, reviewed by Joseph M. Siracusa, Royal Melbourne Institute of Technology, in http://www.h-net.org/~diplo/reviews/PDF/AR419.pdf.

81. Trachtenberg, *History and Strategy*, 198; Gaddis, *Strategies of Containment*, 90.

82. Gaddis, *Strategies of Containment*, 94–95.

83. Gaddis, 89.

84. On the problematic application of defensive perimeter in the Truman administration, see Brands, *What Good Is Grand Strategy?*, 39.

85. See Miller, *When Opponents Cooperate*, 106–7: this is related to the tension between balancing versus bandwagoning as the dominant image of international politics.

86. Mitrovich, *Undermining the Kremlin*, 12, last paragraph: NSC 68 as a policy to achieve nuclear superiority.

87. Gaddis, *Strategies of Containment*, 98; on NSC 68 opposition to preventive war, see Silverstone, *Preventive War and American Democracy*, 68–71 .

88. Although the preventive war option was "advocated with much more vigor" than two of four alternatives discussed in the report (Trachtenberg, *History and Strategy*, 108n25).

89. Trachtenberg, 108.

90. Gaddis, *Strategies of Containment*, 104.

91. Gaddis, 106.

92. Krebs, *Dueling Visions*, 11 and 127nn22 and 23.

93. For a brief overview, see Joseph S. Nye, ed., *The Making of America's Soviet Policy (Council of Foreign Relations Book)* (New Haven, CT: Yale University Press, 1984), 67–72. For recent analyses, see Brands, *What Good Is Grand Strategy?*; and Sestanovich, *Maximalist*.

94. Gaddis, *Strategies of Containment*, 10–16. The argument about Truman's continuation of FDR's conciliatory policy until the end of 1946 is documented most comprehensively in Miscamble, *From Roosevelt to Truman*, chap. 7.

95. Although with Byrnes as Truman's secretary of state, the policy moved to a greater reliance on bargaining and horse-trading. Leffler, *For the Soul of Mankind*, 4, for his part, argues that during 1946 Truman and Stalin wavered between toughness and conciliation.

96. Gaddis, *Strategies of Containment*, 11–12.

97. Kissinger, *Diplomacy*, 410.

98. Gaddis, *The Long Peace*, 50.

99. Larson, *Origins of Containment*, 74.

100. Gaddis, *The Long Peace*, 52–53.

101. Gaddis, *Strategies of Containment*, 10; Kissinger, *Diplomacy*, 412.

102. Gaddis, *We Now Know*, 20–21.

103. Larson, *Origins of Containment*, 70. Leffler, *For the Soul of Mankind*, 42–44—Truman's willingness to collaborate with Stalin at the end of the war: "Stalin, Truman thought, was someone you could deal with. He would respect American power. Agreement was still possible."

104. Krebs, *Dueling Visions*, 8. On a distinction between a security seeker and an expansionist power, see Charles L. Glaser, "The Security Dilemma Revisited," *World Politics* 50, no. 1 (1997): 171–201.

105. Gaddis, *The Long Peace*, 38. Wallace tried to revive this image of the Soviets in spring and summer 1946. Gaddis, *The Long Peace*, 39.

106. Gaddis *The Long Peace*, 254n82.

107. Larson, *Origins of Containment*, 69–70.

108. On FDR's belief in reassurance, see Larson, 75–76.

109. Larson, 76–78.

110. Gaddis, *The Long Peace*, 51.

111. Krebs, *Dueling Visions*, 8. See also on Byrnes's visit to Moscow at the end of 1945, Miscamble, *From Roosevelt to Truman*, 270–74.

112. Miscamble, *From Roosevelt to Truman*, 262–64.

113. May, *American Cold War Strategy*, 2.

114. This paragraph relies heavily on Robert Jervis's review of Miscamble (*From Roosevelt to Truman*) in H-Diplo at https://networks.h-net.org/system/files/contributed-files/fromtrumantoroosevelt-jervis.pdf (accessed February 13, 2020).

115. Kissinger, *Diplomacy*, 433; Gaddis, *The Long Peace*, 53; Larson, *Origins of Containment*, 301; Miscamble, *George F. Kennan and the Making of American Foreign Policy*, 27. More specifically, Kissinger (*Diplomacy*, 433) points out the collapse of the Four Policemen at the Potsdam Conference. In 1946 there was a move toward the "get tough" approach (Miscamble, *George F. Kennan and the Making of American Foreign Policy*, 27); Gaddis (*The Long Peace*, 53) highlights the emerging consensus as early as 1946 in favor of tougher methods in relation to Moscow. Still, 1946 ended with Truman's renewed, but wary, commitment to US-Soviet cooperation (Larson, *Origins of Containment*, 301), though by the end of 1946 many US officials had reached the conclusion that the Soviet adversarial conduct threatened US security (Miscamble, *George F. Kennan and the Making of American Foreign Policy*, 3, citing Gaddis, *The Long Peace*, 20–47).

116. Acheson, *Present at the Creation*, cited in Miscamble, *From Roosevelt to Truman*, 309. Leffler *For the Soul of Mankind*, 68: By the fall of 1947, US officials felt they didn't have the time to try cooperation with the Soviets.

117. On the Truman Doctrine, see Larson, *Origins of Containment*, 3–4, 316–23; Leffler, *A Preponderance of Power*, 121–27, 142–47, 503, 513.

118. Cited in Ernest May, *American Cold War Strategy*, 2; Thompson, *The Hawk and the Dove*, 71.

119. May, *American Cold War Strategy*, 2; Gaddis, *The Long Peace*, 56–57; Brands, *What Good Is Grand Strategy?*, 32–34.

120. Gaddis, *The Long Peace*, 60; Sestanovich, *Maximalist*, 19.

121. May, *American Cold War Strategy*, 2.

122. Brands, *What Good Is Grand Strategy?*, 34–36.

123. Dueck *Reluctant Crusaders*, 86, references in 190n11; Trachtenberg, "Preventive War and US Foreign Policy"; Krebs, *Dueling Visions*, 11.

124. Thompson, *The Hawk and the Dove*, 72.

125. Gaddis, *Strategies of Containment*, 56–59.

126. Gaddis, 60–62.

127. Sestanovich, *Maximalist*, 42.

128. Sestanovich, 42–46.

129. On the centrality of the economic/nonmilitary means, see Brands, *What Good Is Grand Strategy?*

130. Gaddis, *Strategies of Containment*, 60–62.

131. Brands, *What Good Is Grand Strategy?*, 28–29; Gaddis, *Strategies of Containment*, 62–63.

132. Brands, *What Good Is Grand Strategy?*, 30.

133. Brands, 30.

134. On this "wedge" strategy and its great limitations, see Brands, 37–38.

135. Brands, 32; Gaddis, *Strategies of Containment*, 65.

136. Gaddis, *Strategies of Containment*, 66.

137. See Gaddis, 67–68; on the problems of this strategy vis-à-vis China, see Brands, *What Good Is Grand Strategy?*, 37–38.

138. Gaddis, *Strategies of Containment*, 68–9.

139. Gaddis, 69, 77.

140. Gaddis, 44.

141. Sestanovich, *Maximalist*, 29–30, 34; Gaddis, *Strategies of Containment*, 70–81.

142. Gaddis, *Strategies of Containment*, 81–82.

143. Gaddis, 106–15.

144. Barrass, *The Great Cold War*, 63–64, 71, based on Leffler, *A Preponderance of Power*, 355–60; May, *American Cold War Strategy*, 23–81.

145. Leffler, *A Preponderance of Power*, 488.

146. Leffler, 488–89; 636n179 introduces citations on the emphasis on preponderance.

147. Gaddis, *Strategies of Containment*, 111; Brands, *What Good Is Grand Strategy?*, 49.

148. Sestanovich, *Maximalist*, 42–40.

149. Marshall cited in Gaddis, *The Long Peace*, 57.

150. Dueck, *Reluctant Crusaders*, 83.

151. Dueck, 88–89.

152. Dueck, 93.

153. Leffler, *A Preponderance of Power*, 15–19.

154. Leffler cited in G. John Ikenberry, "Rethinking the Origins of American Hegemon," in *American Foreign Policy: Theoretical Essays*, ed. Ikenberry (Boston: Houghton Mifflin, 2005), 85–86.

155. Leffler, *A Preponderance of Power*, 372.

156. May, *American Cold War Strategy*, 9. Barrass, *The Great Cold War*, 63–64: NSC 68 prescribes preponderance of power—both conventional and nuclear.

157. Leffler, *A Preponderance of Power*, 356.

158. John Lewis Gaddis, "Grand Strategies in the Cold War," in *The Cambridge History of*

the Cold War, vol. 2, *Crises and Détente*, ed. Melvyn P. Leffler and Odd A. Westad (Cambridge: Cambridge University Press, 2010), 8.

159. Krebs, *Dueling Visions*, 11–12.

160. Although Krebs argues that there was also a continuation of NSC 20/4: an emphasis on an offensive-minded strategy that characterized US thinking in the late 1940s.

161. Barrass, *The Great Cold War*, 64.

162. Barrass, 68.

163. Barrass, 71–72; Brands, *What Good Is Grand Strategy?*, 48–49.

164. Richard Saull, "American Foreign Policy during the Cold War," in *US Foreign Policy*, ed. Michael Cox and Doug Stokes (Oxford: Oxford University Press, 2008), 78, citing additional sources; see also on the buildup, Leffler, *A Preponderance of Power*, 485–93 — esp. 488–89: the hydrogen bomb; 489: strategic/escalation dominance.

165. Layne, *The Peace of Illusions*.

166. Gaddis, "Grand Strategies in the Cold War," 8.

167. Leffler, *A Preponderance of Power*, 373.

168. Leffler, 372–73.

169. Detailed in Leffler, *A Preponderance of Power*, 373.

170. Barrass, *The Great Cold War*, 71.

171. Brands, *What Good Is Grand Strategy?*, 48; Gaddis, "Grand Strategies in the Cold War," 8.

172. Leffler, *A Preponderance of Power*, 373.

173. Barrass, *The Great Cold War*, 74.

174. Barrass, 111.

175. Barrass, 113.

176. Barrass, 115.

177. Barrass, 125.

178. Gaddis, "Grand Strategies in the Cold War," 8; Brands, *What Good Is Grand Strategy?*, 48.

179. Brands, *What Good Is Grand Strategy?*, 48.

180. Barrass, *The Great Cold War*, 85.

181. Barrass, 89. For a detailed investigation of the US-supported coup in Iran, see Kinzer, *All the Shah's Men*; and the other references cited in chap. 1 on these two cases.

182. Gaddis, *Strategies of Containment*, 200.

183. Mitrovich, *Undermining the Kremlin*; and Peter Grose, *Operation Rollback: America's Secret War behind the Iron Curtain* (New York: Houghton Mifflin, 2000).

184. Mitrovich, *Undermining the Kremlin*, 9.

185. Leffler, *For the Soul of Mankind*, 101, and the related references.

186. Gaddis, *Strategies of Containment*, 152–53.

187. Gaddis, 153. The proposal died because Republicans wanted it to repudiate Yalta, while Democrats didn't like its implied criticisms of FDR and Truman.

188. See sources in Krebs, *Dueling Visions*, 12n26; Mitrovich, *Undermining the Kremlin*; Grose, *Operation Rollback*; and Tim Weiner, *Legacy of Ashes: The History of the CIA* (New York: Anchor Books, 2008); and Sarah-Jane Corke, *U.S. Covert Operations and Cold War Strategy: Truman, Secret Warfare and the CIA, 1945–53* (London: Routledge, 2007)—discussion in *H-Diplo Roundtable Review* 11, no. 29 (June 2010) at https://lists.h-net.org/cgi-bin/logbrowse .pl?trx=vx&list=h-diplo&month=1006&week=b&msg=caTavupZxQ51t5bPae%2BiXA&user=

&pw=. NSC 7 (March 1948) called for the preservation of US atomic superiority and support for underground movements in the communist bloc—an emphasis on aggressive measures to roll back the Iron Curtain, but NSC 7 was never formally considered (Krebs, *Dueling Visions*, 9–10).

189. Krebs, *Dueling Visions*, 10.

190. Krebs, 11.

191. Krebs, 11–12.

192. Krebs, 12; Weiner, *Legacy of Ashes*.

193. Thompson, *The Hawk and the Dove*, 83–86; Miscamble, *George F. Kennan and the Making of American Foreign Policy*, 207–9.

194. Weiner, *Legacy of Ashes*, 32–33.

195. Weiner, 36.

196. Weiner, 37.

197. Weiner, 44.

198. Weiner, 47.

199. Weiner, 48–49.

200. These works are cited in Robert Jervis's introduction to the *H-Diplo Roundtable Review* of Corke's book, *U.S. Covert Operations and Cold War Strategy* (*H-Diplo Roundtable Review* 11, no. 29 [June 2010]). The cited works are Scott Lucas, *Freedom's War: The American Crusade against the Soviet Union* (New York: NYU Press, 1999); Walter Hixson, *Parting the Curtain: Propaganda, Culture and the Cold War, 1945–1961*; Grose, *Operation Rollback* (New York: St. Martin's Press, 1997); and Mitrovich, *Undermining the Kremlin*.

201. Jervis's introduction to the H-Diplo Roundtable Review of Corke's book.

202. Jervis.

203. Robert Legvold, review of Mitrovich, *Undermining the Kremlin*, and Grose, *Operation Rollback*, *Foreign Affairs*, May–June 2000, 158–59.

204. Garthoff, review of Grose, *Operation Rollback*, and Mitrovich, *Undermining the Kremlin*. Krebs shows the great limitations to the offensive rollback even under the administration that supposedly advocated it. See on rollback or Finlandization, Krebs, *Dueling Visions*: The presidential election of 1952, unlike most others before and since, was dominated by foreign policy. Krebs argues that two very different images of Eastern Europe's ultimate status competed to guide American policy during this period: Finlandization and rollback. Rollback, championed by the Joint Chiefs of Staff and the CIA, was synonymous with liberation as the public understood it—detaching Eastern Europe from all aspects of Soviet control. Surprisingly, the figure most often linked to liberation—Secretary of State John Foster Dulles—came to advocate a more subtle and measured policy that neither accepted the status quo nor pursued rollback. This American vision for the region held up the model of Finland, imagining a tier of states that would enjoy domestic autonomy and perhaps even democracy but whose foreign policy would toe the Soviet line. Krebs's case studies of the American response to Stalin's death and to the Soviet-Yugoslav rapprochement reveal the eventual triumph of Finlandization both as vision and as policy.

205. Mitrovich, *Undermining the Kremlin*.

206. Mitrovich.

207. Larson, *Origins of Containment*, 71–76.

208. On the adaptability of US policies to new circumstances, see, for example, Leffler, *A Preponderance of Power*, 18: as allied policies faltered, the US decided to deploy mobile forces for intervention in the Third World.

209. Gaddis, *The Long Peace*, 25–26.

210. Kissinger, *Diplomacy*, 429–32.

211. Leffler, *A Preponderance of Power*, 5; on US economic, military and power projection advantages, see 6.

212. Gaddis, *The Long Peace*, 27.

213. Leffler in G. John Ikenberry, "Rethinking the Origins of American hegemon," in *American Foreign Policy: Theoretical Essays*, ed. Ikenberry (Boston: Houghton Mifflin, 2005), 90–96.

214. Leffler, *A Preponderance of Power*, 3–4.

215. Dueck, *Reluctant Crusaders*, 94–95.

216. Acheson's address in late 1945, cited in Sestanovich, *Maximalist*, 21.

217. Miscamble, *From Roosevelt to Truman*, 263.

218. Acheson, *Present at the Creation*, 726, also cited in Miscamble, *From Roosevelt to Truman*, 309.

219. Sebastian Rosato, "Europe's Troubles: Power Politics and the State of the European Project," *International Security* 35, no. 4 (Spring 2011): 45–86, argues that the distribution of power between 1945 and 1960 gave the Europeans the motive, means, and opportunity to establish a balancing coalition against the Soviet Union. France and West Germany had a powerful incentive to cooperate in the early Cold War period.

220. Rosato, n30.

221. Rosato, n31.

222. Rosato, n32.

223. Rosato, n33. The citations are from the Rosato article, which also claims that in 1946 the Soviet Union had a 6:1 military advantage and 3:1 economic advantage over France. Little had changed a decade later: the Soviets now had almost a 7:1 military advantage over the French, and their economic advantage had increased to almost 4:1. In overall (military plus economic) terms, the Soviet Union was five to six times more powerful than France throughout the period. West Germany was even weaker by comparison. It had no military before 1955 and only a token force in the second half of the 1950s. At the same time, it was at a 2:1 to 3:1 economic disadvantage to the Soviet Union throughout the period in question (see table 1 in Rosato).

224. Miscamble, *From Roosevelt to Truman*, 309; Sestanovich, *Maximalist*, 20. Mead, *Special Providence*, 83–84: From 1914 to 1947, the US had to decide whether to reinforce Great Britain, disengage, or replace it for maintaining world order (cited also in Miscamble, *From Roosevelt to Truman*, 263).

225. Gaddis, *The Long Peace*, 56; Gaddis, *Strategies of Containment*, 22–23, 40, 51, 58, 64–65, 284, 38n, 61; Dueck, *Reluctant Crusaders*, 105–6; Leffler, *For the Soul of Mankind*, 61–62—citation of Truman.

226. Mearsheimer, *The Tragedy of Great Power Politics*. In this context, Mearsheimer's realist argument makes a lot of sense: it was the consistent strategy of the US to prevent the rise of a single hegemon in Eurasia as manifested in American interventions in WWI (against Germany), WWII (against Germany and Japan), and the Cold War. In all these cases, "buckpassing" couldn't work—in the absence of a powerful coalition, which could prevent the rise of a hegemon without a leading US role.

227. Walt, *The Origins of Alliances*.

228. Thomas J. Christensen, *Useful Adversaries: Grand Strategy, Domestic Mobilization, and Sino-American Conflict, 1947–1958* (Princeton, NJ: Princeton University Press, 1996).

229. See Miscamble, *From Roosevelt to Truman*, 308, on the causes of the collapse of FDR's defensive liberalism vision.

230. Dueck, *Reluctant Crusaders*, 106.

231. Barrass, *The Great Cold War*.

232. Kissinger, *Diplomacy*, 420–22.

233. Kenneth N. Waltz, "The United States: Alone in the World," in *Imbalance of Power: US Hegemony and World Order*, ed. I. William Zartman (Boulder: Lynne Rienner, 2009), 29.

234. See chap. 2 above.

235. According to Kissinger, the puzzle was how the Soviet Union transformed from an ally to the "international public enemy number one"; Kissinger, *Diplomacy*, chaps. 16 and 17, cited in Caroline Kennedy-Pipe, *The Origins of the Cold War* (New York: Palgrave Macmillan, 2007), 28. In *Diplomacy*, 397, Kissinger presents the causes of the failure of the Four Policemen (in contrast to the Concert of Europe).

236. Leffler, *A Preponderance of Power*, 3.

237. See the theoretical works by Charlie Glaser (for example, "The Security Dilemma Revisited").

238. See Jervis's deterrence model, *Perception and Misperception in International Politics*, chap. 3.

239. Gaddis, *Strategies of Containment*, 16: Truman believed in accommodation with the Soviet Union—a quid pro quo strategy. It failed due to domestic constraints, but mainly due to a lack of Soviet responsiveness (p. 18). See also Miscamble, *George F. Kennan and the Making of American Foreign Policy*, 3, citing Gaddis, *The Long Peace*, 20–47. However, Leffler (*A Preponderance of Power*, 100) argues that such an assessment took place even earlier: "In early 1946, US officials defined the Soviet Union as the enemy." On the British foreign minister's—Bevin's—concerns in 1946 about Soviet expansion, see Miscamble, *From Roosevelt to Truman*, 277.

240. Kissinger, *Diplomacy*, 398.

241. Kissinger, 415.

242. Gaddis, *Strategies of Containment*, 14, 18. Some leading researchers of the Cold War highlight Stalin's lack of responsiveness following the post–Cold War opening of Soviet documents. Gaddis, *We Now Know*, 25: the key role of Stalin's distrust (see also Leffler, *For the Soul of Mankind*, 75) in leading to the Cold War—such a distrust was not the prevailing attitude in the West in 1945. See also Gaddis, *We Now Know*, 292–93: So long as Stalin was running the Soviet Union, the Cold War was unavoidable. He and authoritarianism are responsible for the Cold War. See Gaddis, *We Now Know*, 31, on Stalin's pattern: advance that stops after provoking a strong US response; thus, if the West bears responsibility for the Cold War, it is that it didn't try containment earlier.

Leffler, however, has a more mixed position: Leffler, *For the Soul of Mankind*, 51: "Stalin's ideological preconceptions and personal paranoia made him suspect enemies everywhere"—this is also argued by Barrass, *The Great Cold War*, 73–74—thus the Cold War was inevitable; Leffler (*For the Soul of Mankind*, 52) claims that there were real threats to Stalin/Soviet Union, and that Stalin's incoherent foreign policy reflected a hard-line but also moderate steps on his part because he didn't want a rift with the West (53). He instead wanted a communist takeover in East Central Europe by peaceful means, while preserving cooperation with the West (55).

243. Gaddis, *We Now Know*, 38, citing Leffler, *A Preponderance of Power*, 10–24, and also Robert A. Pollard, *Economic Security and the Origins of the Cold War, 1945–1950* (New York: Columbia University Press, 1985), 246–47. Gaddis claims that in contrast to the US empire, the Soviet one was established due to internal causes. One might argue that the Soviets did have good security reasons for a security belt on their Western borders—from where Napoleon and Hitler invaded Russia. Yet, the Soviets also imposed a communist ideological order in Eastern

Europe, while the US gave much more freedom to its allies in the western part of the continent (Korina Kagan, PhD diss., Hebrew University, 2000).

244. Krebs, *Dueling Visions*, 7, citing Leffler, *A Preponderance of Power*.

245. Robert Jervis's review of Miscamble, *From Roosevelt to Truman*, in Roundtable review, H-Diplo 10 September 2007, 17–24, at https://issforum.org/roundtables/PDF/From TrumantoRoosevelt-Roundtable.pdf (accessed February 25, 2020); Gaddis, *The Long Peace*, 29–31; Kissinger, *Diplomacy*, 413.

246. Gaddis (*We Now Know*, 16–19) suggests that the US and Britain accepted a Soviet sphere, but asymmetries in the spheres of influence constituted the origins of Cold War; the Western allies hoped that Stalin didn't desire to extend his own system, but the Soviet leader followed a unilateral approach to security; the fears Stalin created in the West by his suppression of Poland raised doubts about cooperation with him.

247. Miller, *When Opponents Cooperate*, 117.

248. Gaddis, *The Long Peace*, 53.

249. Gaddis, 32.

250. Gaddis, *We Now Know*, 31–32.

251. Tony Judt, *PostWar: A History of Europe since 1945* (New York: Penguin, 2005).

252. Leffler, *A Preponderance of Power*, 7.

253. Leffler.

254. Leffler, *For the Soul of Mankind*, 57–59. See figures in Leffler, *A Preponderance of Power*, 7, also 101–3. See also the related concerns of Kennan about conquest by psychological means due to demoralization in Europe and Japan—Gaddis, *Strategies of Containment*, 34.

255. Leffler, *For the Soul of Mankind*, 62.

256. Leffler, *A Preponderance of Power*, 102.

257. Leffler, *For the Soul of Mankind*, 63–64.

258. Leffler, 69.

259. Leffler, 65–66.

260. Leffler, 69.

261. Leffler, *A Preponderance of Power*, 8.

262. Leffler.

263. Gaddis, *The Long Peace*, 33–34.

264. Gaddis, 38.

265. Gaddis, 54–55.

266. Gaddis, 62.

267. Gaddis, *We Now Know*, 32, citing also Larson, *Origins of Containment*, 325–26.

268. Miscamble, *From Roosevelt to Truman*, 308.

269. Miscamble, chap. 8.

270. Gaddis, *Strategies of Containment*, 56.

271. Dueck, *Reluctant Crusaders*, 99.

272. Dueck, 195–96, references in nn85, 86.

273. Dueck.

274. Dueck, 100–105.

275. Christensen, *Useful Adversaries*, 34–36.

276. Dueck, *Reluctant Crusaders*, 102.

277. Leffler, *For the Soul of Mankind*, 68. The economic dimension was important as American policy makers believed that Japan and Germany could remain independent of the

Soviet Union only if there was viable trade within the free world (Leffler, *A Preponderance of Power*, 8–9).

278. May, *American Cold War Strategy*, 3.

279. May, 4; Gaddis, *Strategies of Containment*, 80.

280. May, *American Cold War Strategy*, 3.

281. Barrass, *The Great Cold War*.

282. Gaddis, *Strategies of Containment*, 81–83.

283. May, *American Cold War Strategy*, 3, 10.

284. Gaddis, *Strategies of Containment*, 110.

285. Gaddis, 106–7.

286. Gaddis, 107.

287. John Lewis Gaddis, "Was the Truman Doctrine a Real Turning Point?," *Foreign Affairs* 52, no. 2 (January 1974): 386–402, cited in Larson, *Origins of Containment*, 4.

288. Gaddis, *Strategies of Containment*, 107–9.

289. Gaddis, 110–11.

290. Leffler, *A Preponderance of Power*, 18.

291. Dueck, *Reluctant Crusaders*, 94.

292. Dueck, 103.

293. Barrass, *The Great Cold War*, 64.

294. Snyder (*Myths of Empire*, 256); Benjamin Fordham, "Partisanship, Macroeconomic Policy, and U.S. Uses of Force, 1949–1994," *Journal of Conflict Resolution* 42, no 4 (1998): 418–39, agrees.

295. Barrass, *The Great Cold War*, 74.

296. On the levels of analysis and the Cold War, see Larson, *Origins of Containment*, 18–23.

297. See Joseph S. Nye Jr., *Presidential Leadership and the Creation of the American Era* (Princeton, NJ: Princeton University Press, 2013), 42–43; for an individual-level explanation of Truman, see Kissinger, *Diplomacy*.

298. It is a bit unclear whether Truman actually read it. Secretary Forrestal (at the time secretary of the navy) got the telegram from Harriman, made copies, and brought them personally to the cabinet members, including Truman (John Lewis Gaddis, *George F. Kennan: An American Life* [New York: Penguin Press, 2011], 218–19). But it seems that there isn't hard evidence that Truman in fact read it. In his *Memoirs, 1925–1950*, Kennan wrote that "the President, I believe, read it" (310). But Miscamble, *From Roosevelt to Truman*, 280, writes that "Truman apparently neither read nor commented" on it. Robert Schulzinger, *US Diplomacy since 1900* (Oxford: Oxford University Press, 1998), 206, argues that Truman had read it. In sum, it is unclear if Truman read the telegram.

299. Thompson, *The Hawk and the Dove*, 59.

300. Thompson, 35–36.

301. Thompson, 37.

302. Gaddis, *Strategies of Containment*, 19; see also Gaddis, *The Long Peace*, 39.

303. On the Long Telegram, see Miscamble, *George F. Kennan and the Making of American Foreign Policy*, 25–28; and Gaddis, *George F. Kennan*, 201–24.

304. Gaddis, *The Long Peace*, 39.

305. Gaddis, *George F. Kennan*, 225–26; Miscamble, *George F. Kennan and the Making of American Foreign Policy*, 27–28; and Miscamble, *From Roosevelt to Truman*, 308.

306. Gaddis, *The Long Peace*, 38–39, esp. 254n82.

307. Miscamble, *George F. Kennan and the Making of American Foreign Policy*, 27–28; Larson, *Origins of Containment*, 257, 301, 352, has the same point.

308. Gaddis, *Strategies of Containment*, 107–11.

309. On public opinion and US foreign policy, see Ole R. Holsti, *Public Opinion and American Foreign Policy* (Ann Arbor: University of Michigan Press, 2004).

310. According to Dean Acheson, a primary aspiration of the US public following the war was to "bring the boys home" and also "don't be a Santa Clause," though also "don't be pushed around" (Sestanovich, *Maximalist*, 21).

311. Gaddis, *Strategies of Containment*, 107.

312. Sestanovich, *Maximalist*, 21–23.

313. Leffler, *For the Soul of Mankind*, 70–72.

314. Leffler, 72.

315. Leffler, 72.

316. Gaddis, *Strategies of Containment*, 84; May, *American Cold War Strategy*, 8–9, highlights the domestic pressures toward anticommunism, culminating with McCarthyism.

317. Larson, *Origins of Containment*, 331.

318. Dueck, *Reluctant Crusaders*, 83, 88.

319. Gaddis, *The Long Peace*, 51.

320. See Odd Arne Westad, *The Global Cold War* (Cambridge: Cambridge University Press, 2007).

321. Larson *Origins of Containment*, 329.

322. Larson, 330.

Chapter Four

1. Earlier instances of American thoughts of preventive wars appear in Marc Trachtenberg, "Preventive War and U.S. Foreign Policy," *Security Studies* 16, no. 1 (2007): 1–31.

2. For a short comparison of the danger of inadvertent escalation in the Cuban missile crisis and in the current Iranian nuclear crisis, see the citations of Graham Allison in Scott Shane, "After 2 Wars, Drums Again Beat over Iran," *International Herald Tribune*, February 22, 2012, 1 and 5; and Graham Allison, "The Cuban Missile Crisis at 50," *Foreign Affairs* 91, no. 4 (2012).

3. The policy of détente was the peak of the grand strategy of détente. Most of the accounts of American foreign policy that relate to détente focus on Nixon's policy. This study looks at the strategy that began in Kennedy's term.

4. This distinction partly draws on Miller, *When Opponents Cooperate*.

5. Geoffrey Blainey, *The Causes of War* (New York: Free Press, 1973), chap. 9; Evan Luard, *War in International Society* (New Haven, CT: Yale University Press, 1986), chap. 5. Yet, it seems that their main criticism is directed not so much against the plausibility of inadvertent wars as they are defined here but against the concept of "accidental wars," which will be differentiated from inadvertent wars.

6. See the extremely useful studies by Jack Levy, "The Causes of War: A Review of Theories and Evidence," in *Behavior, Society and Nuclear War*, ed. P. Tetlock et al. (New York: Oxford University Press, 1989); M. I. Midlarsky, ed., *Handbook of War Studies* (Boston: Unwin Hyman, 1989); R. Rotberg and T. Rabb, eds., *The Origin and Prevention of Major Wars* (Cambridge: Cambridge University Press, 1989); and K. J. Holsti, *Peace and War: Armed Conflicts and International Order, 1648–1989* (Cambridge: Cambridge University Press, 1991).

7. This definition is derived from Levy's analysis of preventive wars. Jack Levy, "Declining Power and the Preventive Motivation for War," *World Politics* 40, no. 1 (1987): 82–107.

8. Alternative names of this phenomenon are spiral model, security dilemma wars, and uncontrolled escalation. On inadvertent war, see Thomas Schelling, *Arms and Influence* (New Haven, CT: Yale University Press, 1966); and Alexander L. George, *Avoiding War: Problems of Crisis Management* (Boulder, CO: Westview Press, 1991). Richard Smoke, *War: Controlling Escalation* (Cambridge, MA: Harvard University Press, 1977), deals with the question of controlling escalation.

9. George, *Avoiding War*, 8.

10. Jack Levy, *War in the Modern Great Power System, 1495–1975* (Lexington: University Press of Kentucky, 1983), chap. 3, offers an extended discussion of great-powers wars.

11. Jack Levy, "Long Cycles, Hegemonic Transitions, and the Long Peace," in *The Long Postwar Peace*, ed. Charles Kegley (New York: Harper Collins, 1991), 71.

12. Jervis, *Perception and Misperception in International Politics*, 62–83.

13. Daniel Frei, *Risks of Unintentional Nuclear War* (Totowa, NJ: Rowman & Allanheld, 1983); Graham Allison et al., eds, *Hawks, Doves, and Owls: An Agenda for Avoiding Nuclear War* (New York: Norton, 1985); Richard Ned Lebow, *Nuclear Crisis Management* (Ithaca, NY: Cornell University Press, 1987); Kurt Gottfried and Bruce G. Blair, eds., *Crisis Stability and Nuclear War* (New York: Oxford University Press, 1988); and George, *Avoiding War*.

14. Herman Kahn, *Thinking about the Unthinkable* (New York: Horizon Press, 1962), 44, cited in Frei, *Risks of Unintentional Nuclear War*, 3; Lebow, *Nuclear Crisis Management*, 26.

15. Levy, "Preventive War and the Bush Doctrine"; Levy, "Preventive War: Concept and Propositions," *International Interactions* 37, no. 1 (2011): 87–96; Jonathan Renshon, *Why Leaders Choose War: The Psychology of Prevention* (Westport, CT: Praeger, 2006); Michael W. Doyle, *Striking First: Preemption and Prevention in International Conflict* (Princeton, NJ: Princeton University Press, 2008); Douglas Lemke, "Investigating the Preventive Motive for War," *International Interactions* 29, no. 4 (2003): 273–92; David Luban, "Preventive War," *Philosophy & Public Affairs* 32, no. 3 (2004): 207–48; Karl P. Mueller et al., *Striking First: Preemptive and Preventive Attack in U.S. National Security Policy* (Santa Monica, CA: RAND, 2006); Paul W. Schroeder, "Preventive Wars to Restore and Stabilize the International System," *International Interactions* 37, no. 1 (2011): 96–107; Scott A. Silverstone, *Preventive War and American Democracy* (New York: Routledge, 2007); Trachtenberg, "Preventive War and U.S. Foreign Policy."

16. Examples included the 1945–49 era (before the Soviets eliminated the American nuclear monopoly), the ideas of striking China before it achieved nuclear weapons in the early 1960s under Kennedy, and other instances. Trachtenberg, "Preventive War and U.S. Foreign Policy."

17. George, *Avoiding War*, 8–9, 31. The following discussion is based on Levy, "Declining Power and the Preventive Motivation for War."

18. Trachtenberg, "Preventive War and U.S. Foreign Policy."

19. Secretary of State Daniel Webster, cited in Michael Walzer, *Just and Unjust Wars: A Moral Argument with Historical Illustrations* (New York: Basic Books, 1977), 74.

20. "Fear that the other may be about to strike in the mistaken belief that we are about to strike gives us a motive for striking, and so justifies the other's motive." Thomas C. Schelling, *The Strategy of Conflict* (Cambridge, MA: Harvard University Press, 1960), 207.

21. Levy, "Declining Power and the Preventive Motivation for War," 92n23.

22. In the case of World War I, Fritz Fischer (*Germany's Aims in the First World War* [New York: Norton, 1967]) challenged the prevalent interpretation of the war as inadvertent, pre-

senting it instead as an aggressive war intended and planned by Germany, striving for world domination. A. J. P. Taylor (*The Origins of the Second World War* [New York: Atheneum, 1961]) challenged the dominant view of World War II as an aggressive war caused by Germany, and his interpretation in fact emphasizes several inadvertent elements.

23. Trachtenberg, "Preventive War and U.S. Foreign Policy," and Levy, "Preventive War and the Bush Doctrine," 185–86, and the citations therein.

24. Jonathan Renshon, "Assessing Capabilities in International Politics: Biased Overestimation and the Case of the Imaginary 'Missile Gap,'" *Journal of Strategic Studies* 32, no. 1 (2009): 115–47; Christopher A. Preble, *John F. Kennedy and the Missile Gap* (DeKalb: Northern Illinois University Press, 2004); Peter J. Roman, *Eisenhower and the Missile Gap* (Ithaca, NY: Cornell University Press, 1995); Gaddis, *Strategies of Containment*, 205.

25. George C. Herring, *From Colony to Superpower: U.S. Foreign Relations since 1776* (Oxford: Oxford University Press, 2008), 704. See details on the Soviet and American long-range nuclear systems for the years 1958–62 in Daryl G. Press, *Calculating Credibility: How Leaders Assess Military Threats* (Ithaca, NY: Cornell University Press, 2005), 87–88, 92.

26. Herring, *From Colony to Superpower*, 704–5. Kennedy's initial grand strategy (flexible response) then was based on a symmetrical capability to act in all levels of violence, an ability to respond without either escalation or humiliation. Gaddis, *Strategies of Containment*, 212–14, and on p. 226 provides a short summary of the differences between Eisenhower's "New Look" and Kennedy's flexible response.

27. As early as 1953–54 as a junior senator, Kennedy suggested defense proposals that did not alter the Eisenhower defense budgets but improved his massive retaliation policy. Robert Dallek, *An Unfinished Life: John F. Kennedy, 1917–1963* (Boston: Little, Brown and Company, 2003), 184–85.

28. Marc Trachtenberg, "The Structure of Great Power Politics, 1963–1975," in *The Cambridge History of the Cold War*, vol. 2, *Crises and Détente*, ed. Melvyn P. Leffler and Odd Arne Westad (Cambridge: Cambridge University Press, 2010), 428.

29. Stephen G. Rabe, "John F. Kennedy and the World," in James N. Giglio and Stephen G. Rabe, *Debating the Kennedy Presidency* (Lanham, MD: Rowman & Littlefield Publishers, 2003), 6–7. See also Dallek, *An Unfinished Life*, 343–44: "However strong his determination to avoid a nuclear conflict with the Soviet Union, Kennedy could not rule out the possibility. The Soviet acquisition of a nuclear arsenal had provoked American military planners into advocacy of a massive first-strike stockpile, or what they called 'a war-fighting capability over a finite deterrent [or] (retaliatory) posture.' They believed that the more pronounced the United States' nuclear advantage over Moscow was, the more likely it would be 'to stem Soviet cold war advances.' But such a strategy would also mean an arms race, which seemed likely to heighten the danger of a war. It was a miserable contradiction from which Kennedy was never able entirely to escape." Still, we argue that in the aftermath of the missile crisis, Kennedy did initiate a major change in the grand strategy.

30. Nelson N. Lichtenstein on Stevenson in Thomas Parker, *America's Foreign Policy, 1945–1976: Its Creators and Critics* (New York: Facts on File, 1980), 154–56.

31. Alison and Zelikow, *Essence of Decision*, 114.

32. McGeorge Bundy, *Danger and Survival: Choices about the Bomb in the First Fifty Years* (New York: Random House, 1988), 554–55.

33. Gaddis, *Strategies of Containment*, 212–14.

34. Gaddis, 215–17.

35. Lawrence Freedman, *The Evolution of Nuclear Strategy* (New York: St. Martin's Press, 1981), 195. The idea of arms control was heavily influenced by the writings of Thomas Schelling (*The Strategy of Conflict, Arms and Influence* and, with Morton Halperin, *Strategy and Arms Control*).

36. Freedman, *The Evolution of Nuclear Strategy*, 196–200.

37. Freedman, 252–53, citing Jerome B. Wiesner and Herbert F. York, "National Security and the Nuclear Test Ban," *Scientific American* 221, no. 4 (October 1964): 27–35; see also the discussion in chap. 1.

38. Benjamin Miller, *When Opponents Cooperate*, 148.

39. Freedman, *The Evolution of Nuclear Strategy*, 200–207.

40. Gaddis, *Strategies of Containment*, 224.

41. G. Calvin Mackenzie and Robert Weisbrot, *The Liberal Hour: Washington and the Politics of Change in the 1960s* (New York: Penguin Books, 2009), 241.

42. John F. Kennedy, "Special Message to the Congress on the Defense Budget," March 28, 1961, available online in Gerhard Peters and John T. Woolley, *The American Presidency Project*, http://www.presidency.ucsb.edu/ws/?pid=8554 (accessed January 8, 2012).

43. Dallek, *An Unfinished Life*, 307–21, provides details on the appointments of secretaries of state, defense, treasury, and justice and the ambassador to the UN.

44. Philip A. Goduti Jr., *Kennedy's Kitchen Cabinet and the Pursuit of Peace: The Shaping of American Foreign Policy, 1961–1963* (Jefferson, NC, and London: McFarland & Company, 2009), 13.

45. Mackenzie and Weisbrot, *The Liberal Hour*, 251.

46. Mackenzie and Weisbrot, 254. See also Lloyd Gardner, "Walt Whitman Rostow: Hawkeyed Optimist," in *The Policy Makers: Shaping American Foreign Policy from 1947 to the Present*, ed. Anna Kasten Nelson (Lanham, MD: Rowman & Littlefield Publishers, 2009), 59–82.

47. Gaddis, *Strategies of Containment*, 227.

48. Lichtenstein on Stevenson in Parker, *America's Foreign Policy*, 154–56. The quote from Kennedy regarding Stevenson is from Thomas G. Paterson, "Introduction: John F. Kennedy's Quest for Victory and Global Crises," in *Kennedy's Quest for Victory: American Foreign Policy, 1961–1963*, ed. Thomas G. Paterson (New York: Oxford University Press, 1989), 19.

49. Gaddis, *Strategies of Containment*, 217.

50. Talbott, *The Master of the Game*, 81.

51. Eleanora W. Schoenebaum on Nitze in Parker, *America's Foreign Policy*, 131.

52. Gaddis, *Strategies of Containment*, 217–18.

53. Freedman, *The Evolution of Nuclear Strategy*, 200.

54. Freedman, 253–56.

55. Leffler, *For the Soul of Mankind*, 159–60.

56. Bundy, *Danger and Survival*, 545.

57. Bundy, 545.

58. Mackenzie and Weisbrot, *The Liberal Hour*, 270.

59. Joseph C. Holub on Jackson, in Parker, *America's Foreign Policy*, 69.

60. Mackenzie and Weisbrot, *The Liberal Hour*, 273.

61. John D'Emilio on Fulbright, in Parker, *America's Foreign Policy*, 55–56.

62. John D'Emilio on McGovern, in Parker, 123.

63. Meeting of October 16, 1962, 18:30. Timothy Naftali and Philip Zelikow, eds., *The Presidential Recordings: John F. Kennedy, the Great Crises*, vol. 2 (New York: Norton, 2001), 450.

64. Naftali and Zelikow, 458.

65. See several of the recent accounts: Michael Dobbs, *One Minute to Midnight: Kennedy, Khrushchev, and Castro on the Brink of Nuclear War* (New York: Knopf, 2008); Sheldon M. Stern, *The Week the World Stood Still: Inside the Secret Cuban Missile Crisis* (Stanford, CA: Stanford University Press, 2005); Max Frankel, *High Noon in the Cold War: Kennedy, Khrushchev, and the Cuban Missile Crisis* (New York: Ballantine Books, 2005); and plenty of documents are available to the public at the National Security Archives and the JFK Library.

66. For a recent reference to the Soviets' motivations for placing the missiles in Cuba, see Dobbs, *One Minute to Midnight*, 344.

67. Marc Trachtenberg, *The Cold War and After: History, Theory, and the Logic of International Politics* (Princeton, NJ: Princeton University Press, 2012), 254–62.

68. The draft of Kennedy's speech in case an air strike took place is available online at http://www.jfklibrary.org/Asset-Viewer/Archives/RFKAG-217-001.aspx, 144–154 (accessed October 29, 2012). Levy, "Preventive War and the Bush Doctrine," 186, presents citations on this issue. Trachtenberg criticizes Kennedy administration veterans who attempted to refute the Bush administration's argument that Kennedy was indeed considering a preventive attack on the missiles. Trachtenberg, "Preventive War and U.S. Foreign Policy," 9, 11–12.

69. Philip Nash, *The Other Missiles of October: Eisenhower, Kennedy, and the Jupiters, 1957–1963* (Chapel Hill: University of North Carolina Press, 1997). See also the interesting process tracing of the placing of the Jupiters in Turkey that Gaddis has in *We Now Know*, 263–64.

70. Robert A. Divine: "The Cuban missile crisis had been a sobering turning point in the president's intellectual journey. Having come to the brink of a nuclear holocaust, the president now resolved to work to reduce international tensions." Rabe, "John F. Kennedy and the World," 65; refers to Robert A. Divine, "The Education of John F. Kennedy," in *Makers of American Diplomacy: From Theodore Roosevelt to Henry Kissinger*, ed. Frank J. Merli and Theodore A. Wilson (New York: Charles Scribner's Sons, 1974), 317–44.

71. Bundy, *Danger and Survival*, 544–45.

72. Bundy, 461.

73. Leffler, *For the Soul of Mankind*, 151–60; James Hershberg, "The Cuban Missile Crisis," in *The Cambridge History of the Cold War*, 83.

74. Gaddis, *We Now Know*, 270.

75. James Blight and Janet Lang, *The Armageddon Letters: Kennedy, Khrushchev, Castro in the Cuban Missile Crisis* (Lanham, MD: Rowman & Littlefield, 2012), 231. Quoted in Alexa van Sickle, "The Myths of October," *Survival* 55, no. 1 (2013): 160.

76. One expression of that was in December 1962 (Freedman, *The Evolution of Nuclear Strategy*, 249n10); and then in February 1963, see Gaddis, *Strategies of Containment*, 218; Bundy, *Danger and Survival*, 544–48.

77. Bundy, *Danger and Survival*, 549.

78. "Status report on the implementation of agreement with Soviet Union after removal of IL-28's, Press conference November 20, 1962," in Papers of Robert F. Kennedy, Attorney General Papers, Attorney General's Confidential File, 6-4, Cuba: Cuban Crisis, 1962, White House. Available online at http://www.jfklibrary.org/Asset-Viewer/Archives/RFKAG-216-005.aspx, 55 (accessed October 26, 2012).

79. "The military threat is not presently the real threat; press conference February 7, 1963," in Papers of Robert F. Kennedy, 41.

80. Papers of Robert F. Kennedy, 43–44.

81. Papers of Robert F. Kennedy, 94.

82. Leffler, *For the Soul of Mankind*, 182.

83. Leffler, 185.

84. Jeffrey D. Sachs, *To Move the World: JFK's Quest for Peace* (London: Bodley Head, 2013).

85. Quoted in Alan Neidle, "Nuclear Test Bans: History and Future Prospects," in *U.S.-Soviet Security Cooperation: Achievements, Failures, Lessons*, ed. Alexander L. George, Philip J. Farley, and Alexander Dallin (New York: Oxford University Press, 1988), 179, origin: William G. Hyland, *Soviet-American Relations: A New Cold War?* (Santa Monica, CA: RAND, 1981), 19.

86. It is also true that Walt Rostow, for his part, doubted détente's utility. See Leffler, *For the Soul of Mankind*, 191.

87. Leffler, 188.

88. Leffler, 188.

89. Hershberg, "The Cuban Missile Crisis," 86.

90. Hershberg, 85.

91. Leffler, *For the Soul of Mankind*, 176–84; Sachs, *To Move the World*.

92. Gaddis, *Strategies of Containment*, 227, 232–33.

93. Hershberg, "The Cuban Missile Crisis," 85.

94. Neidle, "Nuclear Test Bans," 177–79.

95. According to Marc Trachtenberg, the treaty was intended to make it harder for West Germany to build nuclear weapons, and Germany was essentially forced to sign it. Trachtenberg, "The Structure of Great Power Politics," 484.

96. Glenn T. Seaborg, *Kennedy, Khrushchev, and the Test Ban* (Berkeley: University of California Press, 1981), cited in Bundy, *Danger and Survival*, 460.

97. Stanley Hoffmann, "Détente," in *The Making of America's Soviet Policy*, ed. Joseph S. Nye Jr. (London: Yale University Press, 1984), 234.

98. Leffler, *For the Soul of Mankind*, 188.

99. Hershberg, "The Cuban Missile Crisis," 85.

100. Barrass, *The Great Cold War*, 144.

101. Hershberg, "The Cuban Missile Crisis," 86.

102. *FRUS, 1961–1963*, vol. 8, 458n3. Quoted in David G. Coleman, *The Fourteenth Day: JFK and the Aftermath of the Cuban Missile Crisis* (New York and London: W. W. Norton: 2012), 170.

103. Coleman, *The Fourteenth Day*, 191.

104. Gaddis, *The Long Peace*; Gaddis, *We Now Know*, 279–80.

105. Gaddis, *The Long Peace*, 195–214.

106. See Daryl Press on credibility during the Cuban crisis. Press, *Calculating Credibility*, 117–41.

107. Gaddis, *Strategies of Containment*, 228–29.

108. Gaddis, *We Now Know*, 271 and 381n66.

109. *FRUS, 1961–1963*, vol. 5, *Soviet Union*, document 259 (October 31 1962).

110. *FRUS, 1961–1963*, vol. 5, *Soviet Union*, document 259.

111. *FRUS, 1961–1963*, vol. 5, *Soviet Union*, document 261 (November 8 1962).

112. Bundy, *Danger and Survival*, 460; Barrass, *The Great Cold War*, 144.

113. Barrass, *The Great Cold War*, 144–45; Bundy, *Danger and Survival*, 460.

114. George, *Avoiding War*, 548; Hershberg, "The Cuban Missile Crisis," 65–66.

115. Hershberg, "The Cuban Missile Crisis,", 83.

116. Hershberg, 83–84.

117. Barton J. Bernstein, "Reconsidering the Perilous Cuban Missile Crisis 50 Years Later," *Arms Control Today*, October 2012.

118. Bernstein.

119. Hershberg, "The Cuban Missile Crisis," 80; Dobbs, *One Minute to Midnight*, 345.

120. Dobbs, *One Minute to Midnight*, 345–46, 350–51.

121. Allison, "The Cuban Missile Crisis at 50," 14.

122. Dobbs, *One Minute to Midnight*, 346.

123. Yuen Foong Khong, *Analogies at War: Korea, Munich, Dien Bien Phu, and the Vietnam Decisions of 1965* (Princeton, NJ: Princeton University Press, 1992), 5n10.

124. Gaddis, *Strategies of Containment*, 240; Khong, *Analogies at War*, chap. 7; Ernest R. May, *"Lessons" of the Past: The Use and Misuse of History in American Foreign Policy* (Oxford: Oxford University Press, 1973), chap. 3 on Truman and Munich.

125. Mackenzie and Weisbrot, *The Liberal Hour*, 270.

126. Hershberg, "The Cuban Missile Crisis," 81.

127. Bundy, *Danger and Survival*, 461–62.

128. Gaddis, *Strategies of Containment*, 210.

129. Gaddis, 228.

130. T. V. Paul, *The Tradition of Non-Use of Nuclear Weapons* (Stanford, CA: Stanford University Press, 2009), 66.

131. Bundy, *Danger and Survival*, 461.

132. Hoffmann, "Détente," 234.

133. Dobbs, *One Minute to Midnight*, 349–50.

134. William Burr and David Alan Rosenberg, "Nuclear Competition in an Era of Stalemate, 1963–1975," in *The Cambridge History of the Cold War*, 91. See also Nina Tannenwald, *The Nuclear Taboo: The United States and the Non-Use of Nuclear Weapons since 1945* (Cambridge: Cambridge University Press, 2007), 206–7.

135. Barrass, *The Great Cold War*, 151.

136. Freedman, *The Evolution of Nuclear Strategy*, 256.

137. Bundy, *Danger and Survival*, 545–6.

138. Freedman, *The Evolution of Nuclear Strategy*, 234–44; Marc Trachtenberg, *A Constructed Peace: The Making of the European Settlement, 1945–1963* (Princeton, NJ: Princeton University Press, 1999), 316.

139. Bundy, *Danger and Survival*, 546.

140. Freedman, *The Evolution of Nuclear Strategy*, 249; see also Hershberg, "The Cuban Missile Crisis," 86.

141. Quoted in Sachs, *To Move the World*.

142. Freedman, *The Evolution of Nuclear Strategy*, 251.

143. On the scientific opposition, see Freedman, *The Evolution of Nuclear Strategy*, 252–53.

144. Bundy, *Danger and Survival*, 547.

145. Bundy, 549; Freedman, *The Evolution of Nuclear Strategy*, 254–56.

146. Bundy, *Danger and Survival*, 549.

147. Barrass, *The Great Cold War*, 165.

148. Bundy, *Danger and Survival*, 550.

149. Bundy, 547–48.

150. Gaddis, *The Long Peace*, 205.

151. Gaddis, 195–214; John Lewis Gaddis, "The Evolution of a Reconnaissance Satellite Re-

gime," in *U.S.-Soviet Security Cooperation: Achievements, Failures, Lessons*, ed. Alexander L. George, Philip J. Farley, and Alexander Dallin (New York and Oxford: Oxford University Press, 1988), 353–72.

152. John Lewis Gaddis, "Grand Strategies in the Cold War," in *The Cambridge History of the Cold War*, 14.

153. Trachtenberg, "The Structure of Great Power Politics," 482; Sachs, *To Move the World*.

154. On the initiation of arms control thinking, see Freedman, *The Evolution of Nuclear Strategy*, 190–207.

155. Emanuel Adler, "Arms Control, Disarmament, and National Security: A Thirty Years Retrospective and a New Set of Anticipations," in *The International Practice of Arms Control*, ed. Emanuel Adler (Baltimore, MD: Johns Hopkins University Press, 1992), 7–8.

156. Adler, 8–9.

157. Gaddis, *Strategies of Containment*, 218; Bundy, *Danger and Survival*, 546–47.

158. William C. Wohlforth, "Realism and the End of the Cold War," *International Security* 19, no. 3 (1994–95): 91–129.

159. Freedman, *The Evolution of Nuclear Strategy*, 197.

160. Freedman, 206–7.

161. Emmanuel Adler, "The Emergence of Cooperation: National Epistemic Communities and the International Evolution of the Idea of Nuclear Arms Control," *International Organization* 46, no. 1 (1992): 101–45.

162. According to Kempe, the Berlin crisis of 1961 attested to Khrushchev that Kennedy was weak, and he tried to exploit this notion in Cuba. Kennedy's resolve on Cuba made Khrushchev understand his earlier mistake. Khrushchev's surrender on Cuba signaled to Kennedy that the Soviets were seeking compromise, and this established the benign environment that allowed the US to change course to defensive realism. Frederick Kempe, *Berlin 1961: Kennedy, Khrushchev, and the Most Dangerous Place on Earth* (New York: G. P. Putnam's Sons, 2011), 482–502.

163. Walt, *The Origins of Alliances*.

164. Brands, *What Good Is Grand Strategy?*, 66.

165. On the realpolitik logic, see Miller, *American Power and Liberal Order*, 45.

166. See, for example, the classic book by Gaddis, *Strategies of Containment*, 238–41, 275.

Chapter Five

1. Frank Costigliola, "US Foreign Policy from Kennedy to Johnson," in *The Cambridge History of the Cold War*, 124–25.

2. Leffler, *For the Soul of Mankind*, 204–5; Costigliola, "US Foreign Policy from Kennedy to Johnson," 128.

3. Leffler, *For the Soul of Mankind*, 205.

4. Leffler, 210.

5. Frank H. Milburn and Nelson N. Lichtenstein on Johnson, in Parker, *America's Foreign Policy*, 72.

6. Costigliola, "US Foreign Policy from Kennedy to Johnson," 129.

7. Leffler, *For the Soul of Mankind*, 221–22.

8. Freedman, *The Evolution of Nuclear Strategy*, 253.

9. Barrass, *The Great Cold War*, 162–63.

10. Trachtenberg, "The Structure of Great Power Politics," 496.

11. On the Nixon-Ford era, see Robert D. Schulzinger, "Détente in the Nixon-Ford years, 1969–1976," in *The Cambridge History of the Cold War*, 373–94.

12. Trachtenberg, "The Structure of Great Power Politics," 491.

13. Trachtenberg, 492.

14. Trachtenberg, 500.

15. Bundy, *Danger and Survival*, 554–55.

16. Kissinger, *Diplomacy*, 739.

17. Kissinger, 743–47, 754–57. Nancy Mitchell raises an interesting point about détente: It "did introduce an element of confusion: it made it difficult to maintain a sharp focus on the conflict. Was the Soviet Union a mortal enemy, as the US defense budget continued to indicate, or was it, as the rhetoric of détente claimed, a partner in creating a 'stable structure of peace'?" Nancy Mitchell, "The Cold War and Jimmy Carter," in *The Cambridge History of the Cold War*, ed. Melvyn P. Leffler and Odd Arne Westad, vol. 3 (Cambridge: Cambridge University Press, 2010), 72.

18. David F. Schmitz and Vanessa Walker, "Jimmy Carter and the Foreign Policy of Human Rights: The Development of a Post–Cold War Foreign Policy," *Diplomatic History* 28, no. 1 (2004): 113–43; Christian Philip Peterson, "The Carter Administration and the Promotion of Human Rights in the Soviet Union, 1977–1981," *Diplomatic History* 38, no. 3 (2014): 628–56; Debbie Sharnak, "Sovereignty and Human Rights: Re-Examining Carter's Foreign Policy towards the Third World," *Diplomacy & Statecraft* 25, no. 2 (2014): 303–30; Luca Trenta, "The Champion of Human Rights Meets the King of Kings: Jimmy Carter, the Shah, and Iranian Illusions and Rage," *Diplomacy & Statecraft* 24, no. 3 (2013): 476–98.

19. Brian J. Auten, *Carter's Conversion: The Hardening of American Defense Policy* (Columbia, and London: University of Missouri Press, 2008), 82–83.

20. Auten, 83.

21. Auten, 84.

22. Auten, 95.

23. Auten, 95.

24. Auten, 96.

25. Auten, 96.

26. Auten, 96–97.

27. Auten, 97–111.

28. Stuart E. Eizenstat, *President Carter: The White House Years* (New York: St. Martin's Press, 2018), 612 and 613–14, citing Edward C. Keefer, *Harold Brown, Offsetting the Soviet Military Challenge, 1977–1981*, Secretaries of Defense Historical Series (Washington, DC: Government Printing Office, 2017), xvi.

29. Eizenstat, 622.

30. Betty Glad, *An Outsider in the White House: Jimmy Carter, His Advisors, and the Making of American Foreign Policy* (Ithaca, NY: Cornell University Press, 2009), 47.

31. Glad, 1; for a comprehensive analysis of Brzezinski's strategy and effects on policies, see Charles Gati, ed., *Zbig: The Strategy and Statecraft of Zbigniew Brzezinski* (Baltimore, MD: Johns Hopkins University Press, 2013).

32. Glad, *An Outsider in the White House*, 25.

33. Cyrus R. Vance, *Hard Choices: Critical Years in America's Foreign Policy* (New York: Simon and Schuster, 1983), 45.

34. Vance, 46.

35. Vance, 48–49.

36. Vance, 49.

37. Brzezinski to Carter, June 24, 1977. Quoted in Leffler, *For the Soul of Mankind*, 271.

38. Jussi M. Hanhimaki, *The Rise and Fall of Détente: American Foreign Policy and the Transformation of the Cold War* (Washington, DC: Potomac Books, 2013), 106.

39. While Carter did not try coercing the Soviet Union to change its human rights policy by force (military or economic), he did do that vis-à-vis less powerful countries that depended on the US in many respects, namely, Pakistan. But the American sanctions on Pakistan did not cause a dramatic change in Islamabad, and were reversed shortly after the Soviet invasion of Afghanistan on Christmas Day of 1979, in order to recruit Pakistan into assisting the mujahidin for the US. But Pakistan was unwilling to cooperate to the extent the US wanted until Carter was replaced by Reagan.

40. Gati, preface, *Zbig*, xvii; Warren I. Cohen and Nanct Bernkopf Tucker, "Beijing's Friend, Moscow's Foe," in Gati, 85–103.

41. Gati, xviii.

42. *FRUS, 1977–1980*, vol. 6, document 92 (304).

43. *FRUS, 1977–1980*, vol. 6, document 130 (424).

44. *FRUS, 1977–1980*, vol. 6, document 1 (1–2).

45. *FRUS, 1977–1980*, vol. 6, document 1 (2).

46. *FRUS, 1977–1980*, vol. 6, document 4 (14).

47. *FRUS, 1977–1980*, vol. 6, document 4 (14).

48. *FRUS, 1977–1980*, vol. 6, document 7 (21).

49. *FRUS, 1977–1980*, vol. 6, document 7 (21).

50. *FRUS, 1977–1980*, vol. 6, document 7 (21–22).

51. *FRUS, 1977–1980*, vol. 6, document 17 (50).

52. Mitchell, "The Cold War and Jimmy Carter," 74.

53. Eizenstat, *President Carter*, 626–27.

54. Zbigniew Brzezinski, *Power and Principle: Memoirs of the National Security Adviser, 1977–1981* (London: Weidenfeld and Nicolson, 1983), 54 (italics in origin).

55. Brzezinski, 146.

56. Brzezinski, 146.

57. Vance indeed was an "establishment" person. He served in several positions under Kennedy and Johnson and in fact was one of the more experienced among the cabinet members.

58. Brzezinski, *Power and Principle*, 147.

59. Brzezinski, 147.

60. *FRUS, 1977–1980*, vol. 6, document 58 (219).

61. Brzezinski, *Power and Principle*, 167.

62. Brzezinski.

63. Nancy Mitchell claims that "Carter's view of the Soviets had always been hard-line. 'I've never doubted the long-range policy or the long-range ambitions of the Soviet Union,' he told *Meet the Press* days after Soviet troops entered Afghanistan. *Meet the Press*, January 20, 1980. His courting of Soviet dissidents and his refusal to accept the Vladivostok draft of SALT II had signaled this early in his presidency, and his China policy had continued the trend. But he had not imagined that Brezhnev would betray him. And, as Mondale explained, 'Carter had been worn down by all these constant challenges and political bruises. He needed to show strength.'" Mitchell, "The Cold War and Jimmy Carter," 84.

64. *FRUS, 1977–1980*, vol. 8, *Arab-Israeli Conflict*, document 113 (595).

65. Benjamin Miller, *When Opponents Cooperate*, chap. 6; Steinberg and Rubinovitz, *Menachem Begin and the Israel-Egypt Peace Process*, chap. 3.

66. http://www.jimmycarterlibrary.gov/documents/pddirectives/pd18.pdf (accessed on June 18, 2014).

67. Brzezinski, *Power and Principle*, 177–78.

68. *FRUS, 1977–1980*, vol. 8, document 103 (336).

69. *FRUS, 1977–1980*, vol. 8, document 120 (387).

70. *FRUS, 1977–1980*, vol. 8, document 120 (388–89).

71. Details in Vance, *Hard Choices*, chap. 3.

72. Romesh Ratnesar, *Tear Down This Wall: A City, a President, and the Speech That Ended the Cold War* (New York: Simon & Schuster, 2009), 45.

73. Ratnesar, 47.

74. "Ronald Reagan's announcement for presidential candidacy." Available online: http://www.reagan.utexas.edu/archives/reference/11.13.79.html (accessed on June 18, 2014).

75. Herring, *From Colony to Superpower*, 830.

76. Herring, 830.

77. Herring, 830.

78. Vance, *Hard Choices*, 101.

79. Vance, 102.

80. Vance, 103.

81. Vance, 109–13, 131.

82. Vance, 131–33.

83. Vance, 135–37.

84. Vance, 358–64.

85. Vance, 367.

86. Brzezinski, *Power and Principle*, 188.

87. Brzezinski, 189.

88. Mitchell, "The Cold War and Jimmy Carter," 69.

89. This is also Eizenstat's argument. Eizenstat, *President Carter*, 635. He makes an even stronger argument that Brzezinski "checkmated" Vance, telling Carter, in Eizenstat's words, that "while members of his administration stood solidly behind him against the Soviets, there were two conflicting interpretations—one that saw it as an aberration from Soviet behavior and the other as a clear symptom of it. He did not need to name names." Eizenstat, 639.

90. Keren Yarhi-Milo, "In the Eye of the Beholder: How Leaders and Intelligence Communities Assess the Intentions of Adversaries," *International Security* 38, no. 1 (2013): 20–28.

91. *Time*, January 14, 1980, quoted in Mitchell, "The Cold War and Jimmy Carter," 84, and in Eizenstat, *President Carter*, 639.

92. Jimmy Carter, "Foreword," in Gati, *Zbig*, viii.

93. Auten, *Carter's Conversion*, 18.

94. *FRUS, 1977–1980*, vol. 6, document 96 (311).

95. *FRUS 1977–1980*, vol. 6, document 98 (316).

96. Auten, *Carter's Conversion*, 17.

97. Auten, 18.

98. Auten, 25–26.

99. Auten, 143.

100. Auten, 149.

101. Auten, 257.

102. Auten, 308.

103. Yarhi-Milo, "In the Eye of the Beholder," 21.

104. Yarhi-*Milo*.

105. Yarhi-Milo, 23 (quoting memos by Brzezinski to Carter).

106. Yarhi-Milo, 23 (quoting Vance, *Hard Choices*, 84 and 101).

107. Yarhi-Milo, "In the Eye of the Beholder," 25, quote from Jimmy Carter, *White House Dairy* (New York: Farrar, Straus and Giroux, 2010), 383.

108. Yarhi-Milo, "In the Eye of the Beholder," 26.

109. Brzezinski, *Power and Principle*, 335.

110. Brzezinski to Carter, memo, May 29, 1979, "Summit Strategy," *FRUS, 1977–1980*, vol. 6, document 197 (567).

111. *FRUS, 1977–1980*, vol. 6, document 197 (568).

112. *FRUS, 1977–1980*, vol. 6, 572.

113. Brzezinski, *Power and Principle*, 345.

114. Brzezinski, 345.

115. Brzezinski, 430.

116. *FRUS, 1977–1980*, vol. 6, document 248 (715).

117. Carter to Brezhnev, December 28 1979, Box 17, Plains files, Carter Library. Quoted in Leffler, *For the Soul of Mankind*, 335.

118. Leffler, *For the Soul of Mankind*, 335.

119. Hanhimaki, *The Rise and Fall of Détente*, 120.

120. Hanhimaki, 125–38.

121. Hanhimaki, 137.

122. Auten, *Carter's Conversion*, 2–3.

123. *FRUS, 1977–1980*, vol. 6, document 302 (888).

124. *FRUS, 1977–1980*, vol. 6, document 302.

125. *FRUS, 1977–1980*, vol. 6, document 302 (889–90).

126. *FRUS, 1977–1980*, vol. 6, document 302 (890).

Chapter Six

1. These changes, as discussed in chap. 5, "virtually assured that the 1980s elections would be contested in a post-détente atmosphere, with the candidates competing over who could best stand up to the Russians." Brown, *Faces of Power*, 361.

2. Robert Mason, "The Domestic Politics of War and Peace: Jimmy Carter, Ronald Reagan, and the Election of 1980," in *US Presidential Elections and Foreign Policy: Candidates, Campaigns, and Global Politics from FDR to Bill Clinton*, ed. Andrew Johnstone and Andrew Priest (Lexington: University Press of Kentucky, 2017), 259, citing Martin P. Wattenberg, *The Rise of Candidate-Centered Politics: Presidential Elections of the 1980s* (Cambridge, MA: Harvard University Press, 1991), 111.

3. Mason, "The Domestic Politics of War and Peace," 263, citing Walter Dean Burnham, "The 1980 Earthquake: Realignment, Reaction, or What?," in *The Hidden Election: Politics and Economics in the 1980 Presidential Campaign*, ed. Thomas Ferguson and Joel Rogers (New York: Pantheon, 1981), 123.

4. See Peter Gourevitch, "The Second Image Reversed: The International Sources of Domestic Politics," *International Organization* 32, no. 4 (1978): 881–912.

5. Haig cited unhappiness with the direction of foreign policy as his reason for resignation, but it seems clear that Reagan found his temperament intolerable and was relieved that Haig resigned. Moreover, it became clear to the Reagan White House that Haig did not accept that the president made foreign policy decisions, not Haig. Kevin V. Mulcahy, "The Secretary of State and the National Security Adviser: Foreign Policymaking in the Carter and Reagan Administrations," *Presidential Studies Quarterly* 16, no. 2 (1986): 292.

6. There was speculation that Weinberger resigned because of his opposition to Reagan's policy toward the Soviet Union, specifically the arms control deal. But Weinberger stated: "I'm all for it and I have been for it from the beginning." Joel Brinkley and Special to the *New York Times*, "Weinberger, as Expected, Resigns Post," *New York Times*, November 6, 1987. Available online at https://www.nytimes.com/1987/11/06/us/weinberger-as-expected-resigns-post.html (accessed June 28, 2018).

7. See details in Daniel Wirls, *Buildup: The Politics of Defense in the Reagan Era* (Ithaca, NY: Cornell University Press, 1992), 31–46. Interestingly, in a private letter to the *Washington Post*'s publisher in December 1987 Reagan wrote: "We haven't had a budget since I've been here. Yes the law says I must present a budget every January. And every January the Congress throws my budget away and passes a 'continuing resolution' with all the appropriations in that one resolution. If I veto, the government shuts down. Yes I've asked for increases in defense spending. Rebuilding our national security was a must. Even Carter had projected a five-year military buildup to begin in 1982. Well the Congress cut my budget by $125 billion. But at the same time, they added $250 billion to my domestic budgets in those 'continuing resolutions.'" Kiron K. Skinner, Annelise Anderson, and Martin Anderson. eds., *Reagan: A Life in Letters* (New York: Free Press, 2003), 385.

8. James Mann, *The Rebellion of Ronald Reagan: A History of the End of the Cold War* (New York: Viking, 2009), 39–40; Francis H. Marlo, *Planning Reagan's War: Conservative Strategists and America's Cold War Victory* (Washington, DC: Potomac Books, 2012), 16–17, 23–24.

9. Marlo (*Planning Reagan's War*, 135) quotes Reagan favoring a constant confrontation with the Soviets "based on the belief (supported so far by all evidence) that in an all out race our system is stronger, and eventually the enemy gives up the race as a hopeless cause." Quoted from Kiron K. Skinner, Martin Anderson, and Annelise Anderson, eds., *Reagan, in His Own Hand* (New York: Free Press, 2001), 442.

10. Douglas Brinkley, ed., *The Reagan Diaries* (New York: Harper, 2009), 142. Quoted in Brands, *What Good Is Grand Strategy?*, 117.

11. Brands, *What Good Is Grand Strategy?*, 117.

12. Marlo, *Planning Reagan's War*, 24.

13. Marlo, 24.

14. Brands, *What Good Is Grand Strategy?*, 117–23.

15. Brands, 124–25.

16. Brands, 130.

17. Brands, 131.

18. Barbara Farnham, "Reagan and the Gorbachev Revolution: Perceiving the End of Threat," *Political Science Quarterly* 116, no. 2 (2001): 232; Svetlana Savraskaya and Thomas Blanton, *The Last Superpower Summits: Gorbachev, Reagan, and Bush, Conversations That Ended the Cold War* (Budapest: Central European University Press, 2016), 7. About Able Archer 83 and its critical role in changing Reagan's perception, see Dueck, *Hard Line*, 218; Beth A. Fischer, *The*

Reagan Reversal: Foreign Policy and the End of the Cold War (Columbia: University of Missouri Press, 1997), 122–31; Jonathan M. DiCicco, "Fear, Loathing, and Cracks in Reagan's Mirror Images: Able Archer 83 and an American First Step toward Rapprochement in the Cold War," *Foreign Policy Analysis* 7, no. 3 (2011): 253–74; Arnav Manchanda, "When Trust Is Stranger than Fiction: The Able Archer Incident," *Cold War History* 9, no. 1 (2009): 111–33; Vojtech Mastny, "How Able was 'Able Archer'? Nuclear Trigger and Intelligence in Perspective," *Journal of Cold War Studies* 11, no. 1 (2009): 108–23; Dmitry Dima Adamsky, "The 1983 Nuclear Crisis—Lessons for Deterrence Theory and Practice," *Journal of Strategic Studies* 36, no. 1 (2013): 12–30. Curiously, Brands does not mention Able Archer at all in his biography of Reagan. H. W. Brands, *Reagan: The Life* (New York: Doubleday, 2015), 420–23.

19. Farnham, "Reagan and the Gorbachev Revolution," 234.

20. Lawrence Freedman, *A Choice of Enemies: America Confronts the Middle East* (New York: Public Affairs, 2008), 114.

21. Vojtech Mastny, "The Soviet Non-Invasion of Poland in 1980–1981 and the End of the Cold War," *Europe-Asia Studies* 51, no. 2 (1999): 189–211.

22. See *FRUS, 1981–1988*, vol. 3, *Soviet Union, January 1981–January 1983*, ed., James Graham Wilson (Washington, DC: Government Printing Office, 2016), document 4. Richard Pipes offers a different reason for the Soviet behavior. He argues that the Polish government convinced Moscow to allow it to crack down on Solidarity. Richard Pipes, "On the National Security Council Staff," in *The Grand Strategy That Won the Cold War: Architecture of Triumph*, ed. Douglas E. Streusand et al. (Lanham, MD: Lexington Books, 2016), 39–51, at 40.

23. Don Oberdorfer, *From the Cold War to a New Era: The United States and the Soviet Union, 1983–1991*, updated ed. (Baltimore, MD: Johns Hopkins University Press, 1998), 15–21.

24. Jack F. Matlock Jr., *Reagan and Gorbachev: How the Cold War Ended* (New York: Random House, 2004), chap. 4, esp. 103.

25. Beth A. Fischer, "Reagan and the Soviets: Winning the Cold War?," in *The Reagan Presidency: Pragmatic Conservatism and Its Legacies*, ed. W. Elliot Brownlee and Hugh Davis Graham (Lawrence: University Press of Kansas, 2003), 116–20; Fischer, *The Reagan Reversal*. Fischer in fact argues that the change in strategy occurred in January 1984 as a result of Able Archer 83, which frightened Reagan with the possibility of an inadvertent devastating nuclear war.

26. Norman A. Graebner, Richard Dean Burns, and Joseph M. Siracusa, *Reagan, Bush, Gorbachev: Revisiting the End of the Cold War* (Westport, CT: Praeger Security International, 2008), 59.

27. Brands, *Reagan*, 461.

28. Oberdorfer, *From the Cold War to a New Era*, 90.

29. Oberdorfer, 90.

30. Ronald Reagan, *An American Life* (London: Arrow Books, 1991), 611.

31. Farnham, "Reagan and the Gorbachev Revolution," 250 (and sources in nn160–61).

32. It is not so much that Reagan forced the Soviet Union to change, but rather he was helping Gorbachev to ignite domestic change that Gorbachev saw as vital for the existence of the Soviet Union. See Wohlforth, "Realism and the End of the Cold War," 111–12; Archie Brown, *The Rise and Fall of Communism* (New York: Ecco, 2011), and *The Gorbachev Factor* (Oxford: Oxford University Press, 1996). See also Robert Service, *The End of the Cold War, 1985–1991* (London: Macmillan, 2015).

33. Matlock, *Reagan and Gorbachev*, 104.

34. Matlock, 104.

35. Matlock, 105.

36. Matlock, 90.

37. William C. Wohlforth, ed., *Witnesses to the End of the Cold War* (Baltimore, MD, and London: Johns Hopkins University Press, 1996), 11.

38. "The President's News Conference," September 17, 1985, available at www.reagan.utexas .edu /archives /speeches /1985/91785c.htm, accessed February 19, 2013 — cited in James Graham Wilson, *The Triumph of Improvisation: Gorbachev's Adaptability, Reagan's Engagement, and the End of the Cold War* (Ithaca, NY, and London: Cornell University Press, 2014), 95.

39. Oberdorfer, *From the Cold War to a New Era*, 129. Reagan wrote in his diary regarding the meeting with Shevardnadze that his "goal was to send him back to Gorbachev with a message that I really meant 'arms reductions' and I wasn't interested in any détente nonsense. For the 1st time they talked of real verification procedures." Brinkley, ed., *The Reagan Diaries*, 500.

40. Oberdorfer, *From the Cold War to a New Era*, 129–30.

41. Oberdorfer, 141.

42. Oberdorfer, 153.

43. Matlock, *Reagan and Gorbachev*, 166–67.

44. Graebner, Burns, and Siracusa, *Reagan, Bush, Gorbachev*, 61.

45. Graebner, Burns, and Siracusa, 67.

46. Graebner, Burns, and Siracusa, 67.

47. Oberdorfer, *From the Cold War to a New Era*, 156–57.

48. Wilson, *The Triumph of Improvisation*, 111.

49. Matlock, *Reagan and Gorbachev*, 213.

50. Mann, *The Rebellion of Ronald Reagan*, 45.

51. Matlock, *Reagan and Gorbachev*, 94 and 219.

52. Matlock, 96.

53. Brands, *What Good Is Grand Strategy?*, 132. On this point see also Mann, *The Rebellion of Ronald Reagan*, 118.

54. Matlock, *Reagan and Gorbachev*, 252–53.

55. Matlock, 253–54.

56. Matlock, 96; Brands, *What Good Is Grand Strategy?*, 132–33.

57. Matlock, *Reagan and Gorbachev*, 96.

58. James H. Broussard, *Ronald Reagan: Champion of Conservative America* (New York and London: Routledge, 2015), 173.

59. Archie Brown, "Gorbachev and the End of the Cold War," in *Ending the Cold War: Interpretations, Causation, and the Study of International Relations*, ed. Richard K. Hermann and Richard Ned Lebow (New York: Palgrave Macmillan, 2004), 51.

60. Marlo, *Planning Reagan's War*, 134 (quotes from Skinner, Anderson, and Anderson, eds., *Reagan: A Life in Letters*, 546, 384).

61. Marlo, *Planning Reagan's War*, 134–35.

62. Brands, *What Good Is Grand Strategy?*, 137.

63. Brands, 138.

Chapter Seven

1. Stephen Burgess, "Operation Restore Hope: Somalia and the Frontiers of the New World Order," in *From Cold War to New World Order: The Foreign Policy of George H. W. Bush*, ed. Meena Bose and Rosanna Perotti (Westport, CT: Greenwood Press, 2002), 259–73, esp. 266–67.

2. Bruce Russett, *Grasping the Democratic Peace* (Princeton, NJ: Princeton University Press, 1993), 128–29.

3. Then national security advisor Anthony Lake, cited in Thomas J. Wright, *All Measures Short of War: The Contest for the 21st Century and the Future of American Power* (New Haven, CT: Yale University Press, 2017), 9.

4. President Clinton cited in Joanne Gowa, "Democratic States and International Disputes," *International Organization* 49, no. 3 (1995): 511n2.

5. On this policy, see Alastair Johnston and Robert Ross, eds., *Engaging China: The Management of an Emerging Power* (London: Routledge, 1999).

6. Michael Mandelbaum, *Mission Failure: America and the World in the Post–Cold War Era* (New York: Oxford University Press, 2016), 52–74.

7. James Mann, *About Face* (New York: Knopf, 1999), cited in Mandelbaum, *Mission Failure*, 24.

8. Mandelbaum, *Mission Failure*; Wright, *All Measures Short of War*.

9. Wright, *All Measures Short of War*, 6–7.

10. Derek Chollet and James Goldgeier, *America between the Wars: From 11/9 to 9/11* (New York: PublicAffairs, 2008).

11. Philip Zelikow and Condoleezza Rice, *Germany Unified and Europe Transformed* (Cambridge, MA: Harvard University Press, 1995).

12. On Bush Sr. as a (defensive) realist, see Goldgeier and McFaul, *Power and Purpose*, 9–11.

13. Hal Brands, *Making the Unipolar Moment: U.S. Foreign Policy and the Rise of the Post–Cold War Order* (Ithaca, NY: Cornell University Press, 2016), 332.

14. Brown, *Faces of Power*, 552.

15. Patrick J. Maney, *Bill Clinton: New Gilded Age President* (Lawrence: University Press of Kansas, 2016), 119.

16. James D. Boys, *Clinton's Grand Strategy: US Foreign Policy in a Post–Cold War World* (London: Bloomsbury, 2015), 54.

17. Boys, 54, quoting Clinton's speech on May 29, 1993, at West Point.

18. See Goldgeier and McFaul, *Power and Purpose*, 11–12; Brown, *Faces of Power*, 569–71; Mandelbaum, *Mission Failure*, 17; Brands, *Making the Unipolar Moment*, 333; and Gowa, "Democratic States and International Disputes," 511–22, 511n1.

19. On this policy, see Johnston and Ross, eds., *Engaging China*; David M. Lampton, *Same Bed, Different Dreams: Managing U.S.-China Relations, 1989–2000* (Berkeley: University of California Press, 2001); Yangmin Wang, "The Politics of U.S.-China Economic Relations: MFN, Constructive Engagement, and the Trade Issue Proper," *Asian Survey* 33, no. 5 (1993): 441–62.

20. Mandelbaum, *Mission Failure*, 26.

21. Mandelbaum, 347.

22. Gideon Rachman, *Easternization: Asia's Rise and America's Decline from Obama to Trump and Beyond* (New York: Other Press, 2016), 76; Wright, *All Measures Short of War*, 10.

23. Kurt M. Campbell and Ely Ratner, "The China Reckoning: How Beijing Defied American Expectations," *Foreign Affairs* (March–April 2018): 62.

24. On the market and democracy, see Michael Mandelbaum, *Democracy's Good Name: The Rise and Risks of the World's Most Popular Form of Government* (New York: Public Affairs, 2007), chap. 3. In a 2000 speech aimed to encourage Congress to dismantle trade barriers with China before its joining the WTO, Clinton drew a direct line between free enterprise and pressure for

accountable government. When individuals have the power to realize their dreams, he argued, "they will demand a greater say." Cited in "China and the West," *Economist*, March 3, 2018, 19.

25. Campbell and Ratner, "The China Reckoning," 64.

26. On democracy and peace, see Russett, *Grasping the Democratic Peace*.

27. James Mann, *The China Fantasy* (New York: Penguin, 2007); Aaron Friedberg, *A Contest for Supremacy: China, America, and the Struggle for Mastery in Asia* (New York: W. W. Norton, 2011), esp. 91–92, cited in Hal Brands and Peter Feaver, "Stress-Testing American Grand Strategy," *Survival* 58, no. 6 (2016): 102; Rachman, *Easternization*, 76. Brown (*Faces of Power*, 560–61) cites Secretary of State Albright's various reasons to integrate China in the world economy even while it violates human rights—the economic reasons and especially domestic political reasons in China and potential Chinese contributions to the international order.

28. Mann, *The China Fantasy*; Polity IV dataset and Freedom House cited in Brands and Feaver, "Stress-Testing American Grand Strategy," 103; Campbell and Ratner, "The China Reckoning," 64.

29. Goldgeier and McFaul, *Power and Purpose*, 18–40, 331.

30. A comprehensive treatment of US strategy toward Russia in the 1990s is Goldgeier and McFaul, *Power and Purpose*. See also Boys, *Clinton's Grand Strategy*, 235–37, and Maney, *Bill Clinton*, 120–23.

31. Brown, *Faces of Power*, 552–53.

32. On US and Russia in the 1990s, see Mandelbaum, *Mission Failure*, 52–74,

33. Goldgeier and McFaul, *Power and Purpose*, 11.

34. Goldgeier and McFaul, 12.

35. Goldgeier and McFaul, 111–16.

36. Goldgeier and McFaul, 334.

37. Goldgeier and McFaul, 13; Mandelbaum, *Mission Failure*, 60–62.

38. Mandelbaum, *Mission Failure*, 64n93.

39. Michael Mandelbaum, *The Dawn of Peace in Europe* (New York: Twentieth Century Fund Press, 1996).

40. Joshua R. Itzkowitz Shifrinson, "Deal or No Deal? The End of the Cold War and the U.S. Offer to Limit NATO Expansion," *International Security* 40, no. 4 (2016): 7–44.

41. Goldgeier and McFaul, *Power and Purpose*, 15; Mandelbaum, *Mission Failure*, 70–71; Maney, *Bill Clinton*, 121–22.

42. Goldgeier and McFaul, *Power and Purpose*, 15.

43. On these humanitarian interventions, see Jon Western, "Sources of Humanitarian Intervention: Beliefs, Information and Advocacy in the US Decisions on Somalia and Bosnia," *International Security* 26, no. 4 (2002): 112–42; Finnemore, *The Purpose of Intervention*; Lawrence Freedman, "Iraq, Liberal Wars and Illiberal Containment," *Survival* 48, no. 4 (2006): 51–65, esp. 51. On Somalia, see also Burgess, "Operation Restore Hope," 266, and DiPrizio, *Armed Humanitarians*, 44–47. The first Gulf War of 1990–91 is not considered here as a primarily humanitarian intervention, because the US had major material interests in the oil-rich Persian Gulf, in addition to the humanitarian motive of liberating Kuwait. The first Gulf War fits the mainly defensive realist era in which it occurred—it took place before the Soviet disintegration and the transition to unipolarity at the end of 1991.

44. This section draws on Benjamin Miller, "The Logic of U.S. Military Intervention in the Post–Cold War Era," *Contemporary Security Policy* 19, no. 3 (December 1998): 72–109.

45. Boys, *Clinton's Grand Strategy*, 55–60.

46. Burgess, "Operation Restore Hope," 259; see also DiPrizio, *Armed Humanitarians*, 52–60, for a refutation of alternative explanations of this intervention (such as the "CNN effect").

47. Jon Meacham, *Destiny and Power: The American Odyssey of George Herbert Walker Bush* (New York: Random House, 2015), 529.

48. Boys, *Clinton's Grand Strategy*, 59; Flavia Gasbarri, "Revisiting the Linkage: PDD 25, Genocide in Rwanda and the US Peacekeeping Experience of the 1990s," *International History Review* 40, no. 4 (2018): 792–813; Alan P. Dobson, "The Dangers of US Interventionism," *Review of International Studies* 28 no. 3 (2002): 587.

49. DiPrizio, *Armed Humanitarians*, 4.

50. DiPrizio, 4.

51. Alan McPherson, *A Short History of U.S. Interventions in Latin America and the Caribbean* (Chichester, West Sussex: Wiley Blackwell, 2016), 179–83; David M. Malone and Sebastian von Einsiedel, "Haiti," in *United Nations Interventionism, 1991–2004*, ed. Mats Berdal and Spyros Economides (Cambridge: Cambridge University Press, 2007), 168–91; Sarah E. Kreps, "The 1994 Haiti Intervention: A Unilateral Operation in Multilateral Clothes," *Journal of Strategic Studies* 30, no. 3 (2007): 449–74; Sebastian von Einsiedel and David M. Malone, "Peace and Democracy for Haiti: A UN Mission Impossible?," *International Relations* 20, no. 2 (2006): 153–74; Daniel P. O'Neill, "When to Intervene: The Haitian Dilemma," *SAIS Review* 24, no. 2 (2004): 163–74; Henry F. Carey, "U.S. Domestic Politics and the Emerging Humanitarian Intervention Policy: Haiti, Bosnia, and Kosovo," *World Affairs* 164, no. 2 (2001): 72–82.

52. For an overview, see Sestanovich, *Maximalist*, 259–62.

53. Ivo H. Daalder and Michael E. O'Hanlon, *Winning Ugly: NATO's War to Save Kosovo* (Washington, DC: Brookings Institution Press, 2000).

54. See Dusko Doder, "Yugoslavia: New War, Old Hatreds," *Foreign Policy* 91 (1993): 3–23, esp. 4; and Richard Ullman, *The World and Yugoslavia's Wars* (New York: Council on Foreign Relations, 1996). The statement "we don't have a dog in this fight" is attributed to Bush's secretary of state, James Baker. See, for example, Steven Weisman, "In Kosovo, Another Setback for the Multiethnic Ideal," *International Herald Tribune*, June 18, 1999, 8.

55. See Western, "Sources of Humanitarian Intervention"; Finnemore, *The Purpose of Intervention*; Mandelbaum, *Mission Failure*, 75–132; and Maney, *Bill Clinton*, 242.

56. "Albright: Milosevic Has Created 'Horror of Biblical Proportions,'" CNN, April 7, 1999, http://www.cnn.com / WORLD/europe/9904/07/albright/index.html (accessed November 28, 2017).

57. Steven L. Burg and Paul S. Shoup, *The War in Bosnia-Herzegovina: Ethnic Conflict and International Intervention* (Armonk, NY: M. E. Sharpe, 1999), 11, 13, 46–47, 60, 195–96, cited in Mandelbaum, *Mission Failure*, 103n63.

58. Mandelbaum, *Mission Failure*, 109–10n79 (citing Ivo H. Daalder, *Getting to Dayton: The Making of America's Bosnia Policy* [Washington, DC: Brookings Institution Press, 2000, 180]).

59. Citation of Clinton in Chollet and Goldgeier, *America between the Wars*, 221.

60. Maney, *Bill Clinton*, 242.

61. On the difficulties of stabilizing weak and deeply divided states, see Miller, *State, Nations, and the Great Powers*; Miller, "Does Democratization Pacify the State?"

62. This section draws on Benjamin Miller, "The Sources and Effects of Humanitarian Interventions: Realism, Liberalism and the State-to-Nation Balance," in Daniel Terris and Galia Golan, *R2P in Ten* (online publication, January 2016): brandeis.edu /ethics/pdfs/internationaljustice/ r2p/march%202015%20papers/r2p-miller.pdf (accessed February 24, 2020).

63. Daniel L. Byman and Matthew C. Waxman, "Kosovo and the Great Air Power Debate," *International Security* 24, no. 4 (2000): 5–38; Dag Henriksen, "Inflexible Response: Diplomacy, Airpower and the Kosovo Crisis, 1998–1999," *Journal of Strategic Studies* 31, no. 6 (2008): 825–58.

64. DiPrizio, *Armed Humanitarians*, 151–53.

65. Doug Bandow, "NATO's Hypocritical Humanitarianism," in *NATO's Empty Victory: A Postmortem on the Balkan War*, ed. Ted Galen Carpenter (Washington, DC: CATO Institute, 2000), 43.

66. The Security Council was not asked to authorize. The US knew it would not get an authorization. Madeleine Albright, *Madam Secretary: A Memoir* (New York: Miramax Books, 2003), 489.

67. On the qualification of NATO as multilateral alongside the UNSC, see Sarah E. Kreps, "Multilateral Military Interventions: Theory and Practice," *Political Science Quarterly* 123, no. 4 (2008–9): 587n39, cited in Miller, "Explaining Changes in U.S. Grand Strategy," 33n8.

68. Martha Finnemore, "Constructing Norms of Humanitarian Intervention," in Katzenstein, *The Culture of National Security*, 153–85.

69. Mandelbaum, *Mission Failure*, 78.

70. Citations of Mueller in Mandelbaum, *Mission Failure*, 84–85.

71. On the emergence of a unipolar world in the aftermath of the Soviet collapse, see Charles Krauthammer, "The Unipolar Moment," *Foreign Affairs* 70, no. 1 (1990–91): 23–33; Charles Krauthammer, "The Unipolar Moment Revisited," *National Interest* 70 (2002–3): 5–17, and esp. Wohlforth, "The Stability of a Unipolar World." Key indicators for US military and economic hegemony are cited in Dueck, *Reluctant Crusaders*, 125–26; see also Layne, *The Peace of Illusions*, and Stephen G. Brooks and William C. Wohlforth, "American Primacy in Perspective," *Foreign Affairs* 82, no. 4 (July–August 2002). For a more refined argument about American leadership in the 1990s, see Nye, *The Paradox of American Power*. For the debate about the endurance of a unipolar world, see Kenneth Waltz, "The Emerging Structure of International Politics," *International Security* 18, no. 2 (1993): 44–79; John G. Ikenberry, ed., *America Unrivaled: The Future of the Balance of Power* (Ithaca, NY: Cornell University Press, 2002); T. V. Paul, Michel Fortmann, and James Wirtz, eds., *Balance of Power: Theory and Practice in the 21st Century* (Stanford, CA: Stanford University Press, 2004); and Christopher Layne, "The Unipolar Illusion Revisited," *International Security* 31, no. 2 (2006): 7–41.

72. On US superiority, see Brands and Feaver, "Stress-Testing American Grand Strategy," 97–102.

73. Stefan Halper and Jonathan Clarke, *America Alone: The Neo-Conservatives and the Global Order* (Cambridge: Cambridge University Press, 2004), 160.

74. Mandelbaum, *Mission Failure*, 83, 88.

75. Notably the Srebrenica massacre—the July 1995 killing of more than eight thousand Muslim Bosnians, mainly men and boys, in and around the town of Srebrenica during the Bosnian War.

76. DiPrizio, *Armed Humanitarians*, 150, 153; additional citations in Miller, "The Logic of US Military Interventions in the Post–Cold War Era," 96.

77. Mandelbaum, *Mission Failure*, 39–40.

78. Mandelbaum, 40.

79. See Wesley Clark, *Waging Modern War: Bosnia, Kosovo and the Future of Combat* (New York: Public Affairs, 2001).

80. Karin Von Hippel, *Democracy by Force: US Military Intervention in the Post–Cold War*

World (Cambridge: Cambridge University Press, 2000), 72–74; Burgess, "Operation Restore Hope," 268.

81. See DiPrizio, *Armed Humanitarians*, chap. 4.

Chapter Eight

1. This chapter draws on Benjamin Miller, "Explaining Changes in U.S. Grand Strategy: 9/11, the Rise of Offensive Liberalism, and the War in Iraq," *Security Studies* 19, no. 1 (2010): 26–65.

2. Public opinion on the invasion of Afghanistan in 2001 is usually supportive. Gallup polls have indicated such support, except for the poll of February 2014 where there were more respondents who thought the war was a mistake (49 percent) than who thought it was not a mistake (48 percent). But overall, it seems like an outlier. See http://www.gallup.com/poll/116233/afghanistan.aspx (accessed on July 27, 2017).

3. Hawaii was an American territory when Japan attacked Pearl Harbor on December 7, 1941. It became a state only in 1959.

4. Colin Dueck, "Ideas, American Grand Strategy, and the War In Iraq," in *Why Did the United States Invade Iraq?*, ed. Jane K. Cramer and A. Trevor Thrall (London and New York: Routledge, 2012), 49–72.

5. Daniel Deudney and G. John Ikenberry, "Realism, Liberalism and the Iraq War," *Survival* 59, no. 4 (2017): 8. For a critique of their argument that is partly similar to the argument made in this chapter, see Patrick Porter, "Iraq: A Liberal War After All; A Critique of Dan Deudney and John Ikenberry," *International Politics* 55, no. 2 (March 2018): 334–48.

6. They erroneously write that Rumsfeld had a prominent role in the 1991 Gulf War (Deudney and Ikenberry, "Realism, Liberalism and the Iraq War," 17). He was out of government during that era.

7. Deudney and Ikenberry, 18.

8. Potentially unintended implications might have included on the domestic level—the 2008 electoral victory of Barack Obama and in a different way we might speculate that it might have even contributed to the victory of Trump eight years later and the rise of antielitist populism in the US; on the regional level—we can't understand the current turmoil in the Middle East without taking into account the major effects of the Iraq invasion, notably the Sunni-Shiite clash and the rise of Iranian power in the region; and on the international level—the regime-change policy in Iraq added to the preexisting fears of the Russians and the Chinese about US commitment to advance "regime change" also in their neighborhoods, including potentially their own regimes.

9. Monten, "The Roots of the Bush Doctrine," 147.

10. Bob Woodward, *Plan of Attack* (New York: Simon & Schuster, 2004), 155; Ivo Daalder and James Lindsay, *America Unbound: The Bush Revolution in Foreign Policy* (New York: John Wiley & Sons, 2005), 136; Michael Gordon and Bernard Trainor, *Cobra II: The Inside Story of the Invasion and Occupation of Iraq* (New York: Pantheon Books, 2006), 71.

11. See chap. 1.

12. Chollet and Goldgeier, *America between the Wars*, 13–16.

13. Chollet and Goldgeier, 222–25. See also Daalder and O'Hanlon, *Winning Ugly*, 221.

14. Jervis, "Understanding the Bush Doctrine," 7. On the distinction between preemptive and preventive wars, see chap. 4 and Mandelbaum, *Mission Failure*, 199–200. On the Bush

Doctrine, see George W. Bush, *The National Security Strategy of the United States of America* (Washington, DC: National Security Council, 2002); George W. Bush, *Remarks by the President at 2002 Graduation Exercise of the United States Military Academy* (June 1, 2002), both accessed on September 19, 2008, http://www.whitehouse.gov/administration/eop/nsc/ and http://www.whitehouse.gov/briefing_room/, respectively. See also Jervis, *American Foreign Policy in a New Era*; Jervis, "Understanding the Bush Doctrine"; Daalder and Lindsay, *America Unbound*; Monten, "The Roots of the Bush Doctrine"; Dueck, *Reluctant Crusaders*, 158–9, and Gurtov, *Superpower on Crusade*, chap. 2.

15. According to Jervis, the Bush Doctrine shows that "Bush and his colleagues are liberal in their beliefs about the sources of foreign policy." See Jervis, "Understanding the Bush Doctrine," 5.

16. Lawrence Kaplan and William Kristol, *The War over Iraq: Saddam's Tyranny and America's Mission* (New York: Encounter Books, 2003), 104.

17. Cited in Monten, "The Roots of the Bush Doctrine," 145.

18. Hal Brands, *What Good Is Grand Strategy?*, 151.

19. Kaplan and Kristol, *The War over Iraq*, 95.

20. Cited in Thomas Powers, "Tomorrow the World," *New York Review of Books*, March 11, 2004, 4–6 (a review of David Frum and Richard Perle, *An End to Evil: How to Win the War on Terror* [Random House, 2004]).

21. Cited in Woodward, *Plan of Attack*, 89.

22. Jervis, "Understanding the Bush Doctrine," 6–7; Monten, "The Roots of the Bush Doctrine," 149–51.

23. "Dr. Condoleezza Rice Discusses the President's National Security Strategy," Waldorf Astoria Hotel, October 1, 2002, available at http://z22.whitehouse.gov/news/releases/2002/10/20021001-6.html (accessed March 2, 2009).

24. The unilateralist tendencies of the new Bush administration were manifested in the US withdrawal from several major international agreements before 9/11. For useful overviews of Bush's early foreign policy, see Halper and Clarke, *America Alone*, 121–35; Daalder and Lindsay, *America Unbound*, 61–76; Dueck, *Reluctant Crusaders*, 148–52; and Hal Brands, *What Good Is Grand Strategy?*, 150–51.

25. Condoleezza Rice, "Promoting the National Interest," *Foreign Affairs* 79, no. 1 (2000): 45–62, esp. 45–47, 49, 53–55.

26. Kaplan and Kristol, *The War over Iraq*, 63, 68, 69; Halper and Clarke, *America Alone*, 133–35; Dueck, *Reluctant Crusaders*, 148–52, and Gordon and Trainor, *Cobra II*, 14.

27. For Powell's staunch defensive realist positions, see Michael Hirsh, *At War with Ourselves* (Oxford: Oxford University Press, 2003), 37–38. While Rice was also a defensive realist at this time, Cheney and Rumsfeld tended to more hawkish offensive realist views.

28. Thomas Ricks, *Fiasco: The American Military Adventure in Iraq* (New York: Penguin Press, 2006), 25. For Cheney's opposition to the invasion of Iraq and the removal of Saddam Hussein at the end of the first Gulf War in 1991, see Ricks, 6.

29. Gary Dorrien, *Imperial Designs: Neoconservatism and the New Pax Americana* (New York: Routledge, 2004), 2, 142–43; Halper and Clarke, *America Alone*, 113–21, and Gurtov, *Superpower on Crusade*, 34.

30. Daalder and Lindsay, *America Unbound*, 14–15, 46.

31. Daalder and Lindsay, 127–28; Ricks, *Fiasco*, 6–7, 15–17, 27–28.

32. Dueck, *Reluctant Crusaders*, 156; Gordon and Trainor, *Cobra II*, 15; Woodward, *Plan of Attack*, 11, 13–14, 16; Ricks, *Fiasco*, 28; Kaplan and Kristol, *The War over Iraq*, 70–71.

33. Daalder and Lindsay, *America Unbound*, 127–28; Dueck, *Reluctant Crusaders*, 156; Ricks, *Fiasco*, 27–28. Wolfowitz had the support of the other offensive liberals within the administration, particularly Cheney's chief of staff, "Scooter" Libby. For an expanded study of Wolfowitz's views and deeds, see. Immerman, *Empire for Liberty*, chap. 6.

34. Immerman, *Empire for Liberty*, 224.

35. Ricks, *Fiasco*, 28; Freedman, *A Choice of Enemies*, 401–2.

36. Cited in Freedman, *A Choice of Enemies*, 402.

37. Daalder and Lindsay, *America Unbound*, 127.

38. George W. Bush's Address to a Joint Session of Congress and the Nation, September 20, 2001. Available online at http://www.washingtonpost.com/wp-srv/nation/specials/attacked/transcripts/bushaddress_092001.html (accessed July 15, 2017). See the 9/11 Commission, *The 9/11 Commission Report: Final Report of the National Commission on Terrorist Attacks upon the United States* (New York: W. W. Norton, 2004), 336, 362–63. Gaddis has similarly written that after September 11, the United States found itself living "in a suddenly more dangerous world." John Lewis Gaddis, "Grand Strategy in the Second Term," *Foreign Affairs* 85, no. 1 (2005): 2–15, cited in Steven Miller, "The Iraq Experiment and US National Security," *Survival* 48, no. 4 (2006): 17–50, at 18; see also Steven Miller, "Terrifying Thoughts: Power, Order, and Terror After 9/11," *Global Governance* 11, no. 2 (2005): 247–71.

39. NBC News, *Meet the Press* show transcript, November 8, 2002. See also Brands, *What Good Is Grand Strategy?*, 152. As the prominent historian of American foreign policy suggested recently, "In my ongoing research about the response to 9/11, what stood out was the level of fear about another prospective attack." See Melvyn P. Leffler, *Safeguarding Democratic Capitalism* (Princeton, NJ: Princeton University Press, 2017), 282.

40. Francis Fukuyama, *America at the Crossroads* (New Haven, CT: Yale University Press, 2006), 166–68; Freedman, *A Choice of Enemies*. Indeed, various intelligence reports and some evidence from Afghanistan were showing that al-Qaeda was planning, among other things, to produce "dirty" nuclear bombs. See Woodward, *Plan of Attack*, 45–46.

41. Miller, "The Iraq Experiment and US National Security," 21. See also Hal Brands and Peter Feaver, "The Case for Bush Revisionism: Reevaluating the Legacy of America's 43rd President," *Journal of Strategic Studies* 41, no. 1–2 (2018): 242.

42. Dueck, *Reluctant Crusaders*, 156.

43. Woodward, *Plan of Attack*, 27; Brands and Feaver, "The Case for Bush revisionism," 8.

44. Peter Baker, *Days of Fire: Bush and Cheney in the White House* (New York: Doubleday, 2013), 135.

45. Mandelbaum, *Mission Failure*, 198.

46. Douglas J. Feith, *War and Decision: Inside the Pentagon at the Dawn of the War on Terrorism* (New York: Harper, 2008), 19, 56, 81; Gordon and Trainor, *Cobra II*, 18–19, 73–74.

47. Mark Danner, "In the Darkness of Dick Cheney," *New York Review of Books*, March 6, 2014, 49. Cited in Mandelbaum, *Mission Failure*, 419n51.

48. Mandelbaum, *Mission Failure*, 198.

49. Mandelbaum, 198.

50. Mandelbaum, 198–99. Freedman makes a similar point in *A Choice of Enemies*, 397–402.

51. Mandelbaum, *Mission Failure*, 199.

52. Mandelbaum, 199, citing Feith, *War and Decision*, 391.

53. Tommy Franks, *American Soldier* (New York: Regan Books, 2004), 356–57. Quoted in Gideon Rose, *How Wars End: Why We Always Fight the Last Battle; A History of American Intervention from World War I to Afghanistan* (New York: Simon and Schuster, 2010), 256.

54. On Bush's view that 9/11 discredited the doctrines of deterrence and containment, see Bush, *Remarks by the President at 2002 Graduation Exercise*, cited also in Andrew Flibbert, "The Road to Baghdad: Ideas and Intellectuals in Explanations of the Iraq War," *Security Studies* 15, no. 2 (2006): 310–52, at 324n42.

55. Miller, "The Iraq Experiment and US National Security," 20.

56. For a useful ideational explanation of the Iraq War, which, however, fails to take into sufficient account the systemic/material factors that enabled the post-9/11 rise of a certain set of ideas, see Flibbert, "The Road to Baghdad."

57. Two major studies of the neoconservatives are Halper and Clarke, *America Alone*, and Dorrien, *Imperial Designs*. Another study that emphasizes their influence on post-9/11 US foreign policy is Gurtov, *Superpower on Crusade*. Key post-9/11 neoconservative works include Kaplan and Kristol, *The War over Iraq*, and Frum and Perle, *An End to Evil*. See also Michael Lind, "Neoconservatism and American Hegemony," in *Why Did the United States Invade Iraq?*, ed. Jane K. Cramer and A. Trevor Thrall (London and New York: Routledge, 2012), 114–17; Immerman, *Empire for Liberty*.

58. Thus, according to Halper and Clarke, "there is a case to be made that, far from being conservative, modern neo-conservatism is better understood as a phenomenon of the 'humanitarian, liberal, Wilsonian' left. . . . It is a new political animal born of an unlikely mating of humanitarian liberalism and brute force." Halper and Clarke, *America Alone*, 18, 181, see also 74, 76–7, 160, and 180. See also Gurtov, *Superpower on Crusade*, 86, who calls the neoconservative strategy "a mixture of evangelical spirit and flexing of military power."

59. See Krauthammer quoted in Halper and Clarke, *America Alone*, 76, 78; Muravchik quoted in Dorrien, *Imperial Designs*, 216. For an analysis of the views of Krauthammer and Muravchik, see Dorrien, chap. 3. On the neoconservative support of global democracy promotion, see also Joshua Muravchik, *Exporting Democracy: Fulfilling America's Destiny* (Washington, DC: American Enterprise Institute, 1991).

60. Robert Tucker and David Hendrickson, *The Imperial Temptation: The New World Order and America's Purpose* (New York: Council on Foreign Relations, 1992), 35. On "rogue" states in post–Cold War US foreign policy, see also Michael Klare, *Rogue States and Nuclear Outlaws: America's Search for a New Foreign Policy* (New York: Hill and Wang, 1995); and Robert Litwak, *Rogue States and U.S. Foreign Policy: Containment after the Cold War* (Baltimore, MD: Johns Hopkins, 2000).

61. For the neoconservative analysis of the Middle East in this vein, see Kaplan and Kristol, *The War over Iraq*, 101–3, 106. See also John Lewis Gaddis, "A Grand Strategy of Transformation," *Foreign Policy* 133 (2002): 50–57.

62. Halper and Clarke, *America Alone*, 101–2, 147–48, 218, 220, 308. Ricks (*Fiasco*, 98) discusses Wolfowitz's expectation that the Iraqis will welcome the Americans as "liberators." On this expectation in the administration, see also Baker, *Days of Fire*, 207 (CIA head George Tenet), 253 (Cheney).

63. Kaplan and Kristol, *The War over Iraq*, 99–100; Halper and Clarke, *America Alone*, 148.

64. Freedman, *A Choice of Enemies*, 397–402. On the "Liberation Strategy," see Woodward, *Plan of Attack*, 20–22.

65. Freedman, *A Choice of Enemies*, 402. Bush's quote from a press conference with Blair, January 31, 2003 (Freedman, 541n18).

66. Rose, *How Wars End*, 259–60n71 (at the end of this paragraph): Assistant Secretary of Defense Peter Rodman articulated the point in August 2002:

The State Department has proposed a Transitional Civil Authority (TCA) led by the United States to govern Iraq once Saddam is gone. . . . My concern is that this occupation government may unintentionally prolong the vacuum in Iraq and enable the wrong people to fill it. . . . While Iraq has no de Gaulle, the [post–World War II] French experience seems to me more instructive than that of [post–World War II] Germany and Japan:

* There are bad guys all over Iraq—radical Shia, Communists, Wahhabis, al-Qaeda—who will strive to fill the political vacuum.
* An occupation government will only delay the process of unifying the moderate forces.
* The best hope for filling the vacuum is to prepare the Iraqis to do it.

Thus, I see Afghanistan as the model to be emulated, even if the Iraqis are not yet ready for their Bonn process.

"Who Will Govern Iraq?," Rodman to Rumsfeld, August 15, 2002, in Feith, *War and Decision*, 546–48.

67. George W. Bush, *Decision Points* (New York: Broadway Paperbacks, 2010), 397. On the agenda, see Bruce Gilley, "Did Bush Democratize the Middle East? The Effects of External-Internal Linkages," *Political Science Quarterly* 128, no. 4 (2013–14): 658–63.

68. Bush, *Decision Points*, 397.

69. For a comparative analysis of the effects—and why the intervention failed to democratize Iraq, see Miller, "Does Democratization Pacify the State?," 455–69.

70. "Project for the New American Century, Letter to President Clinton, January 26, 1998," in *The Iraq Papers*, ed. John Ehrenberg et al. (Oxford: Oxford University Press, 2010), 24–25.

71. Dorrien, *Imperial Designs*, 69; and Gurtov, *Superpower on Crusade*, 29.

72. Halper and Clarke, *America Alone*, 102; Dorrien, *Imperial Designs*, 85.

73. As Daalder and Lindsay remark about their persuasion attempts, "for all the intellectual power behind this effort, it gained little traction in the first months of Bush's tenure"; see Daalder and Lindsay, *America Unbound*, 128. On the neoconservatives' frustration with the Bush administration before 9/11, see also Dorrien, *Imperial Designs*, 141–50, 226; Halper and Clarke, *America Alone*, 129–31; and Gurtov, *Superpower on Crusade*, 30.

74. Cited in Dorrien, *Imperial Designs*, 137–38; Gurtov, *Superpower on Crusade*, 30.

75. Gurtov, *Superpower on Crusade*, 37. On the parallels between Pearl Harbor and 9/11, see also John Lewis Gaddis, *Surprise, Security and the American Experience* (Cambridge, MA: Harvard University Press, 2004).

76. Miller, "The Iraq Experiment and US National Security," 21.

77. Halper and Clarke, *America Alone*, 205; see 4, 33, 40, 113, 138–39, and 144.

78. Bush, *Decision Points*, 228.

79. Bush, 229.

80. Sean Kay, *America's Search for Security: The Triumph of Idealism and the Return of Realism* (Lanham, MD: Rowman & Littlefield, 2014), 160, citing Bush's interview with ITN, April 5, 2002.

81. Kay, 160, citing Ricks, *Fiasco*, 17–18.

82. Ricks, *Fiasco*, 17–18.

83. Condoleezza Rice, *No Higher Honor: A Memoir of My Years in Washington* (New York: Broadway Paperbacks, 2011), 170.

84. Rice, 170.

85. Bush, *Decision Points*, 189; 9/11 Commission, *The 9/11 Commission Report*, 335–36; Woodward, *Plan of Attack*, 24–26; Halper and Clarke, *America Alone*, 149–54; Dorrien, *Imperial Designs*, 151, 153; Daalder and Lindsay, *America Unbound*, 128; Dueck, *Reluctant Crusaders*, 156.

86. Ricks, *Fiasco*, 32.

87. Daalder and Lindsay, *America Unbound*, 128.

88. Bush discusses his conversion to democratization as part of his administration grand strategy in his memoirs—*Decision Points*, chap. 13, esp. 396–97.

89. Cramer and Duggan argue that there was no internalization of Wilsonian ideas on democratization and Bush, Cheney, and Rumsfeld were committed to remove Saddam long before 9/11 or even before taking office. Thus, they claim, the neoconservatives had no effect on going to war with Iraq. Jane K. Cramer and Edward C. Duggan, "In Pursuit of Primacy: Why the United States Invaded Iraq," in *Why Did the United States Invade Iraq?*, ed. Jane K. Cramer and A. Trevor Thrall (London and New York: Routledge, 2012), 201–43. However, there is a major flaw in this line of argument. Removing Saddam Hussein from power was consensual in the United States before 9/11. A law for the liberation of Iraq was passed in Congress and signed by President Clinton already in 1998, and during the 2000 elections, both nominees for president, Bush and Gore, were fully committed. However, until 9/11 this commitment was not operational, and both Clinton and Bush—until 9/11—preferred sanctions and containment. In other words, it was 9/11—and the rising level of (perceived) threat—that increased dramatically the influence of the neocons' ideas about regime change and made them operational.

90. Thus, as Wolfowitz told *Time*, "Dick Cheney is someone whose view of the need to get rid of Saddam Hussein was transformed by Sept. 11. . . . And, of course, the attacks had a major impact on the President." Daalder and Lindsay, *America Unbound*, 128. On the significant changes in the positions of key administration officials following 9/11, see also Kaplan and Kristol, *The War over Iraq*, 71–75; Daalder and Lindsay, *America Unbound*, 127–39. On Cheney and Rice, see the remarks by Brent Scowcroft in Jeffrey Goldberg, "Breaking Ranks," *New Yorker*, October 31, 2005. Powell is a notable exception among the key members of the Bush administration in not having converted to offensive liberalism.

91. Bush, *Decision Points*, 397; Gurtov, *Superpower on Crusade*, 38.

92. Mearsheimer and Walt, *The Israel Lobby and US Foreign Policy*, 245, who criticize Richard Clarke's *Against All Enemies* and Ron Suskind's *The Price of Loyalty* for arguing that Bush and Cheney were bent on invading Iraq from the moment they assumed office in early 2001.

93. George Packer, *The Assassins' Gate: America in Iraq* (New York: Farrar, Straus and Giroux, 2006), 38. See also 37–65 on the changes in the positions of key policy makers in the Bush administration. On the changes in Cheney's view from the 1991 Gulf War to the post-9/11 era, see 42–43.

94. Cited in Halper and Clarke, *America Alone*, 141; on neoconservative elements in the Bush Doctrine, see 143–44.

95. Thomas Carothers, "Promoting Democracy and Fighting Terror," *Foreign Affairs* 82, no. 1 (2003): 84–97, esp. 91–92; Packer (*The Assassins' Gate*, 200) argues that this type of thinking was not confined only to neocons, but rather shared by supporters on both the left and the right; on this point, see also Mandelbaum, *Mission Failure*, 200, who is citing also Ricks, *Fiasco*.

96. Norman Friedman, *Terrorism, Afghanistan, and America's New Way of War* (Annapolis, MD: Naval Institute Press, 2003), 246–47, 306; Gordon and Trainor, *Cobra II*, 73.

97. Cited in Dueck, *Reluctant Crusaders*, 157.

98. Dueck, "Ideas, American Grand Strategy, and the War in Iraq," 63.

99. Dueck, 63–64.

100. Dueck, 64.

101. Dueck, 64, citing Nicholas Lemann, "How It Came to War", *New Yorker*, March 31, 2003, 37.

102. Rice, *No Higher Honor*, 170.

103. Rice, 171.

104. Rice, 181.

105. Dick Cheney with Liz Cheney, *In My Time: A Personal and Political Memoir* (New York: Threshold Editions, 2011), 387.

106. George W. Bush, State of the Union Address, January 28, 2003, cited in Amhed Ijaz Malik, *US Foreign Policy and the Gulf Wars: Decision-Making and International Relations* (London: I. B. Tauris, 2015), 183.

107. Robert Jervis, "Explaining the War in Iraq," in Cramer and Thrall, *Why Did the United States Invade Iraq?*, 32–33.

108. Halper and Clarke, *America Alone*, 144; Gurtov, *Superpower on Crusade*, 37 and 78.

109. James Dobbins, "Who Lost Iraq?," *International Herald Tribune*, April 17, 2007.

110. Sixty-eight percent of the American public supported the war when it broke out in March 2003. See the findings of the Gallup poll and the Pew Research Center for the People and the Press, cited in Flibbert, "The Road to Baghdad," 346.

111. For comprehensive catalogs of the faulty expectations, misplanning, and failures of the US pre- and postinvasion efforts in Iraq until late 2005, see Ricks, *Fiasco*; Gurtov, *Superpower on Crusade*; Gordon and Trainor, *Cobra II*. For a persuasive argument that the democratization of unstable societies might aggravate conflicts rather than reduce them, at least in the initial stages of democratization, see Edward Mansfield and Jack Snyder, *Electing to Fight: Why Emerging Democracies Go to War* (Cambridge, MA: MIT Press, 2005). On the destabilizing effects of democratization in ethnically divided societies, see Miller, "Does Democratization Pacify the State?"

112. Gordon and Trainor, *Cobra II*, 72–73; Woodward, *Plan of Attack*, 154–55. Smith, *A Pact with the Devil*, criticizes the centrality of democracy promotion in the Bush agenda.

113. On these points, see Halper and Clarke, *America Alone*, 219–20, 222–24; Dorrien, *Imperial Designs*, 177, 188; Larry Diamond, *Squandered Victory: The American Occupation and the Bungled Effort to Bring Democracy to Iraq* (New York: Times Books, 2005), 286–87; Monten, "The Roots of the Bush Doctrine," 145, 151, 154. For rosy neoconservative estimates of the ease of installing democracy in Iraq, see Kaplan and Kristol, *The War over Iraq*, 95–99.

114. For suggestions in this vein, see Dorrien, *Imperial Designs*, 234.

115. For such an interpretation, see Halper and Clarke, *America Alone*, 148, 155–56, 202, 206, 308–9, who argue that regime change in Iraq "was clearly an important part of the neoconservative rationale for the Iraq war," and indeed the real and decisive reason for the war, while the WMD issue was a pretext. See also Dorrien, *Imperial Designs*, 3–4, 181–82; and Gurtov, *Superpower on Crusade*, 57, who calls the WMD issue "a false front." For the manipulation of the WMD evidence by the administration, see Halper and Clarke, *America Alone*, 7, and Gurtov, *Superpower on Crusade*, 3. Robert Jervis suggests that the administration knew that sup-

port for the war would decline if the cost of reconstructing Iraq would be known, thus they made it sound casual. The consequence was that the planning toward the war was based on a worst-case scenario, while the postwar era was painted in best-case scenario colors. Jervis, "Explaining the War In Iraq," 33. Yet, Bush needed to overcome strong disapproval—domestic and international—of the war, and Powell's suggestion to return to the UN Security Council for another vote was a path to that end. Jervis, "Explaining the War In Iraq," 36–38.

116. Mandelbaum, *Mission Failure*, 196.

117. Cited in Gurtov, *Superpower on Crusade*, 85.

118. Packer, *The Assassins' Gate*, 60–61.

119. Halper and Clarke, *America Alone*, 230. On 9/11 as an indispensable factor in the neo-conservatives' political success and the resultant change in US strategy, see also Gurtov, *Superpower on Crusade*, 9, 33, 37, 210.

120. Halper and Clarke, *America Alone*, 40.

121. Halper and Clarke, 138.

122. John J. Mearsheimer and Stephen M. Walt, "An Unnecessary War," *Foreign Policy* 134 (January–February 2003): 50–59.

123. Brent Scowcroft, "Don't Attack Saddam," *Wall Street Journal*, August 15, 2002.

124. Bartholomew Sparrow, *The Strategist: Brent Scowcroft and the Call of National Security* (New York: Public Affairs, 2015), 592–93.

125. Mandelbaum, *Mission Failure*, 194–95.

126. Mandelbaum, 417n31.

127. Rice, *No Higher Honor*, 187.

128. Mandelbaum, *Mission Failure*, 200–201.

129. Mandelbaum, 201. In the preparation for war, Rice points out, the postwar era was taken seriously, and it was given to the Department of Defense to plan and manage, the only agency that in fact could run this. Feith was in charge, and shortly before the war began he presented the plan to virtually dismantle the whole Iraqi military. Rice, *No Higher Honor*, 19–195.

130. Monten, "The Roots of the Bush Doctrine."

131. Susan B. Epstein et al., *Democracy Promotion: Cornerstone of U.S. Foreign Policy?* (Congressional Research Service, 2007), 18. Available at http://fas.org/sgp/crs/row/RL34296.pdf (accessed July 2, 2009).

132. In this sense, we disagree with Rose (*How Wars End*, 270) that "with different decisionmakers in power in Washington in 2002–2003, there would not have been an invasion of Iraq," although we agree that "if for some reason there had been, the aftermath would have been handled differently."

133. Frank P. Harvey, "President Al Gore and the 2003 Iraq War: A Counterfactual Test of Conventional 'W'isdom," *Canadian Journal of Political Science* 45, no. 1 (2012): 1–32.

134. Harvey, 5.

135. Frank P. Harvey, *Explaining the Iraq War: Counterfactual Theory, Logic and Evidence* (New York: Cambridge University Press, 2012), 180.

136. Harvey, 81.

137. As the then CIA head, Tenet, commented, "[Saddam] was a fool for not understanding, especially after 9/11, that the US was not going to risk underestimating his WMD capabilities as we had done once before." George Tenet, *At the Center of the Storm: My Years at the CIA* (New York: HarperCollins, 2007), 331–33, cited in Harvey, "President Al Gore and the 2003 Iraq War," 22.

138. Harvey, "President Al Gore and the 2003 Iraq War," 13–19.

139. Harvey, 22.

140. Harvey, 24.

141. Harvey, *Explaining the Iraq War*, 91.

142. Harvey, 104, citing Holbrooke, "High Road to Baghdad: Bush Must Return to the UN if He Wants International Backing," *Guardian*, August 29, 2002. Available at www.guardian.co .uk/world/2002/aug/29/Iraq.comment1 (accessed October 2010).

143. A short while after the occupation of Iraq, as things evidently were not going according to plan and were getting out of control, the neocons lost their influence and began leaving their posts.

144. For neoconservative lists of future targets for US democracy promotion after Iraq, see Dorrien, *Imperial Designs*, 242–46.

Chapter Nine

1. Dueck, *The Obama Doctrine*, 44–45. An insider's comprehensive book about Obama's foreign policy is by one of his key assistants in this domain; see Derek Chollet, *The Long Game: How Obama Defied Washington and Redefined America's Role in the World* (New York: Public Affairs, 2016).

2. Dueck, *The Obama Doctrine*, 36n51.

3. On Obama and the Middle East, see Fawaz A. Gerges, *Obama and the Middle East* (New York: Palgrave Macmillan, 2012); and Marc Lynch, "Obama and the Middle East: Rightsizing the US Role," *Foreign Affairs* 94, no. 5 (September–October 2015): 18–27.

4. On the differences between hard power and soft power, see Joseph Nye Jr., *Bound to Lead* (New York: HarperCollins, 1990); and Nye, *Soft Power*.

5. Mandelbaum, *Mission Failure*, 369.

6. Dueck, *The Obama Doctrine*, 67–68.

7. Sestanovich, *Maximalist*, 312; Rachman *Easternization*, 76.

8. Mandelbaum, *Mission Failure*, 178–83 and 414n188.

9. See Gerges, *Obama and the Middle East*; Lynch, "Obama and the Middle East"; and Wright, *All Measures Short of War*, 101–10.

10. Nicolas Bouchet, "Hard Choices in Democracy Promotion: Obama and Egypt," in *The Obama Doctrine: A Legacy of Continuity in US Foreign Policy?*, ed. Michelle Bentley and Jack Holland (London: Routledge, 2017), 150–63.

11. Mikael Blomdahl, "Bureaucratic Roles and Positions: Explaining the United States Libya Decision," *Diplomacy & Statecraft* 27, no. 1 (2016): 142–61; Aidan Hehir, "The Permanence of Inconsistency: Libya, the Security Council, and the Responsibility to Protect," *International Security* 38, no. 1 (2013): 137–59; Alan J. Kuperman, "A Model Humanitarian Intervention? Reassessing NATO's Libya Campaign," *International Security* 38, no. 1 (2013): 105–36; Simon Chesterman, "'Leading from Behind': The Responsibility to Protect, the Obama Doctrine, and Humanitarian Intervention after Libya," *Ethics and International Affairs* 25, no. 3 (2011): 279–85.

12. R2P refers to the commitment of the international community for the "responsibility to protect" civilians who are violently attacked on a massive scale—including by their own government. Alex J. Bellamy, "The Responsibility to Protect and the Problem of Military Intervention," *International Affairs* 84, no. 4 (2008): 615–39; Hannes Peltonen, "Modelling International Collective Responsibility: The Case of Grave Humanitarian Crises," *Review of International Studies* 36, no. 2 (2010): 239–55; Thomas G. Weiss, "The Sunset of Humanitarian Intervention? The Responsibility to Protect in a Unipolar Era," *Security Dialogue* 35, no. 2 (2004): 135–53. For

a critique, see Jeremy Moses, "Sovereignty as Irresponsibility? A Realist Critique of the Responsibility to Protect," *Review of International Studies* 39, no. 1 (2013): 113–35.

13. For the accounts of Obama's assistants, see Chollet, *The Long Game*; and Ben Rhodes, *The World as It Is: Inside the Obama White House* (London: Bodley Head, 2018): 223–40; see also Wright, *All Measures Short of War*, 106–7.

14. Mandelbaum, *Mission Failure*, 348–51; Wright, *All Measures Short of War*, 67–98. For details on the growing aggression of China in the South China Sea in recent years, see Ely Ratner, "Course Correction: How to Stop China's Maritime Advance," *Foreign Affairs* (July–August 2017). See also Kurt M. Campbell and Ely Ratner, "The China Reckoning: How Beijing Defied American Expectations," *Foreign Affairs* (March–April 2018).

15. Madelbaum, *Mission Failure*, 351–53; Rachman, *Easternization*, 79. On 72–73 Rachman analyzes the key statements on the new policy: Obama's address to the Australian parliament in November 2011 and Secretary of State Hillary Clinton's article "America's Pacific Century" in *Foreign Policy* a month earlier. See also Chollet, *The Long Game*, 60–61.

16. Chollet, *The Long Game*, 55–56; David E. Sanger, *Confront and Conceal: Obama's Secret Wars and Surprising Use of American Force* (New York: Crown Publishers, 2013), 412.

17. Rhodes, *The World as It Is*, 164–65. On soft balancing, see Robert A. Pape, "Soft Balancing against the United States," *International Security* 30, no. 1 (2005): 7–45; T. V. Paul, "Soft Balancing in the Age of U.S. Primacy," *International Security* 30, no. 1 (2005): 46–71.

18. Rachman, *Easternization*, 75, cites a senior White House official who said that the relations became "80 percent competition and 20 percent cooperation."

19. See chap. 7. See also Brands and Feaver, "Stress-Testing American Grand Strategy," 102–4.

20. Sanger, *Confront and Conceal*, 371, 374, 377, 379; Sestanovich, *Maximalist*, 312; Chollett, *The Long Game*, 58–59.

21. Rachman, *Easternization*, 78; Sanger, *Confront and Conceal*, 394.

22. Mandelbaum, *Mission Failure*, 351. Oliver Turner terms the relations with China "cautious engagement." Oliver Turner, "The US and China: Obama's Cautious Engagement," in *The Obama Doctrine: A Legacy of Continuity in Us Foreign Policy?*, ed. Michelle Bentley and Jack Holland (London: Routledge, 2017), 180–93.

23. Mandelbaum, *Mission Failure*, 343–53.

24. See the defense of the administration's policy as both resolute and cautious in Chollet, *The Long Game*, 162–79 versus Obama's critic—Dueck, *The Obama Doctrine*, 8, 41, 71—who highlights what he views as the failure of Obama's accommodating strategy vis-à-vis Russia, culminating with the invasion of Ukraine. For more criticism, see Robert G. Kaufman, *Dangerous Doctrine: How Obama's Grand Strategy Weakened America* (Lexington: University Press of Kentucky, 2016).

25. Dueck, *The Obama Doctrine*, 41.

26. For details of the sanctions, see Robert Legvold, *Return to Cold War* (Cambridge, UK, and Malden, MA: Polity Press, 2016), 10–12; and also on the military response, see Chollet, *The Long Game*, 164–69.

27. Legvold, *Return to Cold War*, 11.

28. Michal Wozniak, "The Ukraine Crisis and Shift in US Foreign Policy," *International Studies: Interdisciplinary Political and Cultural Journal* 18, no. 2 (2016): 87–102 at 93.

29. Dueck, *The Obama Doctrine*, esp. 221.

30. Chollet, *The Long Game*, 171–72, citing also the US ambassador to Moscow, Michael McFaul.

31. Maxine David refers to Obama's Russia policy as "damage limitation policy," which he hoped will "do the least amount of damage in the hope of keeping the doors open for a more productive relationship with Putin's successor." Maxine David, "US-Russia Relations in Obama's Second Term: A Damage Limitation Exercise," in *The Obama Doctrine: A Legacy of Continuity in US Foreign Policy?*, ed. Michelle Bentley and Jack Holland (London: Routledge, 2017), 150–79.

32. Wozniak, "The Ukraine Crisis and Shift in US Foreign Policy," 94–95.

33. Jason Douglas and Andrew Futter, "Plus ca Change? Reflecting on Obama's Nuclear Agenda and Legacy," in *The Obama Doctrine: A Legacy of Continuity in US Foreign Policy?*, ed. Michelle Bentley and Jack Holland (London: Routledge, 2017), 117–30.

34. Partly based on such criticisms, the US under President Trump withdrew unilaterally from the nuclear deal with Iran (the Joint Comprehensive Plan of Action [JCPOA]) in May 2018. This issue is also discussed in the next chapter.

35. Ian Black and Simon Tisdall, "Saudi Arabia Urges US Attack on Iran to Stop Nuclear Programme," *Guardian*, November 28, 2010, available online at https://www.theguardian.com/world/2010/nov/28/us-embassy-cables-saudis-iran (accessed July 27, 2018); James Dobbins, "Negotiating with Iran: Reflections from Personal Experience," *Washington Quarterly* 33, no. 1 (2010): 160. See also Sanger, *Confront and Conceal.*

36. Walter C. Clemens Jr., *North Korea and the World: Human Rights, Arms Control, and Strategies for Negotiations* (Lexington: University Press of Kentucky, 2016), chaps. 15–16; Mark Fitzpartick, "Obama's Prime Nonproliferation Failure," *Arms Control Today* 46, no. 10 (December 2016): 11.

37. On Obama's drone usage, see Christopher Fuller, "The Assassin in Chief: Obama's Drone Legacy," in *The Obama Doctrine: A Legacy of Continuity in US Foreign Policy?*, ed. Michelle Bentley and Jack Holland (London: Routledge, 2017), 131–49. On its effectiveness against al-Qaeda, see Javier Jordan, "The Effectiveness of the Drone Campaign against Al Qaeda Central: A Case Study," *Journal of Strategic Studies* 37, no. 1 (2014): 4–29.

38. On the changing balance, see Hal Brands, *American Grand Strategy in the Age of Trump* (Washington, DC: Brookings Institution Press, 2018), 127–52.

39. Robert S. Ross, "US Grand Strategy, the Rise of China, and US National Security Strategy for East Asia," *Strategic Studies Quarterly* 7, no. 2 (2013): 36.

40. Brands and Feaver, "Stress-Testing American Grand Strategy," 98–99.

41. Brands and Feaver, 98–100.

42. World Bank Dataset, July 23, 2016, cited in Wright, *All Measures Short of War*, 19–20.

43. Gideon Rachman, *Zero-Sum Future: American Power in the Age of Anxiety* (New York: Simon and Schuster, 2011), 179–85; Mandelbaum, *Mission Failure*, 321, citing Martin Wolf, *The Shifts and the Shocks: What We've Learned—and Have Still to Learn—from the Financial Crisis* (New York: Penguin Press, 2014), 9.

44. Mandelbaum, *Mission Failure*, 322.

45. Mandelbaum, 324.

46. This is somewhat similar to the first few years of the Cold War—at the beginning of the second half of the 1940s before the Soviet threat emerged very clearly following the 1948 Berlin crisis and certainly the 1950 Korean invasion; see chap. 3.

47. On the debate inside the Obama administration on the nature and the extent of the Russian threat, see Chollet, *The Long Game*, 163–64.

48. Wright, *All Measures Short of War*, 70–76.

Chapter Ten

1. See also Barry Posen, "The Rise of Illiberal Hegemony," *Foreign Affairs*, March–April 2018; Layne, "The US-Chinese Power Shift and the End of Pax Americana," 89–111; Walt, "US Grand Strategy after the Cold War: Can Realism Explain It? Should Realism Guide It?," 3–22; and Brands, *American Grand Strategy in the Age of Trump*, 153–55, and citations there.

2. Relative gains refer to the state's gains in relation to how other states are doing. This is in contrast to the liberal focus on absolute gains—the state's gains in relation to its own past gains. On the importance of relative gains, see Joseph M. Grieco, "Anarchy and the Limits of Cooperation: A Realist Critique of the Newest Liberal Institutionalism," *International Organization* 42, no. 3 (1988): 485–507; Grieco, *Cooperation among Nations: Europe, America, and Non-Tariff Barriers to Trade* (Ithaca, NY: Cornell University Press, 1990).

3. Brands, *American Grand Strategy in the Age of Trump*, 157.

4. On Trump's abandonment of human rights, see Sarah Margon, "Giving Up the High Ground: America's Retreat on Human Rights," *Foreign Affairs*, March–April 2018. On his opposition to democracy promotion and the reasons for that, related to his opposition to "American exceptionalism," see Stephen Wertheim, "Donald Trump versus American Exceptionalism: Toward the Sources of Trumpian Conduct," February 1, 2017, https://issforum.org/roundtables/policy/1-5k-trump-exceptionalism. On Trump's reservations about protecting human rights, see Allissa J. Rubin, "In Trump's America, a Toned-Down Voice for Human Rights," *New York Times*, March 10, 2017, https://www.nytimes.com/2017/03/10/world/europe/in-trumps-america-a-toned-down-voice-for-human-rights.html?ribbon-ad idx=5&rref=world/europe&module=Ribbon&version=context&region=Header&action=click&contentCollection=Europe&pgtype=article.

5. Paul D. Miller, "Mapping Ideology in the age of Trump," *War on the Rocks*, February 5, 2018, available online at https://warontherocks.com/2018/02/mapping-ideology-in-the-age-of-trump/ (accessed July 31, 2018). For his earlier classification of grand strategies, see *American Power and Liberal Order*.

6. Thus, for example, just before the G-7 meeting in June 2018, Trump, while being very critical toward the Western liberal partners of the US (the Western Europeans, Canada, and Japan), called for the readmission of authoritarian Russia back to the club of the leading Western industrialized countries, thus turning it again into a G-8. Moscow was expelled from the group following its 2014 invasion of Ukraine and annexation of Crimea. Trump's support for Russia joining the exclusive economic club is a puzzle also because of the latter's relative lack of economic importance (it is the twelfth largest economy in the world). Shortly after the G-7 meeting, Trump held a summit with the North Korean dictator, Kim. Again, it is noteworthy to view his criticism of the Western allies in contrast to the admiring and flattering attitude toward the North Korean dictator. Similarly, in July 2018 there was a huge difference between Trump's almost hostile attitude to the EU and NATO allies and his extremely friendly and appeasing, if not submissive, attitude to Putin in their Helsinki Summit a few days later.

7. Colum Lynch, "Trump Administration Eyes $1 Billion in Cuts to U.N. Peacekeeping," *Foreign Policy*, March 23, 2017, available online at https://foreignpolicy.com/2017/03/23/trump-administration-eyes-1-billion-in-cuts-to-u-n-peacekeeping/.

8. This paragraph draws on Paul Wladman, "Trump's Effort to Isolate Us from the World Is Going Great," *Washington Post*, June 8, 2018.

9. Walter Russell Mead, "How Trump Plans to Change the World," *Wall Street Journal*, July 9, 2018.

10. Cited in Brands, *American Grand Strategy in the Age of Trump*, 162.

11. Mearsheimer and Walt, "Off-Shore Balancing."

12. Posen, *Restraint*; Stephen M. Walt, "Is Trump's America the Safest Country in the World?," *Foreign Policy*, June 21, 2018.

13. Stephen Wertheim, "Quit Calling Donald Trump an Isolationist. He's Worse than That," *Washington Post*, online, February 17, 2017.

14. Posen, *Restraint*.

15. Posen; and Posen, "The Rise of illiberal Hegemony."

16. See the recent studies on Trump supporters conducted by Andrew L. Whitehead, Joseph O. Baker, and Samuel L. Perry, overviewed in the Monkey Cage column, "Despite Porn Stars and Playboy Models, White Evangelicals Aren't Rejecting Trump. This Is Why," *Washington Post*, March 26, 2018. See also Francis Fukuyama, *Identity: The Demand for Dignity and the Politics of Resentment* (New York: Farrar, Straus and Giroux, 2018).

17. On the crucial importance of tribal identity in America, see Amy Chua, *Political Tribes* (New York: Penguin Press, 2018).

18. There are three major explanations for the rise of populism in the West: the identity/cultural explanation (the fear of changing demographics due to the decline of white/Christian dominance and related decline of "traditional values"), the economic (globalization), and the political (the preference for "strongmen"). For a useful collection of quite a few recent scholarly articles on nationalist populism, see Michael Bernhard and Daniel O'Neill, "Trump: Causes and Consequences," Special Sections of *Perspectives on Politics* 17, no. 2 (June 2019): 317–479. On nationalist populism esp. in the age of Brexit and Trump, see also Ian Bremmer, *US vs. Them: The Failure of Globalism* (New York: Penguin, 2018); Barry Eichengreen, *The Populist Temptation: Economic Grievances and Political Reaction in the Modern Era* (New York: Oxford University Press, 2018); Steven Levitsky and Daniel Ziblatt, *How Democracies Die?* (New York: Crown, 2018); Joshua Green, *Devil's Bargain: Steve Bannon, Donald Trump, and the Nationalist Uprising* (New York: Penguin, 2018); John B. Judis, *The Populist Explosion: How the Great Recession Transformed American and European Politics* (New York: Columbia Global Projects, 2016); Michiko, Kakutani, *The Death of Truth: Notes on Falsehood in the Age of Trump* (New York: Tim Duggan, 2018); Robert Kuttner, *Can Democracy Survive Global Capitalism?* (New York: Norton, 2018); Edward Luce, *The Retreat of Western Civilization* (New York: Atlantic, 2017); Milanovic Branko, *Global Inequality: A New Approach for the Age of Globalization* (Cambridge, MA: Belknap Press, Harvard University Press, 2016); Mishra Pankaj, *Age of Anger: A History of the Present* (New York: Farrar, Straus and Giroux, 2017); Yasscha Mounk, *The People vs. Democracy: Why Our Freedom Is in Danger and How to Save It* (Cambridge, MA; Harvard University Press, 2018); Cas Mudde and Cristobal Rovira Kaltwasser, *Populism: A Very Short Introduction* (Oxford: Oxford University Press, 2017); Ashesh Mukherjee, *The Internet Trap: Five Costs of Living Online* (Toronto: University of Toronto Press, 2018); Jan-Werner Muller, *What Is Populism?* (Philadelphia: University of Pennsylvania Press, 2016); Diana C. Mutz, "Status Threat, Not Economic Hardship, Explains the 2016 Presidential Vote," PNAS, April 23, 2018, 201718155; published ahead of print April 23, 2018, https://doi.org/10.1073/pnas.1718155115 (accessed August 9, 2018).

19. The BRICS include Brazil, Russia, India, China, and South Africa. While most members of this group are far from being great powers for the foreseeable future, China is by far the most important rising great power: China's share of global output rose to about 15 percent from less than 4 percent in the past two decades. Roger Cohen, "Year One in Donald Trump's World," *New York Times*, international ed., January 23, 2018, 13.

20. Layne, "The US-Chinese Power Shift and the End of the Pax Americana"; Rachman, *Easternization*. But see also a counterview that highlights enduring American power advantages, esp. in the military field: Brooks and Wohlforth, *America Abroad*.

21. According to SIPRI (Stockholm International Peace Research Institute) 2018, the US and China lead the increase in world military expenditure. US military spending grew—for the first time since 2010—by 4.6 percent, to reach $649 billion in 2018. The US remained by far the largest spender in the world, and spent almost as much on its military in 2018 as the next eight largest-spending countries combined. "The increase in US spending was driven by the implementation from 2017 of new arms procurement programmes under the Trump administration," writes Dr. Aude Fleurant, the director of the SIPRI AMEX program. China, the second-largest spender in the world, increased its military expenditure by 5.0 percent to $250 billion in 2018. This was the twenty-fourth consecutive year of increase in Chinese military expenditure. Its spending in 2018 was almost ten times higher than in 1994, and accounted for 14 percent of world military spending. The growth in Chinese military spending tracks with the country's overall economic growth. China has allocated 1.9 percent of its GDP to the military every year since 2013.

22. See John Mearsheimer, *The Great Delusion: Liberal Dreams and International Realities* (New Haven, CT: Yale University Press, 2018).

23. Leading primacists include Lieber, *Power and Willpower in the American Future*; Michael Beckley, "China's Century? Why America's Edge Will Endure," *International Security* 36, no. 3 (Winter 2011–12): 41–78; Josef Joffe, *The Myth of American Decline*; and Joseph S. Nye Jr., *Is the American Century Over?* (Cambridge: Polity Press, 2015); while the declinists include Christopher Layne, "The Unipolar Illusion Revisited: The Coming End of the United States' Unipolar Moment," *International Security* 31, no. 2 (Fall 2006): 7– 41; Steven Walt, "The End of the American Era," *National Interest* (November–December 2011): 6–16; Mandelbaum, *Mission Failure*; and Posen, *Restraint*.

24. Hal Brands et al., *Critical Assumptions and American Grand Strategy* (Washington, DC: Center for Strategic and Budgetary Assessments, 2017), 12–13, and their citations; Brands, *American Grand Strategy in the Age of Trump*, chap. 6.

25. Brands et al., *Critical Assumptions and American Grand Strategy*, 14.

26. Rachman, *Easternization*, 32.

27. Wayne M. Morrison, "China's Economic Rise: History, Trends, Challenges, and Implications for the United States," *Congressional Research Service*, February 5, 2018; citations in Layne, "The US-Chinese Power Shift and the End of Pax Americana," 95.

28. IMF Datasets 2018.

29. Michael Mandelbaum, *The Rise and Fall of Peace on Earth* (New York: Oxford University Press, 2019), 51.

30. Cited in Layne, "The US-Chinese Power Shift and the End of Pax Americana," 95; Brands, "The Chinese Century," *National Interest*, March–April 2018, citing Rand Corporation report (p. 36).

31. Hal Brands et al., *Critical Assumptions and American Grand Strategy*; Brands, "The Chinese Century."

32. Even though there were debates on the severity of the threat and esp. how to respond to it.

33. For a partly related point, though not addressing the competing threat conceptions, see Brands, *American Grand Strategy in the Age of Trump*, 133, who cites also the director of national intelligence from February 29, 2016. See also the Expert Debate in *Foreign Affairs* on the evalu-

ation of the Russia threat in comparison with other threats: "How Big a Challenge Is Russia?," *Foreign Affairs*, November 13, 2017.

34. Mearsheimer, *The Tragedy of Great Power Politics* (2nd ed.).

35. On the strong fear of Muslims by white Christian supporters of Trump, see the studies by Andrew L. Whitehead, Joseph O. Baker, and Samuel L. Perry overviewed in "Despite Porn Stars and Playboy Models, White Evangelicals Aren't Rejecting Trump. This Is Why," *Washington Post*, Monkey Cage, online, March 26, 2018.

36. See John Mueller and Mark G. Stewart, "Why Are Americans Still So Afraid of Islamic Terrorism?," Monkey Cage, *Washington Post*, March 23, 2018, https://www.washingtonpost .com /news /monkey-cage /wp /2018/03/23/ why-are-americans-still-so-afraid-of-islamic -terrorism /?utm_term=.c5f212324301&wpisrc=nl_politics&wpmm=1. Some of their key findings show that the fears grew in the years preceding the 2016 elections: "40 percent of Americans both in 2001 and today fear that they or a family member might become a victim of terrorism. Our data also show that in 2013 and 2014 many Americans saw the country as less safe than before 9/11—even more than had said so a decade earlier. And the percentage who were confident (for the most part, only fairly so) that the government could protect them from such attacks has, if anything, waned some over the decade and a half since 9/11." This article is a short review of some major studies conducted by the two authors that show the persistent fear of large sectors of the US public of Islamic terrorism from 9/11 until today.

37. Arnold Isaacs, "The Trump Administration Is Using Fake Terrorism Statistics to Scare You about Immigrants: Inflated Numbers Tell a False Story of a Nation under Attack," *Nation*, March 5, 2018.

38. Pippa Norris and Ronald Inglehart, *Cultural Backlash: Trump, Brexit, and Authoritarian Populism* (Cambridge: Cambridge University Press, 2019), esp. 44–49; Diana C. Mutz, "Status Threat, Not Economic Hardship, Explains the 2016 Presidential Vote," PNAS, April 23, 2018, 201718155, published ahead of print, April 23, 2018, https://doi.org/10.1073/pnas .1718155115 (accessed August 9, 2018); Francis Fukuyama, *Identity: The Demand for Dignity and the Politics of Resentment* (New York: Farrar, Straus and Giroux, 2018); John Sides, Michael Tesler, and Lynn Vavreck, *Identity Crisis: The 2016 Presidential Campaign and the Battle for the Meaning of America* (Princeton, NJ: Princeton University Press, 2018); Jennifer Rubin notes in her *Washington Post* article "The Ugly Face of Ethno-Nationalists" (January 22, 2018) that "antagonism toward immigrants and a preference for white Europeans over brown and black people remain the default setting for Trump and increasingly for his party." See also "The New Nationalism," *Economist*, November 19, 2016; Mirren Gidda, "How Donald Trump's Nationalism Won over White Americans," *Newsweek*, November 15, 2016; Stephen Wertheim, "Donald Trump's Plan to Save Western Civilization," *New York Times*, online, July 22, 2017.

39. Ivan Krastev, "Could 2018 Be Europe's new 1968?," *International New York Times*, February 22, 2018, 1.

40. Posen, "The Rise of Illiberal Hegemony." On the Post–Cold War "liberal hegemony," see chaps. 7–9 above.

41. Brands, *American Grand Strategy in the Age of Trump*, 159–60; Steven Walt, "Trump's Sound and Fury Has Signified Nothing," *Foreign Policy*, January 30, 2018.

42. Posen, "The Rise of illiberal Hegemony."

43. Eric Schmitt, "On Ground and Online, a Counter to Russia," *New York Times*, July 5, 2018, 1; Jim Goldgeier, "President Trump Goes to Europe This Week. Its Leaders Are Bracing for the Impact," *Washington Post*, Monkey Cage, July 9, 2018.

44. Steven Erlanger, Julie Hirschfeld Davis, and Katie Rogers, "NATO Survives Trump, but the Turmoil Is Leaving Scars," *New York Times*, online, July 12, 2018.

45. Daniel Deudney and G. John Ikenberry, "Liberal World: The Resilient Order," *Foreign Affairs*, July–August 2018, 23.

46. Peter Baker and Ana Swansonmarch, "Trump Authorizes Tariffs, Defying Allies at Home and Abroad," *New York Times*, online, March 8, 2018.

47. Trump had denied that this was a trade war. For a useful analysis, see Sourabh Gupta, *The Art of the China Deal: Trump's Section 301 China IPR-Related Tariffs and Investment Measures* (Washington, DC: Institute for China-America Studies, June 2018), available online at http://chinaus-icas.org/wp-content/uploads/2018/06/Section-301-Report-FINAL.pdf (accessed July 31, 2018). See also Manik Mehta, "'America First' or 'America Alone'?," *Steel Times International* 42, no. 2 (March 2018): 15–16, available online at https://search.proquest.com/openview/a5f1b2b6a21280a1bd58246eb7685e4d/1?pq-origsite=gscholar&cbl=1056347 (accessed July 31, 2018); Minghao Li, Wendong Zhang, and Chat Hart, "Lessons from Previous U.S.-China Trade Disputes," *Agricultural Policy Review* (Ames: Iowa State University, Spring 2018), 1–3, available online at https://www.card.iastate.edu/ag_policy_review/pdf/spring-2018 .pdf (accessed August 1, 2018). For a broader perspective, see C. Donald Johnson, *The Wealth of a Nation: A History of Trade Politics in America* (New York: Oxford University Press, 2018).

48. Shrutee Sarkar, "Economists United: Trump Tariffs Won't Help the Economy," *Reuters*, March 13, 2018, available online at https://www.reuters.com/article/us-usa-economy-poll/economists-united-trump-tariffs-wont-help-the-economy-idUSKCN1GQ02G (accessed August 1, 2018).

49. Keith Johnson, "Trump's $12 Billion Bailout Is No Remedy for Farmers Caught in Trade War," *Foreign Policy*, July 31, 2018, available online at https://foreignpolicy.com/2018/07/31/trumps-12-billion-bailout-no-i-remedy-for-farmers-caught-in-trade-war/ (accessed August 1, 2018).

50. Chad P. Bown, "What We Do and Don't Know after Trump's Tariff Announcement," *Harvard Business Review*, March 9, 2018, available online at https://hbr.org/2018/03/what-we -do-and-dont-know-after-trumps-tariff-announcement (accessed August 1, 2018); Jacob M. Schlesinger, Peter Nicholas, and Louise Radnofsky, "Trump to Impose Steep Aluminum and Steel Tariffs," *Wall Street Journal*, March 1, 2018, available online at https://www.wsj.com/articles/trump-wont-quickly-announce-new-tariffs-on-aluminum-steel-1519921704 (accessed August 1, 2018).

51. Ana Swanson and Keith Bradsher, "Chinese Goods May Face 25% Tariffs, Not 10%, as Trump's Anger Grows," *New York Times*, August 1, 2018, available online at https://www.nytimes .com/2018/08/01/business/china-tariffs-trump.html (accessed August 2, 2018). See also Chad P. Bown, "The Accumulating Self-Inflicted Wounds from Trump's Unilateral Trade Policy," in PIIE Briefing 18-1, *US-China Economic Relations: From Conflict to Solutions*, ed. Ha Jiming and Adam S. Posen (Washington, DC: Peterson Institute for International Economics, June 2018), 7–21. Later Trump even further escalated the tariffs on imports from China.

52. Data from the Peterson Institute for International Economics, cited in Ana Swanson, "Tariffs Push China Links to US into 'Free Fall,'" *New York Times*, September 2, 2019, 1.

53. Stephen M. Walt, "It Still Doesn't Get Worse than Afghanistan," *Foreign Policy*, July 9, 2018.

54. Posen, "The Rise of illiberal Hegemony."

55. Matthew Kroenig, "The Return of the Pressure Track: The Trump Administration and the Iran Nuclear Deal," *Diplomacy and Statecraft* 29, no. 1 (2018): 94–104.

56. Thomas Wright, "Trump Wants Little to Do with His Own Foreign Policy: The Clash between America First and the Global Shift to Great-Power Competition," *Atlantic*, January 31, 2018.

57. Brands, *American Grand Strategy in the Age of Trump*, 159.

58. Julian E. Barnes, Eric Schmitt, and Katie Benner, "Spies Shake Their Heads as Gap Grows with Trump," *New York Times*, July 23, 2018, 1.

59. See the analysis by Mark Landler in the *New York Times* of August 3, 2018, https://www.nytimes.com/2018/08/03/us/politics/trump-foreign-policy.html?nl=top-stories&nlid=29775677ries&ref=headline (accessed on August 4, 2018).

60. James Kirchick, "Trump Wants to Destroy the World Order. So What?," *Foreign Policy*, July 26, 2018.

61. Stewart Patrick, "The World Order Is Starting to Crack," *Foreignd Policy*, July 25, 2018.

62. Fareed Zakaria, "The Trump Two-Step Strikes Again," *Washington Post*, July 26, 2018.

63. On the meaning and implications of his resignation, see Elizabeth N. Saunders, "Three Reasons That Jim Mattis's Resignation Is Not Just Unusual—but Startling," *Washington Post*, December 21, 2018, https://www.washingtonpost.com/news/monkey-cage/wp/2018/12/21/these-are-the-3-reasons-that-jim-mattiss-resignation-is-not-just-unusual-but-startling/?wpisrc=nl_most&wpmm=1.

Chapter Eleven

1. James Gerstenzang and Robert Shogan, "Conservatives Hit Reagan on Treaty: One Calls President 'a Useful Idiot' of Soviets; Criticism of Accord Mounts," *Los Angeles Times*, December 5, 1987.

2. For partly related points, see Samuel P. Huntington, *The Clash of Civilizations and the Remaking of World Order* (New York: Simon & Schuster, 1996).

3. On Chinese and American military and economic capabilities, see also chap. 10.

4. According to one definition, hybrid warfare "exploits domestic weaknesses via non-military means (such as political, informational, and economic intimidation and manipulation), but is backed by the threat of conventional military means." See Julio Miranda Calha, "Hybrid Warfare: NATO's New Strategic Challenge?," *NATO Parliamentary Assembly: Defence and Security Committee* (2015): 1.

Index

The letter *t* following a page number denotes a table.